HANDBOOK OF INTUITION RESEARCH

Handbook of
Intuition Research

Edited by

Marta Sinclair

Senior Lecturer, Griffith University, Australia

Edward Elgar
Cheltenham, UK • Northampton, MA, USA

Published by
Edward Elgar Publishing Limited
The Lypiatts
15 Lansdown Road
Cheltenham
Glos GL50 2JA
UK

Edward Elgar Publishing, Inc.
William Pratt House
9 Dewey Court
Northampton
Massachusetts 01060
USA

A catalogue record for this book
is available from the British Library

Library of Congress Control Number: 2011925707

ISBN 978 1 84844 888 9 (cased)

Typeset by Servis Filmsetting Ltd, Stockport, Cheshire
Printed and bound by MPG Books Group, UK

Contents

Contributors

Alessandro Antonietti is Full Professor of Cognitive Psychology and head of the Department of Psychology at the Catholic University of the Sacred Heart in Milan, Italy. He has carried out experimental studies on creativity, problem-solving and learning, and investigated the role played by the media in cognition. He is interested in the applications of cognitive issues in the field of instruction and rehabilitation and has devised tests to assess thinking skills and programs to train cognitive abilities.

Bjørn T. Bakken is PhD Fellow in Leadership and Organization at the Norwegian School of Management, Oslo, and currently employed by the Norwegian Defence University College, in the Department of Military Psychology and Leadership Development. His research interests include behavioral decision making, cognitive psychology, personality and individual differences, human factors in information technology, system dynamics, organizational learning, business and military ethics, and military leadership and organization. He has published his research in journals such as the *Journal of Behavioral Decision Making*, *Military Operations Research*, the *Leadership & Organization Development Journal*, and the *International Journal of Organizational Analysis*.

Cornelia Betsch is Scientific Manager at the interdisciplinary Center for Empirical Research in Economics and Behavioral Sciences (CEREB) at the University of Erfurt, Germany. She received her PhD at the University of Heidelberg in 2006. Her research interests are individual differences in decision making, intuition, risk perception and communication in health decisions. Dr Betsch is the co-editor (with H. Plessner and T. Betsch) of the book *Intuition in Judgment and Decision Making* (2008).

Raymond Trevor Bradley (PhD, Columbia University, New York, USA) has been pioneering the multi-disciplinary application of physics, information science, neuropsychology, psychophysiology, and sociology in research on social systems for more than 35 years. His work has included studies on charismatic and entrepreneurial systems, experts and novices, communication and holographic social organization, experiments on nonlocal intuition, a quantum-holographic theory of nonlocal interaction, and most recently a work on the collective identity signature of secret social groups. He has (co)authored over 60 publications. He is Director of the Institute for Whole Social Science, Northland, New Zealand, and

Chief Scientist and Director of Research, Center for Advanced Research (CFAR), Neuron Dynamics, Appleton, WI, USA.

Lisa A. Burke is Professor of Management in the College of Business at the University of Tennessee at Chattanooga, TN, USA. She has published more than 60 articles in the area of management training, development, and education in journals such as the *Academy of Management Learning & Education, Human Resource Development Quarterly, Human Resource Management*, the *Decision Science Journal of Innovation in Education*, and the *Journal of Management Education*. Prof. Burke teaches primarily in the area of human resources.

Jean-Francois Coget is Associate Professor of Management at the Orfalea College of Business at Cal Poly, San Luis Obispo, CA, USA, where he teaches Organizational Behavior. He earned his PhD from the Anderson School at UCLA, and was previously a faculty member at HEC Paris. His research interests include emotions, intuition, and charismatic leadership. His overarching professional goal is to create and disseminate actionable knowledge that can help managers-citizens to organize a productive, creative, ethical, and sustainable cooperation among people.

Erik Dane is Assistant Professor of Management at the Jesse H. Jones Graduate School of Business, Rice University, Houston, TX, USA. He received his PhD from the University of Illinois at Urbana-Champaign. His current research explores the nature of intuition, its role in organizational decision making, and its connections with related concepts including expertise and mindfulness. His research on intuition has been published in such outlets as the *Academy of Management Review, International Review of Industrial and Organizational Psychology*, and *Psychology of Aesthetics, Creativity, and the Arts*.

Ap Dijksterhuis is Professor of Psychology at the Radboud University Nijmegen, the Netherlands. He has published widely on unconscious processes and has won many scientific awards such as the *APA Award for Early Career Contributions* and the *SESP Career Trajectory Award*. Prof. Dijksterhuis is a member of the board of reviewing editors of *Science*. In 2007, he published the trade book *Het Slimme Onbewuste (The Smart Unconscious)* which became a bestseller in the Netherlands. That same year, the influential magazine HP/De Tijd named him one of the 100 most influential people in the Netherlands.

William Duggan is Senior Lecturer at Columbia Business School, New York, USA. He is the author of three books on strategic intuition: *Napoleon's Glance* (2002), *The Art of What Works* (2003), and *Strategic*

Intuition (2007) which was named the 'Best Strategy Book of the Year' in 2007 by the journal *Strategy+Business.* He has BA, MA and PhD degrees from Columbia University.

Irena D. Ebert earned her PhD at the University of Jena, Germany, where she has worked as Postdoctoral Fellow since 2010. Her research topics include implicit cognition with a special focus on gender issues, and the field of applied psychology.

Seymour Epstein is Professor Emeritus of Psychology at the University of Massachusetts at Amherst, MA, USA, where he has been since obtaining his PhD degree in clinical psychology from the University of Wisconsin in 1953. Prof. Epstein is certified by the *American Psychological Association* as a diplomat in clinical psychology. His research has been supported by the *National Institute of Mental Health* for over 40 years. His major interest is in the development of a unified theory of personality. His most recent previous publication on intuition is 'Demystifying intuition: What it is, what it does, and how it does it' in *Psychological Inquiry* (2010: 21).

Andreas Glöckner earned his PhD at the University of Erfurt, Germany. He is Head of the Intuitive Experts research group at the Max Planck Institute for Research on Collective Goods, Bonn. His research focuses on the cognitive processes underlying judgment and decision making with a special focus on intuition, expertise and implications for legal institutions. Dr Glöckner is the co-editor (with C. Witteman) of the book *Foundations for Tracing Intuition: Challenges and Methods* (2010).

Bernhard Graf, MD, is Professor and Head of the Department of Anesthesiology, University Hospital Regensburg, Germany. During his academic career he has worked at various university hospitals in Germany (Heidelberg, Göttingen) and the United States (Children's Hospital of Wisconsin, Milwaukee). He has received multiple awards for his research and academic teaching. He has established and directed simulation laboratories at Heidelberg, Göttingen, and now at Regensburg. He is editor of the journal *Anästhesiologie & Intensivmedizin* which is the official journal of the German Association of Anesthesiology and Intensive Care.

Lisa K. Gundry is Professor of Management in the Charles H. Kellstadt Graduate School of Business at DePaul University, Chicago, IL, USA, where she teaches courses in Creativity and Innovation in Business, and Entrepreneurship. She is Director of the Center for Creativity and Innovation, which facilitates training, research and outreach. Prof. Gundry has authored several books, including *Entrepreneurship Strategy: Changing Patterns in New Venture Creation, Growth, and Reinvention*

(2007, co-authored with J. Kickul). She has published many articles and book chapters, and conducts research on issues related to innovation strategies and entrepreneurial processes in organizations. She received her PhD from Northwestern University.

James Richard Guzak is Assistant Professor of Management at Oklahoma City University, OK, USA. He holds a Master of Business Administration from the University of Nebraska, a Master of Management from the University of Dallas, and a PhD in Management from the University of Texas at Arlington. He is a former United States Naval Officer with over 25 years of private sector business experience in a variety of industries, both manufacturing and service.

Thorvald Haerem earned his PhD at Copenhagen Business School in Denmark and is currently Associate Professor of Organization Psychology at the Norwegian School of Management, Oslo. His research interests include technology in organizations, organizational and individual routines, behavioral decision making, and expertise. He has published his research in journals such as the *Journal of Applied Psychology*, the *Journal of Behavioral Decision Making*, *Organizational Studies*, and *Organization Science*.

M. Blake Hargrove is Tenured Instructor at McLennan Community College in Waco, TX, USA. He is also Graduate Teaching Assistant and Dean's Fellow at the University of Texas at Arlington where he is a Doctoral Candidate in Management. He holds an MA in Management from Webster University. In addition to teaching, he has 20 years of business experience in the real estate, construction, and manufacturing industries. Prior to his business career he served in the United States Navy as a submarine sonarman.

Christian Harteis, PhD, is Professor of Educational Science at the University of Paderborn, Germany. His research is in the field of workplace learning and professional development. The topic of his dissertation was *Competence Supporting Working Conditions* and his habilitation was on *Professional Learning – Theoretical and Empirical Analyses*. He has conducted several German and international research projects on individual and organizational features of work-related learning. He has published two monographs and several edited books and is Associate Editor of the Springer journal *Vocations and Learning – Studies in Vocational and Professional Education*. He is a member of the AERA-SIG *Workplace Learning* and member of the EARLI-SIG *Learning and Professional Development*.

Gerard P. Hodgkinson, PhD, AcSS, is Professor of Organizational Behaviour and Strategic Management and Director of the Centre for Organizational Strategy, Learning and Change (COSLAC) at Leeds University Business School in the UK. A Fellow of both the British Psychological Society and the British Academy of Management, his research and professional interests centre primarily on the analysis of cognitive processes in work organizations. The (co-)author and/or (co-) editor of 11 books, he has published over 60 scholarly journal articles and chapters in edited volumes on this and related topics.

Paola Iannello is Post-Doctoral Fellow at the Center for Empirical Research in Economics and Behavioral Sciences (CEREB) – University of Erfurt, Germany, and Lecturer in Personality Psychology at the Catholic University of the Sacred Heart in Milan, Italy. Her main research interests are individual differences in decision making (with particular interest in cognitive and decision styles), intuition, metacognition, and mindreading processes.

Karl-Peter Ittner, MD, is Senior Physician at the Department of Anesthesiology, University Hospital Regensburg, Germany.

Jill R. Kickul is Director of the Stewart Satter Program in Social Entrepreneurship in the Berkley Center for Entrepreneurship and Innovation at New York University Stern School of Business, USA. In her faculty position, Prof. Kickul teaches courses in both entrepreneurship and social entrepreneurship. Her primary research areas of interest include innovation and strategic processes within new ventures, micro-financing practices and wealth creation in transitioning economies, and more recently, social entrepreneurship. She received her PhD from Northern Illinois University.

Gary Klein is Senior Scientist at MacroCognition LLC, Yellow Springs, OH, USA. He was instrumental in founding the field of Naturalistic Decision Making. Dr Klein received his PhD in experimental psychology from the University of Pittsburgh in 1969. He was Assistant Professor of Psychology at Oakland University and worked as a research psychologist for the US Air Force. He founded Klein Associates in 1978, and subsequently sold it to Applied Research Associates (ARA) in 2005. Dr Klein is the author of *Sources of Power: How People Make Decisions* (1998), *The Power of Intuition* (2004) and *Streetlights and Shadows* (2009). He developed a Recognition-Primed Decision (RPD) model to describe how people actually make decisions in natural settings.

Christine Kugler, MA, is a staff member of the Institute for Educational Science at the University of Regensburg, Germany. She wrote her xii *Handbook of intuition research*

Magister thesis on the topic of intuition of emergency physicians. Her main areas of research are intuition and expertise.

Claudia Kuhnle has earned her PhD while conducting research as part of the project *Values, Motivational Interference and Studying* at the University of Mannheim, Germany. She received her Diploma in Psychology in 2007 from the University of Mannheim. She has experience in the area of personnel selection, personnel and organization development. Her research focuses on motivational interferences, the role of self-control, regret and life balance in adolescents, the usability of intuition within the area of personnel selection and the linkage of intuition with the area of motivational interference and learning.

Janice Langan-Fox is Organizational Psychologist and Professor of Management at Swinburne University, Melbourne, Australia, where she has held executive roles including Head of Group. After 10 years in industry, she earned a BEd (Hons 1st class) at University of East Anglia, an MPhil at Nottingham University in the UK and a PhD at University of Melbourne where she was on staff for 15 years. Her research in health and human factors and HRM has resulted in more than 130 publications. She has received numerous national competitive grants and currently leads a team investigating hospital adverse events, part of an Australian Research Council grant.

Malia Mason is Assistant Professor at Columbia Business School and Decision Science Fellow at Columbia University's Brain Imaging Center, New York, USA. Using behavioral and brain imaging-based approaches, her research identifies strategies for managing attention and explains how the brain mediates cognitive control. She has a BA from Rice University, and MA and PhD degrees from Dartmouth College.

Barbara Morgenthaler, Dipl.-Päd., is a member of the Institute for Educational Science at the University of Regensburg, Germany. In 2009 she participated in the research project *Intuition as a Component of Professional Performance* directed by Prof. Harteis. Her major areas of interest and research are intuition, professional learning, and expertise.

Jean E. Pretz is Associate Professor in the Psychology Department at Elizabethtown College in Elizabethtown, PA, USA. She received her MS, MPhil, and PhD degrees in Psychology from Yale University in New Haven, CT, and her BA in Psychology and Music from Wittenberg University, Springfield, OH. Her research is focused on the relationship between intuition and expertise, the use of intuition in nursing, individual differences in implicit cognition, and cognitive processes in creativity. Her work has appeared in journals such as *Memory and Cognition, Personality and Individual Differences, Thinking and Reasoning,* and *Behavior Research Methods.*

Dean Radin is Senior Scientist at the Institute of Noetic Sciences (IONS), CA, and Adjunct Faculty at Sonoma State University, Rohnert Park, CA, USA. He earned an MS in Electrical Engineering and a PhD in Psychology from the University of Illinois, Urbana-Champaign. He held appointments at Princeton University, the University of Edinburgh, the University of Nevada, and three Silicon Valley think-tanks, including SRI International, where he worked on a classified program investigating psychic phenomena for the US government. He is (co-)author of over 200 articles in such journals as *Foundations of Physics* and *Psychological Bulletin* and several books including the bestselling *The Conscious Universe* (1997) and *Entangled Minds* (2006).

Gabriel Roth, MD, is Senior Physician at the Department of Anesthesiology, University Hospital Regensburg, Germany. He studied medicine at the University of Regensburg and at the Universities of Vienna and Munich, where he graduated in 1988. After postgraduate education in internal medicine at the University Hospital in Munich, he moved to the Department of Anesthesiology at LMU Munich. Since 1998 he has been working at the Department of Anesthesiology, University Hospital Regensburg where he is also an academic teacher and head of the *Medical Simulation Center.* His main fields of interest are airway management, critical care and emergency medicine, medical education and simulation.

Eugene Sadler-Smith is Professor of Management Development and Organizational Behaviour in the School of Management at the University of Surrey, Guildford, UK. His research interests are centred currently on the role of intuitive judgement in management decision making and management learning and education. His research has been published widely in leading peer-reviewed journals, he is the author of several books including *Inside Intuition* (2008) and *The Intuitive Mind* (2010), and is joint editor-in-chief of *Management Learning.*

Marta Sinclair received an MA in Education from George Washington University, USA, and a PhD in Organizational Behavior from the University of Queensland, Australia. At present she is Senior Lecturer in Griffith Business School at Griffith University, Brisbane, Australia. Her research interests include the role of intuition in managerial decision making, creative processes and learning, and effects of emotional climate on creativity and innovation. She has (co-) authored a number of articles and edited chapters in these areas; she is also editor of this handbook. Dr

Sinclair has over 20 years of management experience from a number of industries in Europe and the USA, including Silicon Valley.

Madelijn Strick is Post-Doctoral Researcher at the Psychology Department of the Radboud University Nijmegen, the Netherlands. She received her PhD with honors in 2009. Her graduate work on unconscious influences of humorous advertising on consumer behavior was awarded the *Best Dissertation 2009* of the ASPO (Dutch organization for social psychology). Her current research focuses on the benefits and pitfalls of unconscious thought on decision making. She also studies the automatic effects of advertising and social influence techniques on consumer behavior.

Dana Elisa Tomasino is Research Associate at the Institute for Whole Social Science, Northland, New Zealand, and Co-Director at the Center for Advanced Research (CFAR), Neuron Dynamics, Appleton, WI, USA. With her colleagues at the Institute of HeartMath in Boulder Creek, CA, USA, she has studied heart–brain interactions, the heart's role in intuition, and the psycho-physiological mechanisms by which positive emotions influence cognitive processes, intuition, behavior, and health. This research has informed the development of heart-based tools and technologies to optimize individual and organizational health and performance. Her current interests encompass the energetic interactions involved in nonlocal communication, including intuitive perception and nonlocal agency.

Vedran Vranic is an Honours Graduate in Business from Swinburne University of Technology in Melbourne, Australia. Working as Research Assistant for Prof. Langan-Fox, he has contributed to and co-authored three book chapters and two journal articles. He has also completed a degree in Business, majoring in Management and Marketing and a minor in Business Law.

Acknowledgements

First, I would like to thank all contributing authors for their enthusiastic support of this project and their dedication to providing new perspectives that are truly on the cutting edge. My heartfelt thanks go to Francine O'Sullivan, Acquisitions Editor, who showed an unwavering belief in the handbook since its very inception, and to all her colleagues at Edward Elgar who provided assistance. I would also like to pay respects to my mentor, Weston Agor, who dared to research intuition way before most of us did. Finally, all my love goes to my husband Carl who has always been there for me and whose artwork adorns the cover of this book.

Marta Sinclair, Editor

Introduction

Welcome to the first edition of the *Handbook of Intuition Research*. This is by no means an all-encompassing volume on the topic. Rather, it showcases new developments in this field of inquiry, contrasting streams of research embedded in various disciplines. It presents different, often conflicting views on what intuition is and how it works. The handbook offers a glimpse into what is currently happening in the field with the aim of cross-pollinating our knowledge so that intuition research can consolidate and progress to the next, truly multi-disciplinary level. The chapters are meticulously researched and provocative, which will hopefully stimulate our thinking about 'what next'. The views of some authors are not compatible, but it is important to present them in a single volume in order to grasp fully the breadth and depth of intuition research. This is in accordance with consensus reached at the first Intuition Caucus at the Academy of Management meeting in 2009: we need to 'respectfully disagree' in order to expand our understanding beyond the confines of individual disciplines.

The diversity of the presented research will help us appreciate the danger of new theory being developed on conclusions from conceptually incongruous findings. This not only questions rigorousness but, more importantly, it affects the validity of the proposed inferences. That may be why there is a proliferation of theoretical papers, followed by a relative paucity of empirical research, especially that carried out by researchers other than the originators of a particular theory. A collateral of this is the silence about non-significant results that many authors self-censor or deem unimportant to report and, if they dare to do so, they may not find an outlet to publish them. Hence we remain uninformed because these are often the findings that move the field forward as they stimulate our thinking and inform the formulation of future research design. This is not specific to intuition research. Nevertheless, it is particularly damaging in an emerging discipline that is still forming its boundaries. That is why this handbook also includes reports of inconclusive results that point to conceptual or methodological issues to be addressed in subsequent studies. Another unhelpful factor is the overemphasis on quantitative research that may not always be suitable for the study of such a non-conscious phenomenon as intuition and pushes us into a very narrow paradigm, evaluating intuition mostly through the lens of psychology. This has been partially remedied by the emergence of neuroscience research, mapping parts of the brain. However, caution has to be exercised when attributing the 'lit-up' regions of the brain categorically to intuition or its specific functions. Overall, more qualitative studies with inclusion of other disciplines and their investigative methods, such as phenomenology, sociology or quantum physics, should be *integrated* into intuition research, not held in separate compartments.

Sadly, a truly multi-disciplinary perspective on intuition is still lacking. That is why this volume opens with a chapter proposing an overarching framework for intuition research, inviting those active in the field to fill in the blanks and corroborate the outlined differentiations. The ensuing chapters in Part I explore different facets of the intuiting process and its outcome, examining the type of processing, the role of consciousness and affect, and alternative ways of capturing intuition. Part 2 deals with various functions of intuition and how they relate to expertise, strategy, entrepreneurship, and ethics. The chapters in Part 3 outline intuitive decision making in selected practices, such as critical occupations, the legal profession, medicine, the film and wine industries, and teaching. They also examine conceptual issues encountered in the studied context, which have far-reaching implications for other areas of intuition research. Part 4 pushes the boundaries of our current understanding by suggesting the possibility of nonlocal intuition, based on the principles of quantum holography. Finally, the chapters in Part 5 investigate from different perspectives how to develop our intuitive skills and capture fleeting intuitions more effectively.

The learning that can be drawn from this volume is that intuition may be viewed differently if we understand it in its broadest sense as 'direct knowing', which offers an opportunity to reconcile conflicting views by focusing on their *relationships* instead of their differences. This opens a possibility for a new breed of interdisciplinary collaboration projects. The theoretical focus of many chapters in this handbook also highlights the need for more empirical studies that would test the proposed conceptualizations and develop streams of research validating the models in different settings. Another area of concern is the heavy emphasis on decision making while the role of intuition in problem solving and creativity seems to receive less attention, especially in the business and management context. Similarly, more methodological studies are welcome in future volumes, fueling a systematic development of new ways to investigate this fascinating yet elusive phenomenon. And last but not least, there seems to be a lack of cross-cultural research that would examine whether intuition is indeed a universal phenomenon and how its use varies across cultures and professional domains. Overall, this handbook gives us an opportunity to reflect how much intuition research has advanced in the past twenty or so years, and where we should channel our effort next. Let the chapters speak for themselves.

Marta Sinclair, PhD
June 2011

PART 1

CONCEPTUALIZING INTUITION

1 An integrated framework of intuition
Marta Sinclair

One of the reasons why conceptualizations of intuition vary so much is the absence of a comprehensive, overarching framework that would reconcile different views. This void is particularly worrying as individual interpretations often do not contradict but rather focus on specific aspects of intuition, oblivious to the big picture in which they are all embedded. Hence, there is a need for a unifying framework that outlines the relationships of discordant views rather than disqualifying them. In other words, instead of having a debate about what is *not* intuition, we shall shift our focus to how various perspectives complement each other. Creating such a framework requires that we view the construct in its broadest sense as 'direct knowing'. This is, in a way, a return to the original understanding of intuition (Behling & Eckel, 1991; Osbeck, 2001), before we started exploring and defining it in modern times – in an attempt to grasp it. But somewhere along the way we got lost in the myriad of qualifying factors. It is time to reclaim the big picture that will allow us to examine not only different perspectives but also how they relate to each other – and possibly interact. This 'return to basics' will free us to think about intuition in new, fresh terms.

This is a rather speculative chapter, the labels and categories are tentative, and most links are yet to be developed. Some boxes are still empty, waiting for results from future studies. I hereby invite colleague researchers to fill in the blanks: to amend, expand, and modify the proposed framework, which is meant to serve as a starting point for our discussion. Its goal is to help categorize various facets of intuition more clearly and select appropriate tools to capture them. Interestingly, from practitioners' perspective, the usefulness of intuition and the means to develop it may depend on the 'box' we are dealing with. Recent research into the role of emotions and expertise also indicates that intuition is more contextual than we thought (see, e.g., Baylor, 2001; Coget, 2004; Sinclair, 2011). It refers to both how we interact with our environment and what transpires inside us. The identified between- and within-person differences should draw attention to the development of links across categories that would make the proposed framework dynamic. Otherwise we shall end up with another static model that does not reflect accurately what is happening in real life.

'Direct knowing' implies the absence of conscious information processing. It does *not* specify how the information was gleaned, which factors influenced it, and how accurate or effective is the outcome. Paraphrasing Frances Vaughan (1979), it simply states that we know something without knowing how. All 'knowing' is about information. Naturally, questions arise: where do we get this information from, along which channels does it 'travel', and how does it become available to us? This raises a fundamental question for intuition research: does intuitive processing rely exclusively on a separate system or can it use the deliberative system as well? And does the latter scenario imply that intuition could also be inferential, not only holistic? Although Seligman and Kahana (2009) assert that the cognitive architecture of intuition remains mostly a mystery, many advances in mapping the structure have been made. The challenge is rather how to disentangle the confusion stemming from nebulous boundaries among its various facets. Let us start by reviewing the commonly used distinctions and use them as building blocks of the framework.

PROCESSING SYSTEMS

With the onset of dual processing theories (see Evans, 2007; Stanovich & West, 2000), there has been a growing consensus that information is processed by two independent systems that interact seamlessly – until we consciously intervene. Following on that, intuition is believed to be handled by the experiential system (System 1) that is 'preconscious, rapid, automatic, holistic, primarily nonverbal, [and] intimately associated with affect' (Pacini & Epstein, 1999: 972). This view implies that any processing that uses neural pathways for deliberation should be disqualified as intuition. Not necessarily so – if we view intuition in the broad sense of 'direct knowing'. Proponents of naturalistic decision making suggest, for instance, that intuitive expertise is based on quick pattern matching that is too fast for us to register consciously (Klein, 1998, 2003). The information could then very well be processed through the deliberative system. It would mean though that the process is merely non-conscious, rather than preconscious, as stipulated by experientiality. Also, the theory of unconscious thought (Dijksterhuis, 2004) implies that our mind processes information when we divert our conscious attention elsewhere, which does not exclude the employment of a rational/deliberative system (System 2). We somehow assume that deliberation requires awareness – but does it always? Research suggests that humans are capable of complex behavior and activities without conscious awareness (Dijksterhuis & Aarts, 2010), it is yet to be determined whether deliberation is one of them.

Even if some intuiting does utilize the deliberative system, it is not clear whether the processing is structured the same way as conscious deliberating or whether it is organized differently. For instance, could it be more holistic since we do not have to follow the rules of inferential logic that we would impose consciously? Intriguingly, this argument may be tailored to Western cultures where the emphasis is placed on logical reasoning. Social conditioning in some non-Western cultures where intuition is taught from an early age (Iannello, Antonietti, & Betsch, ch. 15 this volume) could result in a reliance on different knowledge structures for both conscious and non-conscious processes. This raises questions about universality of intuition and possible effects of social conditioning on its use. Sadly, a comparative cultural view on intuition in the Western management literature is missing.

PROCESSING TYPE AND STYLE

Inferential Processing

Some researchers make a distinction between an inferential and a holistic type of intuiting which process information differently (e.g., Hill, 1987; Pretz & Totz, 2007). Inferential processing is sometimes likened to 'analysis frozen into habit' in that it relies on automated responses based on a quick recognition of memory patterns accumulated through experience (see Hammond et al., 1987; Pretz, ch. 2 this volume; Simon, 1987). This is the type discussed most frequently in expertise because it requires extensive practice. Nevertheless, its functioning appears to be more fine-grained than that (see Glöckner & Ebert, ch. 14 this volume). It can draw on a quick impression triggered by previous experiences (*associative style*), which presumes minimum processing and its associonistic nature implies involvement of the experiential system. Or it can be more complex in that it compares the current situation with stored mental schemas and searches for a match or an anomaly (*matching style*) (see also Kahneman & Klein, 2009; Klein, ch. 6 this volume). This requires a deeper level of processing that could very well use the deliberative system suited for drawing inferences.

Holistic Processing

The holistic type of intuiting, on the other hand, processes information non-sequentially, in a jigsaw puzzle-like manner (Sinclair & Ashkanasy, 2005). It usually deals with synthesis of 'unconnected memory fragments into a new information structure' (Mintzberg et al., 1998: 164) and is often mentioned in terms of integrating complex information, too complex for a speedy conscious deliberation (Pretz, ch. 2 this volume). Since the intuitive outcome represents something new, it necessitates a more sophisticated processing mechanism than matching. Many authors consider the resulting type of intuition entrepreneurial (Crossan et al., 1999) and creative (Dörfler, 2010). On closer examination of their characteristics, it seems prudent to distinguish between the two.

Borrowing from Dane's (2010) differentiation between incremental and radical idea generation as prevention mechanisms for cognitive entrenchment of experts, I propose a similar distinction here. Incremental intuiting seems to connect information in a new but predictable manner that builds on the existing domain knowledge, which opens the possibility that it could be mediated by the deliberative system. It is amenable to experts relying on extensive schemas (ibid.) and possibly entrepreneurs with experience in spotting opportunities (Sinclair, 2010). This seems to correspond broadly to the description of 'constructive style' offered by Glöckner and Ebert (ch. 14 this volume). It is also plausible that such processing could accommodate the dynamics of unconscious thought (Dijksterhuis, 2004), which was demonstrated even among novices. Radical intuiting, on the other hand, departs dramatically from the existing knowledge patterns and generates a surprising novum in a truly 'creative style' (Dörfler, 2010), which requires a certain predisposition and talent (Kahneman & Klein, 2009). It appears therefore that this processing might be anchored in the experiential system.

Contrary to Dane and Pratt (2009), I have categorized creative intuiting as a style that can be utilized in decision making or problem solving rather than a function itself, as their typology would be understood in the context outlined here. Nevertheless, I concur with their description and characteristics. All labels in the proposed framework are tentative, and the assumptions need to be tested rigorously. Some researchers also identified affective and moral intuition as separate entities (e.g., Dane & Pratt, 2009; Guzak & Hargrove, ch. 9 this volume; Pretz, ch. 2 this volume). I have organized them differently and discuss each in turn in the following sections on processing components and functions.

Nonlocal Processing

There is also the intriguing possibility, implied by theories underpinning *nonlocal* intuition (see Bradley, ch. 17 and Radin, ch. 16 this volume), that no information processing occurs at all – since we receive 'prepackaged' information from somewhere. *Local* intuition assumes that intuitive answers are a result of processed information that we contain in the raw form already (as mental schemas or affectively coded memories; Damasio, 1994, 1999; Simon, 1987) or we have been in contact with (through reading, learning, noticing our environment or other form of cursory exposure; Duggan, 2007; Sinclair, 2010). But what if, in some instances, we tap into an external source of information that does not require any additional modification? A certain extent of processing would be likely even here, especially in the case of goal-directed intuiting (see Strick & Dijksterhuis, ch. 3 this volume). Nonlocalists propose that this could be achieved by means of passionate attention, which is consistent with the question of passion raised in entrepreneurial intuition research (Kickul & Gundry, ch. 8 this volume). And the information would have to be identified through some sort of environmental scanning in order to be 'received'. Of course, all of this is highly speculative but we should reserve space in our framework for this possibility.

Mode of Reception

Putting aside the location of the processed information, there is a higher-order question about the mode of reception – which may not be related to the actual processing at all. Intuition can emerge into our consciousness in various ways. We may register it as a thought, a feeling, or through any of our senses (Vaughan, 1979). The reception mode appears to be very personal and clearly distinct from processing *per se* (Sinclair, 2010). The former refers to how we become aware of intuition as the *outcome* of our information processing while the latter enables the *process* of intuiting that remains 'hidden' from our awareness. As discussed elsewhere (Sinclair, 2010: 3), another distinction has to be made between the lack of awareness of how intuiting occurs and our ability to facilitate the process consciously or even trigger it. There appear to be four levels of awareness in this respect, ranging from an accidental non-conscious situation (when intuition emerges at whim) to an actively conscious approach (when we enter a relaxed mental state with a clear intention to intuit a desired outcome). It seems therefore that 'we can learn how to invoke intuiting at will without knowing how it generates the answer'.

In summary, from the perspective of 'direct knowing', intuiting can utilize experiential *or* deliberative processing; it can be of a holistic *or* an inferential nature in various degrees of complexity, or maybe even received 'prepackaged' from an external source. The resulting intuition can be received through a number of channels, dictated by individual preferences and sensitivities. And while we can learn to intuit we are not aware of its inner workings.

PROCESSING COMPONENTS

Until recently, there has been a split view between proponents of experience-based intuiting who stress its cognitive component or even consider affect detrimental (e.g., Simon, 1987), and those in favor of affect-based intuiting who highlight the emotional and sensory nature of the process (e.g., Epstein, 1990). As I argued elsewhere, these seem to focus merely on different components of the same multifaceted construct (Sinclair & Ashkanasy, 2005). More recent research has taken on a similar perspective and tends to acknowledge the importance of both. I am not qualified to even speculate whether intuiting proper (not the resulting intuition) could occur in the absence of cognition. Let us leave this conclusion to cognitive psychologists and neuroscientists. The more palatable questions at the moment are whether affect is present at all and which function it fulfills. The connection of intuition to the experiential system implies a strong affective component in the embedded styles by default, although as Epstein (ch. 4 this volume) points out, even deliberative processing can be infused with affect (see also Forgas, 1995). While the presence of affect alone does not guarantee intuiting, it remains of interest how prevalent it is in the process.

Affect in Processing Styles

One instance where researchers suggest a dominant role of affect is the associative style which operates via 'relatively direct affective responses to stimuli that result from previous experiences with sufficiently similar stimuli' (Glöckner & Ebert, ch. 14 this volume; see also Slovic et al., 2002). This mechanism could be attributed to somatic markers which are affectively encoded memories reactivated in a context-congruent situation (Damasio, 1994; see also Sinclair et al., 2009). The associative style therefore appears to function as simple 'affective matching' between the received stimulus and its counterpart in the 'somatic bank'. Interestingly, somatic states seem to activate different parts of the brain depending on the provenance of the stimulus (Reimann & Bechara, 2010), which implies that the underpinning mechanism may be less straightforward than it appears at first sight. Moreover, the above discussion does not preclude the possibility that this simple matching mechanism may also be triggered by a different, non-affective kind of a cue.

   In more complex intuiting, the importance of affect may depend on the novelty of the faced problem or decision. As Bechara (2004) suggests, dealing with an unfamiliar situation may require a stronger presence of affect as the information 'travels' via the (affect-rich) 'body loop' while less novel situations are assessed via the (affect-poor) 'as-if' loop. There is a possibility that affect can be absent altogether, for instance, in some kind of super-speed inferential processing. This could be the case of the matching style that draws on habitual mental schemas. Following on this argument, affect is likely to be found in both constructive and creative intuiting, although one would expect it to be less prevalent in the constructive style that relies on a new arrangement of established *convergent* patterns (see Dane & Pratt, 2009). On the contrary, since creative intuiting deals with a markedly new constellation of *divergent* associations, affect is likely to play a more important role in this style, which is consistent with its proposed embeddedness in holistic processing of the experiential system. Reports about affective intensity of creative intuiting abound in the literature (e.g., Hayashi, 2001; Monsay, 1997) but it is yet to be determined whether affect is *inherent* in the processing or whether it acts merely as a conduit. 'In other words', as I asked recently (Sinclair, 2010: 4), 'is the affective component built in the stored information that is processed intuitively – or is it "hard-wired" in the pathway along which intuiting proceeds?'.

Affect as Antecedent or Attribute

The above discussion relates to intuiting proper, which is distinct from what happens *before* and *after* it. In the antecedent stage, affective factors were found to be influential (see Epstein, ch. 4 this volume; Sinclair et al., 2010). Although a comprehensive summary of factors facilitating intuition is beyond the scope of this chapter, I would like to mention a few new developments on the affective front where research to date has focused mostly on the influence of generic mood. More attention should be paid to mood intensity that may override the opposite effects of positive vs. negative mood (see Sinclair et al., 2010). New findings also indicate that discrete moods (such as happy vs. glad) and emotions (such as angry vs. fearful) could have different effects that might even be contextual. This could be the case of emotional intuitive decision making reported by Coget (ch. 12 this volume). Intense anger or fear as determinants of information processing can hinder intuiting if the decision maker focuses on the emotion itself. This may result in substandard deliberation, if not paralysis. Alternatively, the decision maker may activate effective intuiting if he/ she 'channels the emotional charge' into the intention to reach the desired goal (see Sinclair et al., 2002). In the post-processing stage, or at the onset of intuition emergence into consciousness, its most commonly mentioned attribute is a confirmatory feeling, which is usually of an affective nature but not always (see Sinclair, 2010).

PROCESSING FUNCTIONS

Traditional Perspective: Decision Making and Problem Solving

It seems that, like other information processing, intuiting serves predominantly two functions: decision making and problem solving. There appears to be a different dynamic in each, although these functions are usually intertwined (Dane & Pratt, 2009; Dörfler, 2010). Most research in management has been conducted in the decision-making paradigm, which may be the reason for the emphasis on expertise and speed. With the exception of quick holistic associations (associative style), it appears to be more closely linked to the convergent variants of intuiting that may utilize the deliberative system, such as matching and constructive styles.

Decision making, however, offers a rather narrow view of intuiting. Complex problem solving often requires a protracted incubation period (Goldberg, 1983), hence the discrepancy regarding the role of speed. Also, it often involves dealing with new situations, otherwise the problem would be treated routinely; consequently there is a higher likelihood that an experiential system with affect infusion will be activated (see Sinclair, 2010). However, like in decision making, it depends on how the retrieved information is used. If the situation is simply matched to stored patterns (matching style), then inferential and deliberative aspects are more likely to be at play. If schemas are 'reshuffled' in a new but predictable way, an incremental innovation may be generated (constructive style). And if the process is used to create something fundamentally new, then the likely outcome will be a creation, an invention, or a scientific discovery, as a result of creative intuiting. As discussed previously, the more novel the situation, the more likely it is that experiential processing will be used with a stronger presence of affect.

Although I use different labels, the above distinction is overall consistent with Dane and Pratt's (2009) differentiation between problem-solving intuition (here decision-making function) and creative intuition (here problem-solving function). As elucidated above, the key distinction between the two approaches is that I do not view these as intuition types but rather as processing functions that can be applied to any type (and its embedded styles).

As mentioned earlier, some researchers also recognize moral intuition as a separate type (ibid.; Guzak & Hargrove, ch. 9 this volume) but I see it as an affect-driven variant of the decision-making function. In the case of individual, personal decisions, it is likely to rely on a simple associative style, matching quickly the given situation with a socially conditioned schema. Since the sense of rightness usually evokes strong feelings in individuals, one would expect the association to occur by means of the previously discussed 'affective matching'. In the case of law professionals adjudicating morality, the style is likely to be more complex, usually that of constructive intuiting (Glöckner & Ebert, ch. 14 this volume). Since this type of processing relies heavily on the social construction of what we consider right or wrong, I concur with Dane and Pratt (2009) that it is likely to be heavily influenced by culture. This accentuates my previous call for more comparative cultural research.

Neglected Perspective: Interpersonal Interaction

Not much has been written in the academic literature about intuiting between/among people, probably because it implies a transpersonal interaction. Naturally, a lot of information can be gleaned non-consciously from non-verbal cues, such as facial expressions, gestures, or tone of voice (e.g., Kahneman & Klein, 2009). These are usually expressions of an underlying emotion; hence one would consider it likely that people-related intuiting will be affect-infused. Other than that, there is no substantiation so far to assume that the gathered information would be processed differently from task-related intuiting. That applies to the local variant of the process.

Should we be able to receive information from or about another person (or event, for that matter) externally, as the nonlocal perspective proposes (see Radin, ch. 16 this volume), then an interpersonal connection is needed. That goes for interaction in the same physical location as well as at a distance. If this is indeed the case, then more research into the dynamic of the processing will be needed. Heart studies also indicate that we might be able to intuit events before they actually occur (see Bradley ch. 17 and Tomasino, ch. 21 this volume). Although the current research has identified a lead-time only in terms of seconds, it opens an intriguing possibility for redefining our understanding of foresight, both in people- and task-related intuiting.

AN INTEGRATED FRAMEWORK: INFORMATION-BASED FUNCTIONALITY

Another way of categorizing intuitive processes is according to the nature of the processed information. Extending the previously outlined differentiation (see Sinclair, 2010, for an overview), I reviewed (i) type of information, (ii) point of time when the information was acquired, and (iii) location of the information. Based on combinations of the first two factors, I grouped intuitive functions into intuitive expertise, intuitive creation, and intuitive foresight. The third factor has been added in this chapter. Although I agree with Dane and Pratt (2009) that these labels may confound the discussion since they confuse intuiting with its antecedents (expertise) or possible outcomes (creativity), the intention was to create generic categories that would reconcile previously conflicting views. The labels, however, are arbitrary and open to suggestions. Labeling debate aside, let us focus first on the information typology:

Type of information   One way to distinguish the provenance of information, common in the literature, is among (i) domain-specific expertise, (ii) general experience, and (iii) cursory exposure. While expertise presupposes an extensive network of information patterns in a specific domain (e.g., chemistry) and/or practice (e.g., conflict resolution) (Klein, 1998; Simon, 1987), general experience relates to accumulated bits of information from unrelated domains or life in general, which seem to provide additional stimuli in more complex intuiting (see Dane, 2010; Monsay, 1997). Furthermore, we should take into account the impact of a cursory exposure that may act as a catalyst, especially for the creative style (Sinclair, 2010). In summary, when intuiting, we draw on different 'pools' of stored information in a varied depth – but also breadth if we combine information from various pools.

Time acquisition of information   This relates to the point of time when the processed information is integrated into our knowledge structure. The obvious benchmarks on the time continuum are (i) past, (ii) present, and (iii) future. Most information we accumulated in the past, through learning, practice, or other type of exposure, and stored in schemas or somatic markers in our brain or other parts of the body (see, e.g., Damasio, 1994; Duggan & Mason, ch. 7 and Klein, ch. 6 this volume). Some information, as mentioned above, we appropriate at the moment of processing in the form of a current stimulus or fleeting exposure (Sinclair, 2010). It may be the missing 'piece of the puzzle' we have been waiting for in order to process, as often reported by artists or inventors. Another mind-boggling possibility suggested by nonlocal presentiment experiments, is that we might be able to connect to information residing in the future (see Bradley, ch. 17, and Radin, ch. 16, this volume).

Location of information   Also there appear to be three categories, depending on where the information is located in relation to us: (i) local internal, (ii) local external, and (iii) nonlocal. Large amounts of information have already been stored in our system; hence most of the intuiting is focused inward (local internal) (Kahneman & Klein, 2009). As outlined above, some elements may be gleaned from the surrounding environment at the present moment. These are the outward stimuli incorporated into the processing as it occurs (local external) (Sinclair, 2010). And following on the nonlocal perspective argument, it is to be determined whether we may tune into information that is outside of our mental and physical presence.

Intuitive Expertise, Creation, and Foresight

Using the tentative labels (see Table 1.1) it becomes obvious that each of the three intuitive functions relies on a different combination of information in terms of the above categories (see Sinclair, 2010). *Intuitive expertise* draws mostly on locally stored domain-specific patterns accumulated in the past. Following on the prior discussion about its convergent focus, it is likely that it will utilize predominantly the matching and constructive styles with little or no involvement of affect. *Intuitive creation* also tends to handle domain-specific information (however, not always), but it usually incorporates general experience, and cursory exposure. This means that the information has more breadth, and although it can be sourced from the past, it has a critical present element. Being of a local nature, it remains to be seen whether it can also tap into nonlocal sources, as implied by findings from entrepreneurial research. Depending on whether the processed patterns are combined in a convergent or divergent manner, it is likely to utilize the constructive or creative style with lower and higher presence of affect, respectively. Least is known about the inner workings of *intuitive foresight*. It appears that it uses the broadest scope of information, possibly encompassing expertise, experience, and cursory exposure. Although it may utilize locally stored information from the past, conclusions from strategic intuition research hint at the coalescing effect of a present stimulus, while entrepreneurial research even suggests the possibility of sensing from the future. A collateral implication is that some of the information might be sourced nonlocally. A question remains whether foresight could be accommodated by the constructive style, drawing on expertise in spotting opportunities, or whether it is reliant on the creative style, combining diverse stimuli along the time continuum. In this case, the role of passionate attention would call for a strong presence of affect. These conclusions are, of course, speculative and warrant a research scrutiny. I hereby invite everybody's contribution.

Table 1.1   Integrated Framework of Intuition – Tentative Categorization

	Intuitive expertise	Intuitive creation	Intuitive foresight
Type of information			
Domain-specific expertise	xx	x	xx
General experience	x	xx	xx
Cursory exposure	?	xx	xx
Time acquisition of information			
Past	xx	x	x
Present	x	xx	xx
Future	?	?	??
Location of information			
Local internal	xx	xx	x?
Local external	x	xx	xx
Nonlocal	?	?	??
Processing style			
Associative	x	?	?
Matching	xx	?	?
Constructive	xx	x?	x?
Creative	?	xx	x?
Processing type			
Inferential	xx	?	x?
Holistic	x	xx	x?
Processing system			
Deliberative	xx	?	x?
Experiential	x	xx	x?
Involvement of affect			
Low to none	xx	?	?
Some	x	x	x
Dominant	?	xx	xx
Main function			
Decision making	xx	x?	x?
Problem solving	x	xx	x?
Personal interaction	x	?	x?
Type of outcome			
Decision about existing issue/dilemma	xx	x?	n/a
Solution to existing problems	xx	x	n/a
Creation of new knowledge	?	xx	x?
Relationship impact	?	?	?
Information about future	?	?	xx

Table 1.1   (continued)

	Intuitive expertise	Intuitive creation	Intuitive foresight
Area of application	Professional domain and/ or practice	Creation Innovation Invention	Future opportunities and/or issues
Influential antecedents	Complexity etc.	Novelty etc.	Passionate attention ?
Outcome attributes	Speed etc.	Aha moment etc.	?

Note: xx = highly likely; x = probably; x? = maybe; ? = to be determined; ?? = to be determined but theorized.

REFERENCES

Bechara, A. 2004. The role of emotion in decision-making: Evidence from neurological patients with orbitofrontal damage. *Brain and Cognition*, 55: 30–40.

Behling, O., & Eckel, N. L. 1991. Making sense out of intuition. *Academy of Management Executive*, 5(1): 46–54.

Baylor, A. L. 2001. A U-shaped model for the development of intuition by level of expertise. *New Ideas in Psychology*, 19: 237–244.

Coget, J. F. 2004. *Leadership in motion: An investigation into the psychological processes that drive behavior when leaders respond to 'real-time' operational challenges*. Doctoral dissertation. Anderson School of Management, UCLA.

Crossan, M. M., Lane, H., & White, R. E. 1999. An organizational learning framework: From intuition to institution. *Academy of Management Review*, 24(3): 522–537.

Damasio, A. R. 1994. *Descartes' error: Emotion, reason and the human brain*. New York: HarperCollins.

Damasio, A. R. 1999. *The feeling of what happens: Body, emotion and the making of consciousness*. London: Vintage.

Dane, E. 2010. Reconsidering the trade-off between expertise and flexibility: A cognitive entrenchment perspective. *Academy of Management Review*, 35: 579–603.

Dane, E., & Pratt, M. G. 2009. Conceptualizing and measuring intuition: A review of recent trends. *International Review of Industrial and Organizational Psychology*, 24: 1–40.

Dijksterhuis, A. 2004. Think different: The merits of unconscious thought in preference development and decision making. *Journal of Personality and Social Psychology*, 87: 586–598.

Dijksterhuis, A., & Aarts, H. 2010. Goals, attention, and (un)consciousness. *Annual Review of Psychology*, 61: 467–490.

Dörfler, V. 2010. *Creative intuition*. Manuscript in preparation. Strathclyde University, Glasgow.

Duggan, W. 2007. *Strategic intuition*. New York: Columbia Business School Publishing.

Epstein, S. 1990. Cognitive–experiential self-theory. In L. Pervin (Ed.), *Handbook of personality theory and research*: 165–192. New York: Guilford Press.

Evans, J. St. B. T. 2007. *Hypothetical thinking: Dual processes in reasoning and judgment*. Hove, UK: Psychology Press.

16   *Handbook of intuition research*

Forgas, J. P. 1995. Mood and judgment: The Affect Infusion Model (AIM). *Psychological Bulletin*, 117: 39–66.
Goldberg, P. 1983. *The intuitive edge: Understanding and developing intuition*. Los Angeles: Jeremy P. Tarcher.
Hammond, K. R., Hamm, R. M., Grassia, J., & Pearson, T. 1987. Direct comparison of the efficacy of intuitive and analytical cognition in expert judgment, *IEEE Transactions on Systems, Man, and Cybernetics*, 17(5): 753–770.
Hayashi, A. M. 2001. When to trust your gut. *Harvard Business Review*, 79: 59–65.
Hill, O. W. 1987. Intuition: Inferential heuristic or epistemic mode? *Imagination, Cognition, and Personality*, 7(2): 137–154.
Kahneman, D., & Klein, G. 2009. Conditions for intuitive expertise: A failure to disagree. *American Psychologist*, 64: 515–526.
Klein, G. 1998. *Sources of power: How people make decisions*. Cambridge, MA: MIT Press.
Klein, G. 2003. *Intuition at work*. New York: Doubleday.
Mintzberg, H., Ahlstrand, B., & Lampel, J. 1998. *Strategy safari: A guided tour through the wilds of strategic management*. New York: Free Press.
Monsay, E. H. 1997. Intuition in the development of scientific theory and practice. In R. Davis-Floyd, & P. S. Arvidson (Eds.), *Intuition: The inside story*: 103–120. New York: Routledge.
Osbeck, L. M. 2001. Direct apprehension and social construction: Revisiting the concept of intuition. *Journal of Theoretical and Philosophical Psychology*, 21(2): 118–131.
Pacini, R., & Epstein, S. 1999. The relation of rational and experiential information processing styles to personality, basic beliefs, and the ratio-bias phenomenon. *Journal of Personality and Social Psychology*, 76: 972–987.
Pretz, J. E., & Totz, K. S. 2007. Measuring individual differences in affective, heuristic, and holistic intuition. *Personality and Individual Differences*, 43: 1247–1257.
Reimann, M., & Bechara, A. 2010. The somatic marker framework as a neurological theory of decision-making: Review, conceptual comparisons, and future neuroeconomics research. *Journal of Economic Psychology*, 31(5): 767–776.
Seligman, M. E. P., & Kahana, M. 2009. Unpacking intuition: A conjecture. *Perspectives on Psychological Science*, 4(4): 399–402.
Simon, H. A. 1987. Making management decisions: The role of intuition and emotion. *Academy of Management Executive*, February: 57–64.
Sinclair, M. 2010. Misconceptions about intuition. *Psychological Inquiry*, 21: 1–9.
Sinclair, M. 2011. *Intuitive profile of film makers*. Paper presented at the Academy of Management annual meeting, San Antonio, TX, August, 12–16.
Sinclair, M., & Ashkanasy, N. M. 2005. Intuition: Myth or a decision-making tool. *Management Learning*, 36(3): 353–370.
Sinclair, M., Ashkanasy, N. M., & Chattopadhyay, P. 2010. Affective antecedents of intuitive decision making. *Journal of Management and Organization*, 1: 382–398.
Sinclair, M., Ashkanasy, N. M., Chattopadhyay, P., & Boyle, M. V. 2002. Determinants of intuitive decision-making in management: The moderating role of affect. In N. M. Ashkanasy, W. J. Zerbe, & C. E. J. Härtel (Eds.), *Managing emotions in the workplace*: 143–163. Armonk: M. E. Sharpe.
Sinclair, M., Sadler-Smith, E., & Hodgkinson, G. P. 2009. The role of intuition in strategic decision making. In L. Costanzo & R. B. McKay (Eds.), *The handbook of research on strategy and foresight*: 393–417. Cheltenham, UK and Northampton, MA, USA: Edward Elgar.
Slovic, P., Finucane, M., Peters, E., & MacGregor, D. G. 2002. The affect heuristic. In T. Gilovich, D. Griffin, & D. Kahneman (Eds.), *Heuristics and biases: The psychology of intuitive judgment*: 397–420. New York: Cambridge University Press.
Stanovich, K. E., & West, R. F. 2000. Individual differences in reasoning: Implications for the rationality debate? *Behavioral and Brain Sciences*, 23: 645–65.
Vaughan, F. E. 1979. *Awakening intuition*. New York: Doubleday.

2 Types of intuition: inferential and holistic
Jean E. Pretz

For decades, psychologists have viewed intuition as primarily irrational and unreliable. Research in the heuristics and biases paradigm has consistently shown that intuitive judgments resulting from the use of heuristics (mental short cuts) are inaccurate and systematically biased (Tversky & Kahneman, 1974). However, recent work challenges this pessimistic view, documenting conditions under which intuitions are not only accurate, but actually more reliable than judgments resulting from analysis (Dijksterhuis, 2004; Kahneman & Klein, 2009; Klein, 1998; McMackin & Slovic, 2000).

In order to organize and interpret the contradictory evidence in the psychological literature, we must clarify what is meant by 'intuition' and examine the circumstances that affect its reliability and accuracy. In this chapter, I shall argue for a distinction between 'inferential intuition' and 'holistic intuition' and use this distinction to show that intuition is accurate for highly complex tasks and for individuals on either end of the novice/expert continuum. I define inferential intuition as judgments based on analytical processes that have become automatic through practice. In contrast, classical intuitions are holistic judgments that integrate complex information. This Gestalt perspective on intuition emphasizes that the whole is greater than the sum of the parts. Holistic intuition is qualitatively non-analytical (Betsch, 2008; Hill, 1987–88; Pretz & Totz, 2007).

THEORETICAL VIEWS OF INTUITION

Both types of intuition can be identified in historical work on the construct. Jung (1971) viewed intuition as a holistic mode of perception. Intuitive types prefer to engage in inward-focused, subconscious processing of information, whereas sensate types are focused outward on sensory experiences. Intuition involves imagining abstract possibility, not necessarily concrete reality, and intuitive types are adept at sensing patterns rather than focusing on precise details. In Jung's view, intuition can be a valuable source of insight, and is not seen as a source of bias or error. In contrast, Westcott and Ranzoni (1963: 595) viewed intuition as an automatic inference, defining it as 'the process of reaching a conclusion on the basis of little information which is normally reached on the basis of significantly more information'. Westcott (1961: 267) calls such judgments 'intuitive leaps', and explains that these judgments 'may be differentiated from "ordinary" inference primarily by the size of the gap between evidence and conclusion'.

The difference between Jung's and Westcott's notions of intuition was noted by Hill (1987–88), who contrasted the 'classical' notion of intuition with an 'inferential' understanding of the construct. Classical intuition, according to Hill, is a holistic, non-analytical judgment which is based on an integration of complex information. Inferential intuition, in contrast, is an analytical judgment that has become automatic through practice. In the inferential sense, intuition is 'a heuristic that represents a logical (inferential) process in which several intermediary steps have been omitted or obscured' (ibid.: 138). Both types of intuition can result in quick judgments, but they result from distinct cognitive processes. Though some have used the term 'heuristic' to describe inferential intuition (Hill, 1987–88; Pretz & Totz, 2007), inferential intuition is assumed to rely on a great deal of information that has been automatized, unlike a heuristic judgment that is based on a small subset of relevant information, as in the heuristics and biases paradigm.

Intuition has also been defined in contrast to analysis. Hammond (1996: 60) described intuition in its classical sense, arguing that intuitions are the result of the holistic integration of multiple cues without awareness or the availability of an explicit rule, defining intuition as the opposite of analysis, 'a cognitive process that somehow produces an answer, solution, or idea without the use of a conscious, logically defensible, step-by-step process'. Recent dual process models of mind contrast implicit, intuitive processing with explicit, analytical processing (Epstein, 1991; Hogarth, 2001; Sloman, 1996). The implicit, intuitive system operates largely without conscious awareness, requires little attention or effort, and processes information associatively and holistically, whereas the explicit, rational system operates with awareness, attention, and effort. Explicit processing is rule based and analytical. Intuition can be placed in this larger theoretical context; however, dual process theory does not distinguish between inferential and holistic processing in the implicit mode.

EMPIRICAL EVIDENCE FOR THE DISTINCTION

Inferential and holistic intuition rely on different mechanisms. Inferential intuitive judgments rely on automated analyses whereas holistic intuitive judgments rely on holistic integration of cues. Evidence for the distinction between analytical and holistic mechanisms comes from the literatures in experimental cognitive psychology, neuroscience, and personality psychology.

Cognitive Psychology

A classic paper in the cognitive literature demonstrated the successful use of holistic intuition on a timed word association task (Bowers et al., 1990). In the 'Dyads of Triads' task, participants attempted to solve simultaneously two sets of three words, one of which was an item from the Remote Associates Test, by finding a fourth word that was associated with one of the triads (only one triad had a solution). Evidence for the automatic and holistic integration of the stimuli was found when participants were able to reliably guess which triad had a solution, even when they could not consciously derive a solution in the allotted time. More recent work has confirmed the power of holistic intuition in other paradigms (Dijksterhuis, 2004; McMackin & Slovic, 2000).

Evidence from the literature on expertise shows the value of inferential intuition. Expert knowledge is chunked in a meaningful way, allowing experts to rely on long-term memory of typical configurations of pieces and knowledge of strategies, freeing up short-term memory for additional processing (Chi et al., 1988). Experts automatically recognize familiar situations and intuitively know how to respond (Chase & Simon, 1973; Klein, 1998).

Neuroscience

Neuroscientific evidence shows that holistic and analytic processing rely on different neural systems. Lieberman (2007) has outlined two systems that may underlie behavior in each of the dual processing modes – the reflexive and reflective systems. The reflexive or 'X' system involves processing in the amygdala, basal ganglia, lateral temporal cortex, ventromedial prefrontal cortex (VMPFC), and the dorsal anterior cingulate cortex. Activation in the basal ganglia and VMPFC has been associated with implicit learning, the non-conscious acquisition of knowledge. The reflective or 'C' system involves processing in the rostral anterior cingulate cortex (rACC), the lateral prefrontal cortex (LPFC), posterior parietal cortex, hippocampus, and medial temporal lobe. Activation in the LPFC is associated with working memory, which involves effortful, serial processing, and the rACC is involved in consciously overriding automatic processes. The two systems operate independently. Activation in one system is uncorrelated (or negatively correlated) with activation in the other.

The process of automatizing analytic, serial processes also results in changes in neural activity, as shown in studies of skill acquisition. As a process becomes automatic, overall activation lessens and becomes more focused (Hill & Schneider, 2006). In early stages of skill acquisition, a domain general control network is activated that directs attention and effort to various aspects of the novel task. The control network consists of structures associated with the C system. As the task becomes more familiar and automated, activation in the control network decreases, whereas activation in areas required for task performance (e.g., motor areas, modality-specific regions) remains comparable across all stages of skill acquisition (Chein & Schneider, 2005 as cited in Hill & Schneider, 2006). Experts recruit more specific, focused areas of relevant neural systems to complete a task, whereas broader brain areas are recruited in novices to complete the same task. These findings support the argument that inferential and holistic intuition rely on distinct mechanisms and suggest that neural processing associated with inferential intuition should be more focused than that associated with holistic or analytical processing among individuals with less experience.

Personality Psychology

Additional evidence for the distinction between holistic and inferential intuition comes from the personality literature. Pretz and Totz (2007) compared two commonly used measures of intuition, the Myers Briggs Type Indicator (MBTI; Myers et al., 1998) and the Rational Experiential Inventory (REI; Pacini & Epstein, 1999), and discovered that the two did not tap identical constructs in their assessment of preferences for 'intuition'. The MBTI intuitive/sensate subscale uniquely measured holistic intuition, whereas the REI experiential subscale assessed intuition in a more general sense, with no distinction between holistic and inferential intuition. Further examination of the relationship between the MBTI and the REI subscales revealed that MBTI intuition was more strongly related to REI rational favorability than REI experiential scores. This was based on the fact that the two scales tapped a preference for abstract, conceptual thinking, essentially holistic intuition.

A newly developed measure, the Types of Intuition Scale (TIntS; Pretz et al., 2010), aims to assess individual differences in preference for three types of intuition: holistic, inferential, and affective. Affective intuition refers to judgments based on feeling as opposed to thinking, whereas holistic intuition and inferential intuition do not necessarily rely on emotion. Results have shown that the scores on the three types are uncorrelated and that the three are differentially related to other self-report measures, supporting their uniqueness. Specifically, holistic intuition was moderately positively correlated with REI rational favorability, MBTI intuition, and openness to experience, whereas inferential intuition was correlated only weakly with these constructs. Tolerance for ambiguity was moderately positively correlated with holistic intuition but unrelated to inferential. Inferential intuition was correlated with extraversion and agreeableness, but holistic was not. These preliminary findings suggest that not only are holistic and inferential intuition theoretically distinct constructs, but that individuals can make a distinction between them in reporting their decision-making preferences as well.

ACCURACY OF INTUITION DEPENDS ON TASK COMPLEXITY AND EXPERIENCE

Intuition and Task Complexity

Several researchers have proposed that the validity of intuition depends on task complexity (Hammond et al., 1987; Hogarth, 2005). If a problem is relatively straightforward, with a small set of variables, decisions can be made using an analytical 'formula'. However, some problems may involve so many relevant factors that the explicit system is too challenged to compute the solution. In such cases, an intuitive decision will be necessary.

Hogarth (2005) has articulated predictions for the success of the tacit (intuitive) and deliberate (analytical) systems as a function of task complexity. Specifically, he expects that deliberate thought will be most accurate for problems with relatively low complexity and when tacit processes give rise to relatively large bias or error. In contrast, the tacit system will produce more accurate responses for items with relatively high analytical complexity and when the bias implied by the tacit system is relatively small. Specifically, I argue that the high complexity problems are best approached with holistic intuition.

Much evidence exists for the superiority of holistic over analytical judgments. In a now classic study, Wilson and Schooler (1991) asked participants to rate several kinds of strawberry jam. Some were asked to give overall ratings, whereas others were first asked to indicate their reasons for liking or disliking each jam. Results showed that overall, holistic judgments corresponded more closely to expert judgments than those given after explicitly evaluating the jam. The authors argued that the reasons manipulation directed participants' attention to various aspects of the jam that may not have been an accurate representation of the factors discriminating good from bad jam. It is possible that merely considering a subset of jam features caused participants to implicitly overweight those features in their judgment and potentially exclude others that they did not consider as reasons. McMackin and Slovic (2000) reinforced this explanation, showing that asking participants to provide reasons for their ratings interfered with intuitive judgments but facilitated analytical judgments. More recent work by Dijksterhuis (2004) has shown that in tasks requiring the integration of a great deal of information, analytical deliberation resulted in more suboptimal judgments than did 'unconscious' deliberation (a period of distraction). It is clear that holistic, intuitive judgments are not necessarily biased and error prone, but can instead yield accurate responses, especially for tasks that require the weighting and integration of many pieces of information.

Other evidence suggests that implicit, intuitive processing may be superior to analytic processing because it is less susceptible to fixation on incorrect or misleading information. Classic research by Berry and Broadbent (1988) showed that instructions to explicitly seek a rule resulted in worse performance in a process-control task than instructions that did not mention the existence of a rule. When the rule was relatively simple, the explicit approach facilitated performance, but when the rule was relatively complex, rule-seeking instructions led to worse performance. A replication and extension of this work explained the pattern of results, showing that rule seeking on complex problems may have led to fixation on an incorrect rule, whereas those who did not seek a rule were better able to passively acquire complex knowledge of the structure of the learning environment (Pretz & Zimmerman, 2009).

Intuition and Experience

A corollary argument to this view of the relationship between intuition and complexity regards the relationship between intuition and experience. To the extent that an individual has more experience in a domain, he or she will perceive problems in that domain as less complex. Therefore, if analysis facilitates the processing of relatively simple tasks, experts should have more success with an explicit, analytical approach than those with less experience in that domain. In the same vein, to the extent that a person has very little experience in a domain, an intuitive approach may be superior to an analytical one.

Evidence for the benefit of a holistic intuitive approach for novices comes from a study of medical reasoning (Norman et al., 1999). Undergraduate psychology students were asked to make diagnoses on the basis of electrocardiograms. The forward-reasoning strategy required participants to examine the data first and then apply given rules to create a diagnosis.

The backward-reasoning strategy encouraged participants to first create a hypothesized diagnosis and then seek data that supported that diagnosis. Accuracy rates were higher for the backward-reasoning group, showing the advantage of holistic judgment among those with little experience.

Evidence for the benefit of an analytical approach for experts has been found in a study of everyday problem solving (Pretz, 2008). Undergraduate students solved everyday problems about college life (e.g., how to get along with a roommate, manage time, interact with professors) using a situational judgment task. Strategy use (holistic intuition vs. analysis) was manipulated to observe its effect on problem solving for novice and experienced participants. Results showed that experienced students who used holistic intuition scored worse than those who used analysis. In contrast, undergraduates in the first few weeks on campus performed slightly better when using the intuitive strategy than when using the analytical strategy, although this was not a significant effect. This interaction between strategy and experience was replicated when comparing participants based on their self-reported preferred strategy (as measured by the REI). These findings support the view that novices benefit from holistic intuition, whereas experts benefit from analysis.

Yet there is a great deal of psychological literature showing that the highly organized knowledge base of experts yields accurate intuitive responses. Klein (1998) has described numerous stories illustrating how expert firefighters and nurses make decisions with remarkable speed and accuracy by trusting intuition. In these cases in which judgments are time-sensitive and involve high stakes, it is likely that adopting an analytical strategy will not improve the decision outcome and may actually interfere with successful intuitive decision making. In such cases, experts rely on inferential intuition. Their expert knowledge is organized into sophisticated schemas based on their extensive experience in the domain. Although experts' highly organized knowledge allows them to recognize patterns in their domain of expertise, this knowledge is not necessarily impermeable to consciousness. Schmidt and Boshuizen (1993) showed that although medical experts recalled fewer details about a set of cases, presumably because of their encapsulated expert knowledge, probing questions revealed that experts actually remembered more details about the cases than did those with less experience.

How do we reconcile the evidence that experts have powerful intuition with the findings that those with experience benefit from the use of analysis? It is likely that the experts sampled in the college student study were intermediate experts. Baylor (2001) has proposed a developmental theory of the relationship between experience and availability of intuition. This theory predicts that this relationship will be U-shaped, with intuition highest for novices and experts and lowest for intermediate experts. She explains that novices have too little knowledge on which to base an analytical approach to a problem, forcing them to rely on an intuitive sense when responding. As experience is gained, intermediate experts practice invoking the rules of the field, facilitating an analytical response. Finally, when mastery is achieved, experts no longer need to work through the steps of the analysis and can instead rely on a sophisticated, knowledge-based intuition. This view of intuition and experience supports the idea that there are two kinds of intuition, one that is used by those with little experience (holistic intuition) and one that is used by those with a great deal of experience (inferential intuition). Whereas intuition is typically associated with high levels of experience, I argue that holistic intuition in particular can be successfully used by those with little experience in a domain.

ACCURACY OF HOLISTIC AND INFERENTIAL INTUITION

Theory and evidence support the assertion that accuracy of intuition depends on both task complexity and experience. Intuition is likely to be most reliable for novices, experts, and for highly complex problems, whereas analysis is most likely to be reliable for intermediate experts and for the least complex problems. Figure 2.1 proposes a new model of the relationship between appropriateness of intuition and analysis as a function of task complexity and experience. This model builds on a synthesis of theory proposed by Hogarth (2005) and Baylor (2001). Intuition is best for the least complex and for the most complex tasks, with tasks of intermediate complexity being best approached analytically. This U-shaped relationship between strategy and complexity also depends on experience level. The same problem may be best approached analytically by a novice yet intuitively by an expert because perceived complexity is relative to the experience of the individual.

Using this model, we can further predict when each type of intuition will be accurate on the basis of complexity and experience. Holistic intuition is likely to be the most appropriate strategy when problems are perceived as highly complex, whether due to lack of experience or simply the large number of variables involved. In such instances, attempts to analyze are likely to emphasize a subset of cues that may not be the most diagnostic. Holistic intuition is represented in the model as the left side of each U-curve. In contrast, inferential intuition is likely to be best when problems are perceived as relatively simple, whether due to expertise or because the problem is relatively straightforward. An expert can trust inferential

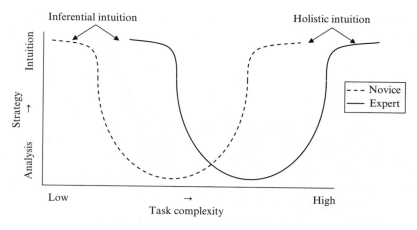

Note: Strategy appropriateness depends on task complexity and expertise. At relatively low levels of task complexity, inferential intuition can be used (left side of the U). As complexity increases, analysis becomes more appropriate (trough of the U). For highly complex tasks, holistic intuition is best (right side of the U). Perceived task complexity depends on level of experience, with novices perceiving problems as more complex than experts do.

Figure 2.1   *Inferential and Holistic Intuition as a Function of Task Complexity and Experience Level*

intuition because of his or her extensive practice with the task. Inferential intuition is represented in the model as the right side of each U-curve. We can also make predictions for cases that lie in-between these extremes on a continuum of complexity and experience.

This model has implications for future work in cognition, neuroscience, and personality. Researchers must consider both the task complexity and the experience of the individual when predicting the accuracy of intuition. In future work, cognitive psychologists should manipulate task complexity to examine its effect on intuitive judgment among individuals of a similar level of experience. Longitudinal designs can be used to observe changes in intuition on the same task as expertise is developed. If the model is correct, an intermediate effect (Schmidt & Boshuizen, 1993) should be observed as a task becomes more complex and as experience is gained. Research in neuroscience should confirm the proposed mechanism underlying the two types of intuition. Brain imaging should be used to detect predicted changes in patterns of activation from the X system to the C system and back again as a task becomes more complex or as expertise develops. Current work on preferences for intuition as a personality variable is examining the validity of the types of intuition scale, with an aim to examine its predictive validity on cognitive tasks involving implicit learning, classic judgment and decision making, insight problem solving, and creativity (Pretz et al., 2010). However, the value of this approach to measuring global preferences may be limited, given the fact that the appropriateness of intuition is a function of task complexity and experience. Measures of preference may need to specify a domain of expertise in order to accurately assess individual differences in preference for intuition.

For decades, most psychologists have viewed intuition with skepticism, but this view is now challenged by evidence that intuitions can be powerful and adaptive. The theoretical distinction between inferential and holistic intuition clarifies these contradictions in the literature and directs future research in the field. Intuition researchers are encouraged to consider the new model proposed in this chapter, derive and test its predictions, and thereby refine our understanding of the mechanisms underlying this elusive construct.

REFERENCES

Baylor, A. L. 2001. A U-shaped model for the development of intuition by level of expertise. *New Ideas in Psychology*, 19: 237–244.

Betsch, T. 2008. The nature of intuition and its neglect in research on judgment and decision making. In H. Plessner, C. Betsch, & T. Betsch (Eds.), *Intuition in judgment and decision making*: 3–22. New York: Lawrence Erlbaum Associates.

Berry, D. C., & Broadbent, D. E. 1988. Interactive tasks and the implicit–explicit distinction. *British Journal of Psychology*, 79: 251–272.

Bowers, K. S., Regehr, G., Balthazard, C., & Parker, K. 1990. Intuition in the context of discovery. *Cognitive Psychology*, 22: 72–110.

Chase, W. C., & Simon, H. A. 1973. Perception in Chess. *Cognitive Psychology*, 4: 55–81.

Chi, M. T. H., Glaser, R., & Farr, M. J. 1988. *The nature of expertise*. Hillsdale, NJ: Erlbaum.

Dijksterhuis, A. 2004. Think different: The merits of unconscious thought in preference development and decision making. *Journal of Personality and Social Psychology*, 87: 586–598.

Epstein, S. 1991. Cognitive–experiential self-theory: An integrative theory of personality. In R. C. Curtis (Ed.), *The relational self: Theoretical convergences in psychoanalysis and social psychology*: 111–137. New York: Guilford.

Hammond, K. R. 1996. *Human judgment and social policy*. New York: Oxford University Press.

Hammond, K. R., Hamm, R. M., Grassia, J., & Pearson, T. 1987. Direct comparison of the efficacy of intuitive and analytical cognition in expert judgment. *IEEE Transactions on Systems, Man, and Cybernetics*, 17: 753–770.

Hill, N. M., & Schneider, W. 2006. Brain changes in the development of expertise: Neuroanatomical and neurophysiological evidence about skill-based adaptations. In K. A. Ericsson, N. Charness, P. J. Feltovich, & R. R. Hoffman (Eds.), *The Cambridge handbook of expertise and expert performance*: 653–682. New York: Cambridge University Press.

Hill, O. W. 1987–88. Intuition: Inferential heuristic or epistemic mode? *Imagination, Cognition, and Personality*, 7: 137–154.

Hogarth, R. M. 2001. *Educating intuition*. Chicago, IL: University of Chicago Press.

Hogarth, R. M. 2005. Deciding analytically or trusting your intuition? The advantages and disadvantages of analytic and intuitive thought. In T. Betsch & S. Haberstroh (Eds.), *Routines of decision making*: 67–82. Mahwah, NJ: Erlbaum.

Jung, C. J. 1971. Psychological types. In H. Read, M. Fordham, G. Adler, & W. McGuire (Eds.), *Collected works of C.G. Jung*: vol. 6. Princeton, NJ: Princeton University Press.

Kahneman, D., & Klein, G. 2009. Conditions for intuitive expertise: A failure to disagree. *American Psychologist*, 64: 515–526.

Klein, G. 1998. *Sources of power*. Cambridge, MA: MIT Press.

Lieberman, M. D. 2007. The X- and C-systems: The neuronal basis of automatic and controlled social cognition. In E. Harmon-Jones, & P. Winkielman (Eds.), *Social neuroscience: Integrating biological and psychological explanations of social behavior*: 290–315. New York: Guilford Press.

McMackin, J., & Slovic, P. 2000. When does explicit justification impair decision making? *Applied Cognitive Psychology*, 14: 527–541.

Myers, I., McCaulley, M. H., Quenk, N. L., & Hammer, A. L. 1998. *Manual: A guide to the development and use of the Myers–Briggs Type Indicator* (2nd ed.). Palo Alto, CA: Consulting Psychologists Press.

Norman, G. R., Brooks, L. R., Colle, C. L., & Hatala, R. M. 1999. The benefit of diagnostic hypotheses in clinical reasoning: Experimental study of an instructional intervention of forward and backward reasoning. *Cognition and Instruction*, 17: 433–488.

Pacini, R., & Epstein, S. 1999. The relation of rational and experiential information processing styles to personality, basic beliefs, and the ratio-bias phenomenon. *Journal of Personality and Social Psychology*, 76: 972–987.

Pretz, J. E. 2008. Intuition versus analysis: Strategy and experience in complex everyday problem solving. *Memory and Cognition*, 36: 554–566.

Pretz, J. E., Brookings, J. B., & Carlson, L. A. 2010. Development and validation of a new measure of intuition: The Types of Intuition Scale. Manuscript in preparation.

Pretz, J. E., & Totz, K. S. 2007. Measuring individual differences in affective, heuristic, and holistic intuition. *Personality and Individual Differences*, 43: 1247–1257.

Pretz, J. E., & Zimmerman, C. 2009. When the goal gets in the way: The interaction of goal specificity and task difficulty. *Thinking and Reasoning*, 15: 405–430.

Schmidt, H. G., & Boshuizen, H. P. A. 1993. On the origin of intermediate effects in clinical case recall. *Memory and Cognition*, 21: 338–351.

Sloman, S. A. 1996. The empirical case for two systems of reasoning. *Psychological Bulletin*, 119: 3–22.

Tversky, A., & Kahneman, D. 1974. Judgment under uncertainty: Heuristics and biases. *Science*, 185: 1124–1131.

Westcott, M. R. 1961. On the measurement of intuitive leaps. *Psychological Reports*, 9: 267–274.

Westcott, M. R., & Ranzoni, J. H. 1963. Correlates of intuitive thinking. *Psychological Reports*, 12: 595–613.

Wilson, T. D., & Schooler, J. W. 1991. Thinking too much: Introspection can reduce the quality of preferences and decisions. *Journal of Personality and Social Psychology*, 60: 181–192.

3 Intuition and unconscious thought
Madelijn Strick and Ap Dijksterhuis[1]

Some people possess remarkable intuition. Gary Kasparov is the greatest chess player in the world because he has a better 'chess sense' than other grandmasters. He can anticipate his competitor's moves, calculate all possible positions, and decide on the most appropriate next move, all in a very brief period of time. Warren Buffet, the 'oracle of Omaha', is one of the most successful investors in the world because he has a better 'market sense' than other traders. He has the mysterious ability to know when to buy and when to sell. More importantly, he is able to pick stocks that become clear winners in the long run.

How do these people arrive at such great decisions? Clearly, they have a very high level of intelligence and a lot of expert knowledge and experience. Precisely because they are so experienced and skilled, they can trust their intuition to arrive at sound decisions without much deliberation. They easily grasp the essence of complicated issues and come up with the appropriate answer relatively quickly. Although we may not become as brilliant as Kasparov or Buffet, there is reason to believe that we can improve our intuition by adopting a decision-making style that fosters the reliability of intuition.

We define intuition as the feeling of knowing what one has to do – go right instead of left, buy stock A rather than B, or not quite trust the person approaching – without necessarily being able to verbalize why (Dijksterhuis & Nordgren, 2006; Lieberman, 2000). Defined as such, intuition is not by definition good or bad. Laypeople's knowledge regarding intuition is often one-sided: some see it as something highly useful that one should obey, while others see it as an irrational process leading people away from sound decisions. In our view, it is neither. The quality, so to speak, of an intuition is determined by the knowledge it was based on and the psychological process that led up to it. A quick feeling telling you that you should buy stock A rather than B can be extremely reliable when it comes from Warren Buffet, but completely useless when it comes from one of the authors of this chapter.

In our work on unconscious thought theory (UTT, Dijksterhuis & Nordgren, 2006), we try to shed light on the processes leading to an intuition. According to UTT, the best way to find an appropriate solution to a complex problem is often to first gain expert knowledge by absorbing all possible information about the problem, then distract oneself from the problem for a period of time, and finally make the decision according to one's 'gut feeling'. During the distraction period, unconscious processes are assumed to deal with the problem, a process termed 'unconscious thought' (UT). Unconscious thought is thought without conscious attention and related to the notion of 'incubation' in creativity research. As said before, the outcome of unconscious thought is intuition, the inner conviction, gut feeling or hunch that something is the way it is without (yet) knowing exactly why.

UNCONSCIOUS THOUGHT THEORY

UTT describes various characteristics of both conscious and unconscious thought on the basis of which specific hypotheses can be derived that are applicable to decision making, attitude formation, impression formation, and creativity. For example, whereas unconscious thought works 'bottom up' and can integrate large amounts of information, conscious thought is very limited in its capacity and works 'top down'. One of the central principles of the model is the observation that consciousness has limited capacity. This limited capacity of consciousness had led to the hypothesis that conscious thought often leads to relatively poor decisions (see Dijksterhuis et al., 2006).

Many studies have confirmed the hypothesis that unconscious thought can lead to superior decisions relative to conscious thought. In various experiments, participants made decisions under three different experimental conditions. After participants had read information about a decision problem (for example, information about three different apartments), they had to decide immediately, after a few minutes of conscious thought about the choice alternatives, or after a few minutes of distraction. Unconscious thinkers (i.e., distracted people) made superior decisions relative to participants in the other two conditions (for a recent meta-analysis, see Strick et al., 2010a).

Importantly, research has shown that the superior decisions made by unconscious thinkers are caused by a goal-directed thought process, and not simply by the effects of distraction *per se*. Distraction can lead to the change of a 'mental set' (Schooler & Melcher, 1995). In such a case, the role of the unconscious is merely passive. People often approach a problem with wrong cues, wrong heuristics and/or wrong information. Following a period of distraction, wrong approaches become less accessible or are forgotten altogether. One could lump these processes together under the umbrella of the 'fresh look' explanation: putting a problem aside for a while allows for a fresh, unbiased new start.

The importance of this work notwithstanding, unconscious thought is more than distraction. It is an active thought process. Recent evidence (Bos et al., 2008) shows that such unconscious thought is goal directed. In their experiments, participants first read information pertaining to a decision problem. Subsequently, all participants were distracted, but some were told that they would later have to choose between the various decision alternatives, whereas others were told they could forget the information and that they would not be asked any questions about it. As it turned out, the former group produced a better decision than the latter group. In sum, only participants who knew they had to choose between the apartments sometime later engaged in unconscious thought. Moreover, Dijksterhuis (2004) demonstrated that unconscious thought renders information better organized in memory (as assessed by clustering scores). Further evidence for the goal-directedness of unconscious thought was found by Lerouge (2009) and by Strick et al. (2010b). Thus, by appointing a goal to the unconscious, one can to some extent steer intuitive processes.

Although more research is needed to understand exactly how unconscious thought produces superior decisions and what kind of problems it applies to, several important insights have been obtained over recent years. In the remainder of this chapter we shall give a brief overview of the most significant findings of six years of UT research. First we shall specify the different domains and types of problems that the theory applies to. Then we shall describe some significant moderators and implications for the underlying processes. We end with a brief conclusion regarding the relation among expertise, information acquisition, and intuition, from the perspective of UTT.

THE GENERALIZABILITY OF UNCONSCIOUS THOUGHT

The first empirical findings on unconscious thought were mainly in the context of consumer choice (i.e., between cars or apartments), but a growing body of evidence shows that unconscious thought can improve decisions in various other domains. For example, Ham et al. (2009) showed that unconscious thought improves moral decision making. They presented participants with a complex version of the well-known footbridge dilemma, in which the life of a large man on a railway bridge must be sacrificed in order to save the lives of five other people on the railway track, and showed that unconsciously thinking about the dilemma led to more utilitarian decisions (that is, approving harmful actions that maximize good consequences) than consciously thinking or deciding immediately.

De Vries et al. (2010) provided evidence for the merits of unconscious thought in clinical decision making. They presented students of clinical psychology with case descriptions from the DSM-IV casebook, and found that unconscious thinking about the case descriptions significantly increased the number of correct classifications compared to conscious thinking.

There are also recent studies showing that unconscious thought helps to avoid racial bias in decision making (Strick et al., 2010b). In these experiments White participants chose a new roommate out of four candidates, two of which had Black facial features, and two had White facial features. The evaluations of participants in the conscious- and unconscious-thought conditions were less racially biased – that is, they preferred White to Black candidates to a lesser extent – than participants in the immediate-decision condition.

In another vein there are already several studies showing that unconscious thought also promotes creative processes (Dijksterhuis & Meurs, 2006; Zhong et al., 2008). For example, Zhong et al. demonstrated that unconscious thought increased the mental activation of correct solutions to items of the remote association test (RAT). Although unconscious thought increased the *accessibility* of the correct answers, it did not increase the *reporting* of correct answers compared to an equal duration of conscious thought or mere distraction. Hence, although unconscious thought appears better at associative search than conscious thought, the products of this creative process may not always be immediately available to consciousness, which may prevent its merits from becoming directly apparent.

Ritter et al. (2010) found further evidence for the benefits of unconscious thought for creative processes. They asked participants to generate a list of creative ideas such as unusual uses for bricks or ways for making queuing in a shop less boring. They observed that those who unconsciously thought about these problems differed neither in the number of ideas listed, nor in the average originality of their ideas from those who consciously thought about these problems. However, unconscious thinkers had an important advantage: they were much better than conscious thinkers in choosing the most creative idea among all their ideas.

MODERATORS OF UT: WHEN DOES IT WORK BEST?

Several experiments have been conducted to examine moderators that may determine when unconscious thought (and conscious thought) are more or less effective. In addition, we recently conducted a meta-analysis (Strick et al., 2010a) that included all available studies on unconscious thought published in either peer-reviewed journals or conference proceedings. In this analysis the performance of participants thinking unconsciously was compared to participants thinking consciously, or to participants who did not think at all (immediate decision makers). Below we shall discuss the three most interesting moderators that experimental research and meta-analysis have identified. All three are immediately relevant for an appreciation of the conceptual relation between unconscious thought and intuition.

Complexity of the Decision Problem

In the unconscious-thought literature, complexity is defined as the amount of information a choice involves. A choice between objects for which one or two attributes are important (such as oven mitts or toothpaste) is simple, whereas a choice between objects for which many attributes are important (cars or houses) is complex. Conscious thought is hypothesized, due to its precision, to lead to good choices in simple matters. However, because of its low capacity, conscious thought leads to progressively worse choices with more-complex issues. Unconscious thought is expected, because of its relative lack of precision, to lead to choices of lower quality. However, the quality of choice does not deteriorate with increased complexity, allowing unconscious thought to lead to better choices than conscious thought under complex circumstances, this latter idea being the core of UTT.

This 'complexity hypothesis' was tested in a series of studies (Dijksterhuis et al., 2006). In the first experiment, participants were given information about four hypothetical Japanese cars with the goal to choose the best one. The amount of information involved in the decision differed. The problem was either relatively simple (each car was described by four aspects, for a total of 16 pieces of information), or very difficult (12 aspects per car). Participants indicated their choice either after a few minutes of conscious thought, or after a few minutes of unconscious thought. Conscious thinkers performed well under simple conditions, but progressively worse under more demanding circumstances. Unconscious thinkers showed a different pattern. Both under very demanding and under moderately demanding circumstances, unconscious thinkers often chose the right car. Under simple conditions, however, they fared less well.

In a field study, we interviewed people outside two shops in Amsterdam, one where people predominantly buy 'complex' products (IKEA, which sells furniture) and one where people predominantly buy simple products (the 'Bijenkorf', which sells clothes or small accessories). Here complexity was defined by the number of attributes people like to take into account when buying a certain product. Pilot-testing had revealed that when people buy furniture, they weigh many aspects, whereas when they buy small accessories, they are interested in only a few aspects. People were asked what they bought, whether they had seen it before, and whether they had thought about it a lot before buying it. A few weeks later, we contacted them to ask how satisfied they were. As expected, IKEA customers were generally more happy the less they had consciously thought about what to buy, whereas Bijenkorf customers were more happy the more they had consciously thought. Again, the complexity hypothesis was confirmed.

In our meta-analysis, a second form of complexity was also shown to influence effects of unconscious thought. In most experiments, participants had to choose between alternatives described solely by verbal information. In some studies however, the information was presented in both verbal as well as pictorial format (for example, Ham & van den Bos, 2010; Strick et al., 2010b), significantly increasing the complexity of the decision information. Our meta-analysis showed that unconscious thought is especially apt in tackling such decision problems.

Expertise

Recently we have begun to investigate the role of expertise and its relation to unconscious thought (Dijksterhuis et al., 2009). In two experiments, participants were asked to predict upcoming soccer games immediately after being presented with the fixture list, or after a few minutes of conscious thought, or after a few minutes of unconscious thought. We also assessed people's knowledge of soccer. For people who did not know much about soccer, it did not matter whether they thought consciously, or unconsciously, or not at all. However, 'experts' benefited from unconscious thought – their predictions were more accurate than those made by experts who thought consciously or not at all. The correlation between expertise and accuracy was statistically reliable only for unconscious thinkers.

These findings were replicated in a second experiment: participants predicted results from World Cup soccer games and we also assessed people's knowledge of the World Ranking List – the single most diagnostic predictor for the results of these games. Again, experts who thought unconsciously outperformed those who thought consciously or not at all. Importantly, however, unconscious thinkers who knew a lot about the World Ranking List applied this knowledge and used it to arrive at sound predictions. This was not the case for conscious thinkers.

Given that these results are the only ones on expertise thus far, they should be interpreted with care. However, they do show that, at least in this domain, expertise manifests itself during unconscious thought, and less so, or not at all, during conscious thought. That being said, more research is needed before more firm conclusions can be drawn.

Information Acquisition

It seems that the way the information is encoded before people think unconsciously is important for the quality of the UT process. Multiple datasets point in this direction. First, Lassiter et al. (2009) asked their participants to choose between various alternatives after unconscious thought or after conscious thought. However, the information the decision had to be based on was encoded under two different conditions. Some people were asked to form an impression of the alternatives (as in most UT studies), whereas others were merely asked to memorize the information. The results showed that under impression instructions, unconscious thought led to better results than conscious thought. However, the reverse was true for memory instructions.

A likely reason why an impression formation goal enhances the UT process is that impression formation inherently involves integrating the available information into an organized cognitive representation. Such organization of information would facilitate later evaluation and choice. Participants with a memory instruction will not integrate the information in such a way (and therefore, ironically, show poorer memory than participants with an impression instruction; Chartrand & Bargh, 1996; Hamilton et al., 1980). The results of our meta-analysis confirm this idea. In some UT studies, the information about the decision alternatives is presented in random order, whereas in other studies, the information is presented blocked by choice alternative. The latter studies show larger UT effects than the former, suggesting again that structured encoding of the information is a necessity for unconscious thought to flourish.

Another possible reason why structured information encoding enhances unconscious thought is that it resembles the way people experience most problems in their daily lives. When people decide between real cars, houses, or roommates they usually process most or all information about one choice alternative before moving to the next one. This similarity with real life may enhance involvement and cognitive engagement, which is crucial for unconscious thought. In sum, structured information encoding probably helps unconscious thought because it enhances both integrative and thorough information processing. These effects are reminiscent of the 'garbage in–garbage out' axiom used to explain the 'behavior' of computers. Unconscious thought can lead to excellent results, but the system has to be fed information in an orderly manner.

CONCLUSION

The three moderators discussed above speak to the quality of unconscious thought and hence, of intuition. Intuition – conceptualized as a result of a process of unconscious thought – excels under circumstances where lots of information has to be taken into account. Furthermore, it benefits from a clear representation of the information and it benefits from expertise. When all parameters are optimal, such as in the case of Gary Kasparov playing chess, the UT process can be truncated to such an extent that it seems as if hardly any thought is needed at all. However, from the perspective of UTT, what underlies such great intuition is extremely efficient unconscious thought.

NOTE

1. This chapter was supported by a VICI-grant from NWO (453-05-004).

REFERENCES

Bos, M. W., Dijksterhuis, A., & van Baaren, R. B. 2008. On the goal-dependency of unconscious thought. *Journal of Experimental Social Psychology*, 44: 1114–1120.
Chartrand, T. L., & Bargh, J. A. 1996. Automatic activation of impression formation and memorization goals: Nonconscious goal priming reproduces effects of explicit task instructions. *Journal of Personality and Social Psychology*, 71: 464–478.
De Vries, M., Witteman, C., Holland, R. W., & Dijksterhuis, A. 2010. The unconscious thought effect in clinical decision making: An example in diagnosis. *Medical Decision Making*, Published online: doi:10.1177/0272989X09360820.
Dijksterhuis, A. 2004. Think different: The merits of unconscious thought in preference development and decision making. *Journal of Personality and Social Psychology*, 87: 586–598.
Dijksterhuis, A., Bos, M. W., Nordgren, L. F., & van Baaren, R. B. 2006. On making the right choice: The deliberation-without-attention effect. *Science*, 311: 1005–1007.
Dijksterhuis, A., Bos, M. W., van der Leij, A., & van Baaren, R. B. 2009. Predicting soccer matches after unconscious and conscious thought as a function of expertise. *Psychological Science*, 20: 1381–1387.
Dijksterhuis, A., & Meurs, T. 2006. Where creativity resides: The generative power of unconscious thought. *Consciousness and Cognition*, 15: 135–146.
Dijksterhuis, A., & Nordgren, L. F. 2006. A theory of unconscious thought. *Perspectives on Psychological Science*, 1: 95–109.
Ham, J., & van den Bos, K. 2010. The merits of unconscious processing of directly and indirectly obtained information about social justice. *Social Cognition*, 28: 180–190.
Ham, J., van den Bos, K., & van Doorn, E. 2009. Lady Justice thinks unconsciously: Unconscious thought can lead to more accurate justice judgments. *Social Cognition*, 27: 510–522.
Hamilton, D. L., Katz, L. B., & Leirer, V. O. 1980. Organizational processes in impression formation. In R. Hastie, T. M. Ostrom, E. B. Ebbesen, R. S. Wyer Jr., D. L. Hamilton,

& D. E. Carlston (Eds.), *Person memory: The cognitive basis of social perception*: 121–153. Hillsdale, NJ: Erlbaum.

Lassiter, G. D., Lindberg, M. J., Gonzalez-Vallejo, C., Belleza, F. S., & Phillips, N. D. 2009. The deliberation-without-attention effect: Evidence for an artifactual interpretation. *Psychological Science*, 20: 671–675.

Lerouge, D. 2009. Evaluating the benefits of distraction on product evaluations: The mindset effect. *Journal of Consumer Research*, 36: 367–379.

Lieberman, M. D. 2000. Intuition: A social cognitive neuroscience approach. *Psychological Bulletin*, 126: 109–137.

Ritter, S. M., Dijksterhuis, A., & van Baaren, R. B. 2010. *Creativity: Incubation does not produce better ideas but better selection of ideas.* Manuscript submitted for publication. Radboud University, Nijmegen.

Schooler, J. W., & Melcher, J. 1995. The ineffability of insight. In S.M. Smith, T.B. Ward, & R.A. Finke (Eds.), *The creative cognition approach*: 97–134. Cambridge, MA: MIT Press.

Strick, M., Dijksterhuis, A., Bos, M. W., Sjoerdsma, A., van Baaren, R. B., & Nordgren, L. F. 2010a. *A meta-analysis on unconscious thought effects.* Radboud University, Nijmegen. Manuscript submitted for publication. Available from www.unconsciouslab.com/publications/Paper_Meta.doc.

Strick, M., Dijksterhuis, A., & van Baaren, R. B. 2010b. *Racial bias in conscious and unconscious thinkers.* Manuscript submitted for publication. Radboud University, Nijmegen.

Strick, M., Dijksterhuis, A., & van Baaren, R. B. 2010c. Unconscious thought effects take place off-line, not on-line. *Psychological Science*, 21: 484–488.

Zhong, C. B., Dijksterhuis, A., & Galinsky, A. D. 2008. The merits of unconscious thought in creativity. *Psychological Science*, 19: 912–918.

4 The influence of valence and intensity of affect on intuitive processing
Seymour Epstein[1]

Most research on intuition fails to consider it within a broadly meaningful context that is necessary for understanding its operating rules and its boundary condition. Rather, researchers too often view intuition as an isolated phenomenon that can be distinguished not so much by what it is but by what it is not, describing it as knowledge acquired without analytical reasoning or awareness. Others who attempt to explain what intuition is do not agree on the principles by which it operates (Epstein, 2010; Sinclair et al., 2002). Cognitive–experiential self-theory (CEST, Epstein, 2003) provides a remedy for this situation by proposing a dual process theory in which an automatic associative learning system that operates outside of awareness and that is shared by all higher-order animals is used to explain what intuition is, what it does, and how it does it (Epstein, 2010).

This chapter is divided as follows. The next section provides a summary of the most relevant aspects of CEST for understanding intuition, followed by a presentation of research influenced by CEST on the influence of the valence and intensity of affect on intuitive and analytical information processing. The final section concludes with a summary of the more important inclusions.

COGNITIVE–EXPERIENTIAL SELF-THEORY

According to CEST, humans operate with two information-processing systems, an experiential system, which is an automatic learning system that humans share with other higher-order animals and a rational/analytic system, which is a verbal reasoning system unique to humans. The systems operate by different rules and have different attributes. Although the experiential system encompasses a domain more extensive than intuition (i.e., it also accounts for a variety of other kinds of behavior, including superstitious thinking, irrational fears, unusual beliefs, and religious beliefs), the operating rules and attributes of intuitive processing, which is a subset of the experiential system, are identical with it. Thus, to draw attention to the focus in this chapter on intuition, I refer to an 'experiential/

intuitive system' that elsewhere when considering its broader domain, I have referred to as an 'experiential system'.

Operating Principles and Attributes of Two Processing Systems

The experiential/intuitive system operates by the rules that govern automatic learning from experience. There are three forms of such learning: classical conditioning, operant conditioning, and observational learning, all of which operate through association, contiguity, similarity and affective reinforcement. Through these forms of automatically learning from experience, higher-order animals, including people, construct an implicit working model of the world. In addition to an experiential/intuitive system, humans also operate with a rational/analytic system, which is a verbal reasoning system. I use the word 'rational' here to refer to a process that may or may not produce desirable or reasonable results. Rational/analytical processing does not necessarily imply the most appropriate decision-making process, as sometimes experiential/intuitive processing provides more reasonable solutions. Given two modes of information processing, humans have two models of the world, one consisting of their implicit beliefs automatically acquired from experience and the other of their explicit beliefs derived from conscious reasoning. The two models of the world, or theories of reality as I alternatively refer to them, are mainly congruent, but they sometimes include significant divergences, which can be a significant source of conflict and stress.

Both kinds of models of the world determine people's feelings and behavior, but they do so in different ways and for different purposes. The experiential/intuitive system is a highly efficient system for effortlessly directing behavior in everyday life. The rational/analytic system is a more effortful system that is well suited for abstract thinking and solving problems by reasoning with verbal symbols but is too effortful for effectively directing most everyday behavior.

Table 4.1 provides a comparison of the attributes of the two systems. It can be seen that almost all the attributes of the experiential/intuitive system are as applicable to the information processing of higher non-human animals as to humans. The exceptions are narrative processing and metaphors as they include a speech component and are therefore not present in non-human animals. They are included in the table because of the assumption in CEST that all behavior in humans is influenced by both systems, with their relative influence varying along a dimension from negligible to near total influence. Thus although the experiential/intuitive attributes in the table refer primarily to experiential/intuitive processing, they also include a minor component of rational/analytic processing. It should also be noted that almost all the attributes of the experiential/

Table 4.1 Comparison of the Experiential/Intuitive and Rational/Analytic Systems

Experiential/intuitive system	Rational/analytic system
1. Pleasure–pain oriented (what feels good)	1. Reality oriented (what is accurate and logical)
2. Implicit beliefs encoded in cognitive–affective networks	2. Conscious beliefs encoded in affect-free cognitive networks
3. Holistic	3. Analytic
4. Associative relations	4. Cause-and-effect relations
5. More outcome oriented	5. More process oriented
6. Behavior mediated by feelings from past experience	6. Behavior mediated by conscious appraisal of events
7. Encodes reality in concrete images, metaphors, & narratives	7. Encodes reality in abstract symbols, words, & numbers
8. More rapid processing: oriented toward immediate action	8. Slower processing: oriented also toward delayed action
9. Resistant to change: changes with repetitive or intense experience	9. Changes more readily: changes with speed of thought
10. More crudely differentiated: broad generalization gradient, categorical thinking	10. More highly differentiated: thinking is more nuanced, qualified, and dimensional
11. More crudely integrated: organized by context-specific representations	11. More highly integrated: organized by context-general principles
12. Experienced passively and preconsciously: people feel seized by their emotions	12. Experienced actively and consciously: people feel in control of their conscious thoughts
13. Self-evidently valid: 'experiencing is believing'	13. Requires justification by logic or evidence

Note: This table is a revised and expanded version of a table initially presented in an early article on CEST (Epstein, 1989).

intuitive system in the table are consistent with the assumption that it is a non-verbal, automatic, learning system.

The Advantages and Disadvantages of the Systems

It is commonly assumed that the rational/analytic system is superior to the experiential/intuitive system as it is responsible for humankind's unique accomplishments. In comparison, the experiential/intuitive system is regarded as a crude system that provides adequate solutions when quick and dirty methods are sufficient. This view is not only prevalent among

Table 4.2   Correlates of Rational/Analytic and Experiential/Intuitive Thinking Styles

Rational/analytic thinking style	Experiential/intuitive thinking style
Positive attributes	*Positive attributes*
High level of intellectual performance	Favorable interpersonal relationships
High meaningfulness in life	High social popularity
Realistic thinking	Imaginative thinking
Low stress in living	High agreeableness
High self-esteem	High empathy
Positive worldview	High spontaneity
Low neuroticism	Emotionally expressive
Low anxiety	Good esthetic sense
Low depression	Good sense of humor
Conscientious	Creative
Open-minded	Open-minded
High person growth	High personal growth
Negative attributes	*Negative attributes*
Weak tendency of a dismissive	Naive optimism
relationship style	Polyannaish thinking
	Stereotyped thinking
	Unrealistic beliefs
	Superstitious beliefs

cognitive psychologists, it is supported by a considerable body of research. However, there is a problem with this position as other research (e.g., Dijksterhuis, 2004; Norris & Epstein, in press; Reber, 1993; Wilson, 2002), reveals that the experiential/intuitive system is superior to the rational/analytic system in several important ways. Moreover, as previously noted, it is a much more efficient system than the rational/analytical system for directing everyday behavior.

Table 4.2 presents a summary of the correlates of scores on the experiential/intuitive and rational/analytic styles of thinking, as found in several studies (Epstein et al., 1996; Norris & Epstein, in press; Pacini & Epstein, 1999a; Pacini et al., 1998). The Rational – Experiential Inventory (REI) is a questionnaire that provides independent scales of rational/analytic and experiential/intuitive thinking styles (Epstein et al., 1996; Pacini & Epstein, 1999a). Although some of the attributes and abilities that are significantly correlated with the REI are based on self-reported information, others are based on objective performance measures (e.g., Epstein et al., 1996; Norris & Epstein, in press; Pacini & Epstein, 1999a; Pacini et al., 1998). The objective measures include performance in experimental situations, intelligence test scores, and performance on tasks that measure creativity, sense of humor, intuitive ability, and aesthetic judgment.

It can be seen in Table 4.2 that a rational/analytic thinking style is more strongly related to intellectual performance and to a variety of measures indicative of good adjustment, including low anxiety, low depression, low stress, low neuroticism, high self-esteem and high meaningfulness of life. An experiential/intuitive thinking style is positively associated with a variety of non-intellective favorable attributes, including creativity, empathy, aesthetic judgment, intuitive ability, and establishing satisfactory interpersonal relationships. It is also associated with several unfavorable attributes, including naive optimism, 'Pollyannaish' beliefs, stereotyped thinking, superstitious beliefs, and unrealistic beliefs. It is obvious from the relations in the table that no meaningful statement can be made about the general superiority of either thinking style, as each is superior in some important abilities and attributes and inferior in others.

In interpreting the information in Table 4.2 it is important to recognize that a high score on an experiential thinking style can be obtained in different ways. For example, it can be obtained by endorsing all the desirable criterion variables and none of the undesirable criterion variables, or by endorsing most of the undesirable criterion variables and few of the desirable ones. It is also important to recognize that, as the two thinking styles have been found to be independent (e.g., Epstein et al., 1996; Norris & Epstein, in press; Pacini & Epstein, 1999a; Pacini et al., 1998), it is possible to be high on both thinking styles, high on either thinking style and low on the other thinking style, or low on both thinking styles.

Another interesting way to compare the two systems is by the role they play in establishing an accurate working model of the environment that allows for effective adaptation. The experiential/intuitive system establishes such a model by empirically learning from experience and the rational/analytic system does so by reasoning. Each of these modes of adaptation has its advantages and disadvantages. Humans could not exist as viable organisms if they did not have an experiential/intuitive system, and they could not achieve their unique accomplishments if they did not have a rational/analytic system.

RESEARCH ON THE INFLUENCE OF VALENCE OF AFFECT ON PROCESSING MODE

In this section I first discuss the importance of distinguishing between overt responses and the underlying information processing that produces the responses. Next I present two kinds of research on the relations between valence of affect and processing mode that produce different results, laboratory research with induced affect and reports of affect in everyday life.

The Influence of Valence of Affect on Processing Mode as Distinguished from Overt Responses

It has consistently been demonstrated in laboratory research that positive affect promotes heuristic processing and negative affect promotes deliberative processing (e.g., Bodenhausen et al., 1994; Elsbach & Barr, 1999; Epstein, 1994; Epstein & Pacini, 2006; Forgas, 1995; King et al., 2007; Pacini & Epstein 1999a; Pacini et al., 1998; Ruder & Bless, 2003; Sinclair et al., 2002). However, the translation of deliberative and heuristic responses into modes of information processing is not as straightforward as it might seem. Consider, for example, the following statement by Sinclair et al. (2002: 159), 'The heuristic and substantive decision-making strategies of the AIM (Forgas, 1995) correspond respectively to Epstein et al.'s (1996) analytical and intuitive information processing modes'. However, according to CEST, heuristic responses are not necessarily attributable to experiential/intuitive processing and deliberative responses are not necessarily a result of rational/analytic processing. This equation is unwarranted for the following reasons. First, there are two kinds of heuristics, only one of which is attributable to experiential/intuitive processing as the other is the result of limited processing in the rational/analytic system. As no distinction is usually made between the two kinds of heuristic processing (e.g., Chaiken & Trope, 1999; Kahneman et al., 1991) it is impossible in such research to determine whether the obtained heuristic responses are the result of reduced processing in the rational/analytic system or processing in the experiential/intuitive system. To determine this, it is necessary to indicate that the responses can be attributed to the rules and attributes of the experiential/intuitive system or involve content, such as a belief in magic or other kinds of belief indicative of associative rather than logical thinking, that is clearly in the domain of the experiential/intuitive system (e.g., King et al., 2007). As will be demonstrated shortly, research with the ratio-bias (RB) phenomenon provides a useful experimental paradigm for demonstrating that the processing that produced the phenomenon was in the experiential/intuitive mode.

Second, as some reasoning can occur by experiential/intuitive processing, such as by trial-and-error behavior in imagery (Epstein, 2010), it is incorrect to assume that deliberative reasoning can always be attributed to rational/analytic processing. Third, although the rational/analytic system is an affect-free system, it can operate with infused affect from the experiential/intuitive system. Thus, intellectual behavior can be charged with affect because of past favorable or unfavorable experiences regarding intellectual performance. In such situations the affect that is an aspect of experiential/intuitive processing influences intellectual thinking and behavior as it does any other kind of response. It is therefore important to recognize that because affect is present in intellectual behavior, it does not necessarily follow that it originated in the rational/analytic system, which according to CEST is simply a verbal reasoning system.

In summary, there is considerable evidence in laboratory research that induced sad mood promotes deliberative responding and induced happy mood promotes heuristic responding. However, heuristic responses do not necessarily indicate experiential/intuitive processing as such responses can also be produced by a reduced level of rational/analytic processing. Also, deliberative responses do not necessarily indicate rational/analytical processing as such responses can be produced by experiential/intuitive processing.

The Influence of Valence of Affect on Processing Mode in the Ratio-Bias Phenomenon

Conducting research on processing mode with the RB phenomenon has an advantage over other procedures as the phenomenon can be attributed to experiential/intuitive processing rather than to reduced rational/analytic processing. The RB phenomenon refers to people behaving non-optimally in a game of chance because they find frequency-advantaged information more compelling than probability-advantaged information. Moreover, they do so despite recognizing that such behavior is irrational. Of further interest, the phenomenon is exhibited in a situation in which the frequency and probability information are equally accessible so neither requires more cognitive effort to access than the other. Most people simply find the heuristic responses more compelling than the deliberative responses.

There are two versions of the RB phenomenon, one in which the probabilities remain the same and only the frequencies vary in the choices that are offered in two trays of red and white jellybeans (e.g., 1 in 10 vs. 10 in 100) and the other in which both the frequencies and the probabilities differ (e.g., 1 in 10 vs. 8 in 100), with the choices always being between a frequency- and a probability-advantaged offering. In all RB experiments that we have conducted, most participants have irrationally preferred to make frequency- over probability-advantaged selections (e.g., Denes-Raj & Epstein, 1994; Epstein & Pacini, 2000–01; Kirkpatrick & Epstein, 1992; Pacini & Epstein, 1999a, 1999b; Pacini et al., 1998).

The RB phenomenon can be explained by the experiential/intuitive system representing events concretely and therefore being more responsive to frequencies than to probabilities. That a sensitivity to and comprehension of frequency information is an extremely fundamental reaction is indicated by its presence in non-human animals and preverbal children (e.g., Gallistel, 1989; Gallistel & Gelman, 1992; Hasher & Zacks, 1984). Probabilities and ratios, on the other hand, are less fundamental than frequencies as they consist of relations between frequencies and accordingly are more abstract (less easily visualized) and complex than frequencies.

Additional support for the interpretation that the RB phenomenon can be explained by a different mode of processing being preferred to processing in the mode of the rational/analytic system is provided by conflict that participants report between the two kinds of processing. For example, they make comments such as, 'I know it is foolish to go against the probabilities, but I feel I have a better chance of getting a red jellybean when there are more of them'. It is noteworthy that although most of the participants who make such statements make frequency-advantaged choices, some make probability-advantaged choices. That the conflict people commonly report is between the two processing systems is also supported by the consideration that such a conflict could not exist between recognized inferior and superior outcomes within a single processing system.

A study was conducted in which valence was manipulated by inducing happy and sad moods with the active cooperation of the participants. Participants were informed that the research was about the influence of emotions on behavior, and they were invited to be collaborators in the study (Epstein & Pacini, 2006). One group was instructed to put themselves into and maintain a happy frame of mind by recalling happy events, thinking happy thoughts, and assuming a happy posture and facial expression which they were carefully instructed in how to accomplish. Happy-sounding music was played throughout the session. Participants were requested to maintain their mood during the game of chance they were about to play and to respond naturally according to how they felt and not to attempt to discount the influence of their feelings. The sad group was given corresponding instructions and conditions.

In the sad and happy conditions strong RB effects were observed both in trials in which the probabilities were the same and in those in which the probabilities were different as most participants preferred to make non-optimal frequency-advantaged choices rather than optimal probability-advantaged choices. There was also a strong valence effect, with the number of heuristic, frequency-advantaged responses being much greater in the happy than in the sad condition. The heuristic responses were greater in the happy condition and fewer in the sad condition than in other studies in which there was no mood induction. Thus the results in the present study are consistent with the results in other research on the influence of induced positive and negative affect on mode of information processing.

Two additional RB studies were conducted in which valence of affect was manipulated in a manner intrinsic to the jellybean task by inducing positive and negative affect, respectively, by having some trials designated as win trials and other trials designated as lose trials (Pacini & Epstein, 1999a; Pacini et al., 1998). On lose trials, drawing a red jellybean cost the participants the same amount of money as they received when drawing a red jellybean on win trials. So that they would not lose any of their own money, participants were given a sufficient sum to cover any loses they might sustain. In both studies a significant RB effect (greater frequency- than probability-advantaged responses) was obtained on both win and lose trials and on trials in which the two trays offered equal or unequal probabilities. Of particular interest, the RB effect in both studies was significantly much stronger on win than on lose trials.

Based on the results of all three RB studies (Epstein & Pacini, 2006; Pacini & Epstein, 1999a; Pacini et al., 1998), it can be concluded that there are strong and consistent valence effects, with positive affect promoting heuristic responding and negative affect promoting deliberative responding. Although these results are consistent with the findings by others, they differ in one important respect. The results from the RB studies can be attributed to experiential/intuitive processing and not, as in other research, either to experiential/intuitive processing or to reduced rational/analytic processing. Nevertheless, given the consistency of the findings in research by others it is highly likely that the generality that positive affect promotes heuristic processing and negative affect promotes deliberative processing is true for both kinds of heuristics.

Research on the Relation of Negative Affect and Processing Mode in Reports of Everyday Life

The strong evidence that positive affect promotes heuristic responding and negative affect promotes deliberative responding is based on laboratory studies inducing relatively mild, transient, and personally uninvolving feelings through the use of procedures such as having participants listen to sad or happy music, recall sad or happy events, observe sad or happy scenes in movie segments, or read about them in literary passages. The feelings generated by such procedures are much milder, more transient, and less personally involving than the kinds of feelings often experienced in everyday life from events such as doing poorly on a test or job interview, being reprimanded by an authority figure, or being admonished or rejected by a loved one.

An advantage of laboratory experiments is that they are able to establish causal relations under controlled conditions. They have an important limitation, however, in that they cannot involve procedures that greatly disturb or harm the participants in the experiments. In contrast, investigation of real-life reactions, whether directly observed or reported, have opposite advantages and disadvantages. The advantage of real-life data is that they can involve intense, enduring, and personally significant events, feelings, or behavior. The disadvantage is that such procedures cannot establish causal relations. One can hope to find correspondences between the two kinds of relations, which would strengthen any generalizations that are made. This raises the question of whether the relations between valence of affect and processing mode found in laboratory research can be replicated with reports of real-life behavior.

In an investigation of the correlates of experiential/intuitive and rational/analytic thinking styles, college students were administered the REI and a battery of personality and adjustment questionnaires (Epstein et al., 1996). For present purposes only relations with measures indicative of negative affect will be reported. These measures consisted of scales of anxiety, depression, and stress in college life.

To the extent that negative affect is positively associated with deliberative processing and unrelated to heuristic processing, as found in laboratory research, all three measures of negative affect should be positively correlated with a rational/analytic thinking style and unrelated to an experiential/intuitive thinking style. Instead, all three measures were significantly inversely related to a rational/analytic thinking style. All the measures of negative affect were also weakly but significantly inversely related to an experiential/intuitive thinking style. Thus both findings are different from what has consistently been found in laboratory research. The inverse relation of negative affect with a rational thinking style is consistent with other research we have conducted in which we found that a rational thinking style was inversely associated with a wide variety of measures related to maladjustment (e.g., ibid.). The significant inverse relation of an experiential/intuitive thinking style as well as a rational/analytic thinking style with negative affect is consistent with the view in CEST that both thinking styles are usually adaptive, which is also consistent with other investigations using self-report data and normal participants (e.g., ibid.; Pacini & Epstein, 1999a). An important implication from this research is that because the psychological experiment is very highly esteemed there is a tendency to overestimate the generality of its results.

Influence of Intensity of Affect on the Two Processing Modes in the RB Phenomenon

Affect intensity was manipulated in three RB studies by variations in incentive level (Denes-Raj & Epstein, 1994; Pacini & Epstein, 1999a; Pacini et al., 1998). Participants were informed before each trial whether drawing a red jellybean would have a value of ten cents or two dollars. One of the studies included a comparison of depressed and non-depressed college students. Only minimal consideration will be given here to the depressed group, which will be discussed more thoroughly in the next section on intense negative affect.

Incentive level did not produce a significant main effect in any of the three studies, as in each case some participants responded to an increase in incentive by an increased reliance on their experiential/intuitive processing, and a similar number increased their rational/analytical processing. There were significant interactions of incentive level with various individual-difference variables, including gender, depression, experiential/intuitive thinking style, and rational/analytic thinking style. In one study, women made fewer heuristic, non-optimal responses in the high than in the low incentive condition, whereas men exhibited the opposite pattern (Denes-Raj & Epstein, 1994). In another study, among participants high in an experiential/intuitive thinking style, those low in a rational/analytic thinking style made more heuristic, non-optimal responses in the high than in the low incentive condition, whereas those high in a rational/analytic thinking style reacted in the opposite manner (Pacini & Epstein, 1999a). In the study that included a depressed group, the non-depressed participants made fewer heuristic, non-optimal responses in the high than in the low incentive condition on win trials. On lose trials they made relatively few heuristic, non-optimal responses at both incentive levels. Thus, for the non-depressed participants incentive level produced neither a main effect nor a significant interaction.

Summarizing the results from the three RB studies in which incentive level was varied, it may be concluded that there is not a consistent effect of affect intensity on mode of information processing. Rather, there are important individual differences, with some people reacting to an increase in incentive by relying more on their rational/analytic processing and others relying more on their experiential/intuitive processing.

The following incident provides an example of the thinking of a student who was convinced that heuristic responding in the RB paradigm is the optimal way to respond. An undergraduate research assistant came to my office one day saying that she needed to talk to me. 'Professor Epstein', she said, 'I hate to tell you this, but I think you are wrong to score the selection of the tray with more red jellybeans as a non-optimal response. In a statistics class of course I would say you should go with the better probability, but in real life it is better to go with the tray that has more winners'. I asked her what she would do if a million dollars were at stake. She replied, 'Then I certainly would choose from the tray with more red jellybeans because I would really want to win'.

Influence of Depression and Incentive Level on Processing Mode in the RB Phenomenon

Up to now, discussion has focused on the influence of relatively mild affect in the laboratory and on reports of the effects of the stronger negative affect that is commonly experienced in everyday life. The following research examined the influence of much stronger negative affect experienced in depression.

In a study by Alloy and Abramson (1979) that compared the responses of depressed and non-depressed college students to various contingencies presented in a laboratory task, it was found that the depressed students responded in a more realistic, deliberative manner than the non-depressed students, who responded more heuristically. The finding of what became known as the 'depressive realism phenomenon' generated a great deal of interest because it challenged the view of cognitive-behavioral therapists that depressives think more unrealistically than others (Beck, 1976). To obtain information relevant to the occurrence of this phenomenon, we conducted the following study.

A group of college students with very high scores on the Beck Depression Inventory (Beck et al., 1961) was compared to a group with very low depression scores (Pacini et al., 1998). All participants were administered the REI and the Constructive Thinking Inventory (CTI), which is considered to be a measure of individual differences in the efficacy or intelligence of experiential/intuitive information processing (Epstein, 2001).

The depressed students obtained much lower scores on the REI scale of a rational/analytic thinking style than the non-depressed students and marginally higher scores on the REI scale of an experiential/intuitive thinking style. Note that the results on a rational/analytic thinking style are opposite to what would be expected if negative affect were positively related to deliberative processing, as found in laboratory research. Of further interest, depressed students exhibited a poorer quality of experiential/intuitive processing, as measured by the CTI, than non-depressed students. Thus, although the depressed students differed only slightly in the degree of their experiential/intuitive processing, they differed considerably in its quality as indicated by their significantly poorer scores on the following CTI scales: Emotional Coping, Behavioral Coping, Negative Overgeneralization, Dwelling on Unfavorable Events, Superstitious Thinking, Categorical Thinking, and Distrust of Others. It is noteworthy that not only was the content of the thinking of depressed students more negative than the thinking of non-depressed students, but they also thought in more maladaptive ways regarding process as indicated by an elevated degree of categorical thinking and overgeneralization.

The two groups were also compared with regard to the influence of incentive level in their responses to the RB phenomenon. They were informed before each trial whether the trial was a win or a lose trial and whether drawing a red jellybean would result in winning or losing $0.10 or $2.00. Affect valence produced the usual significant main effect, with more heuristic, non-optimal responses occurring on win than on lose trials. The main effects for depression and incentive were not significant. However, there was a significant depression × incentive interaction on win trials. On low incentive win trials, the depressed students made significantly fewer heuristic, non-optimal responses than the non-depressed students, which reproduced the depressive realism phenomenon. However, in response to an increase in incentive level, the depressed students made more heuristic, non-optimal responses and the non-depressed students made more deliberative, optimal responses. As a result, the groups no longer differed and the depressive–realism phenomenon was no longer present. The results were interpreted as an indication that the depressed participants were able to compensate for an awareness of their tendency to think unrealistically when they were minimally emotionally involved in the outcome of a situation but not when they were more emotionally involved. The non-depressed students responded in the opposite, more adaptive manner by processing heuristically when the incentive for performing well was minimal but processing in the rational/analytic mode when the incentive for performing well was significant.

Based on the questionnaire as well as the RB results in the present study, it may be concluded that strong negative affect, as exhibited in depressed students, is associated with deliberative responding only when the consequence of their behavior is trivial. When the consequences are significant their thinking becomes more heuristic and the depressive–realism phenomenon is no longer manifested.

SUMMARY AND CONCLUSIONS

It may be concluded that the results of laboratory research on the influence of the valence of induced mild, transient and uninvolving affect on processing modes cannot be generalized to the influence of the stronger affect commonly experienced in everyday life. Instead of the direct relation between induced negative affect and rational/analytic processing found in laboratory research, in reports of real-life reactions, negative affect was directly associated with experiential/intuitive processing and inversely associated with rational/analytic processing.

Our results on the influence of intensity of affect as manipulated by incentive level on mode of information processing indicated that there is not a uniform effect among participants. Rather, there are important individual differences, with some people relying more on their experiential/intuitive processing and others on their rational/analytic processing in response to an increase in incentive level.

NOTE

1. The research reported in this chapter was supported by National Institute of Mental Health (NIMH) Research Grant MH01293 and NIMH Research Scientist Award 5 K05 MH003635.

REFERENCES

Alloy, L. B., & Abramson, L. Y. 1979. Judgment of contingency in depressed and non-depressed students: Sadder but wiser? *Journal of Experimental Psychology: General*, 108: 441–485.
Beck, A. T. 1976. *Cognitive therapy and the emotional disorders*. New York: International Universities Press.
Beck, A. T., Ward, C. H., Mendelson, M., Mock, J., & Erbaugh, J. 1961. An inventory for measuring depression. *Archives of General Psychiatry*, 4: 561–571.
Bodenhausen, G. V., Kramer, G. P., & Susser, K. 1994. Happiness and stereotypic thinking in social judgment. *Journal of Personality and Social Psychology*, 66: 621–632.
Chaiken, S., & Trope, Y. (Eds.) 1999. *Dual-process theories in social psychology*. New York: Guilford Press.
Denes-Raj, V., & Epstein, S. 1994. Conflict between experiential and rational processing: When people behave against their better judgment. *Journal of Personality and Social Psychology*, 66: 819–829.
Dijksterhuis, A. 2004. Think different: The merits of unconscious thought in preference development and decision-making. *Journal of Personality and Social Psychology*, 87: 586–598.
Elsbach, K. D., & Barr, P. S. 1999. The effects of mood on individuals' use of structures decision protocols. *Organization Science*, 10: 181–198.
Epstein, S. 1989. Values from the perspective of cognitive–experiential self-theory. In N. Eisenberg, J. Reykowski, & E. Staub (Eds.), *Social and moral values*: 3–22. Hillsdale, NJ: Lawrence Erlbaum.
Epstein, S. 1994. Integration of the cognitive and the psychodynamic unconscious. *Journal of Personality and Social Psychology*, 49: 709–724.
Epstein, S. 2001. *Manual for the Constructive Thinking Inventory*. Odessa, FL: Psychological Assessment Resources.

Epstein, S. 2003. Cognitive–experiential self-theory of personality. In T. Millon & M. J. Lerner (Eds.), *Comprehensive handbook of psychology*, vol. 5: 159–184, Personality and Social Psychology, Hoboken, NJ: Wiley.

Epstein, S. 2010. Intuition: What it is, what it does, and how it does it. *Psychological Inquiry*, 21: 295–312.

Epstein, S., & Pacini, R. 2000–2001. The influence of visualization on intuitive and analytical information processing. *Imagination, Cognition, and Personality*, 20: 195–216.

Epstein, S., & Pacini, R. 2006. *The influence of induced positive and negative affect on the ratio-bias phenomenon.* Analyzed data.

Epstein, S., Pacini, R., Denes-Raj, V., & Heier, H. 1996. Individual differences in intuitive–experiential and analytical–rational thinking styles. *Journal of Personality and Social Psychology*, 71: 390–405.

Forgas, J. 1995. Mood and judgment: The Affect Infusion Model (AIM). *Psychological Bulletin*, 117: 39–66.

Gallistel, C. R. 1989. Animal cognition: The representation of space, time, and number. *Annual Review of Psychology*, 40: 155–189.

Gallistel, C. R., & Gelman, R. 1992. Preverbal and verbal counting and computation. *Cognition*, 44: 43–74.

Hasher, L., & Zacks, R. T. 1984. Automatic processing of fundamental information: The case of frequency of occurrence. *American Psychologist*, 39: 1372–1388.

Kahneman, D., Slovic, P., & Tversky, A. (Eds.). 1991. *Judgment under uncertainty: Heuristics and biases*. New York: Cambridge University Press.

King, L. A., Burton, C. M., Hicks, J. A., & Drigotas, S. M. 2007. Ghosts, UFOs, and magic: Positive affect and the experiential system. *Journal of Personality and Social Psychology*, 92: 905–919.

Kirkpatrick, L. A., & Epstein, S. 1992. Cognitive–experiential self-theory and subjective probability: Further evidence for two conceptual systems. *Journal of Personality and Social Psychology*, 63: 534–544.

Norris, P., & Epstein, S. In press. An experiential thinking style: Its facets and relations with objective and subjective criterion-measures. *Journal of Personality*, DOI: 10.1111/j.1467–6494.2011.00718.x

Pacini, R., & Epstein, S. 1999a. The relation of rational and experiential information processing styles to personality, basic beliefs, and the ratio-bias phenomenon. *Journal of Personality and Social Psychology*, 76: 972–987.

Pacini, R., & Epstein, S. 1999b. The interaction of three facets of concrete thinking in a game of chance. *Thinking and Reasoning*, 5: 303–325.

Pacini, R., Muir, F., & Epstein, S. 1998. Depressive realism from the perspective of cognitive–experiential self-theory. *Journal of Personality and Social Psychology*, 74: 1056–1068.

Reber, A. S. 1993. *Implicit learning and tacit knowledge*. New York: Oxford University Press.

Ruder, M., & Bless, H. 2003. Mood and the reliance on the ease of the retrieval heuristic. *Journal of Personality and Social Psychology*, 85: 25–32.

Sinclair, M., Ashkanasy, N. M., Chattopadhyay, P., & Boyle, M. V. 2002. Determinants of intuitive decision-making in management: The moderating role of affect. In N. M. Ashkanasy, W. J. Zerbe, & C. E. J. Härtel (Eds.). *Managing Emotions in the Workplace*: 143–163, Armonk, NY: M. E. Sharpe.

Wilson, T. D. 2002. *Strangers to ourselves: Discovering the adaptive unconscious*. Cambridge, MA: Harvard University Press.

5 Investigating intuition: beyond self-report

Gerard P. Hodgkinson and
Eugene Sadler-Smith

In recent decades the analysis of intuition and related non-conscious cognitive–affective processes has emerged as a legitimate subject of social scientific inquiry with important implications for educational, personal, medical and organizational decision making (Dane & Pratt, 2007, 2009; Hogarth, 2001; Hodgkinson et al., 2008, 2009a; Klein, 1998, 2003; Sadler-Smith, 2008, 2010). However, the elusive nature of the intuition construct raises particular methodological issues, and the purpose of this chapter is to offer a critical appraisal of alternative methods of assessment. Much of the recent methodological discourse pertaining to the study of intuition has centred on the relative merits of basic self-report instruments comprising attitudinal statements that purport to capture individual differences in preferences for intuitive and/or analytical processing (e.g., Allinson & Hayes, 1996; Betsch, 2008; Betsch & Iannello, 2010; Epstein et al., 1996; Hayes et al., 2003; Hodgkinson & Sadler-Smith, 2003a, 2003b; Hodgkinson et al., 2009b). Accordingly, in this chapter we restrict our focus to a range of alternative assessment techniques, ones that in a variety of ways usefully complement such self-report instruments. Our review of the literature does not claim to offer a comprehensive survey of the full range of potentially pertinent tools. Rather, our intention is to reflect upon the current state of scientific progress with regard to what we consider to be some of the principal methodological alternatives for seeking to capture the processes and outcomes of intuition. In particular, we consider the strengths and weaknesses of selected procedures that seek to capture in different ways important elements of non-conscious cognitive–affective information processing and map the physiological and neural correlates of such processing, together with a variety of methods that might enable participants to reflect more deeply on intuitive episodes and capture on a systematic basis the outcomes of intuitive expertise (for additional coverage of these and related procedures, see the recent edited volumes by Plessner et al., 2008 and Glöckner & Witteman, 2010). Our chapter highlights the need for a genuinely interdisciplinary programme of research that develops systematic evidence pertaining to the construct validity and predictive efficacy of task-based, psychophysiological, and neuroimaging techniques alongside the traditional self-report attitudinal instruments more typically employed by researchers in applied settings.

ASSESSING NON-CONSCIOUS PROCESSING

Among the main challenges in intuition research has been the need to distinguish intuition from a range of related but distinct phenomena, not least tacit knowledge and insight, and to identify the roles played by incubation and intuition in the processes leading up to insight (see Dane & Pratt, 2007; Hodgkinson et al., 2008; Hogarth, 2001). The term 'insight' is 'typically reserved for those moments when people suddenly realize that they can "see into" the structure of problems', it is a subjective experience accompanied by a 'strong conviction of certainty' (Hogarth, 2001: 254). It entails a non-conscious incubation period, following which the problem solution suddenly enters conscious awareness. Evidence for the role of incubation and intuition in the processes leading to insight comes from a variety of sources (for an overview, see Sternberg & Davidson, 1995), including laboratory studies using the methods typified below.

Remote Associates Tests

In a typical remote associates test (RAT) participants are presented with three words that can be associated with a common (i.e., solution) word; for example the items 'goat', 'pass', and 'bike' have the solution word of 'mountain'. Solutions to RATs typically arise relatively slowly from remote semantic associations that are not immediately apparent. The RAT was developed originally by Mednick (1962) as a measure of creative (i.e., divergent) thought. Initial fixation on misleading clues and incorrect solutions is frequently followed by subsequent incubation effects and a correct solution (Smith, 1995). RATs exhibit convergent validity to the extent that they are positively associated with performance on classic insight problems such as 'The Prisoner in the Tower' problem (see Isaak & Just, 1995) and have been offered as supporting evidence for the spreading activation hypothesis of insight problem solving (Bowden & Jung-Beeman, 2003; Bowers et al., 1990). In focusing on outcomes rather than processes, RATs have been important in defining what insight is and, correspondingly, what intuition is not.

Feelings of Knowing

Feelings of knowing (FOK) are 'an individual's belief, unsubstantiated by factual information, that he or she is capable of proceeding in a way that will lead to the successful solution of the problem at hand', in other words the 'sense' that the answer is within reach (Ippolito & Tweney, 1995: 447). FOK are experienced when participants are unable to recall a solicited target, which is available in memory, but are able to accurately assess the potential availability of a correct response – correlations between assessments of availability and actual availability are in the range 0.90 to 0.97 (Koriat, 1993). FOK arise as a result of unintentional inferential heuristics that mediate between implicit-automatic (i.e., System 1) processes and explicit-controlled (i.e., System 2) processes (Koriat, 2000) and often manifest as a 'tip-of-the-tongue' phenomenon. Metcalfe and Wiebe (1987) found that non-insight problems exhibited an incremental pattern of increase in FOK over the course of a problem-solving task, whereas insight-problem solutions were characterized by a sudden, unforeseen flash of illumination. The 'imminence' signified by FOK is one of a number of phenomenological attributes of insight, described as a 'feeling that after only brief moments the answer will burst into consciousness' (Smith, 1995: 236). The phenomenological attributes of insight (Bowers et al., 1990) differ from the phenomenological attributes of intuition (Damasio, 1994); however, the precise nature of the differences is an unresolved issue. The assessment of FOK focuses to a greater extent on 'upstream' processes (as is the case with RATs).

Perceptions of Coherence

The suddenness of insight suggests that a potential source of coherence exists, which serves to unite what at first glance appear to be disparate elements (Schooler et al., 1995). Assessments of intuitive perceptions of coherence have typically employed pictorial and verbal stimuli; for example, in a study using the RAT and a gestalt closure task, Bowers et al. (1990: 72) demonstrated that people could intuitively respond to and discriminate as potentially meaningful 'coherences that they could not identify' on the basis of the automatic patterned activation of problem-relevant networks in long-term memory. If, and when, the level of activation is sufficient to cross the threshold of conscious awareness, the subjective sensation of 'hunch' is experienced (Bowers et al., 1990) – a phenomenon equivalent to the so-called 'intimation' stage in Wallas's (1926) model of creative problem solving (see Mayer, 1995). The intuitive 'hunch' in this case is associated with perceptions of potential coherences and not with a fully fledged realization (insight) of actual coherences (although this may follow). As discussed later, more recent research has used neuroimaging techniques to examine the neural correlates of these processes (see 'Mapping the Physiological and Neural Correlates of Intuitive Processing' below).

Assessing Implicit Learning

Implicit learning is generally considered a System 1 process and is intuitive to the extent that individuals may be unaware of the acquisition or the application of rules. Artificial grammar (AG) algorithms have been used extensively in laboratory studies of implicit learning (Litman & Reber, 2005). For example, Matthews et al. (1989) found that participants who had engaged in an AG implicit learning task could make reliable decisions (distinguishing well-formed letter strings) by the end of day one of a four-day study but were unable to explicate what they had learned. In the so-called Tulsa studies, which involved participants tracking the position of an on-screen target (X), the movement of which was governed by complex algorithms, Lewicki et al. observed that participants were able to learn the complex rules for accurately predicting the target's position but could not verbalize what the rules were (Lewicki et al., 1992, 1998). This body of work was interpreted by Lewicki and colleagues as evidence that inaccessible regions of human cognition are not simply assigned routine and mundane ('house-keeping') operations, but are also involved in more sophisticated processing.

Assessing 'Unconscious Thought'

Some researchers have argued that because of the restrictive capacity of System 2 processing when people are faced with complex decisions conscious thought can be 'maladaptive' and unconscious (System 1) thought can lead to better decisions. In support of this highly controversial assertion, Dijksterhuis et al. have undertaken a number of laboratory studies in which they assigned participants to a conscious thought or unconscious thought condition (for example, through the use of a distraction task) and asked them to perform various complex judgemental tasks (see Dijksterhuis et al., 2006). By way of illustration, Dijksterhuis found that unconscious thinkers consistently 'made the best decisions' (Dijksterhuis, 2004: 586) over a series of five experiments centred on a hypothetical problem concerning the choice of a residential apartment. More recently this group of researchers has offered evidence in support of the view that unconscious thought is goal dependent, i.e. 'without a goal, people do not engage in unconscious thought' (Bos et al., 2008: 1114). This stream of work raises some important and complex issues, not least the question of how the non-conscious reasoning processes that Dijksterhuis and his colleagues claim to yield superior decisions might relate to the affectively charged judgements that form the substance of intuition (see Dane, & Pratt, 2007). The question of how this work might be integrated with current understanding of insight is also highly problematic.[1]

ASSESSING HEURISTIC PROCESSING IN LABORATORY AND NATURALISTIC SETTINGS

The Heuristics and Biases Tradition

Following the seminal work of Meehl (1954), which documented inaccuracies in experts' clinical judgement, behavioural decision researchers have identified, primarily (though not exclusively) through laboratory studies, the systematic biases associated with certain types of intuitive judgement. As noted by Hodgkinson and Sparrow (2002), unlike the relatively recent work on naturalistic decision making (e.g., Klein, 1998) and the work of Gigerenzer and colleagues (e.g., Gigerenzer et al., 1999) on fast-and-frugal heuristics that has highlighted the upside of intuitive judgement, this body of research has tended to accentuate the 'downside' of intuitive judgement.

One of the first studies in what has become known as the heuristics and biases (HB) tradition was conducted by Tversky and Kahneman (1971) who concluded: (i) even sophisticated scientists reached incorrect conclusions and made inferior choices when they followed their intuitions; and (ii) faulty statistical intuitions are pervasive and relatively impervious to formal training and actual experience. The sources of errors in intuitive judgement are traceable, through experimental studies involving various types of tasks and manipulations, to the weighting biases that accrue when particular sources of information (for example, availability of information, or attributes such as representativeness) are overweighted, while others are neglected (for example, base rates, or laws of probability) (see, for example, Gilovich et al., 2002; Kahneman, 2000).

In a comprehensive overview of the HB programme and its theory and methods, Gilovich and Griffin (2002) summarized a number of critiques that have been levelled at this work, including the 'we cannot be that dumb', 'it's all parlour games', and the 'frequencies are [in evolutionary terms] good whereas probabilities are bad' arguments, but concluded with the assessment that the research inspired by the HB approach is flourishing in applied as well as in laboratory settings. For example, from the perspective of business and management a number of practical problems are associated with intuitive heuristic judgement, namely: intuitive responses are usually singular; they come effortlessly to mind; managers have no way of knowing where their intuitive responses come from; and there is no 'subjective marker' that can effectively distinguish correct intuitive judgements from 'highly imperfect' heuristics (Kahneman & Klein, 2009: 522).

Until recently the HB tradition, with its roots in Meehl's work and its sceptical tone towards the utility of intuitive judgements, was considered to be largely at odds with the more positive stance towards intuitive judgement to be found in naturalistic decision research (Klein, 1998, 2003) and related work on expert judgement (Hogarth, 2001; Sadler-Smith & Shefy, 2004; Simon, 1987), but there are now some signs of approaching convergence, as reviewed below (see 'Identifying the Sources of Intuitive Expertise').

Fast-and-frugal Heuristics

A somewhat different body of work has emphasised the upside of intuitive judgement, based on studies of so-called 'fast-and-frugal' heuristics (Gigerenzer, 2007). Fast-and-frugal heuristics are adaptive means of taking decisions in real-world settings under conditions of limited time and knowledge, which 'do not involve much computation, and do not compute probabilities and utilities' (Gigerenzer & Todd, 1999: 6). The fast-and-frugal heuristics research programme endeavours to design computational models of the 'simple heuristics that make us smart', analyse the environmental structures under which such heuristics work well, test their performance in real-world (as opposed to laboratory) environments, and determine if and under what conditions people use them (Gigerenzer & Todd, 1999). Whereas the HB and intuitive expertise programmes have begun to cross-fertilize, a theoretical and empirical challenge remains with regard to how the fast-and-frugal programme interfaces with these alternative conceptions. For example, Kahneman (2000: 683) observed that the phrase 'heuristics that make us smart' 'suggests without exactly saying' that fast and frugal heuristics such as 'recognition' 'do not introduce biases': an assertion which 'cannot be true'.

IDENTIFYING THE SOURCES OF INTUITIVE EXPERTISE

The notion of intuitive expertise may be seen as an outgrowth of the naturalistic decision making (NDM) framework and in particular Klein's

(1998) recognition-primed decision (RPD) model. NDM theories are regarded by some as 'radical', given their rejection of traditional subjective expected utility (SEU) theory and laboratory-based procedures, instead being oriented firmly towards the study of how people use their experience to take decisions in everyday field settings (cf., Kahneman & Klein, 2009). One of the central premises of the view of intuition-as-expertise (Hogarth, 2001), or latterly intuitive expertise (Kahneman & Klein, 2009), is that a fundamental component of expert decision making is quick appraisal rooted in an 'intuitive information processing system' (Salas et al., 2010: 944), which often manifests as 'an emotional sense that something is not right' (Klein, 2003: 96). The scientific study of intuition-as-expertise is predicated on the notion that experienced decision makers will deploy their tacit knowledge gained through many years of learning, experience and feedback in specific domains, as the basis for taking action (see Simon, 1987).

Cognitive Task Analysis

A number of NDM researchers use cognitive task analysis (CTA) techniques (Crandall et al., 2006; Schraagen et al., 2000) in order to identify the cues and strategies that experts use to support their intuitive judgements. CTA relies on a variety of techniques including semi-structured interviews to probe incidents and elicit cues and contextual factors as the basis for inferences about experts' decision processes in situ (see Crandall et al., 2006), but with the acknowledgement that 'researchers cannot expect decision makers to accurately explain *why* they made decisions' (Kahneman & Klein, 2009: 517, our emphasis).

Tacit Knowledge Tests

The intuitive expertise of NDM research possesses similarities to the concepts of 'practical intelligence' or 'practical know-how' (Sternberg, 2002) made measurable through the use of scenario-based tests in which participants' responses to complex judgemental problems are judged against those of experts (Wagner & Sternberg, 1985). Sternberg and Wagner's research has identified reliable knowledge that differentiates experts from novices and found that managers' tacit knowledge predicts job performance (Wagner, 2002).

In comparing their views on HB and NDM, Kahneman and Klein (2009: 525) concluded that: (i) whether or not intuitive judgements can be trusted depends on the validity of the environment in which the judgement is made (in high-validity environments there are stable relationships between cues and events), and the opportunity of the decision maker to learn the regularities of that environment (i.e., the anticipated relationships between cues and subsequent events); (ii) irregular and unpredictable (i.e., low-validity) environments militate against the development of true intuitive expertise and in such environments the illusion of intuitive skill as a result of 'lucky' judgement may be a source of potentially catastrophic overconfidence (as in the case of the financial industry); and (iii) despite the aversion of the NDM community to studying 'bias' and the preoccupation of the HB community with errors, 'a psychology of intuitive judgement and decision making that ignores intuitive skills is seriously blinkered' while a 'psychology of professional judgement that neglects predictable errors cannot be adequate'.

RECOVERING INTUITIVE EPISODES

Intuitions and the process of intuiting have a number of intriguing phenomenological characteristics, which present unique challenges and opportunities to intuition researchers who may wish to recover the subjective aspects of intuitions via first-person accounts. In what follows we speculate on the potential of various methods for the retrospective recovery of intuitive episodes, while recognizing that other approaches, such as verbal protocol analysis (Ericsson & Simon, 1993), i.e., 'thinking aloud' techniques, offer a potentially valuable means for the concurrent capturing of intuiting and intuitions at their moments of occurrence.

Phenomenological Approaches

A greater emphasis on phenomenographic research could delve more deeply into managers' lived experiences of intuition in terms of the recovery of both the cognitive and affective facets of intuitive episodes. The nature of the intuitive experience requires the use of methods that are specifically geared towards the phenomenal experience. In phenomenological inquiry the goal of the phenomenological interview is to gain a first-person description of some specified domain of experience, where the course of the dialogue is set largely by the participant (Cope, 2005; Thompson et al., 1989). As well as deploying conventional interview techniques, eliciting first-person accounts of intuitive episodes might also draw on the techniques of guided introspection based on psycho-phenomenological methods which offer the potential for high levels of 'granularity' in the data recovered (Petitmengin, 2006; Tosey & Mathison 2010; Vermersch, 1999).

Capturing Intuitive 'Hits' and 'Misses'

Given that positive instances of intuitive episodes have, in the popular literature at least, tended to be more visible than negative instances, it is imperative that researchers study the full range of intuitive outcomes (i.e., 'misses' as well as 'hits'). For instance, in the domain of business venturing it may be possible to scrutinize successful and unsuccessful entrepreneurial intuitions and in the domain of human resource management to analyse the 'gut feel appointment' that failed. The Critical Incident Technique (CIT) (Flanagan, 1954) could provide insights into the conditions under which intuitive judgements are seen to be effective and ineffective. In exploring the role of attributions to intuition in the business venturing process, Blume and Covin (2011) have asked the question of whether or not entrepreneurs actually use intuition, or 'just say that they do', but also acknowledged that verifying whether or not intuition is actually used is a difficult task.

Improving Retrospective Reporting

The retrospective reporting of intuitive episodes as elicited by techniques such as the CIT are subject to a number of well-documented potential sources of bias and inaccuracy, an inherent limitation of first-person accounts. Other more sophisticated methods in addition to CIT are available; for example, Hodgkinson et al. (2008) suggested that managers' intuitive episodes might be researched by the experience sampling method (ESM) (Csikszentmihalyi & Larson, 1987) and day reconstruction method (DRM) (Kahneman et al., 2004). The former is relatively expensive and involves high levels of 'participant burden', whereas the latter aims to be more efficient than ESM by being less burdensome to participants and investigators, and not disruptive of normal day-to-day activities (ibid.: 1776).

MAPPING THE PHYSIOLOGICAL AND NEURAL CORRELATES OF INTUITIVE PROCESSING

Neuroimaging

In recent years there have been some particularly compelling examples of the use of the latest generation of neuroimaging tools such as functional Magnetic Resonance Imaging (fMRI) to advance understanding of intuition and related non-conscious cognitive and cognitive-affective processes.[2] For instance, in foundational studies in the emerging field of social cognitive neuroscience, Lieberman et al. (2004) used fMRI in the identification of various brain regions associated with reflexive social cognition (which they refer to as the 'X-system') and reflective social cognition (which they referred to as the 'C-system'), analogous to automatic, intuitive (i.e., System 1) and controlled, analytical (i.e., System 2) processing, respectively (for overviews of this and related work, see Lieberman, 2007, 2009). A second convenient illustration is provided by the recent work of Volz and von Cramon (2006), which used a variant of the Waterloo Gestalt Closure Task in conjunction with fMRI studies of intuitive judgements of visual coherences. The orbito-frontal cortex (OFC), the amygdala and several other brain regions, including the ventral occipito-temporal regions (VOT) were activated in coherence judgements, even when participants were unable to name the stimulus object concerned. As a third illustration, Jung-Beeman et al. (2004) used RATs in conjunction with fMRI in a study that compared patterns of neural activity between problems solved through insight and problems solved non-insightfully (i.e., incrementally). An increase in neural activity in the anterior Superior Temporal Gyrus (aSTG) of the right hemisphere was detected when insight occurred. Jung-Beeman et al. postulated that the aSTG region of the right hemisphere facilitates diffuse and overlapping integration of information across wide semantic networks, whereas the same region of the left hemisphere produces more discrete fields of activation. It is particularly encouraging that a growing number of these sorts of studies are showing promising signs of the potential to gather evidence of convergent and discriminant validity between task-based and self-report measures on one hand, and brain-imaging techniques on the other hand. Further work along these lines is urgently needed, both in order to further validate these alternative approaches to assessment and advance understanding of the various basic mechanisms underpinning intuition, insight and related conscious and non-conscious cognitive and cognitive–affective processes.

Electroencephalography (EEG)

The EEG technique is based on the principle that when large populations of neurons are active simultaneously, electrical signals are produced that are of a magnitude sufficient to be measured by electrodes placed on the scalp (Gazzaniga et al., 2002). As an illustration of the potential of this approach, the aforementioned study by Jung-Beeman et al. (2004) incorporated the use of EEG, which revealed a burst of alpha waves over the right posterior parietal–occipital region in insight problem solving (in general terms the presence of alpha activity is associated with a quiescent, meditative state, whereas its dissipation is associated with attention and arousal). Jung-Beeman et al. offered a speculative interpretation of this finding, as follows. Alpha activity in the visual cortex indicates that information from this brain region is subject to 'idling' (hence the 'burst' of alpha activity) in order to protect fragile insight processes from interference by stronger visual information processing signals.

Skin Conductance Responses

In addition to EEG, other potentially illuminating psychophysiological measures in the study of insight, intuition and related non-conscious cognitive and cognitive–affective processes include the assessment of galvanic skin responses, i.e., the analysis of changes in electrical activity that arise from the functioning of the autonomic nervous system. The utility of this approach was demonstrated by Bechara et al. (1997) in the seminal Iowa Gambling Task (IGT) studies, which investigated the underlying neurophysiological mechanisms of intuitive judgement. They compared the skin conductance responses (SCRs) of normal participants engaged in a 'loaded' gambling task with those of patients performing the same task who had previously suffered damage to the ventro-medial region of the prefrontal cortex (VMPC). Bechara and colleagues maintain that the VMPC plays a vital role as the neural substrate underpinning the generation of 'somatic markers', that is, neurophysiological signals that guide decision choices and, therefore, constitute an affective biasing step in decision making, which operates in advance of conscious awareness.

CONCLUDING REMARKS

As recently observed by Hodgkinson and Healey (2008), the study of non-conscious processes at the intersections of cognition and affect has reached a new and exciting stage of development. Recent advances in neuroimaging techniques, especially when used in conjunction with task-based measures, self-report instruments, and conventional psychophysiological procedures, are beginning to generate new and highly insightful findings into the basic mechanics of these fundamental processes that lie at the heart of personal, social and organizational decision making. Accordingly, it seems fitting to conclude our chapter with a plea for a programme of interdisciplinary research on intuition, using multiple and mixed methods in the search for convergent findings among researchers who, even though they may be operating in different disciplines, are seeking collectively to uncover the scientific bases of what are undoubtedly exceedingly complex and intriguing phenomena.

NOTES

1. As observed by Haslam (2007), when viewed from the standpoint of social psychology the main implication of this body of work that complex decisions are best accomplished intuitively is misguided and dangerous, as exemplified by President George W. Bush's decision to invade Iraq, which was apparently justified on the basis of a similar logic. Clearly, there are many occasions when decision processes need to be both extensive and deliberative, involving stakeholders with varying goals and opinions.
2. fMRI techniques do not measure neuronal activity directly; rather, they track changes in blood flow (hemodynamics) on the basis that the more active neurons are, the more blood they need (Churchland, 2002). From the patterns of blood flow it is thus possible to indirectly infer the neural circuits which 'fire' (and thereby consume oxygen from the bloodstream) during specific types of mental activities or tasks.

REFERENCES

Allinson, C. W., & Hayes, J. 1996. The Cognitive Style Index: A measure of intuition-analysis for organisational research. *Journal of Management Studies*, 33(1): 119–135.

Bechara, A., Damasio, H., Tranel, D., & Damasio, A. R. 1997. Deciding advantageously before knowing the advantageous strategy. *Science*, 275: 1293–1294.

Betsch, C. 2008. Chronic preferences for intuition and deliberation in decision making: Lessons learned about intuition from an individual differences approach. In Plessner, H., Betsch, C., & Betsch, T. (Eds.), *Intuition in judgment and decision making*: 231–248. New York: Erlbaum.

Betsch, C., & Iannello, P. 2010. Measuring individual differences in intuitive and deliberate decision making styles: A comparison of different measures. In Glöckner, A., & Witteman, C. (Eds.), *Foundations for tracing intuition: Challenges and method*: 251–271. Hove, UK: Psychology Press.

Blume, B. D., & Covin, J. G. 2011. Attributions to intuition in the venture founding process: Do entrepreneurs actually use intuition or just say that they do? *Journal of Business Venturing*, 26: 137–151.

Bos, M. W., Dijksterhuis, A., & van Baaren, R. B. 2008. On the goal-dependency of unconscious thought. *Journal of Experimental Social Psychology*, 44: 1114–1120.

Bowden, E. M., & Jung-Beeman, M. 2003. Aha! insight experience correlates with solution activation in the right hemisphere. *Psychonomic Bulletin and Review*, 10: 730–737.

Bowers, K. S., Regehr, G., & Balthazard, C. 1990. Intuition in the context of discovery. *Cognitive Psychology*, 22: 72–110.

Churchland, P.S. 2002. *Brain-wise: Studies in neurophilosophy*. Cambridge, MA: Bradford Book/MIT Press.

Cope, J. 2005. Researching entrepreneurship through phenomenological inquiry: Philosophical and methodological issues. *International Small Business Journal*, 23(2): 163–189.

Crandall, B., Klein, G., & Hoffman, R. R. 2006. *Working minds: A practitioner's guide to cognitive task analysis*. Cambridge, MA: MIT Press.

Csikszentmihalyi, M., & Larson, R. W. 1987. Validity and reliability of the Experience Sampling Method. *Journal of Nervous and Mental Disease*, 175: 526–536.

Damasio, A. R. 1994. *Descartes' error: Emotion, reason, and the human brain*. New York: G. P. Putnam & Sons.

Dane, E., & Pratt, M. G. 2007. Exploring intuition and its role in managerial decision making. *Academy of Management Review*, 32(1): 33–54.

Dane, E., & Pratt, M. G. 2009. Conceptualizing and measuring intuition: A review of recent trends. In G. P. Hodgkinson, & J. K. Ford (Eds.), *International Review of Industrial and Organizational Psychology*, 24: 1–40. Chichester, UK: Wiley.

Dijksterhuis, A. 2004. Think different: The merits of unconscious thought in preference development and decision making. *Journal of Personality and Social Psychology*, 87: 586–598.

Dijksterhuis, A., Bos, M. W., Nordgren, L. F., & van Baaren, R. B. 2006. On making the right choice: The deliberation-without-attention effect. *Science*, 311: 1005–1007.

Epstein, S., Pacini, R., Denes-Raj, V., & Heier, H. 1996. Individual differences in intuitive–experiential and analytical–rational thinking styles. *Journal of Personality and Social Psychology*, 71(2): 390–405.

Ericsson, A., & Simon, H. A. 1993. *Protocol analysis: Verbal reports as data* (rev. ed.). Cambridge, MA: MIT Press.

Flanagan, J. C. 1954. The Critical Incident Technique. *Psychological Bulletin*, 51(4): 327–358.

Gazzaniga, M. S., Ivry, R. B., & Mangun, G. R. 2002. *Cognitive neuroscience: The biology of the mind*. New York: W. W. Norton & Co.

Gigerenzer, G. 2007. *Gut feelings*. London: Penguin.

Gigerenzer, G., & Todd, P. M. 1999. Fast and frugal heuristics: The adaptive toolbox. In Gigerenzer et al.: 3–36.

Gigerenzer, G., Todd, P. M., & The ABC Research Group (Eds.). 1999. *Simple heuristics that make us smart*. New York: Oxford University Press.

Gilovich, T., & Griffin, D. 2002. Introduction – heuristics and biases: Then and now. In Gilovich et al. (Eds.): 1–16.

Gilovich, T., Griffin, D., & Kahneman, D. (Eds.) 2002. *Heuristics and biases: The psychology of intuitive judgment*. New York: Cambridge University Press.

Glöckner, A., & Witteman, C. (Eds.) 2010. *Foundations for tracing intuition: Challenges and methods*. Hove, UK: Psychology Press.

Haslam, S. A. 2007. I think, therefore I err? *Scientific American Mind*, April: 16–17.

Hayes, J., Allinson, C. W., Hudson, R. S., & Keasey, K. 2003. Further reflections on the nature of intuition-analysis and the construct validity of the Cognitive Style Index. *Journal of Occupational and Organizational Psychology*, 76(2): 269–278.

Hodgkinson, G. P., & Healey, M. P. 2008. Cognition in Organizations. *Annual Review of Psychology*, 59: 387–417.

Hodgkinson, G. P., Langan-Fox, J., & Sadler-Smith, E. 2008. Intuition: A fundamental bridging construct in the behavioural sciences. *British Journal of Psychology*, 99: 1–27.

Hodgkinson, G. P., & Sadler-Smith, E. 2003a. Complex or unitary? A critique and empirical re-assessment of the Allinson–Hayes Cognitive Style Index. *Journal of Occupational and Organizational Psychology*, 76: 243–268.

Hodgkinson, G. P., & Sadler-Smith, E. 2003b. Reflections on reflections . . . on the nature of intuition, analysis and the construct validity of the Cognitive Style Index. *Journal of Occupational and Organizational Psychology*, 76: 279–281.

Hodgkinson, G. P., Sadler-Smith, E., Burke, L. A., Claxton, G., & Sparrow, P. 2009a. Intuition in organizations: Some implications for strategic management. *Long Range Planning*, 42: 277–297.

Hodgkinson, G.P., Sadler-Smith, E., Sinclair, M., & Ashkanasy, N. 2009b. More than meets the eye? Intuition and analysis revisited. *Personality and Individual Differences*, 47: 342–346.

Hodgkinson, G. P., and Sparrow, P. R. 2002. *The competent organization*. Buckingham, UK: Open University Press.

Hogarth, R. M. 2001. *Educating intuition*, Chicago: University of Chicago Press.

Ippolito, M. F., & Tweney, R. D. 1995. The inception of insight. In Sternberg & Davidson (Eds.): 433–462.

Isaak, M. I., & Just, M. A. 1995. Constraints on thinking and invention. In Sternberg & Davidson (Eds.): 281–325.

Jung-Beeman, M., Bowden, E. M., Haberman, J., Frymiare, J., Arambel-Lui, S., Greenblat, R., Reber, P. J., & Kounios, J. 2004. Neural activity when people solve problems with insight. *Public Library of Science (Biology)*, 2(4): 0500–0510.

Kahneman, D. 2000. A psychological point of view: violations of rational rules as diagnostic of mental processes. *Behavioral and Brain Sciences*, 23: 681–683.

Kahneman, D., & Klein, G. 2009. Conditions for intuitive expertise: A failure to disagree. *American Psychologist*, 64(6): 515–526.

Kahneman, D., Krueger, A. B., Schkade, D. A., Schwarz, N., & Stone, A. A. 2004. A survey method for characterizing daily life experience: The Day Reconstruction Method. *Science*, 306(5702): 1776–1780.

Klein, G. 2003. *Intuition at work*, New York: Doubleday.

Klein, G. 1998. *Sources of power: How people make decisions*. Cambridge, MA: MIT Press.

Koriat, A. 1993. How do we know that we know? The accessibility model of the feeling of knowing. *Psychological Review*, 100(4): 609–639.

Koriat, A. 2000. The feeling of knowing: Some metatheoretical implications for consciousness and control. *Consciousness and Cognition*, 9: 149–171.

Lewicki, P., Hill, T., & Bizot, E. 1998. Acquisition of procedural knowledge about a pattern of stimuli that cannot be articulated. *Cognitive Psychology*, 20: 24–37.

Lewicki, P., Hill, T., & Czyzewska, M. 1992. Non-conscious acquisition of information. *American Psychologist*, 47: 796–801.

Lieberman, M. D. 2007. Social cognitive neuroscience: A review of core processes. *Annual Review of Psychology*, 58: 259–289.

Lieberman, M. D. 2009. What zombies can't do: A social cognitive neuroscience approach to the irreducibility of reflective consciousness. In J. St. B. T. Evans, & K. Frankish (Eds.), *In two minds: Dual processes and beyond*: 293–316. Oxford: Oxford University Press.

Lieberman, M. D., Jarcho, J. M., & Satpute, A. B. 2004. Evidence-based and intuition-based self-knowledge: An fMRI study. *Journal of Personality and Social Psychology*, 87: 421–435.

Litman, L., & Reber, A. 2005. Implicit cognition and thought. In K.J. Holyoak & R.G. Morrison (Eds.), *The Cambridge handbook of thinking and reasoning*: 431–453. Cambridge: Cambridge University Press.

Matthews, R. C., Buss, R. R., Stanley, W. B., Blanchard-Fields, F., Cho, R.J., & Bruhan, B. 1989. Role of implicit and explicit processes of learning from examples: A synergistic effect. *Journal of Experimental Psychology: Learning, Memory and Cognition*, 15: 1083–1100.

Mayer, R. E. 1995. The search for insight. In Sternberg, & Davidson (Eds.): 3–32.

Mednick, S.A. 1962. The associative basis of the creative process. *Psychological Review*, 69: 220–232.

Meehl, P. E. 1954. *Clinical versus statistical prediction*. Minneapolis, MN: University of Minnesota Press.

Metcalfe, J., & Wiebe, D. 1987. Intuition in insight and non-insight problem solving. *Memory and Cognition*, 15(3): 238–246.

Petitmengin, C. 2006. Describing one's subjective experience in the second person: An interview method for the science of consciousness. *Phenomenology and the Cognitive Sciences*, 5(3): 229–269.

Plessner, H., Betsch, C., & Betsch, T. (Eds.) 2008. *Intuition in judgment and decision making*, New York: Erlbaum.

Sadler-Smith, E. 2008. *Inside intuition*. Abingdon: Routledge.

Sadler-Smith, E. 2010. *The intuitive mind*. Chichester: John Wiley & Sons.

Sadler-Smith, E., & Shefy, E. 2004. The intuitive executive: Understanding and applying 'gut feel' in decision-making. *Academy of Management Executive*, 18(4): 76–91.

Salas, E., Rosen, M. A., & DiazGranados, D. 2010. Expertise-based intuition and decision making in organizations. *Journal of Management*, 36, 941–973.

Schooler, J. W., Fallshore, M., & Fiore, S. M. 1995. Epilogue: Putting insight into perspective. In Sternberg, & Davidson (Eds.): 559–588.

Schraagen, J. M. C., Chipman, S. F., & Shalin V. L. (Eds.). 2000. *Cognitive task analysis.* Mahwah, NJ: Erlbaum.

Simon, H. A. 1987. Making management decisions: The role of intuition and emotion. *Academy of Management Executive*, 1(1), 57–64.

Smith, S. M. 1995. Getting into and out of mental ruts: A theory of fixation, incubation and insight. In Sternberg, & Davidson (Eds.): 229–251.

Sternberg, R. J. 2002. *Why smart people can be so stupid.* New Haven, CT: Yale University Press.

Sternberg, R. J., & Davidson, J. E. (Eds.). 1995. *The nature of insight*, Cambridge, MA: MIT Press.

Thompson, C. J., Locander, W. B., & Pollio, H. R. 1989. Putting consumer experience back into consumer research: The philosophy and method of existential phenomenology. *Journal of Consumer Research*, 16(2): 133–146.

Tosey, P., & Mathison, J., 2010. Exploring inner landscapes through psychophenomenology: The contribution of neuro-linguistic programming to innovations in researching first person experience. *Qualitative Research in Organizations and Management*, 5: 63–82.

Tversky, A., & Kahneman, D. 1971. Belief in the law of small numbers. *Psychological Bulletin*, 76(2): 105–110.

Vermersch, P. 1999. Introspection as practice. *Journal of Consciousness Studies*, 6(2–3): 17–42.

Volz, K. G., & von Cramon, D. Y. 2006. What neuroscience can tell about intuitive processes in the context of perceptual discovery. *Journal of Cognitive Neuroscience*, 18(12): 2077–2087.

Wagner, R. K. 2002. Smart people doing dumb things: The case of managerial incompetence. In Sternberg (Ed.): 42–63.

Wagner, R. K., & Sternberg, R. J. 1985. Practical intelligence in real-world pursuits: The role of tacit knowledge. *Journal of Personality and Social Psychology*, 49: 436–458.

Wallas, G. 1926. *The art of thought.* New York: Harcourt Brace Jovanovich.

PART 2

FUNCTIONS OF INTUITION

6 Expert intuition and naturalistic decision making
Gary Klein

The topic of intuition is strongly connected to the naturalistic decision making (NDM) framework, which is why the following chapter is included in the current volume. The NDM framework has emphasized the way people build expertise and apply it to cognitive functions such as judgment and decision making. Expertise depends on different forms of knowledge. Explicit knowledge (knowledge of facts and rules) is the easiest form to describe, teach and track, but is less important than tacit knowledge. Tacit knowledge includes perceptual abilities, pattern recognition, judgments of typicality, and mental models. When skilled decision makers use their tacit knowledge they usually cannot articulate the basis of their judgments and decisions. Tacit knowledge is, by definition, difficult if not impossible to articulate. Therefore, we experience the use of tacit knowledge as intuition. We notice something jarring, or recognize a pattern, and we do not know where these judgments come from so they seem mysterious, as opposed to a logical conclusion based on a deliberated line of reasoning. Klein (2009) uses the example of making a turn against oncoming traffic. There are no rules for judging when to make the turn; with experience we have learned to recognize safe versus unsafe conditions. And this is a difficult judgment. People occasionally get it wrong, as we see when we maneuver around the damaged cars. Thus, every day we make life-and-death decisions using our intuition. Intuition, in the form of tacit knowledge, is essential to expertise, and is central to the kinds of skilled judgments and decisions studied by NDM researchers.

NDM researchers have devised methods and tools for probing tacit knowledge. These methods typically involve forms of cognitive task analysis (Crandall et al., 2006). One of the most powerful of these tools, the critical decision method, examines case accounts from the field. Klein (1998) has described two instances in which people made decisions that were so intuitive that they felt like extrasensory perception (ESP). Both of these informants, a veteran firefighter and a British Naval officer, were unaware of any objective basis for their judgments and concluded that some occult ESP force had provided them with guidance. In both cases, the critical decision method interview was successful in eliciting the actual cues the informants had used.

The Naval officer looked at a radar blip and immediately recognized it as a Silkworm missile that the Iraqis had just fired at his ship toward the end of the 1991 conflict in Kuwait. However, the radar blip was identical for Silkworm missiles and for American A-6 aircraft which were also flying back to sea from Kuwait. They were the same size and flew at the same speed. The Silkworm missiles flew at a lower altitude, around 1,000 feet, whereas the A-6s flew at 2,000 to 3,000 feet, but the initial radar equipment the officer was using did not capture altitude. The officer said that the blip was accelerating as it came off the coast but a careful review of the tapes showed no sign of acceleration. Therefore, the officer felt justified in believing that intuition alone informed his decision to shoot it down. He interrogated it with a second radar suite before engaging it, and verified that it was flying at the lower altitude characteristic of Silkworm missiles, but he knew it was a threat from the very beginning.

However, the cognitive probing unearthed the basis for his decision. The Silkworm missile, flying at the lower altitude, broke out of the ground clutter much further out to sea than the A-6s that the officer was used to tracking. That anomaly had caught his eye. It violated his patterns of typicality. Once the Silkworm missile broke out of ground clutter it continued at the typical speed shown by A-6s, about 600–650 knots. The perceptual impression was of an air contact that was accelerating as it came off the coast. The perception, the tacit knowledge, was accurate even though the facts were wrong. The subjective report held the clue to his intuition and resolved a mystery that analysts and engineers, working with the physical details on the tapes, had been unable to solve.

In this incident, the officer had compiled a sense of typicality based on all the aircraft tracks he had seen. He could not articulate what was typical because it was primarily perceptual and pattern based. Because the pattern was so clear he could immediately detect an anomaly – a track that violated his expectations. Intuition is what provides us with these expectations (Klein & Hoffman, 1993).

The recognition-primed decision (RPD) model, one of the achievements of the NDM framework, demonstrates the application of intuition. It is a blend of intuition and analysis. The pattern matching to rapidly size up a situation and generate a likely course of action is the intuitive part. The mental simulation to evaluate the feasibility of that course of action is the analytical part.

The NDM framework offers a complement to other approaches such as the heuristics and biases tradition (Tversky & Kahneman, 1974). NDM

Expert intuition and naturalistic decision making   71

work illustrates a creative potential, whereas the heuristics and biases tradition cautions us about human potential for mistakes. Klein (2011) has argued that effective performance depends on increasing insights and reducing mistakes. Both are important. However, most organizations only focus on ways to reduce mistakes, by imposing rules and procedures and checklists, by assigning blame and penalties, by establishing standards for carrying out cognitive tasks. The elimination of any mistakes does not result in insights. Even worse, a lop-sided emphasis on reducing mistakes can interfere with insights.

Kahneman and Klein (2009) have described the conditions under which effective intuitions can develop – non-random situations and ample opportunity for practice and feedback. The NDM framework seeks to understand how effective intuitions are developed and applied in natural settings where people can gain the necessary months and years if not decades of experience. The NDM chapter describes the origins of the NDM framework and provides an overview of its applications.

REFERENCES

Crandall, B., Klein, G., & Hoffman, R. R. 2006. *Working minds: A practitioner's guide to cognitive task analysis.* Cambridge, MA: MIT Press.
Kahneman, D., & Klein, G. 2009. Conditions for intuitive expertise: A failure to disagree. *American Psychologist*, 64(6): 515–526.
Klein, G. 1998. *Sources of power: How people make decisions.* Cambridge, MA: MIT Press.
Klein, G. 2009. *Streetlights and shadows: Searching for the keys to adaptive decision making.* Cambridge, MA: MIT Press.
Klein, G. 2011. Critical thoughts about critical thinking. *Theoretical Issues in Ergonomic Science*, 12(3): 210–224.
Klein, G. A., & Hoffman, R. 1993. Seeing the invisible: Perceptual/cognitive aspects of expertise. In M. Rabinowitz (Ed.), *Cognitive science foundations of instruction*: 203–226. Mahwah, NJ: Lawrence Erlbaum Associates.
Tversky, A., & Kahneman, D. 1974. Judgment under uncertainty: Heuristics and biases. *Science*, 185: 1124–1131.

ORIGINS OF NDM[1]

A major contribution of the naturalistic decision making (NDM) community has been to describe how people actually make decisions in real-world settings. This statement might seem odd because decision researchers had conducted experiments and developed models for decades prior to the emergence of NDM in 1989. However, that research primarily identified optimal ways of making decisions (defined as choices among alternatives) in well-structured settings that could be carefully controlled.

The heuristics and biases paradigm (e.g., Kahneman et al., 1982) demonstrated that people did not adhere to the principles of optimal performance; subjects relied on heuristic as opposed to algorithmic strategies even when these strategies generated systematic deviations from optimal judgments as defined by the laws of probability, the axioms of expected utility theory, and Bayesian statistics.

So by 1989, it was fairly clear how people didn't make decisions. They didn't generate alternative options and compare them on the same set of evaluation dimensions. They didn't generate probability and utility estimates for different courses of action and elaborate these into decision trees. Even when they did compare options they rarely employed systematic evaluation techniques.

But what did they do instead? Researchers weren't likely to find out how people actually made decisions by conducting experiments to test hypotheses derived from statistical and mathematical models of ideal choice strategies. Even the decision researchers who performed studies in field settings, using experienced participants, primarily assessed performance according to formal standards. (For a fuller discussion of this history, see Lipshitz et al., 2001.)

Unfortunately, the training methods and decision support systems developed in accord with the formal standards didn't improve decision quality and didn't get adopted in field settings. People found these tools and methods cumbersome and irrelevant to the work they needed to do (Yates et al., 2003).

The initial NDM researchers tried a different approach. Instead of beginning with formal models of decision making, we began by conducting field research to try to discover the strategies people used. Instead of looking for ways that people were suboptimal we wanted to find out how people were able to make tough decisions under difficult conditions such as limited time, uncertainty, high stakes, vague goals and unstable conditions (see Orasanu & Connolly, 1993). Researchers in fields such as medicine (Elstein et al., 1978) and business (Isenberg, 1984) had already been studying these kinds of issues.

The basic research program at the Army Research Institute for the Behavioral and Social Sciences began funding several of the NDM researchers during the mid-1980s. The US Navy became interested in naturalistic decisions following the 1988 *Vincennes* Shootdown incident in which a US Navy Aegis cruiser destroyed an Iranian commercial airliner, mistaking it for a hostile attacker. Both the Army and the Navy wanted to help people make high stakes decisions under extreme time pressure and under dynamic and uncertain conditions.

The first NDM conference in 1989 assembled researchers studying decision making in field settings. In a chapter that emerged from that meeting, Raanan Lipshitz (1993) identified no less than nine models of naturalistic decision making, which had been developed in parallel.

One of these was Hammond's cognitive continuum theory (Hammond et al., 1987) which asserts that decisions vary on the degree to which they rely on intuitive and analytical processes. Conditions such as amount of information and time available determine where decisions fall on this continuum and whether people rely more on patterns or on functional relationships. A second account of decision making was Rasmussen's model of cognitive control (Rasmussen, 1983), which distinguished skill-based, rule-based and knowledge-based behavior operating within the context of a decision ladder that permitted heuristic cut-off paths. A third, the recognition-primed decision (RPD) model (Klein, 1989), is discussed in more detail below.

Working separately, we all reached similar conclusions. People weren't generating and comparing option sets. People were using prior experience to rapidly categorize situations. People were relying on some kind of synthesis of their experience – call it a schema or a prototype or a category – to make these judgments. The categories suggested appropriate courses of action. The static notion of decisions as gambles, which portrays people as passively awaiting the outcomes of their bets, didn't fit leaders who were actively trying to shape events.

The NDM researchers studied people in field settings, such as Navy commanders, jurors, nuclear power plant operators, Army small unit leaders, anesthesiologists, airline pilots, nurses, and highway engineers. From this perspective, making a decision means committing oneself to a course of action where plausible alternatives exist, even if the person doesn't identify or compare these alternatives.

The NDM movement shifted our conception of human decision making from a domain-independent general approach to a knowledge-based approach exemplified by decision makers who had substantial experience. The decision-making process was expanded to include a prior stage of perception and recognition of situations, as well as generation of appropriate responses, not just choice from among given options. This perspective took advantage of advances in cognitive psychology such as knowledge representation concepts of scripts, schemas and mental models to contrast expert versus novice behavior.

To provide a fuller account of the NDM view of decision making I shall describe the RPD model; I am more familiar with it than with the others and it has received a fair amount of attention. However, all of the nine NDM models Lipshitz listed show a strong family resemblance.

RECOGNITION-PRIMED DECISION MODEL

The RPD model describes how people use their experience in the form of a repertoire of patterns (Klein et al., 1986). These patterns describe the primary causal factors operating in the situation. The patterns highlight the most relevant cues, provide expectancies, identify plausible goals, and suggest typical types of reactions in that type of situation. When people need to make a decision they can quickly match the situation to the patterns they have learned. If they find a clear match they can carry out the most typical course of action. In that way, people can successfully make extremely rapid decisions. The RPD model explains how people can make good decisions without comparing options.

However, there is more to the RPD model than pattern matching. How can a person evaluate an option without comparing it to others? We found that the fireground commanders we studied evaluated a course of action by using mental simulation to imagine how it would play out within the context of the current situation. If it would work then the commanders could initiate the action. If it almost worked they could try to adapt it or else consider other actions that were somewhat less typical, continuing until they found an option that felt comfortable. This process exemplifies Herbert Simon's notion of satisficing – looking for the first workable option rather than trying to find the best possible option. Because fires grow exponentially the faster the commanders could react, the easier their job.

Therefore, the RPD model is a blend of intuition and analysis. The pattern matching is the intuitive part and the mental simulation is the conscious, deliberate and analytical part. This blend corresponds to the System 1 (fast and unconscious)/System 2 (slow and deliberate) account of cognition put forward by Epstein (1994), Kahneman (2003), and others (for an overview, see Evans, 2008). A purely intuitive strategy relying only on pattern matching would be too risky because sometimes the pattern matching generated flawed options. A completely deliberative and analytical strategy would be too slow; the fires would be out of control by the time the commanders finished deliberating.

We formulated the RPD model based on in-depth interviews with fireground commanders about recent and challenging incidents, and found that the percentage of RPD strategies generally ranged from 80–90% (Klein, 1989) (see Figure 6.1). Other researchers have replicated these findings (see Klein, 1998).

Most critically, we tested the prediction from the RPD model that for experienced decision makers the first option they consider is usually satisfactory. Klein et al. (1995) found that chess players were not randomly

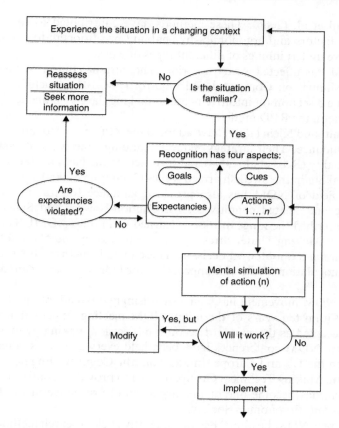

Source: Klein (1989).

Figure 6.1 Model of Recognition-Primed Decision Making

generating moves that they would then evaluate. Rather, the first moves that occurred to them were much better than would be expected by chance. These findings support the RPD hypothesis that the first option considered is usually satisfactory. These results were later replicated by Johnson and Raab (2003).

CONTRIBUTIONS OF NDM

The demands of NDM research have spurred the development of cognitive field research and cognitive task analysis methods, as described by

Crandall et al. (2006). These methods have contributed to the field of human factors and ergonomics by enabling practitioners to explore the cognitive underpinnings of different types of work.

NDM has affected Army doctrine. The current edition of the Army Field Manual on Command and Control (FM 101-5) includes for the first time a section on intuitive decision making, largely influenced by the research on the RPD model.

Schmitt and Klein (1999) have adapted the RPD model to military planning guidance. Their strategy reduces planning time without sacrificing plan quality (Ross et al., 2004) and has become the basis for tactical decision making in the Swedish armed forces (Thunholm, 2006).

The field of NDM has also provided guidance for training decision making and related cognitive skills. Cannon-Bowers and Salas (1998) have described the range of lessons learned from the TADMUS (Tactical Decision Making Under Stress) project initiated by the Navy following the *Vincennes* Shootdown decision. These include methods for providing stress inoculation along with approaches for individual and team decision training.

The NDM movement has seen a surprisingly rapid adoption of its findings. Within ten years of the initial NDM meeting, experiential models were accepted as the standard account of decision making by most practitioners. NDM conferences have been held every 2–3 years, alternating between the US and Europe. In addition, the Cognitive Engineering and Decision Making Technical Group, formed to provide an outlet for NDM research, has become one of the largest and most active in the Human Factors and Ergonomics Society.

Where is NDM heading? Because cognitive field research methods have proven so effective for generating insights about decision making they are being used to study other 'macrocognitive' functions, such as situation awareness, sensemaking, planning and replanning, and the ways they are linked (Klein et al., 2003). Macrocognition, the study of cognitive adaptations to complexity, may reflect the next step in the evolution of NDM. Macrocognitive functions are performed at the level of individuals. These functions are also performed by teams, as emphasized by Letsky et al. (2007), who build on NDM research on shared mental models and team knowledge (e.g., Cooke et al., 2004). The growth of interest in macrocognition suggests that the premises of NDM are stimulating research and applications that cover a broader and interrelated set of cognitive functions at the team, organizational and individual levels.

NOTES

1. Reprinted from *Human Factors*, 50 (3): 456–460, with permission from SAGE Publications, Inc. Copyright 2008 by the Human Factors and Ergonomics Society. All rights reserved. The author would like to thank Robert Hoffman, Danny Kahneman, Beth Veinott, and Raanan Lipshitz for their very helpful comments and criticisms in reviewing an earlier draft of this manuscript. He also appreciates the helpful suggestions of three anonymous reviewers.

REFERENCES

Cannon-Bowers, J. A., & Salas, E. 1998. *Making decisions under stress: Implications for individual and team training.* Washington, DC: American Psychological Association.

Cooke, N. J., Salas, E., Kiekel, P. A., & Bell, B. 2004. Advances in measuring team cognition. In E. Salas & S. M. Fiore (Eds.), *Team cognition: Understanding the factors that drive process and performance.* Washington, DC: APA.

Crandall, B., Klein, G., & Hoffman, R. R. 2006. *Working minds: A practitioner's guide to cognitive task analysis.* Cambridge, MA: MIT Press.

Elstein, A. S., Shulman, L. S., & Sprafka, S. A. 1978. *Medical problem solving: An analysis of clinical reasoning.* Cambridge, MA: Harvard University Press.

Epstein, S. 1994. Integration of the cognitive and psychodynamic unconscious. *American Psychologist,* 49: 709–724.

Evans, J. St. B. T. 2008. Dual-processing accounts of reasoning, judgment and social cognition. *Annual Review of Psychology,* 59: 255–278.

Hammond, K. R., Hamm, R. M., Grassia, J., & Pearson, T. 1987. Direct comparison of the efficacy of intuitive and analytical cognition in expert judgment. *Proceedings of IEEE Transactions on Systems, Man, and Cybernetics, SMC-17:* 753–770.

Isenberg, D. J. 1984. How senior managers think. *Harvard Business Review,* November–December: 80–90.

Johnson, J. G., & Raab, M. 2003. Take the first: Option generation and resulting choices. *Organizational Behavior and Human Decision Processes,* 91(2): 215–229.

Kahneman, D. 2003. Maps of bounded rationality: Psychology for behavioral economics. *American Economic Review,* 93(5): 1449–1475.

Kahneman, D., Slovic, P., & Tversky, A. (Eds.). 1982. *Judgment under uncertainty: Heuristics and biases.* New York: Cambridge University Press.

Klein, G. A. 1989. Recognition-primed decisions. In W. B. Rouse (Ed.), *Advances in man-machine systems research: Vol. 5:* 47–92. Greenwich, CT: JAI Press.

Klein, G. 1998. *Sources of power: How people make decisions.* Cambridge, MA: MIT Press.

Klein, G. A., Calderwood, R., & Clinton-Cirocco, A. 1986. Rapid decision making on the fireground. *Proceedings of the Human Factors and Ergonomics Society 30th Annual Meeting,* 1: 576–580.

Klein, G., Ross, K. G., Moon, B. M., Klein, D. E., Hoffman, R. R., & Hollnagel, E. 2003. Macrocognition. *IEEE Intelligent Systems,* 18(3): 81–85.

Klein, G., Wolf, S., Militello, L., & Zsambok, C. 1995. Characteristics of skilled option generation in chess. *Organizational Behavior and Human Decision Processes,* 62(1): 63–69.

Letsky, M., Warner, N., Fiore, S. M., Rosen, M., & Salas, E. 2007. *Macrocognition in complex team problem solving.* Paper presented at the 12th International Command and Control Research and Technology Symposium (ICCRTS), Newport, RI, June 19–21.

Lipshitz, R. 1993. Converging themes in the study of decision making in realistic settings. In G. A. Klein, J. Orasanu, R. Calderwood, & C. E. Zsambok (Eds.), *Decision making in action: Models and methods:* 103–137. Norwood, NJ: Ablex.

Lipshitz, R., Klein, G., Orasanu, J., & Salas, E. 2001. Focus article: Taking stock of naturalistic decision making. *Journal of Behavioral Decision Making*, 14: 331–352.

Orasanu, J., & Connolly, T. 1993. The reinvention of decision making. In G. A. Klein, J. Orasanu, R. Calderwood, & C. E. Zsambok (Eds.), *Decision making in action: Models and methods*: 3–20. Norwood, NJ: Ablex.

Rasmussen, J. 1983. Skill, rules and knowledge: Signals, signs, and symbols, and other distinctions in human performance models. *IEEE Transactions on Systems, Man and Cybernetics, SMC*-13(3): 257–266.

Ross, K. G., Klein, G., Thunholm, P., Schmitt, J. F., & Baxter, H. C. 2004. The recognition-primed decision model. *Military Review*, 74(4): 6–10.

Schmitt, J. F., & Klein, G. 1999. How we plan. *Marine Corps Gazette*, 83(10): 18–26.

Thunholm, P. 2006. A new model for tactical mission planning for the Swedish Armed Forces. In *Proceedings of the 2006 Command and Control Research and Technology Symposium: The state of the art and the state of the practice*. June 20–22, San Diego, CA. Washington, DC: Command and Control Research Program (CCRP).

Yates, J. F., Veinott, E. S., & Patalano, A. L. 2003. Hard decisions, bad decisions: On decision quality and decision aiding. In S. L. Schneider, & J. Shanteau (Eds.), *Emerging perspectives on judgment and decision research*: 13–63. New York: Cambridge University Press.

7 Strategic intuition
William Duggan and Malia Mason

Strategic intuition is the mental mechanism that produces flashes of insight. Some scholars exclude insight from the definition of intuition, but that distinction is more than a decade out of date, following the 1998 paper by Milner et al., 'Cognitive neuroscience and the study of memory'. Recent research indicates that intuition comes from learning and automatic recall (Edelman, 2004; Gordon & Berger, 2003), in two ways. In *expert* intuition, recall comes quickly, without conscious thought, by drawing from direct experience. In *strategic* intuition, recall includes the experience of others learned through reading, seeing or hearing, which explains why it features slower recall from a wider range of weaker memory. But in both forms of intuition, the mechanism of recall is generally the same.

The precise mechanism of recall, though, differs across the two forms of intuition. These differences are the subject of a growing body of modern research. Simon (1989), in the lab and Klein (1998), in the field, pioneered expert intuition, which has become a significant field of study, as researchers identify experts and measure how they perform expert tasks. Strategic intuition is much farther behind, because it is much more difficult to capture; flashes of insight happen at odd times, in odd places, to experts and non-experts alike. The study of strategic intuition did not make much methodological progress since von Clausewitz first identified flashes of insight as the key to Napoleon's military strategy in the early 1800s (von Clausewitz, 1832 [1968]) until the end of the twentieth century. Over that time, the study of historical examples has been the primary means of capturing the fleeting phenomenon of strategic intuition (Duggan, 2007; Kuhn, 1962).

Over the past decade, however, cognitive and neuroscience research have made significant methodological progress in studying flashes of insight from three different angles. First, psychology experiments show that subjects solve problems better after sleep than both subjects who focus continuously on the problems and subjects who have periods of resting wakefulness (Stickgold et al., 2001; Wagner et al., 2004). Second, research on arousal and stress shows that the physiology of the relaxed mental state fosters this kind of 'off-line' problem-solving (Martindale, 1999; Martindale & Greenough, 1973). Third, neuroelectrical recordings and brain scans provide preliminary evidence that defocused attention contributes to flashes of insight (Dewing & Battye, 1971; Kounios et al., 2007; Mason et al., 2007; Mendelsohn & Griswold, 1964).

INTUITION AND SLEEP

There are numerous historical examples of discoveries made in lucid dream states. Friedrich August Kekule saw benzene's ring-like structure as a snake in his dreams (as cited in Roberts, 1989). Otto Lowei awoke to discover he had penned the mysteries of neurochemical transmission during the previous night's slumber (as cited in Mazzarello, 2000). Although few people experience insights of this caliber, it is not uncommon for people to report gaining perspective on unresolved problems while asleep or in semi-conscious dream states. Scientists have debated the power of the unconscious for centuries, yet until recently few have offered explanations as to why sleep might foster insight. Some speculate that the relaxed attentional state of sleep is associated with flexible or 'fluid' cognition (Horn & Cattell, 1966), a processing mode conducive to linking loosely connected material. From this perspective, sleep promotes creative problem solving because the rigid, rule-based processing that characterizes wakeful states is supplanted by a flexible, associative processing mode (Walker et al., 2002). Others suggest that during certain sleep stages information is restructured in a manner that makes overlooked but meaningful connections (Wagner et al., 2004).

Consistent with relaxed attentional states enabling the detection of loosely connected material, Walker reported that rapid eye movement (REM) sleep, a stage rich in dreams, was associated with significant increases in cognitive flexibility compared to non-REM sleep (Walker et al., 2002). Participants awakened during REM sleep were significantly better at rearranging words to produce new phrases than participants awakened from non-REM sleep. Similarly, Stickgold et al. measured the speed at which participants recognized weak (e.g., thief–wrong) and strong associations (e.g., hot–cold) after a period of REM or non-REM sleep (Stickgold et al., 1999). Whereas performance on the recognition of strong associations was greatest after non-REM sleep, participants excelled at the detection of weak associations after periods of REM sleep. Finally, a recent study by Cai et al. provides compelling evidence that REM sleep helps integrate information. Participants in their study were more likely to identify the associate (e.g., 'salt') of three seemingly unrelated words (e.g., 'mine', 'lick', 'table') following periods of REM (Cai et al., 2009). These findings support the view that hyperassociative processes during REM sleep help people draw connections among loosely related material.

In addition to promoting fluid thinking, sleep is purported to foster intuition by reshuffling associations. Evidence suggests that information recombines during REM sleep such that previously overlooked connections are more apparent. In the most compelling demonstration of this reshuffling, Wagner et al. (2004) had participants perform a stimulus-response task by quickly pressing specific keyboard buttons (e.g., 'F') when relevant stimuli (e.g., an odd digit) appear on a computer screen. The speed at which participants perform this task improves abruptly if they gain insight into the abstract rule governing the sequences. Once uncovered, the hidden rule provides a short cut or simpler method for solving the problem. Wagner et al. found that participants who slept for eight hours following a period of task performance were twice as likely to detect the hidden rule when they resumed the task upon wakening, than both participants who rested in an awake state for eight hours and participants who went about their daily activities for eight hours before resuming the task.

Scientists continue to debate precisely how sleep leads to cognitive restructuring (see Stickgold & Walker, 2004; Vertes & Siegel, 2005). During REM sleep the mind is working but not taking in new information, which may be critical for the integration of new information and the cognitive reshuffling necessary for strategic intuition. A host of evidence suggests that REM sleep is important in memory consolidation, the process by which memories strengthen and become resistant to interference (Huber et al., 2004; Plihal & Born, 1997). It is worth noting evidence which suggests that the strengthening of memories for important information during REM sleep is complemented by the forgetting of unimportant details and the weakening of non-adaptive memory traces during non-REM sleep (Giuditta et al., 1995). According to this view, sleep consists of opposite processes that work in concert to maintain memory housekeeping. In this way, sleep may help people abandon ineffective strategies, consider less obvious solutions, and tease out regularities that exist but have gone undetected.

RELAXATION AND 'OFF-LINE' PROBLEM SOLVING

Impasses in problem solving frequently result because the futility of a favored strategy has gone undetected (Sternberg & Davidson, 1995). Problem solvers who have the key pieces of information at their disposal sometimes fail simply because they abstain from exploring alternative configurations of the problem's parts. The longer the faulty strategy is explicitly considered, the more strongly it becomes associated in memory with the desired outcome. As a result, the problem solver is habitually drawn to consider how the inappropriate strategy can be reworked to produce the solution, despite its ineffectiveness. Although focus is imperative in key stages of intuition – when judging the merit of an insight, for example – it fosters tunnel vision when implemented prematurely. In haste to reach closure, people overfixate on a framework that lacks merit and promise. Attempts at elucidating the conditions under which people experience intuition can therefore benefit from considering the factors that affect the likelihood that people will apply diffuse versus focused attention when 'searching' for the answer to a problem. Two important determinants appear to be the problem solver's level of stress and physiological arousal.

Research on stress paints a bleak picture of its effect on innovation. During periods of heightened anxiety, people default to routinized thinking patterns and well-learned habits (Hull, 1943; Osgood, 1960), making them prone to dogmatically adhere to ineffective problem-solving strategies. Originality is noticeably diminished (Dentler & Mackler, 1964) and people exhibit a mindless, functional fixedness as opposed to mindfulness (Langer, 1992; Pennebaker, 1989). Although stress enhances the *encoding* of memories under certain situations, high stress interferes with the *retrieval* of information from memory (Roozendaal, 2002). This further limits people's capacity for constructing sophisticated solutions to problems. Finally, evidence suggests that stress diminishes innovative problem solving by reducing cognitive flexibility. For example, performance on anagram tasks declines when stress hormones, like norepinephrine, are administered and improves when these hormones are blocked (Beversdorf et al., 1999). Beversdorf et al. suggest that stress hormones exert a modulatory effect on cognitive flexibility in problem solving, such that increases in stress hormone diminish cognitive flexibility. In sum, stress diminishes creative innovation by inducing people to cling to routinized habits, by interfering with effective memory retrieval and by increasing cognitive rigidity.

Research on physiological arousal yields a similar story. For decades scientists have known that arousal improves performance on simple problems while relaxation improves performance on complex problems (Duffy, 1941; Easterbrook, 1959; Yerkes & Dodson, 1908). Complexity can be defined in a myriad of ways but one critical dimension is problem structure. In contrast to structured problems (e.g., 'Which company has the largest share of the market?'), the resolution of unstructured problems (e.g., 'How can we increase our market share?') requires identifying relevant information and developing a framework for thinking about the problem. Solving the latter requires searching a wider conceptual space for a solution. Although people can reach solutions to both types of problems through insight, the sheer scope of unstructured problems necessitates a broader consideration. Arousal funnels attention, reducing the range of cues that an organism processes and uses (Derryberry & Tucker, 1994). Broadly employed attention increases the chances of bringing seemingly irrelevant information into conscious awareness. Indeed, performance on tasks that require a wide search of information (e.g., the Remote Associates Test: RAT; Mednick & Mednick, 1967) worsens when people are highly aroused (Martindale & Greenough, 1973).

DEFOCUSED ATTENTION

Although too much focus inhibits solving complex problems, insights do not come to those who simply ignore problems or wait passively for solutions to bubble to consciousness. On the contrary, focus is essential for key stages of the creative process, especially the elaboration of fragmented, incomplete insights and the verification of a solution's legitimacy (Martindale, 1999; Mendelsohn, 1976). Nevertheless, many researchers speculate that defocused attention in the period leading up to insight fosters novel solutions (Bransford & Stein, 1984; Eysenck, 1995) and complex problem solving (Dijksterhuis et al., 2006; Dijksterhuis & Nordgren, 2006; Dijksterhuis & van Olden, 2005). Evidence suggests that individuals who allocate their attention diffusely or cast broad 'attentional nets' outperform those who focus well, on problems that require the connection of remote problem elements (Dewing & Battye, 1971; Mendelsohn & Griswold, 1964). Similarly, several investigators report that highly creative individuals are more subject to distraction by task-irrelevant cues than their non-creative counterparts, presumably because they habitually employ a wider focus of attention (Ansberg & Hill, 2003; Dykes & McGhie, 1976; Martindale, 2007).

Recent cognitive neuroscience research appears to substantiate these findings. While daydreaming or in a prolonged moment of reflection, the brain enters an alpha wave state, a more relaxed state of mind with a relatively slow, rhythmic electrical activity, distributed across the brain in a specific spatial pattern. The alpha power increases (synchronizes) when people are relaxing and attenuates (desynchronizes) when people engage in difficult tasks that require focus or concentration (Gevins et al., 1997; Pfurtscheller, 1992). Consistent with the view that defocused attention promotes insight, Martindale and Hasenfus (1978) demonstrated that the individuals who exhibited high magnitude alpha waves were more likely to generate a novel solution to an anagram than those who exhibited low magnitude alpha waves. Similarly, more recent work suggests that creative individuals have chronically higher alpha wave signals than non-creative individuals (Kounios et al., 2007). Although the point is still hotly debated, some suggest that attentional control is relaxed during alpha periods, resulting in a heightened capacity for detecting non-obvious connections.

Convergent findings appear to be emerging from functional brain imaging studies. During baseline periods, when directed to 'rest' and 'clear their thoughts', participants exhibit recruitment of a set of brain regions referred to as the 'default network' (Buckner et al., 2008; Mason et al., 2007; Raichle et al., 2001). These brain areas are active when people are resting or engaged in mindless, effortless tasks and are deactivated during tasks that require focus and effort. Recent brain imaging research reveals that activity in this network increases prior to insight experiences. While there is little direct evidence that this network supports diffuse attention, these findings provide additional preliminary evidence that periods of diffuse attention are essential for insight experiences (Kounios et al., 2006).

APPLICATIONS

In all this research, the psychology experiments understandably provide stronger results than the scans. Neuroscience has only begun to reveal the precise workings of the brain. Nevertheless, there are some preliminary applications we can identify for professional domains of various kinds. And these in turn lead to further indications for future psychology and neuroscience research.

First, strategic intuition has application to creativity in all walks of life. The 1998 learning-and-memory model of Milner et al. replaced Sperry's previous model of the two-sided brain, where the left is creative and the right is analytical (Sperry, 1961, 1981). In the years between those two models, formal brainstorming sessions became the primary method of creativity in most professions. In brainstorming, following Sperry, the creative right side of the brain takes over from the analytical left side, and creative thoughts arise spontaneously. The learning-and-memory model, in contrast, argues against this kind of brainstorming. Instead, creative ideas arise at odd times when the mind is relaxed, like in the shower or exercising or falling asleep.

Nevertheless, brainstorming is still widespread in the professional world. Related methods include scattering toys and beanbag chairs around, to stimulate the creative right side of the brain, which again the learning-and-memory model contradicts. Instead this model suggests a host of alternative techniques for practitioners to try and for neuroscience and cognitive research to test. For example, what are the best sequence, timing and means of learning and relaxation to generate insights for various kinds of creative problems? And for social psychology: what are the best organizational, management and leadership practices that follow from that?

Future research can and should seek detailed answers to these questions. Larger lessons may follow as well. When Kandel won the Nobel Prize for Physiology or Medicine in 2000, he stated in his lecture: 'we are who we are in good measure because of what we have learned and what we remember' (Kandel, 2000). For him, the learning-and-memory model covers all forms of conscious and unconscious thought, including 'analysis'. That is, all analysis requires some form of learning and automatic recall: you cannot analyze something that is completely new to you. Even mathematical calculations require you to learn and then recall each number and symbol and the rules of operation, such as addition or division. Further research might well show that underlying all the different modes of thought, such as rational analysis or creative intuition, there is a single 'meta-mode' of learning and memory.

The implications of this single meta-mode of thought could be enormous. At present, expert and strategic intuition sit alongside analysis as junior or even equal partners in problem solving. But perhaps, instead, all problem solving is either expert or strategic intuition, or a combination of the two, and analysis is a part of both. Conscious and unconscious thought might both be impossible without prior learning and automatic recall. Analysis depends on learning and memory for the subject matter analyzed as well as the method of analysis used. Analysis yields greater understanding of a problem, but not a solution, except in a field of pure logic like mathematics. All real-world problem solving requires a leap of cognition beyond analysis. That leap is either the rapid recognition of expert intuition or the flash of insight of strategic intuition, or a combination of the two.

When it comes to human action, a purely rational world is impossible. But with the right research effort, better expert and strategic intuition are very much within our grasp.

REFERENCES

Ansberg, P., & Hill, K. 2003. Creative and analytic thinkers differ in their use of attentional resources. *Personality of Individual Differences*, 34: 1141–1152.

Beversdorf, D., Hughes, J., Steinberg, B., Lewis, L., & Heilman, K. 1999. Noradrenergic modulation of cognitive flexibility in problem solving. *NeuroReport: For Rapid Communication of Neuroscience Research*, 19: 2763–2767.

Bransford, J., & Stein, B. 1984. *The IDEAL problem solver*. New York: W. H. Freeman.

Buckner, R., Andrews-Hanna, J., & Schacter, D. 2008. The brain's default network: Anatomy function and relevance to disease. *Annals of the New York Academy of Sciences*, 1124: 1–38.

Cai, D. J., Mednick, S. A., Harrison, E. M., Kanady, J. C., & Mednick, S. C. 2009. REM, not incubation, improves creativity by priming associative networks. *Proceedings of the National Academy of Sciences of the United States of America*, 106: 10130–10134.

Dentler, R., & Mackler, B. 1964. Originality: Some social and personal determinants. *Behavioral Science*, 9: 1–7.

Derryberry, D., & Tucker, D. 1994. Motivating the focus of attention. In: P. Niedenthal & S. Kitayama (Eds.), *Heart's eye: Emotional influences in perception and attention*: 167–196. New York: Academic Press.

Dewing, K., & Battye, G. 1971. Attention deployment and nonverbal fluency. *Journal of Personality and Social Psychology*, 17: 214–218.

Dijksterhuis, A., Bos, M., Nordgren, L., & Van Baaren, R. 2006. On making the right choice: The deliberation-without-attention effect. *Science*, 311: 1005–1007.

Dijksterhuis, A., & Nordgren, L. 2006. A theory of unconscious thought. *Perspectives on Psychological Science*, 1: 95–109.

Dijksterhuis, A., & van Olden, Z. 2005. On the benefits of thinking unconsciously: Unconscious thought can increase post-choice satisfaction. *Journal of Experimental Social Psychology*, 42: 627–631.

Duffy, E. 1941.The conceptual categories of psychology: A suggestion for revision. *Psychological Review*, 48: 177–203.

Duggan, W. 2007. *Strategic intuition*. New York: Columbia Business School Publishing.

Dykes, M., & McGhie, A. 1976. Cognitive study of attentional strategies of schizophrenic and highly creative normal subjects. *The British Journal of Psychiatry*, 128: 50–56.

Easterbrook, J. 1959. The effect of emotion on cue utilization and the organization of behavior. *Psychological Review*, 66: 183–201.

Edelman, G. 2004. *Wider than the sky*. New Haven, CT: Yale University Press.

Eysenck, H. 1995. Creativity as a product of intelligence and personality. In D. H. Saklofske, & M. Zeidner (Eds.), *International handbook of personality and intelligence*: 231–247. New York: Plenum Press.

Gevins, A., Smith, M., McEvoy, L., & Yu, D. 1997. High-resolution EEG mapping of cortical activation related to working memory: Effects of task difficulty, type of processing, and practice. *Cerebral Cortex*, 7: 374–385.

Giuditta, A., Ambrosini, M., Montagnese, P., Mandile, P., Cotugno, M., Grassi, Z., & Vescia, S. 1995. The sequential hypothesis of the function of sleep. *Behavioral Brain Research*, 69: 157–166.

Gordon, B., & Berger, L. 2003. *Intelligent memory*. New York: Viking.

Horn, J., & Cattell, R. 1966. Refinement and test of the theory of fluid and crystallized intelligence. *Journal of Educational Psychology*, 57: 253–270.

Huber, R., Ghilardi, M., Massimini, M., & Tononi, G. 2004. Local sleep and learning. *Nature*, 430: 78–81.

Hull, C. 1943. *Principles of behavior*. New York: Appleton-Century.

Kandel, E. 2000. *Nobel Lecture*. Stockholm Concert Hall, Stockholm, December 10.

Klein, G. 1998. *Sources of power*. Cambridge, MA: MIT Press.

Kounios, J., Frymiare, J., Bowden, E., Fleck, J., Subramaniam, K., Parrish, T., & Jung-Beeman, M. 2006. The prepared mind: Neural activity prior to problem presentation predicts solution by sudden insight. *Psychological Science*, 17: 882–890.

Kounious, J., Fleck, J., Green, D., Payne, J., Stevenson, J., Bowden, E., & Jung-Beeman, M. 2007. The origins of insight in resting-state brain activity. *Neuropsychologia*, 46: 281–291.

Kuhn, T. 1962. *The structure of scientific revolutions*. Chicago: University of Chicago Press.

Langer, E. 1992. Interpersonal mindlessness and language. *Communication Monographs*, 59: 324–327.

Martindale, C. 1999. Biological bases of creativity. In R. J. Sternberg (Ed.), *Handbook of creativity:* 137–152. New York: Cambridge University Press.

Martindale, C. 2007. Creativity, primordial cognition and personality. *Personality and Individual Differences*, 43: 1777–1785.

Martindale, C., & Greenough, J. 1973. The differential effects of increased arousal on creative and intellectual performance. *Journal of Genetic Psychology*, 123: 325–329.

Martindale, C., & Hasenfus, N. 1978. EEG differences as a function of creativity, stage of creative process and effort to be original. *Biological Psychology*, 6: 157–167.

Mason, M., Norton, M., Van Horn, J., Wegner, D., Grafton, S., & Macrae, C. 2007. Wandering minds: The default network and stimulus-independent thought. *Science*, 315: 393–395.

Mazzarello, P. 2000. What dreams may come? *Nature*, 408: 523.

Mednick, S. A., & Mednick, M. T. 1967. *Examiner's manual: Remote Associates Test*. Boston, MA: Houghton Mifflin.

Mendelsohn, G., & Griswold, B. 1964. Differential use of incidental stimuli in problem solving as a function of creativity. *Journal of Abnormal and Social Psychology*, 68: 431–436.

Mendelsohn, G. 1976. Associative and attentional processes in creative performance. *Journal of Personality*, 44: 341–369.

Milner, B., Squire, L., & Kandel, E. 1998. Cognitive neuroscience and the study of memory. *Neuron*, 20: 445–468.

Osgood, C. 1960. Some effects of motivation and style on encoding. In T. A. Sebeok (Ed.), *Style in language*: 293–306. Cambridge, MA: MIT Press.

Pennebaker, J. 1989. Stream of consciousness and stress: Levels of thinking. In J. Uleman, & J. Bargh (Eds.), *Unintended thought*: 327–350. New York: Guilford Press.

Pfurtscheller, G. 1992. Event-related synchronization (ERS): An electrophysiological correlate of cortical areas at rest. *Electroencephalogr. Clinical Neurophysiology*, 83: 62–66.

Plihal, W., & Born, J. 1997. Effects of early and late nocturnal sleep on declarative and procedural memory. *Journal of Cognitive Neuroscience*, 9: 534–547.

Raichle, M., MacLeod, A., Snyder, A., Powers, W., Gusnard, D., & Shulman, G. 2001. A default mode of brain function. *Proceedings of the National Academy of Sciences of the United States of America*, 98: 676–682.

Roberts, R. 1989. *Serendipity, Accidental Discoveries in Science*: 75–81. New York: John Wiley & Sons.

Roozendaal, B. 2002. Stress and memory: Opposing effects of glucocorticoids on memory consolidation and memory retrieval. *Neurobiology of Learning and Memory*, 78: 578–595.

Simon, H. 1989. *Models of thought: Volume 2*. New Haven, CT: Yale Press.

Sperry, R. 1961. Cerebral organization and behavior. *Science*, 133: 1749–1757.

Sperry, R. 1981. *Nobel Lecture*. Stockholm Concert Hall, Stockholm, December 8.

Sternberg, R., & Davidson, J. 1995. *The nature of insight*. Cambridge, MA: MIT Press.

Stickgold, R., Hobson, J., Fosse, R., & Fosse, M. 2001. Sleep, learning, and dreams: Off-line memory reprocessing. *Science*, 294: 1052–1057.

Stickgold, R., Scott, L., Rittenhouse, C., & Hobson, J. 1999. Sleep-induced changes in associative memory. *Journal of Cognitive Neuroscience*, 11: 182–193.

Stickgold, R., & Walker, M. 2004. To sleep, perchance to gain creative insight? *Trends in Cognitive Sciences*, 8: 191–192.

Vertes, R. & Siegel, J. 2005. Time for the sleep community to take a critical look at the purported role of sleep in memory processing. *Sleep*, 28: 1228–1229.

Von Clausewitz, C. 1832 [1968]. *On war*. New York: Penguin.

Wagner, U., Gais, S., Haider, H., Verleger, R., & Born, J. 2004. Sleep inspires insight. *Nature*, 427: 352–355.

Walker, M., Liston, C., Hobson, A., & Stickgold, R. 2002. Cognitive flexibility across the sleep–wake cycle: REM-sleep enhancement of anagram problem solving. *Cognitive Brain Research*, 14: 317–324.

Yerkes, R., & Dodson, J. 1908. The relation of strength of stimulus to rapidity of habit formation. *Journal of Comparative Neurology and Psychology*, 18: 459–482.

8 Entrepreneurial intuition
Jill R. Kickul and Lisa K. Gundry

Entrepreneurship processes and behaviors tend to transpire within a highly competitive environment characterized by uncertainty and rapid change. Entrepreneurial decisions are often made under conditions in which information is imperfect and risk is persistent. Perhaps due to the very nature of entrepreneurial processes that rely on individuals' abilities to form impressions and grapple with problems or opportunities for which there are no clear, easy solutions, the entrepreneur's intuition plays a significant role. As Joseph Schumpeter recognized:

> Here the success of everything depends on intuition, the capacities of seeing things in a way which afterwards proves to be true, even though it cannot be established at the moment, and of grasping the essential facts, discarding the unessential, even though one can give no account of the principles by which it is done. (Schumpeter, 1983: 85)

Intuition has been defined as 'affectively charged judgments that arise through rapid, non-conscious, and holistic associations' (Dane & Pratt, 2007: 33), and as a form of cognition that operates in two ways: 'knowing' and in a way that connects mind and body through 'feeling' (Sadler-Smith & Shefy, 2004). Much of the understanding of entrepreneurial intuition is linked to cognition, and the cognitive styles of entrepreneurs.

Entrepreneurs' preferred modes of thinking – their cognitive styles – likely influence the ways in which they learn, gather knowledge, process information and make decisions. Cognitive style is viewed as having multiple dimensions, including decision making, learning, personality and awareness. One of these dimensions is especially relevant for entrepreneurs: *awareness* of people, ideas, objects and incidents (Allinson & Hayes, 1996; Leonard et al., 1999). This dimension can be viewed as a continuum ranging from 'intuitive' to 'analytic' (Ornstein, 1977). These modes of thinking have particular significance for entrepreneurs.

The new venture process can be segmented into broad stages that include activities such as the discovery of opportunities, planning for new venture launch, acquiring resources to support the venture, and implementing the plan. Research has shown that these stages are non-linear and iterative, and that entrepreneurs perceive these activities through distinct cognitive lenses. Aspiring entrepreneurs whose intuitive skills are strong are more likely to discover new opportunities by observing unfamiliar, often unorganized cues and information and then synthesizing this information to help them make decisions (Olson, 1985). Such use of heuristics helps entrepreneurs reduce the complexity with which they are confronted, and allows them to make connections and focus on what they feel is critical (Tversky & Kahneman, 1974). Instincts are not infallible, however, and there are pitfalls entrepreneurs must avoid, such as confusing gut reactions (based on emotion and irrationality) with gut decisions (based on instinct and experience) (New Zealand Management, 1998).

Intuitive abilities have been found to be very effective for entrepreneurs in the discovery process as they are searching for ideas and opportunities prior to launch, or even in later stages of the business cycle as they seek to reinvent their organizations and import novel ideas for new products, services, technologies and processes. Thus, entrepreneurial intuition can identify a potentially viable opportunity that others may overlook (Sadler-Smith, 2010). Intuition has emerged as a critical success factor in entrepreneurship (Chapman, 2000). In the entrepreneurial context, therefore, it is closely related to the creative competencies of entrepreneurs and their ability to navigate the often fuzzy front end of innovation and organization formation.

SUMMARY OF LATEST RESEARCH ON ENTREPRENEURIAL INTUITION

As highlighted earlier, entrepreneurial intuition enables individuals to discover opportunities by observing cues or signals through unfamiliar and unorganized information that is processed in a synthetic and holistic manner (Olson, 1985). Miner (1997) found intuition to be a crucial thinking mode of 'expert idea generators'. As described by Allinson et al. (2000), intuitive individuals prefer settings that are flexible and activity oriented. Their preference is to have freedom from daily rules and regulations in order to give them multiple opportunities to create their own ideas without the presence of rigid structure. In their early work in examining some of the work of theorists and empirical researchers, Allinson and Hayes (1996) reported the development and validation of the Cognitive Style Index (CSI). Based on work with the CSI, Allinson et al. (2000) found that people showing entrepreneurial behavior tend to score high on the intuition pole of their intuition/analysis dimensions. Recent examination of the measurement of cognitive style, however, has suggested that there are two incompatible theoretical perspectives: the single dimension, supported by the CSI, and dual process, supported by the Rational–Experiential Inventory (Pacini & Epstein, 1999). The dual process perspective has received support from recent studies such as Hodgkinson et al. (2009). As demonstrated in the research of La Pira and Gillin (2006) and also postulated by Mitchell et al. (2005), entrepreneurs rely more heavily on intuitive abilities than on their analytic abilities in viewing new business opportunities.

Some of the recent research examining the role of intuition and entrepreneurship has examined how individuals perceive their own abilities and self-efficacy regarding the different stages of the new venture process (e.g., searching, evaluating, marshalling of resources, and implementation). Using the CSI, Kickul et al. (2010) found that individuals' cognitive preference for analysis or intuition influences their perception and assessment of their entrepreneurial self-efficacy and intentions. Individuals with an intuitive cognitive style were more confident in their ability to identify and recognize new venture opportunities.

In related research also using the CSI to assess an individual's intuition, Brigham and Sorenson (2008) developed a conceptual model to investigate how an intuitive cognitive style relates to habitual business ownership. They propose and find that the intuitive cognitive style serves as a pull factor and affects other pull and push factors in enabling individuals to be attracted to entrepreneurship and recognize new opportunities. The intuitive individuals also experience negative psychosocial outcomes in traditional organizations. Pull factors include the opportunity to pursue an idea or market opportunity or a financial and performance incentive as opposed to the more negative push factors such as poor job satisfaction or layoff. Both pull and push factors, especially in combination can be seen as 'impelling forces' (Vesper, 1983: 38), that function as a key role in an individual's decision to leave his/her existing organization and embark on his/her own new venture. Thus, intuition serves as a key and pivotal role in motivating individuals (from a pull and push perspective) to consider an entrepreneurial career.

ENHANCING INTUITIVE COMPETENCIES: TOOLS AND PRACTICES FOR ENTREPRENEURS

Traditionally, entrepreneurial training has focused primarily on the acquisition of technical and analytic skills, with inadequate attention paid to the cognition and belief systems of entrepreneurs (Allinson et al., 2000). Courses and programs concentrate on the management and planning skills needed by entrepreneurs to launch and harvest successful ventures, in some cases discounting or even ignoring the creativity, risk-taking and innovation competencies that are deeply connected to the opportunity search process.

As seen in the previous sections, effective entrepreneurial development and growth relies on intuitive dexterity as much as analytic capabilities, and there are methods that educators and trainers can utilize to strengthen the intuition of students and participants. Some of these tools can help individuals learn to use alternative modes of thinking more comfortably, and to become more fluid in their generation of ideas and alternative solutions to situations. Below are a few examples of tools useful to the enhancement of intuitive skills of entrepreneurs:

- *Creative Problem Solving (CPS)* Based on the Osborn–Parnes model of creative problem solving developed in the 1950s, and adapted and refined by researchers over the years, it is designed to help individuals and groups generate the most novel and useful ideas and solutions (Isaksen et al., 2000). The model comprises six primary steps to help facilitate creative problem solving. Osborn pioneered the process of brainstorming, a method by which groups of people share ideas in an open and unstructured fashion, building on the ideas of one another while suspending judgment. Tools are used to stimulate breakthrough thinking, going 'blue sky', and digging to unexpected solutions (Hughes, 2003).
- *Assumption Reversal* This tool (adapted from Michalko, 1991) enables individuals to challenge the facts and information known about a product, service, market, or scenario. Assumptions are listed, reversed, and the reversals provoke generation of ideas and interesting observations that can lead to new opportunities.
- *Backwards Thinking* An opportunity generation tool (Prather & Gundry, 1995) that guides the entrepreneur to ask 'What if?' questions, exploring the ideal state or condition for an idea, hunch, or solution to work. This tool allows for non-linear leaps of thought that enable the development of innovative paths to reach a desired goal (Kickul et al., 2010).

The above tools and others that stimulate intuitive modes of thinking help individuals create new patterns of recognition, make associations across categories and boundaries, and question their prior knowledge. With practice, entrepreneurs are encouraged to become comfortable with the unknown, to adapt ideas from other fields, and to trust their instincts as they experiment and test concepts and solutions for potential value.

FUTURE RESEARCH DIRECTIONS ON INTUITION

Given the dearth of research on entrepreneurial intuition, there may be a number of promising research questions. Although we believe that there are quite a few interesting research opportunities, we chose to focus on four areas that may be fruitful for researchers to further explore:

1. What is the relationship between entrepreneurial passion and intuition?
2. How does intuition influence the bricolage behavior of entrepreneurs?
3. What role does intuition have on the discovery of different types of opportunities and innovations?
4. What is the interaction or association between effectuation and entrepreneurial intuition?

What Is the Relationship between Entrepreneurial Passion and Intuition?

Based on the assumption that the entrepreneur is passionately committed to the new venture idea, how does his/her passion drive their intuitive thinking? Recent work by Cardon and Stevens (2009) has uncovered a multi-dimensional measure of entrepreneurial passion that may influence how an entrepreneur becomes motivated in engaging in entrepreneurial behavior and the determination of the future growth/success or even failure of his/her venture. Entrepreneurial passion is often characterized by a discrete emotion that can be quite intense. Beyond acting as a motivating force in driving decision making and actions, it may be interesting to examine how passion affects the entrepreneur's intuitive thinking and behavior. Cardon and Stevens have validated several scales of passion, including hope, optimism, state positive emotion, state negative emotion, obsessive and harmonious passion, and passion for work that may indeed have both positive and negative consequences of how an entrepreneur intuitively acts to information and changes within his/her environment or industry.

How Does Intuition Influence the Bricolage Behavior of Entrepreneurs?

While intuitive thinking can be advantageous in identifying new ideas and opportunities for the venture, it would seem plausible that it will also assist the entrepreneur in arriving at new ways to tackling existing and ongoing challenges due to resource scarcity encountered by the entrepreneurial firm. Bricolage was developed by Lévi-Strauss (1967) to suggest the creation of something new through involved actors in the process of recombination and transformation of existing resources (Baker & Nelson 2005; Garud et al., 1998; Venkataraman, 1997). Often entrepreneurs need to engage in 'bricolage' behavior, particularly at the early, start-up stages of their business.

Bricolage behavior can be defined as a variety of actions driven by the pursuit of existing and often scarce resources that can be recombined to create novel and interesting solutions of value that impact their respective markets. As Baker and Nelson (2005) assert, it is having a focus on using resources at hand, using existing resources for new purposes, recombining existing resources and making do to provide breakthrough solutions in firm creation. Bricolage is normally directed towards resource processes, relationships, and interconnections among them. Thus, how does intuition influence the degree of bricolage behavior of entrepreneurs as they creatively use existing resources at hand and leverage existing relationships among their stakeholders (team members, suppliers, customers, investors) to develop and sustain the new venture?

What Role Does Intuition Have on the Discovery of Different Types of Opportunities and Innovations?

While research has shown that intuition can be a key precursor to opportunity identification (La Pira & Gillin, 2006; Mitchell et al., 2005), another question that may be relevant to explore is how does intuition factor into the types of new opportunities and innovations? That is, it may be interesting to investigate the role of intuition on the two types of innovation: radical and incremental. Radical innovations can propel entrepreneurial firms into a position of industry leadership and can bring down large incumbents that fail to innovate, thus creating new markets and destroying old ones. Leifer et al. (2000) suggest that radical innovations are characterized by an entirely new set of performance features, significant improvements in known performance features and also by reduction in costs. Radical innovations involve use and development of advanced knowledge or technology that transforms the way similar challenges are solved for the future. On the other hand, incremental innovation is defined as refinements and extensions of designs that result in substantial price or functional benefits to users (Banbury & Mitchell, 1995: 163). While radical innovation transforms, the incremental innovation seeks to improve existing knowledge or technology (Dosi, 1982). Such small improvements add value to the product or service and generate benefits to the customer. While both forms of innovation may be important to the entrepreneurial firm at various stages of growth, it may be a promising area of future research to assess how intuition can be used to stimulate and facilitate both types of innovation. Previous knowledge and experience may also act as an intervening variable between intuition and the type/degree of innovation that is introduced within the entrepreneur's marketplace.

What Is the Interaction or Association between Effectuation and Entrepreneurial Intuition?

There is growing evidence that the essence of entrepreneurial planning is not linear and well-structured, but instead ill-structured and effectuated (Sarasvathy, 2001). As postulated by Sarasvathy, effectuation enables entrepreneurs to make reasoned and informed choices based on the logic of control. For example, given a particular scenario, limited resources, etc., an entrepreneur will choose among possibilities to create a desired outcome. Two well-tested approaches to convey effectuation skills are action learning and problem-based learning. Research has yet to reveal how the effectuation reasoning and process are associated. Future research needs to examine whether intuitives are more prone to effectuational thinking. Moreover, it may be useful to assess whether a strong preference for effectuational thinking actually underlies intuitive thinking.

CONCLUSION

Our chapter provides an overview of the latest research in the area along with tools and practices nascent and experienced entrepreneurs can use to stimulate their own intuitive thinking and skills. We conclude by introducing several new potential areas for researchers to investigate that overlap with other entrepreneurial constructs. While much work remains in examining the role of intuition in the context of entrepreneurship, it is our hope that additional research will shed light on its importance to new venture development and growth. As expressed by Albert Einstein, 'the only real valuable thing is intuition' and for entrepreneurs developing their own set of competencies for their next challenge, intuition may be their competitive advantage in identifying the most promising opportunities for the future.

REFERENCES

Allinson, C. W., Chell, E., & Hayes, J. 2000. Intuition and entrepreneurial behavior. *European Journal of Work and Organizational Psychology*, 9(1): 31–43.
Allinson, C. W., & Hayes, J. 1996. The Cognitive Style Index: A measure of intuition-analysis for organizational research. *Journal of Management Studies*, 33(1): 119–135.

Baker, T., & Nelson, R. E. 2005. Creating something from nothing: Resource construction through entrepreneurial bricolage. *Administrative Science Quarterly*, 50: 329–366.

Banbury, C., & Mitchell, W. 1995. The effect of introducing important incremental innovations on market share and business survival. *Strategic Management Journal*, 16: 161–182.

Brigham, K. H., & Sorenson, R. L. 2008. Cognitive style differences of novice, serial, and habitual entrepreneurs: A two-sample test. In A. Zacharakis, G. George, S. Alvarez, M. S. Cardon, & J. O. De Castro (Eds.), *Frontiers of Entrepreneurship Research: Proceedings of the Twenty-Eighth Annual Entrepreneurship Research Conference*. Babson Park, MA: Babson College.

Cardon, M., & Stevens, C. 2009. The discriminant validity of entrepreneurial passion. In G. T. Solomon (Ed.), *Academy of Management Proceedings*: 1–6, Chicago, IL.

Chapman, M. 2000. 'When the entrepreneur sneezes, the organization catches a cold': A practitioner's perspective on the state of the art in research on the entrepreneurial personality and the entrepreneurial process. *European Journal of Work and Organizational Psychology*, 9(1): 97–101.

Dane, E., & Pratt, M. G. 2007. Exploring intuition and its role in managerial decision making. *Academy of Management Review*, 32(1): 33–54.

Dosi, G. 1982. Technological paradigms and technological trajectories: A suggested interpretation of the determinants and directions of technical change. *Research Policy*, 11(3): 147–162.

Garud, R., Kumaraswamy, A., & Nayyar, P. 1998. Real options or fool's gold: perspective makes the difference. *Academy of Management Review*, 3(2): 212–214.

Hodgkinson, G. P., Sadler-Smith, E., Sinclair, M., & Ashkanasy, N. M. 2009. More than meets the eye? Intuition and analysis revisited. *Personality and Individual Differences*, 47: 342–346.

Hughes, G. D. 2003. Add creativity to your decision processes. *Journal for Quality and Participation*, Summer: 5–13.

Isaksen, S. G., Dorval, B. K., & Treffinger, D. J. 2010. *Creative approaches to problem solving: A framework for innovation and change*. Thousand Oaks, CA: Sage.

Kickul, J., Gundry, L. K., Barbosa, S. D., & Simms, S. 2010. One style does not fit all: The role of cognitive style in entrepreneurship education. *International Journal of Entrepreneurship and Small Business*, 9(1): 36–57.

La Pira, F., & Gillin, M. 2006. Non local intuition and the performance of serial entrepreneurs. *International Journal of Entrepreneurship and Small Business*, 3(1):17–35.

Leifer, R., McDermott, C. M., O'Connor, G. C., Peters, L. S., Rice, M. P., & Veryzer, R. W. 2000. *Radical innovation: How mature companies can outsmart upstarts*. Boston, MA: Harvard Business School Press.

Leonard, N. H., Scholl, R. W., & Kowalski, K. B. 1999. Information processing style and decision making. *Journal of Organizational Behavior*, 20: 407–420.

Lévi-Strauss, C. 1967. *The savage mind*. Chicago: University of Chicago Press.

Michalko, M. 1991. *Thinkertoys*. Berkeley, CA: Ten Speed Press.

Miner, J. B. 1997. *A psychological typology of successful entrepreneurs*. London: Quorum Books.

Mitchell, J. R., Friga, P. N., & Mitchell, R. K. 2005. Untangling the intuition mess: Intuition as a construct in entrepreneurial cognition research. *Entrepreneurship: Theory and Practice*, 30 (November): 653–679.

New Zealand Management. 1998. 'Protect yourself from too much intuition.' *New Zealand Management*, 45(7): 24.

Olson, P. D. 1985. Entrepreneurship: Process and abilities. *American Journal of Small Business*, 10(1): 25–31.

Ornstein, R. E. 1977. *The psychology of consciousness*. New York: Harcourt Brace.

Pacini, R., & Epstein, S. 1999. The relation of rational and experiential information processing styles to personality, basic beliefs, and the ratio-bias phenomenon. *Journal of Personality and Social Psychology*, 76: 972–987.

Prather, C. W., & Gundry, L. K. 1995. *Blueprints for innovation*. New York: American Management Association.

Sadler-Smith, E. 2010. Instinct messaging. Available at: www.peoplemanagement.co.uk/features: 24–26 (accessed February 25, 2010).

Sadler-Smith, E., & Shefy, E. 2004. The intuitive executive: Understanding and applying 'gut feel' in decision-making. *Academy of Management Executive*, 4: 76–91.

Sarasvathy, S.D. 2001. Causation and effectuation: toward a theoretical shift from economic inevitability to entrepreneurial contingency. *Academy of Management Review*, 26: 243–288.

Schumpeter, J. A. 1983. *The theory of economic development*. New Brunswick, NJ: Transaction Publishers.

Tversky, A., & Kahneman, D. 1974. Judgment under uncertainty: Heuristics and biases. *Science*, 185: 1124–1131.

Venkataraman, S. 1997. The distinctive domain of entrepreneurship research: An editor's perspective. In J. Katz, & R. Brockhaus (Eds.), *Advances in entrepreneurship, firm emergence and growth*, Vol. 3: 119–138. Greenwich, CT: JAI Press.

Vesper, K. H. 1983. *Entrepreneurship and national policy*. Chicago: Heller Institute for Small Business Policy.

9 The role of intuition in ethical decision making

James Richard Guzak and M. Blake Hargrove

Ethical decision making has been an important area of theoretical and empirical work within the field of organizational behavior for the past 25 years. To date, most of this work has focused on rationality as the basis of most ethical decisions, while relatively little research attention has centered on the role intuition plays in ethical decisions (Haidt, 2001; Reynolds, 2006; Sonenshein, 2007). The purpose of this chapter is to provide a brief review of the most important theories of ethical decision making within the field, to provide a more in-depth review of the potential importance of non-cognitive intuitive modes of ethical decision making, and to propose some potential opportunities for further research.

The theoretical underpinning for modern ethical decision-making research stems from Rest's (1986) foundational work which suggests that people move sequentially along a four-step process of moral decision making. These steps include (i) moral awareness – being able to interpret the situation as being moral; (ii) moral judgment – deciding which course of action is morally right; (iii) moral intent – prioritizing moral values over other values; and (iv) moral behavior – executing and implementing the moral intention. Subsequent empirical research in ethical decision making has primarily focused on testing Rest's four steps as dependent measures. Various researchers have offered independent variables emphasizing individual constructs, organizational constructs, and Jones's (1991) moral intensity construct (Ford & Richardson, 1994; Loe et al., 2000; McDevitt et al., 2007; O'Fallon & Butterfield, 2005).

Rest's (1986) four-step model suggests a description of a *rational* process in ethical decision making. Rest was explicit in identifying his model as a cognitive model of ethical decision making designed to understand what individuals *think* when they encounter an ethical decision (Reynolds, 2006). Consequentially, research that centers on associations between individual or organizational variables and one or more of Rest's aspects of ethicality must be based on an assumption that people engage in rational decision-making processes, thus they exclude examination of intuitive considerations.

Like Rest, most philosophers have focused on making ethical decisions within a rational or cognitivist model. Plato and Aristotle focused on virtues as the basis of morality; that which was virtuous could be determined by reason (Darwall, 2003). Christian philosophers from Augustine to Aquinas also believed that moral decision making resulted from a rational understanding of the will of God, His natural law, and the pursuit of goodness (Waddell, 2007). Despite the fact that their ethical systems differed greatly, the Enlightenment philosophers Immanuel Kant and John Stuart Mill concurred that reason played the primary role in determining what decision was morally correct, given a set of conditions (Sidgwick, 1981). Many modern philosophers such as Rawls (1999) have followed the cognitivist tradition of placing reason as the principal basis of moral decision making.

Opposed to the many cognitivists within the field of philosophy are the emotivists. Emotivism is the philosophy that feelings and intuition play a substantial role in moral decision making (Gensler, 1998). One of the early proponents of emotivism was the Scottish Enlightenment figure David Hume. In his 1751 work, Hume (2006) argued that in making moral decisions an actor ought to avoid those behaviors which would bring about 'approbation or blame'. Both of these terms, he argued, could not be the work of reason, but rather were 'of the heart' or 'active feeling or sentiment'. Hume, followed by later emotivists, laid the foundation for a non-cognitive model of ethical decision making.

Within the field of organizational behavior, recent research has criticized the prevalent underlying assumption of rationality in the ethical business decision-making literature stream for not taking into account the potentially important role of intuition in the decision-making process (Garcia & Ostrosky-Solis, 2006; Haidt, 2001; Reynolds, 2006; Sayegha et al., 2004; Sonenshein, 2007). Some of these researchers have suggested theoretical frameworks for the inclusion of intuitive processes (e.g., Reynolds, 2006; Sonenshein, 2007) but have not tested their models empirically.

The view of ethical decision making from a strictly rational perspective might be unsatisfactory, considering two important bodies of research. One area of research suggests that both conscious and non-conscious systems are utilized in cognitive decision making (Jacoby, 1996; Sloman, 1996; Stanovich & West, 1998). This 'dual processing' framework for cognition has found substantial support (e.g. Dane & Pratt, 2007; Epstein, 1990, 2008; Hammond, 1981, 1986, 1987, 1990; Hogarth, 2001). Another relevant area is the role of affect in the decision-making process. The concept of 'affect as information' has been documented in research regarding the role of affect in decision making (Schwarz, 1990; Schwarz & Clore, 2003). Emotional associations from prior experiences result in how one feels about an event, object or person (positively or negatively), and that feeling is used directly as information in coming to a judgment (Clore et al., 2001; Daniels, 2008).

At the intersection of the research on dual processing and affect is intuition. Intuition is understood to be the non-conscious component of dual processing (Betsch, 2008; Dane & Pratt, 2007; Epstein, 2008), and it is inextricably linked to affect in the human decision-making process (Damasio, 1994; Hogarth, 2001; Sadler-Smith et al., 2008). Dane and Pratt (2009) suggest that intuition might be categorized into three primary variants: problem-solving intuition, creative intuition, and moral intuition. Following Dane and Pratt, the area of moral intuition might be an important facet of intuition research. Consequently, an examination of dual processing models and affective models is necessary for an understanding of the role intuition plays in ethical decision making.

DUAL PROCESSING MODELS

Epstein (1990, 2008) proposes a framework he labeled 'cognitive experiential self-theory' (CEST) as a model of how rational and intuitive processes might work in tandem. According to CEST, the two systems interact both simultaneously and sequentially, with the intuitive system usually reacting first to a stimulus. If this initial response tendency is identified by the rational system as inappropriate, the rational system will suppress or adjust the response tendency. If it is not identified as inappropriate, the tendency is automatically expressed. Another possible sequence suggested by CEST (Epstein, 2008) is one in which the intuitive system reacts to the rational system. A thought produced by the rational system can instigate emotions or produce associations in the experiential system. Once the process is set in motion, the two systems then work simultaneously to influence each other. Research demonstrates that the mutual influence of the two systems results in conflicts and compromises between the experiential and rational systems (e.g., Denes-Raj & Epstein, 1994; Haidt, 2001; Reber, 1993; Yanko & Epstein, 1999).

Knowing that human decisions are the result of mutual influence between the two systems, an important aspect of the relationship between the intuitive and the rational systems is the extent to which decision makers might rely on one system versus the other. Hammond (1981, 1986, 1990) suggests that a cognitive continuum exists between the poles of intuition and rational analysis in which a decision may fall between these extremes based on the relative influence of each system.

The modes of operation occurring between the intuitive and analytical poles of Hammond's cognitive continuum theory (CCT) represent differing proportions of influence exercised by intuition and analysis in thought processes, and result in what Hammond refers to as 'quasi-rationality'. Quasi-rationality appears to be closely related to Heider's (1958) view of commonsense and to Simon's (1986) concept of bounded rationality. In Hammond's theory, quasi-rationality assumes that neither rationality nor intuition assume lesser importance in the framework, but rather that they work conjointly (Cooksey, 1996).

Hammond (1990) suggests that different tasks, or different types of decisions, might call for one system, intuitive or rational, to be relatively more influential than the other when a person considers a decision. Task properties that will tend to induce more intuitive or more analytical cognitive bias when making judgments include (i) the complexity of the task structure, (ii) the ambiguity of the task structure, and (iii) the form of the task presentation (Cooksey, 1996).

Hammond et al. (1987) empirically tested the cognitive continuum across different types of decisions. They were able to document the cognitive continuum's predictive ability as decision makers used differing levels of intuition and rationality conjointly for different types of tasks in line with the cognitive continuum. More explicitly, highway engineers were asked to render judgments on three different tasks with varying levels of task complexity. Based on the subjects' relative use of intuition conjointly with rationality, the corresponding position of the subjects along the cognitive continuum was predicted by task characteristics (Cooksey, 1996).

CCT therefore suggests that the nature of the problem structure might determine how a decision maker would process a decision, either more intuitively or more rationally. Dane and Pratt (2007) propose that the concept of problem structure is captured in the distinction between intellective and judgmental tasks for individual decision making as suggested by Laughlin (1980) and Laughlin and Ellis (1986). Intellective tasks involve a 'definite objective criterion of success within the rules, operations and relationships of a conceptual system'. Judgmental tasks involve 'political, ethical, aesthetic or behavioral judgments for which there is no objective criterion or demonstrable solution' (Laughlin, 1980: 128). Consistently with Hammond (1990), Laughlin (1980) concludes that the intellective–judgmental task relationship is a continuum rather than a dichotomy.

As dual processing pertains to ethical decision making, research implies that people would not make a purely 'rational' or 'intuitive' decision but rather would be influenced by both systems to some degree. The work of Hammond (1986, 1987, 1990) and Hammond et al. (1987) proposes that tasks high in complexity and ambiguity are processed more intuitively. Moral decisions are often highly complex and ambiguous (Mathieson, 2007) and therefore might be processed more intuitively.

However, Hammond and his associates also propose that the form of presentation of the decision, as either functionally or perceptually organized, has an influence on how people might process an ethical decision. Cooksey (1996: 22) concludes that if information presented to a decision maker is perceptually organized, such as in photographs, recorded messages, or in vividly descriptive text, then those modalities will tend to increase holistic pattern seeking and intuitive processing on the part of the decision maker. If cues are presented in a manner that is pallid, the decision maker will be less inclined to process that information associatively, focusing more on the logical implications of the facts rather than the associative context or holistic meaning of the information. Thus, the decision maker in this case will rely less on intuitive processing and more on rational analysis. On the other hand, if cues are presented in a functionally oriented way, such as with data points, measured quantities, or amounts and rates, then decision makers will be more likely to use rational processing that considers the cues sequentially. Consequently the CCT framework suggests that the modality of information presented to decision makers can influence them to be either more intuitive or more rational in their decision making (Cooksey, 1996).

Additional clarity regarding the role of information modality on decision processes is provided by Paivio (1986, 1991, 2007) who offers a parallel theoretical framework originating from the literature on perception. Paivio's framework, linking verbal and non-verbal perception, similarly proposes that changes in information modality can alter the manner of cognitive processing between the rational and the intuitive. Paivio's (1986, 1991, 2007) dual coding theory (DCT) suggests that cognition involves the cooperative interdependence of two functionally independent but interconnected systems, a verbal system specialized for dealing with language and a non-verbal system specialized for dealing with non-linguistic objects and events (Paivio, 2007: 33). In DCT the two perceptive systems symbolize reality for the perceptor in fundamentally different ways depending upon the modality of information coming to the perceiver.

Information can be conveyed in via both verbal and non-verbal systems. In the verbal system, one experiences and encodes language, which can be perceived from visual, auditory, or even haptic (e.g., Braille) stimuli. The verbal system makes sense of reality indirectly using language symbols that Paivio calls 'logogens', which are interpretable groups of language units (letters, words, phrases) that mean something to us and provide an understandable representation. Some logogens provide us with conceptual meaning (e.g., justice, trust, beauty) and others provide imagery indirectly following recognition (e.g., stick, glove, wrench). In the non-verbal system, visual objects, non-language sounds, emotions and other sensory input give rise to what Paivio refers to as 'imagens', which generate mental imagery directly and unconsciously. These images tap our experiences for associative meaning based on our familiarity with the objects and give rise to a context through associations which are often congruently nested (e.g., justice in courts in government in America; stick with leaves on tree in forest) (Krasny, 2004; Paivio, 2007).

Guzak (2009) tested whether the form of presentation would alter the way people process an ethical decision by presenting case information either in bullet point (functional) or narrative (perceptual) form, and either with or without associative (perceptual) pictures. An ethical case scenario offered two alternative decision outcomes to decision makers, either favoring a 'rights' subjective (intuitive) or a calculative 'utilitarian' (rational) approach. Using Hammond et al.'s (1987) dependent measures for intuition, this research found conflicting results, with one of three measures supporting the hypothesis that functionally presented ethical case material would be processed more rationally than perceptually presented material, a finding which was supported by an additional measure.

While further research in this area is needed, the form of information presented to the decision maker might be an important element in determining whether people use intuition to a greater or lesser degree in ethical decisions. If so, this has important implications for our understanding of ethical decision making, because different decision outcomes might be the result of people processing information more intuitively or more rationally based only on the manner in which information is presented to them.

AFFECT MODELS

There are three important research streams that should be considered in the discussion of the role of affect and intuition in decision-making processes: hedonic tone, activation, and regulatory focus theory (RFT) (Baas et al., 2008). Hedonic tone research suggests that affect can be parsed into two separate valences, positive and negative, and that these affective states respectively promote and attenuate the use of intuition by a decision maker (Fiedler, 1988; Isen, 1984, 1987; Klinger, 1993; Kuhl, 1983; Schwarz, 1990; Taylor, 1991). As an example of the research centered on hedonic tone, Fiedler (1988) proposed that positive affect produces a 'loosening style' which he characterized as creative and intuitive, whereas negative mood produces a 'tightening style' which he described as being systematic and rigid.

A growing body of literature also indicates that affect's relationship to cognition might be understood by distinguishing between arousal activation and deactivation (Barrett, 2006; Heller, 1993; Heller & Nitschke, 1997; Mano, 1992, 1997; Posner et al., 2005). In this research stream, affective states such as happiness and anger, regardless of their opposite valence, are activating, while states such as calmness or sadness are deactivating. Extremely low and high levels of activation appear to inhibit the use of intuitive processes while moderate levels of activation promote them (DeDreu et al., 2008).

Research indicates that an individual's capacity for intuitive processing is altered in a curvilinear manner as arousal activation increases, which is consistent with work on threat rigidity (Staw et al., 1981) and stress performance (Berridge & Waterhouse, 2003; Broadbent, 1972; Yerkes & Dodson, 1908). Low levels of arousal lead to inactivity, avoidance, and neglect of information, while extremely high levels of arousal result in preprogrammed, dominant responses rather than innovative responses (Berlyne, 1967; Easterbrook, 1959). Moderate levels of arousal are associated with release of neurotransmitters in the brain that promote cognitive flexibility, abstract thinking, faster processing of information, cognitive flexibility, restructuring of information, and access to long-term memory (Baas et al., 2008; Baddeley, 2000; Damasio, 2001; Dietrich, 2004). These traits are generally associated with intuitive processing (Betsch, 2008; Epstein, 2008).

In addition to hedonic tone and activation, affective states might also be distinguished in terms of their association with self-regulation. RFT (Higgins, 1997; Idson et al., 2000) distinguishes between promotion and prevention focus, which describe the two self-regulatory and motivational systems underlying approach–avoidance behavior (Baas et al., 2008). Research in RFT suggests that promotion focus states promote flexibility and divergent thinking which are associated with intuitive processing (Friedman & Forster, 2000).

In the research on RFT, promotion states engender broad and global attention and facilitate conceptual access to mental representations with lower *a priori* access. In contrast, prevention states promote a narrow attention scope and a 'choking off' of conceptual access to mental representations (Baas et al., 2008; Derryberry & Tucker, 1994; Forster et al., 2006; Forster & Higgins, 2005; Friedman & Forster, 2000). Affective states such as happiness, sadness, anger and joy that are promotion based might therefore be associated more closely with intuitive processing than prevention states such as fear, relaxation or calmness (Baas et al., 2008).

In their meta-analysis of the body of research on creativity, Baas et al. (2008) found evidence to suggest that RFT was more explanatory than hedonic tone or activation frameworks in research on creativity levels. Considering the close association that creativity has with flexible, parallel processing, it is possible that RFT might be a viable lens for examining intuitive processing as well.

In looking at the relationship between affective states and intuitive processing in ethical decision making, Guzak (2009) hypothesized consistently with research on hedonic tone that decision makers manipulated into a positive affective state (happiness) would use more intuitive processing when considering what to do in an ethical dilemma than people placed in a negative affective state (sadness). He found significant results that were contrary to expectations. Using Hammond's (1986) measures for intuitive and rational processing, decision makers in both a positive and a negative hedonic state used intuitive and rational processing at similar levels, but also at a level significantly higher than those subjects in a neutral affective state. While this result was inconsistent with hedonic tone, it was consistent with RFT as both happiness and sadness are promotion focused. This could suggest that something unique to ethical decisions makes RFT explanatory.

CONCLUSIONS AND RECOMMENDATIONS FOR FUTURE RESEARCH

The body of research in ethical decision making has focused attention on rational models to the exclusion of intuition as an explanatory factor as to how people make ethical decisions. This research has primarily examined individual and organizational traits as independent variables to explain one or more dependent variables in Rest's (1986) four-step model of moral awareness, judgment, intent and behavior (O'Fallon & Butterfield, 2005). Increasingly, researchers are suggesting that intuition should be more closely examined as it relates to ethical decision making (Haidt, 2001; Reynolds, 2006; Sonensheim, 2007) due to the paucity of results in this stream of research.

Considering the important role that intuition plays in dual processing models of cognition, these frameworks might provide a viable perspective from which to examine its role in ethical decision making. Research looking at intuition in decisions of a non-ethical nature has been supportive of the CCT (Dunwoody et al., 2000; Hammond, 1986) framework. This framework could also be used as a lens to examine its explanatory power in ethical decisions, which will require more research in this area.

Likewise, intuition's close association with affect calls attention to affective frameworks as another possible lens from which to examine ethical decision-making processes. While hedonic tone frameworks have been useful in explaining the use of intuition, they have not extensively tested how positive or negative affective valences can explain decision processes. Creativity research, an area closely associated with intuition (Dane & Pratt, 2009), suggests that RFT in particular might be a useful framework through which to examine intuitive processes in ethical decision makers.

This chapter considers a new and potentially important direction for our study of ethical decision making and offers two specific areas that might be fruitful for future research. The focus on rationality to examine ethical decision making to the exclusion of intuition has not yielded a reasonable comprehension of the process. Incorporating models that include intuition could offer additional insight into our understanding of ethical decision making.

REFERENCES

Baas, M., De Dreu, C. K. W., & Nijstad, B. A. 2008. A meta-analysis of 25 years of mood-creativity research: Hedonic tone, activation, or regulatory focus? *Psychological Bulletin*, 134(6): 779–806.

Baddeley, A. 2000. The episodic buffer: A new component of working memory. *Trends in Cognitive Sciences*, 4: 417–423.

Barrett, L. F. 2006. Valence is a basic building block of emotional life. *Journal of Research in Personality*, 40: 35–55.

Berlyne, D. E. 1967. Arousal and reinforcement. In D. Levine (Ed.), *Nebraska Symposium on Motivation*: 1–110. Lincoln, NE: University of Nebraska Press.

Berridge, C. W., & Waterhouse, B. D. 2003. The locus coeruleus–noradrenergic system: Modulation of behavioral state and state-dependent cognitive processes. *Brain Research Reviews*, 42: 33–84.

Betsch, T. 2008. The nature of intuition and its neglect in research on judgment and decision making. In H. Plessner, C. Betsch, & T. Betsch (Eds.), *Intuition in judgment and decision making*: 23–37. New York: Laurence Earlbaum Associates/Taylor & Francis Group.

Broadbent, D. E. 1972. *Decision and stress*. New York: Academic Press.

Clore, G. L., Wyer, R. S., & Dienes, B. 2001. Affective feelings as feedback: Some cognitive consequences. In L. L. Martin, & G. L. Clore (Eds.), *Theories of mood and cognition: A user's handbook*: 27–62. Mahwah, NJ: Erlbaum.

Cooksey, R. W. 1996. *Judgment analysis: Theory, methods and applications*. New York: Academic Press.

Damasio, A. R. 1994. *Descartes' error: Emotion, reason and the human brain*. New York: Grosset/Putnam.

Damasio, A. R. 2001. Some notes on brain, imagination and creativity. In K. Pfenninger, & V. R. Shubik (Eds.), *The origins of creativity*: 59–68. Oxford: Oxford University Press.

Dane, E., & Pratt, M. G. 2007. Exploring intuition and its role in managerial decision making. *Academy of Management Review*, 32(1): 33–54.

Dane, E., & Pratt, M. G. 2009. Conceptualizing and measuring intuition: A review of recent trends. *International Review of Industrial and Organizational Psychology*, 24: 1–40.

Daniels, K. 2008. Affect and information processing. In G. P. Hodgkinson, & W. H. Starbuck (Eds.), *The Oxford handbook of organizational decision making*: 325–341. New York: Oxford University Press.

Darwall, S. (Ed.). 2003. *Virtue ethics*, Oxford: Blackwell.

De Dreu, C. K. W., Baas, M., & Nijstad, B. A. 2008. Hedonic tone and activation in the mood–creativity link: Towards a dual pathway to creativity model. *Journal of Personality and Social Psychology*, 94: 739–756.

Denes-Raj. V., & Epstein, S. 1994. Conflict between experiential and rational processing: When people behave against their better judgment. *Journal of Personality and Social Psychology*, 66: 817–829.

Derryberry, D., & Tucker, D. M. 1994. Motivating the focus of attention. In P. M. Niedenthal, & S. Kitayama (Eds.), *The heart's eye: Emotional influences in perception and attention*: 167–196. San Diego, CA: Academic Press.

Dietrich, A. 2004. The cognitive neuroscience of creativity. *Psychonomic Bulletin & Review*, 11: 1011–1026.

Dunwoody, P. T., Haarbauer, E., Mahan, R. P., Marino, C., & Tang, C. 2000. Cognitive adaptation and its consequences: A test of cognitive continuum theory. *Journal of Behavioural Decision-Making*, 13: 55–59.

Easterbrook, J. A. 1959. The effect of emotion on cue utilization and the organization of behavior. *Psychological Review*, 66: 183–201.

Epstein, S. 1990. Cognitive–experiential self-theory. In L. Pervin (Ed.), *Handbook of personality: Theory and research*: 165–192. New York: Guilford Press.

Epstein, S. 2008. Intuition from the perspective of cognitive-experiential self-theory. In H. Plessner, C. Betsch, & T. Betsch (Eds.), *Intuition in judgment and decision making*: 23–37. New York: Laurence Earlbaum Associates/Taylor & Francis Group.

Fiedler, K. 1988. Emotional mood, cognitive style and behavior regulation. In K. Fiedler, & J. Forgas (Eds.), *Affect, cognition and social behavior*: 100–119. Gottingen, Germany: Hogrefe.

Ford, R. C., & Richardson, W. D. 1994. Ethical decision making: A review of the empirical literature. *Journal of Business Ethics*, 13: 205–221.

Forster, J., Friedman, R. S., Ozelsel, A., & Denzler, M. 2006. Enactment of approach and avoidance behavior influences the scope of perceptual and conceptual attention. *Journal of Experimental Social Psychology*, 42: 133–146.

Forster, J., & Higgins, E. T. 2005. How global vs. local processing fits regulatory focus. *Psychological Science*, 16: 631–636.

Friedman, R. S., & Forster, J. 2000. The effects of approach and avoidance motor actions on the elements of creative insight. *Journal of Personality and Social Psychology*, 79: 477–492.

Garcia, A. E. V., & Ostrosky-Solis, F. 2006. From morality to moral emotions. *International Journal of Psychology*, 41(5): 348–354.

Gensler, H. J. 1998. *Ethics: A contemporary introduction*. New York: Routledge.

Guzak, J. R. 2009. *The role of intuition in ethical decision making*. Unpublished doctoral dissertation, University of Texas at Arlington, Arlington, TX.

Haidt, J. 2001. The emotional dog and its rational tail: A social intuitionist approach to moral judgment. *Psychological Review*, 108(4): 814–834.

Hammond, K. R. 1981. *Principles of organization intuitive and analytical cognition (Report No. 231)*. Center for Research on Judgment and Policy, University of Colorado, Boulder, CO.

Hammond, K. R. 1986. *A theoretically based review of theory and research in judgment and decision making (Report No. 260)*. Center for Research on Judgment and Policy, University of Colorado, Boulder, CO.

Hammond, K. R. 1987. Toward a unified approach to the study of expert judgment. In J. Mumpower, L. Phillips, O. Renn, & R. Uppoluri (Eds.), *Expert judgment and expert systems*: 1–16. Berlin: Springer-Verlag.

Hammond, K. R. 1990. Intuitive and analytical cognition: Information models. In A. P. Sage (Ed.), *Concise encyclopedia of information processing in systems and organizations*: 301–312. Oxford: Pergamon Press.

Hammond, K .R., Hamm, R. M., Grassia, J., & Pearson, T. 1987. Direct comparison of the relative efficiency on intuitive and analytical cognition. *IEEE Transactions on Systems, Man, and Cybernetics*, 17: 753–770.

Heider, F. 1958. *The psychology of interpersonal relations.* New York: John Wiley & Sons.
Heller, W. 1993. Neuropsychological mechanisms of individual differences in emotion, personality, and arousal. *Neuropsychology*, 7: 476–489.
Heller, W., & Nitschke, J. B. 1997. Regional brain activity in emotion: A framework for understanding cognition in depression. *Cognition and Emotion*, 11: 637–661.
Higgins, E. T. 1997. Beyond pleasure and pain. *American Psychologist*, 52: 1280–1300.
Hogarth, R. M. 2001. *Educating intuition.* Chicago: University of Chicago Press.
Hume, D. 2006. An enquiry concerning the principles of morals: A critical edition. Beauchamp, T. (Ed.), New York: Oxford University Press.
Idson, L. C., Liberman, N., & Higgins, E. T. 2000. Distinguishing gains from non-losses and losses from non-gains: A regulatory focus perspective on hedonic intensity. *Journal of Experimental Social Psychology*, 36: 252–274.
Isen, A. M. 1984. Towards understanding the role of affect in cognition. In R. S. Wyler, & T. K. Srull (Eds.), *Handbook of social cognition*, Vol. 3: 179–236. Hillsdale, NJ: Erlbaum.
Isen, A. M. 1987. Positive affect, cognitive processes, and social behavior. In L. Berkowitz (Ed.), *Advances in Experimental Social Psychology*, Vol. 20: 203–253. New York: Academic Press.
Jacoby, L. L. 1996. Dissociating automatic and consciously-controlled effects of study/test compatibility. *Journal of Memory and Language*, 35: 32–52.
Jones, T. M. 1991. Ethical decision making by individuals in organizations: An issue-contingent model. *Academy of Management Review*, 16(2): 368–395.
Klinger, E. 1993. Clinical approaches to mood control. In D. M. Wegner, & J. W. Pennebaker (Eds.), *Handbook of mental control*: 344–369. Englewood Cliffs, NJ: Prentice-Hall.
Krasny, K. A. 2004. *Imagery, affect and the embodied mind: Implications for reading and responding to literature.* Unpublished doctoral dissertation, Texas A&M University College Station, TX.
Kuhl, J. 1983. Emotion, cognition and motivation: The functional significance of emotions to problem solving. *Sprache und Kognition*, 4: 228–253.
Laughlin, P. 1980. Social combination processes of cooperative problem-solving groups on verbal intellective tasks. In M. Fishbein (Ed.), *Progress in social psychology*, vol. 1: 127–155. Hillsdale, NJ: Lawrence Erlbaum Associates.
Laughlin, P. R., & Ellis, A. L. 1986. Acquisition of procedural knowledge about a pattern of stimuli that cannot be articulated. *Cognitive Psychology*, 20: 24–37.
Loe, T. W., Ferrell, L., & Mansfield, P. 2000. A review of empirical studies assessing ethical decision making in business. *Journal of Business Ethics*, 25: 185–204.
Mano, H. 1992. Judgments under distress: Assessing the role of unpleasantness and arousal in judgment formation. *Organizational Behavior and Human Decision Processes*, 52: 216–245.
Mano, H. 1997. Affect and persuasion: The influence of pleasantness and arousal on attitude formation and message elaboration. *Psychology and Marketing*, 14: 315–335.
Mathieson, K. 2007. Towards a design science of ethical decision support. *Journal of Business Ethics*, 76: 269–292.
McDevitt, R., Giapponi, C., & Tromley, C. 2007. A model of ethical decision making: The integration of process and content. *Journal of Business Ethics*, 73: 219–229.
O'Fallon, M. J., & Butterfield, K. D. 2005. A review of the empirical ethical decision-making literature: 1996–2003. *Journal of Business Ethics*, 59: 375–413.
Paivio, A. 1986. *Mental representations: A dual coding approach.* Oxford: Oxford University Press.
Paivio, A. 1991. *Images in mind: The evolution of a theory.* New York: Harvester Wheatsheaf.
Paivio, A. 2007. *Mind and its evolution: A dual coding theoretical approach.* Mahwah, NJ: Lawrence Erlbaum Associates.
Posner, J., Russell, J. A., & Peterson, B. S. 2005. The circumplex model of affect: An integrative approach to affective neuroscience, cognitive development and psychopathology. *Development and Psychopathology*, 17: 715–734.

Rawls, J. 1999. *A theory of justice* (rev ed.). Boston: Harvard University Press.
Reber, A. S. 1993. *Implicit learning and tacit knowledge: An essay on the cognitive unconscious.* New York: Oxford University Press.
Rest, J. R. 1986. *Moral development: Advances in research and theory.* New York: Praeger.
Reynolds, S. J. 2006. A neurocognitive model of the ethical decision-making process: Implications for study and practice. *Journal of Applied Psychology,* 91: 737–748.
Sadler-Smith, E., Hodgkinson, G. P., & Sinclair, M. 2008. A matter of feeling? The role of intuition in entrepreneurial decision-making and behavior. In W. J. Zerbe, C. E. J. Härtel, & N. M. Ashkanasy (Eds.), *Emotion, ethics, and decision-making: Research on emotion in organizations*: 35–51. Bingley, UK: Emerald Group.
Sayegha. L., Anthony, W. P., & Perrewé, P. L. 2004. Managerial decision-making under crisis: The role of emotion in an intuitive decision process. *Human Resource Management Review,* 14(2): 179–200.
Schwarz, N. 1990. Feelings as information: Informational and motivational functions of affective states. In T. Higgins, & R. M. Sorrentino (Eds.), *Handbook of motivation and cognition: Foundations of social behavior*: 527–561. New York: Guilford Press.
Schwarz, N., & Clore. G. L. 2003. Mood as information: 20 years later. *Psychological Inquiry,* 14: 296–303.
Sidgwick, H. 1981. *The methods of ethics.* Indianapolis, IN: Hackett.
Simon, H. A. 1986. Alternative visions of rationality. In H. R. Arkes, & H. K. Hammond (Eds.), *Judgment and decision making: An interdisciplinary reader*: 97–113. Cambridge: Cambridge University Press.
Sloman, S. A. 1996. The empirical case for two systems of reasoning. *Psychological Bulletin,* 119: 3–22.
Sonenshein, S. 2007. The role of construction, intuition, and justification in responding to ethical issues at work: The sensemaking-intuition model. *Academy of Management Review,* 32(4): 1022–1040.
Stanovich, K. E., & West, R. F. 1998. Individual differences in rational thought. *Journal of Experimental Psychology: General,* 127: 161–188.
Staw, B. M., Sandelands, L. E., & Dutton, J. E. 1981. Threat-rigidity effects in organizational behavior: A multilevel analysis. *Administrative Science Quarterly,* 26: 501–524.
Taylor, S. E. 1991. Asymmetrical effects of positive and negative events. The mobilization–minimalization hypothesis. *Psychological Bulletin,* 110: 67–85.
Waddell, P. J. 2007. *Happiness and the Christian moral life: An introduction to Christian ethics.* Landham, MD: Rowman & Littlefield.
Yanko, J., & Epstein, S. 1999. *Compromises between experiential and rational processing as a function of age-level.* Unpublished raw data. University of Massachusetts at Amherst, Amherst, MA.
Yerkes, R. M., & Dodson, J. D. 1908. The relation of strength of stimulus to rapidity of habit formation. *Journal of Comparative Neurology and Psychology,* 18: 459–482.

PART 3

INTUITION IN PROFESSIONAL/ OCCUPATIONAL DOMAINS

10 Life, death, and intuition in critical occupations
Janice Langan-Fox and Vedran Vranic

Throughout history, the construct of intuition has been alluded to with great scepticism, and has been shrouded in mystery. To this very day, there exists a large variety of interpretations of intuition. Since these interpretations emerge from the culmination of various definitions used, the practicality and applicability of intuition is often clouded or misconstrued. Nevertheless, the use of intuition has been reported in a large variety of occupations. This chapter examines its prevalence in critical occupations that often deal with life and death situations. Maybe because of the gravity of their decisions, professionals in these occupations do not take intuition lightly. In what follows, we provide examples and quotes, detailing intuition use in different critical settings.

MEDICAL OCCUPATIONS

Nursing and Emergency Nursing

In a recent qualitative study of 14 experienced emergency nurses, reports similar to the response below were collated:

> At about 11 pm, a 7-month-old baby accompanied by his babysitter arrived with no specific complaint. I suddenly felt my stomach turn. I assessed the infant's basic signs, found nothing unusual yet picked him up and informed the pediatric resident that I was taking him to the resuscitation area. When asked why, I replied that he needed to be there. The resident had no choice but to follow me. Two hours later the baby was admitted to the operating theater requiring a repair to a large previously undiagnosed ventral septal defect. Later, the pediatric resident asked how I knew about the heart failure. I could not provide any answer as I just had a sense of knowing that something was seriously wrong. This experience had disturbed me. (Lyneham et al., 2008a: 101)

Despite a lack of quantitative testing, similar research provides tentative support for an intuitive component of emergency nursing practice. Intuition has also been described as an important type of nursing knowledge (Paterson & Zderad, 1988) and has gained acceptance as a valid way of knowing, not only in emergency but also clinical nursing (Benner & Tanner, 1987; Rew, 1986, 1988a, 1988b; Schraeder & Fischer, 1987; Welsh & Lyons, 2001). Research on intuition in this occupation has mainly been centred on the work of experienced practitioners. As a result the use of intuition has turned into a way of explaining a certain type of professional expertise (Benner, 1984; Easen & Wilcockson, 1996).

Further studies (McCutcheon & Pincombe, 2001) have identified that nursing intuition is an outcome generated through an intricate interaction of attributes, including knowledge, experience and expertise. Its antecedents also constitute personality, environment, acceptance of intuition as a valid 'behaviour' and the presence or absence of a nurse/client relationship. Nursing intuition should not therefore be considered as something that just 'happens'. An outlook of intuition that has recently surfaced is that knowledge, experience and expertise are reciprocally dependent, interacting to yield an effect greater than their sum, often referred to as 'synergy'. The synergy that occurs throughout their interaction produces intuition and is the central tenet that links other categories. Other research appeals for further study in this respect, claiming that intuition is characterized as direct perception, and as an observable, lawful phenomenon is measurable, potentially teachable and appropriately part of nursing science (Effken, 2001).

Three more recent studies of nursing intuition (Lyneham et al., 2008b; Smith, 2009; Smith et al., 2004) acknowledge intuition as a legitimate form of knowing rather than an exclusively expert trait. This should sanction the empowerment of intuitive skills at all levels of experience, as well as the fostering of intuition in academic study.

Clinical Consultation/Diagnosis/Therapy

The use of intuition is not strictly bound to the domain of nursing; it is also evident across other medical occupations. For the field of clinical consultation/diagnosis, Philipp et al. (1999: 40) examine intuition's relevance and conclude that 'an intuitive approach to clinical work can greatly improve the quality of our consultations'. Largely matching these conclusions, physicians seem to equally make use of and recognize the prevalence of intuitive experience (see Edwards, 2004).

Similarly, for the field of psychiatric diagnosis, Srivastava and Grube (2009: 105), utilize a detailed case study to demonstrate that intuition can play a significant role in the field: 'As we have demonstrated, however, intuition is an important component of psychiatric diagnosis and not clearly inferior to other diagnostic tools'. Furthermore Brien et al. (2009) identified that homeopathic practitioners frequently use intuition, and are aware of its significance in their practice. Their findings precisely illustrated that despite differences in clinical practice, homeopaths showed considerable similarities to other medical practitioners in their description and use of intuition in practice.

Finally, psychotherapist Hans Welling (2005) reveals a personal case study, as an example of a highly detailed process of intuition which is often used in treating psychological problems. It involves receiving insight and listening to intuitive reactions during arguments held in consultations. It is neatly used to diagnose imbalance in people's reasoning, which often leads to poor decision making, depression, etc. Thus it seems common across all of these medical professions that intuition is efficient at detecting harmful abnormalities, regardless of whether they are physical or psychological.

Surgical Risk Assessment

Assessing potential risks prior to any surgery often means the difference between life and death. In a prospective observational study by Woodfield et al. (2007), risk assessment was carried out using a 100 millimetre Visual Analog Scale (VAS) undertaken by the surgeons before and after surgery. As a number between 0 and 100, surgeons use this scale to determine the approximate risk for major complications. It was discovered that intuition is not as accurate as structured clinical risk assessment in predicting postoperative complications, but that it is still useful when combined with rational structured risk assessment (ibid.).

Medical occupations described above are not the only beneficiaries of intuition however. Discussed below, intuition is not only efficient in detecting physical or psychological abnormalities but also in detecting instantaneous danger.

FIREFIGHTING

Firefighting is a business where one must make very quick decisions on the basis of very little information. Murgallis (2005), writing in *Harvard Business Review*, claims that intuition is critical to high-performing firefighting teams. It can mean the difference between life and death. However, this kind of intuition is learned. Through training, reading, responding to emergencies, and talking with veterans, firefighters learn the cues and signals that indicate that certain things might occur. They have a vast mental databank that is based on experience and training (ibid.).

Firefighter and trainer Buckman (2006) similarly stresses the importance of the 'first two seconds' in firefighting. Subsequently, he discusses intuition's importance in an attempt to teach other firefighters, officers, chiefs and incident commanders about intuition's usability. Buckman first explains that most firefighters involved in bad situations say they felt something; they were not sure what it was, but they felt something that made them hesitate. Supposedly the brain helped them through an intuitive process (ibid.). Buckman additionally claims that the adaptive unconscious part of the brain quickly and quietly processes information. His concluding notion is that in order for a firefighter to become better at completing a fast size-up of a given situation, and hence produce good decisions, his brain must be trained and given reliable information to make the right intuitive decision in the first two seconds.

ARMY

Writing in the US *Military Review*, Reinwald (2000) emphasizes the term 'tactical intuition' to explain the power of intuitive thought in combat. Tactical intuition's immediate grasp of a situation and penetrating insight remain vital in today's Army. As historian Michael Handel wrote:

> Commanders are rarely in control over events on the battlefield. The successful general is not the one who carefully implements his original plans but rather the one who intuitively 'reads' the chaos on the battlefield well enough to take advantage of passing opportunities . . . Since it is impossible to weigh all of the relevant factors for even the simplest decisions in war, it is the military leader's intuition (his coup d'oeil) that must ultimately guide him in effective decision making. (Handel, 2001: 120–121)

Reinwald (2000) also believes that tactically, intuition enables leaders to make and implement decisions faster than an enemy counterpart and it actualizes the difference between competence and incompetence, victory or defeat. It affords the force as a whole, through the leader's expertise, to gain a critical advantage through increased tempo, sustained initiative and bold action.

Intuition is highly regarded in the army, as further evidenced by their LADP (Leadership Assessment and Development Program), which acknowledges intuition as a key leadership quality, especially for senior commanders, actively encouraging the awareness and development of it (McClean, 1995).

LAW ENFORCEMENT

In a study by the US National Institute of Justice (2004), scientists analysed the results of law enforcement officials' use of intuition, and derived
conclusions that went against the use of intuition. The 2004 report
thoroughly details the outweighing negatives to the use of intuition in
law enforcement. It outlines an informal survey of a National Academy
class in which about 90% of the respondents reported experiencing a 'gut
instinct', 'sixth sense', or a 'hairs rising on the back of your neck' feeling.
However, after the analysis of all the data retrieved, the scientists involved
concluded that intuition might actually be heightened vigilance and that
the use of intuition produces cognitive biases which can create problems in
investigative processes.

> Many times cases went off the rails because someone had a gut instinct and
> acted on it and then the whole thing goes down the tube. We need to be able
> to let go of intuition. Those following their intuitions are usually the ones that
> are most likely to get into trouble and not keep their mouth shut. (US National
> Institute of Justice, 2004: 5)

A more recent study (Tussey, 2007) assessing a sample of 37 municipal
police academy attendees and 37 undergraduate research participants
from a rural university in Western Pennsylvania has generated different
interpretations. Results supported the notion that intuition has a pertinent
role in law enforcement decision making and that, at the very least, it is
influenced through emotional arousal.

An excellent case study example of the use of intuition in law enforcement is provided in an extract from the FBI Law Enforcement Bulletin
(2004):

> During a drug-bust, an officer began calling out to the others, as well as broad-
> casting on the radio, to 'get the one in the red shirt; he's got a gun.' The man
> in the red shirt started to run down the sidewalk after he observed plainclothes
> officers approaching from both sides with their weapons drawn. The male
> surrendered, and the officers removed a .357-caliber revolver from his waist-
> band and placed him under arrest. While the officers were in the station house
> processing the prisoners and, completing the necessary paperwork, the officer
> who originally identified the seller turned to the officer who spotted the gunman
> and asked, 'How did you know he had a gun?' The officer who noticed the
> gunman hesitated for a moment and stated, 'I'm not sure why; I just knew.' As
> he began to recall the details and circumstances of the incident, he had to make
> a conscious effort to remember the observations that led him to conclude that
> the suspect possessed a handgun. First, the officer recalled that when pulling up
> to the scene, he saw the suspect sitting on the curb. As the officers approached
> and the crowd began to scatter, the man stood up and adjusted his waistband.

Next, the officer remembered that although the weather was extremely warm, the suspect had on a long-sleeved dress shirt with the shirttails hanging out. Finally, he recalled that immediately after the male stood up, he turned the right side of his body away from the officer and began to walk in another direction, grabbing the right side of his waistband as if securing some type of object. (Pinizzotto et al., 2004: 1–2).

The combination of these factors (interrelated data) led the officer to intuitively and quickly believe that the individual in the red shirt was armed (Pinizzotto et al.). The officer made these observations so rapidly that he experienced an 'instantaneous recognition' of danger. However, he could not articulate these reasons to his fellow officers until after the incident was resolved.

AIR TRAFFIC CONTROL

An article by Carlin Flora in *Psychology Today* describes a situation when Peter Nesbitt, an air traffic controller at Memphis International Airport, was watching a departing plane under his jurisdiction. With a glance at the radar scope, he noticed that an incoming aircraft seemed to be descending on the same flight path. 'Suddenly, I realised that the two planes were heading right toward each other', he said. 'I told my pilot to stop his climb and turn away. It was a case of instantly seeing it and doing something' (Flora, 2007: 1). Quick thinking is vital to shepherding planes, Nesbitt pointed out:

> We look at a scope with 40 airplanes – each on a different route, at a different altitude, a different speed – and intuitively understand whether things are going well or badly. Someone may later ask, 'Why did you tell that guy to turn?' and I might have to think about it for a minute. (Ibid.: 1)

As argued by Flora, the literature supports the notion that professionals, such as air traffic controllers, who make life and death decisions, almost always use a mix of intuition and analysis (Dane et al., 2005; Dijksterhuis, 2004). However, this does not mean that professional intuition is without limitations. Dane et al. concluded that in highly structured tasks, analytical decision making is superior at producing valuable outcomes. However, intuition is much more effective when the decision makers are domain experts who are facing tasks that are scantily (loosely) structured. Dijksterhuis discovered that when individuals are confronted with complex, yet loosely structured decisions (i.e., their attitudes toward potential roommates or evaluating the attractiveness of a place in which to live) unconscious thought can indeed produce superior decisions. Furthermore, in a truly chaotic and disordered environment, where cause and effect no longer have a linear relationship, the last thing you want to do is attempt to apply patterns to it. This is where intuition prospers.

Thus if intuition were to be placed on continuum of usefulness, ranging from least to most, we would find that the more structured and complex the situation, the more misleading and hence useless intuition becomes (Dane et al., 2005). For instance, deciding whether to invest in new machinery for your business involves looking at your financial stability, at budgets and weighing up costs and benefits. It is a highly structured and complex decision that would not be made best using intuition (ibid.). On this note, it is also important to keep in mind that intuitive influences may at times be invisible to us. This is because: (i) they are not always rapid and immediate and (ii) there can be, and often is, an intuitive component in analytically considered decisions. Individuals faced with complex situations can still produce quality decisions. Such individuals are aware of their intuitive influences and their subsequent effects on the choices of alternatives. They are hence more likely to find an effective balance between consideration of analysed data and alternatives, and the intuitive component.

AVIATION

A pioneering article by pilot Kathleen Bangs (2004) provides real-life examples, and thoroughly examines the impact of intuition's use in aviation. First, Bangs makes a seldom noted observation that a part of intuition that we often fail to realize is that our senses are stronger than we think. Sometimes our 'feelings' are based on fact and we just do not know it (ibid.). We hear things we disregard, catch things out of our peripheral vision that we ignore, notice a scent that smells 'funny' well before we see the smoke. Because we are so accustomed to over-rely on our vision, we all too frequently fail to take into account the ability of our other senses to convey information (ibid.). Bangs provides a personal account of one of her intuitive experiences:

> Almost two hours into the flight, I left the flight deck to go back into the cabin for a little chitchat with the flight attendants and to scrounge up some dinner. Fifteen minutes elapsed before I made it back to the cockpit. That's when it hit me – something was wrong. Standing just inside the roomy area behind the flight engineer's station, I looked around. The second officer and captain were sitting quietly, not doing anything in particular, and looking completely calm, almost drowsy. I climbed over the center console, strapped into my scat, and was overcome with an overwhelming feeling that something was truly amiss. Looking around the cockpit, there was nothing unusual to confirm my suspicions, at least not in my cursory sweep. No illuminated warning lights, no

bells and ringers sounding, no look of concern on anyone's face. Yet, I couldn't shake the feeling, and then it hit me. When I had left the flight deck earlier, the setting sun had been on the west – or right – side of the aircraft, where it should have been. Now below the horizon, the residual light from the sun was to the east – on our left side. We were headed exactly 180 degrees in the wrong direction – we had essentially reversed course.

It seemed so apparent that something was obviously wrong, yet everybody, and everything around me, was an island of calm in a lonely expanse of airspace. 'I think we've somehow gotten way off course,' I said hesitatingly to the captain. Coming to life, he sat up straight, shook his head, looked out the window, and after a few lively words of disbelief, immediately rolled the airplane into a 180-degree course change. Indeed, we had been heading north, back to Alaska, not south as he (and the flight engineer) believed. It turned out that when I had gone back into the cabin, the captain put the airplane into a very slight, almost imperceptible 2- to 3-degree bank turn, and then promptly forgot about it. (Ibid.: 1–2)

The lesson learnt is that when you are flying and you start to lose concentration, by fatigue, confusion or overload, the survival voice of instinct and intuition perseveres. Not only would it be an ideal time to listen, but it is also vital to speak up and take action (Bangs, 2004; Myers, 2007; Reistad-Long, 2009).

MANAGERIAL/ENTREPRENEURIAL (OTHER USES)

It is documented that intuition has been utilized in many other occupations and domains, which do not specifically relate to critical life or death professions. Among many others, some of these include management/executive positions (Sadler-Smith & Shefy, 2004; Sadler-Smith, 2008), education/teaching (Klein, 2004; Thorbjörn & Tomas, 2004), entrepreneurship (Mitchell et al., 2005) and human resource management (Caudron, 2001). It should be noted here that although the applicability of intuition within life or death/critical occupations seems to be mainly concerned with the recognition of danger, managerial and other uses demonstrate its capacity to also aid in the recognition of opportunity (Mitchell et al., 2005; Sadler-Smith, 2008).

CONCLUSIONS

Among the many occupations discussed, nursing, firefighting, aviation, law enforcement and the army appear to benefit appreciably from intuition. These occupations are frequently exposed to life or death and emergency situations. Danger recognition is a vital skill in such professions. Whether you are flying planes, entering into a burning building, surveying a drug-bust scene, or simply tending to a sick baby incapable of communication, recognition of danger proves to be highly related to the use of intuition. In all of the examples provided, intuition has consistently shown to be the prime competency in this respect. It is thus a *vital* construct. As a result of this emergent understanding, numerous academics and industry leaders are arguing that it is possible to teach aspects of intuition and that a move should be made towards obtaining reliable measures and methods for doing so (Effken, 2001; Langan-Fox & Shirley, 2003; Lyneham et al., 2008b; Seligman & Kahana, 2009; Smith et al., 2004; Sundgren & Styhre, 2004; Tesolin, 2007). The future of intuition as a modern construct of decision making rests therefore in the possibility of a unified definition, reliable measures, and methods for testing and teaching of it (Langan-Fox & Shirley, 2003).

REFERENCES

Bangs, K. 2004. Hearing voices: Intuition and accident avoidance. *Business & Commercial Aviation*, 95(3): 44–49.

Benner, P. 1984. *From novice to expert*. Menlo Park, CA: Addison-Wesley.

Benner, P., & Tanner, C. 1987. Clinical judgment: how expert nurses use intuition. *American Journal of Nursing*, 87: 23–32.

Brien, S., Dibb, B., & Burch, A. 2009. *The use of intuition in homeopathic clinical decision making: An interpretative phenomenological study*. Uxbridge, UK: Oxford University Press.

Buckman III, J. M. 2006. Volunteers corner: The first two seconds. *Fire Engineering*, 159(8): 12–16.

Caudron, S. 2001. Instinct basics. *Workforce*, 80(2): 20–21.

Dane, E. I., Rockman, K. W., & Pratt, M. G. 2005. *Should I trust my gut? The role of task characteristics in intuitive and analytical decision-making*. Paper presented at the annual meeting of the Academy of Management, Honolulu, HI, August.

Dijksterhuis, A. 2004. Think different: The merits of unconscious thought in preference development and decision-making. *Journal of Personality and Social Psychology*, 87(5): 586–598.

Easen, P., & Wilcockson, J. 1996. Intuition and rational decision making in professional thinking: A false dichotomy? *Journal of Advanced Nursing*, 24: 667–673.

Edwards, R. 2004. Intuition, evidence, and safety. *The Lancet*, 364: 387.

Effken, J. A. 2001. Informational basis for expert intuition. *Journal of Advanced Nursing*, 34(2): 246–255.

Flora, C. 2007. Intuition: Heads in the clouds – professionals who make life-and-death decisions use intuition and analysis to make judgments under time pressure. *Psychology Today*, 40(3): 12–13. Available at: http://www.psychologytoday.com/articles/200705/intuition-heads-in-the-clouds (accessed December 2, 2009).

Handel, M. I. 2001. *Masters of war – Classical strategic thought*. London: Frank Cass.

Klein, J. 2004. The effectiveness of intuitive and computer-assisted educational decision making in simple and complex educational situations. *Education and Information Technologies*, 9(4): 321–331.

Langan-Fox, J., & Shirley, D. A. 2003. The nature and measurement of intuition: Cognitive and behavioral interests, personality and experiences. *Creativity Research Journal*, 15(2&3): 207–222.

Lyneham, J., Parkinson, C., & Denholm, C. 2008a. Intuition in emergency nursing: A phenomenological study. *International Journal of Nursing Practice*, 14(2): 101–108.

Lyneham, J., Parkinson, C., & Denholm, C. 2008b. Explicating Benner's concept of expert practice: Intuition in emergency nursing. *Journal of Advanced Nursing*, 64(4): 380–387.

McClean, B. C. W. 1995. Intuition in modern command philosophy. *Military Review*, 75(5): 96–99.

McCutcheon, H. H. I., & Pincombe, J. 2001. Intuition: An important tool in the practice of nursing. *Journal of Advanced Nursing*, 35(3): 342–348.

Mitchell, J. R., Friga, P. N., & Mitchell, R. K. 2005. Untangling intuition mess: Intuition as a construct in entrepreneurship research. *Entrepreneurship: Theory and Practice*, 29(6): 653–679.

Murgallis, R. P. 2005. Performance under fire. *Harvard Business Review*, 83(7/8): 44–45.

Myers, D. G. 2007. The powers and perils of intuition. *Scientific American Mind*, 18(3): 24–31.

Paterson, J. G., & Zderad, L. Z. 1988. *Humanistic nursing.* New York: National League for Nursing.

Philipp, R., Philipp, E., & Thorne, P. 1999. The importance of intuition in the occupational medicine clinical consultation. *Occupational Medicine*, 49(1): 37–41.

Pinizzotto, A., Davis, E. F., & Miller III, C. E. 2004. Intuitive policing emotional/rational decision making in law enforcement. *FBI Law Enforcement Bulletin*, 73(2): 1–6.

Reinwald, B. R. 2000. Tactical intuition. *Military Review*, 80(5): 78–89.

Reistad-Long, S. 2009. Is your intuition calling? *Shape*, 29(2): 146–149.

Rew, L. 1986. Intuition: Concept analysis of a group phenomenon. *Advances in Nursing Science*, 8(2): 21–28.

Rew, L. 1988a. Intuition in decision-making. *Image: The Journal of Nursing Scholarship*, 20(3): 150–154.

Rew, L. 1988b. Nurses' intuition. *Applied Nursing Research*, 1(1): 27–31.

Sadler-Smith, E. 2008. The role of intuition in collective learning and the development of shared meaning. *Advances in Developing Human Resources*, 10(4): 494–508.

Sadler-Smith, E., & Shefy, E. 2004. The intuitive executive: Understanding and applying 'gut feel' in decision-making. *Academy of Management Executive*, 18(4): 76–91.

Schraeder, B., & Fischer, D. K. 1987. Using intuitive knowledge in the neonatal intensive care nursery. *Holistic Nursing Practice*, 1(3): 45–51.

Seligman, M. E. P., & Kahana, M. 2009. Unpacking intuition: A conjecture. *Perspectives on Psychological Science*, 4(4): 399–402.

Smith, A. 2009. Exploring the legitimacy of intuition as a form of nursing knowledge. *Nursing Standard*, 23(40): 35–40.

Smith, A. J., Thurkettle, M. A., Dela, C., & Felicitas, A. 2004. Use of intuition by nursing students: Instrument development and testing. *Journal of Advanced Nursing*, 47(6): 614–622.

Srivastava, A., & Grube, M. 2009. Does intuition have a role in psychiatric diagnosis? *Psychiatric Quarterly*, 80(2): 99–106.

Sundgren, M., & Styhre, A. 2004. Intuition and pharmaceutical research: The case of AstraZeneca. *European Journal of Innovation Management*, 7(4): 267–279.

Tesolin, A. 2007. Don't stifle intuition in your workplace. *T+D*, 61(6): 76–78.

Thorbjörn, J., & Tomas, K. 2004. Teacher's intuition-in-action: How teachers experience action. *Reflective Practice*, 5(3): 357–381.

Tussey, C. M. 2007. The role of intuition in decision making among law enforcement officials. *Dissertation Abstracts International: Section B: The Sciences and Engineering*, 68(3-B): 1957–2076.

US National Institute of Justice. 2004. *The nature and influence of intuition in law enforcement: Integration of theory and practice.* American Psychological Association, Marymount University Arlington, VA.

Welling, H. 2005. The intuitive process: The case of psychotherapy. *Journal of Psychotherapy Integration*, 15(1): 19–47.

Welsh, I., & Lyons, C. M. 2001. Evidence-based care and the case for intuition and tacit knowledge in clinical assessment and decision making in mental health nursing practice: An empirical contribution to the debate. *Journal of Psychiatric and Mental Health Nursing*, 8(4): 299–305.

Woodfield, J. C., Pettigrew, R. A., Plank, L. D., Landmann, M., & van Rij, A. M. 2007. Accuracy of the surgeons' clinical prediction of postoperative complications using a Visual Analog Scale. *World Journal of Surgery*, 31(10): 1912–1920.

11 Intuition in crisis management: the secret weapon of successful decision makers?
Bjørn T. Bakken and Thorvald Haerem

What do military commanders, police commissioners, fire marshals, and rescue team leaders have in common? They are frequently engaged in crisis management, that is, they make life-and-death decisions in situations characterized by time pressure, high risk, and ambiguous or lacking information (Sayegha et al., 2004). Superior decision-making skills are argued to be the cornerstone for military operations and unit effectiveness (Hidayat et al., 2009). Consequentially, researchers, educators and practitioners alike have long been in search of the mechanisms behind superior decision-making performance in crisis management. One important characteristic of successful decision making in crises is the use of intuition (Klein, 1998, 2003). The purpose of this chapter is to examine the role of intuition in crisis management decision making, and outline some of the preconditions for its effective use, especially in a military setting.

We define intuition as '[A]ffectively charged judgments that arise through rapid, nonconscious, and holistic associations' (Dane & Pratt, 2007: 33). The contrast to intuition is analysis, which is associated with the rational system described by Epstein et al. (1996) as intentional, primarily conscious and verbal, and relatively affect-free.

Few empirical studies, but several theoretical works (e.g., Sinclair & Ashkanasy, 2005) have highlighted the importance of intuition for managerial decision making in general. There is a growing interest in intuition (e.g., Gigerenzer, 2000; Hogarth, 2001) and in particular the role of experience-based intuition (e.g., Kahneman & Klein, 2009; Salas et al., 2010). Many models of military decision making, however, either omit or diminish the impact of intuitive decision making on the outcome of a military operation (e.g., Hidayat et al., 2009; Seiler, 2009). As a result, there appears to be a common belief among military officers that military decision making continues to be an elaborate process, characterized by clarity, rationality, careful consideration, and an abundance of information (Ramanathnan, 2009).

Military command, however, demands the ability of a decision maker to continuously adapt to a dynamic situation and changing conditions, and taking advantage of new possibilities as they arise, 'even in the face of friction, chaos and uncertainty' (NDCSC, 2007: 130). The situation is similar for the police, where for example the Crisis Management Manual of the Norwegian Police states that police officers should be proactive, rational and effective in the face of extraordinary events (such as a crisis). While activities such as planning and coordination with other actors are essential in a crisis, crisis management also requires rapid and decisive action (NNPD, 2007).

Based on our review of the literature, elaborate, effortful analysis, as well as rapid, experience-based intuition seems to be prescribed for the management of crises (e.g., Klein, 1998, 2003). Sayegha et al. (2004) have developed a model of managerial decision making under crisis, where rational (i.e., analytic) decision-making skills are predecessors to an intuitive decision process and outcome of the crisis. Recently, however, it has been common to conceptualize intuition and analysis within a 'dual process' perspective. In this perspective, intuition and analysis are considered separate ways of information processing that operate in parallel, independently but interconnected (Sinclair & Ashkanasy, 2005). It follows that analysis and intuition work in a complementary manner; and intuition is subconscious and based on experience. Dane and Pratt (2007) give an explicit account of experience and expertise in their model of factors influencing the effectiveness of intuitive decision making.

In the remainder of the chapter we shall use both theoretical and empirical studies to shed light on the following questions: how and why is intuition important in crisis management? Do intuitive people perform better in crises? What is the relationship between intuitive versus analytic cognitive style, and intuition as a cognitive style versus intuition as actual processing? We have structured the chapter in sections according to these questions. For each section we shall first present theoretical research, then we discuss recent studies that focus on the current question, and we conclude the chapter by outlining implications for future research and practice.

WHY AND HOW IS INTUITION IMPORTANT IN CRISIS MANAGEMENT?

Crisis management is what an organization deals with when it handles a major unpredictable event that threatens to harm the organization, its stakeholders, or the general public. Three elements are common to most definitions of crisis: a threat to the organization; the element of surprise; and a short decision time (Seeger et al., 2003). Examples of crises may be found in both the civilian and military domains: large-scale accidents and natural disasters, as well as sudden security threats, terrorist attacks and military strikes. The purpose of crisis management is to respond to, and recover from, such events (Department of Homeland Security, 2007).

The Crisis Management Manual of the Norwegian Police (NNPD, 2007) points out ten common characteristics of a crisis situation: a crisis comes as a surprise; there is a lack of control; vital interests are at stake; many actors are involved; one is subject to time pressure; the regular decision process has broken down; there is a focus on short-term solutions; uncertainty prevails; there is a lack of information; and there is a great interest and 'push' from outsiders. The manual defines crisis management as the sum of activities and actions that have to be carried out in order to secure life, health, vital functions to the society, material assets, damage reduction, and termination of the crisis (ibid.).

Superior decision-making skills are essential for successful operations (Hidayat et al., 2009). From the perspective of a defence organization, a crisis situation is positioned in the middle of the conflict intensity scale, between peace and (full-scale) armed conflict. Such a crisis usually starts with a surprise event, or a gradual escalation of an ongoing conflict, that is perceived as threatening. The time available to decide on a response is usually severely limited. A failure to respond, or making an inadequate response, could lead to catastrophic consequences (NDCSC, 2007).

Despite the focus on rational and deliberate planning in the military literature, we still find notable references to intuition, which indicates that it has been a central element of military strategy and leadership for centuries. During warfare, intuition is the commander's ability to, at a glance, assess the enemy situation and the condition of the terrain (Nyhus, 2000). Frederick II ('the Great') of Prussia (1712–86) is said to have recognized the intuitive thought process, which he believed stemmed from experience (ibid.). Napoleon's (1769–1821) successes on the battlefield were ascribed to his ability to rapidly assess a strategic situation and quickly arrive at possible goals and courses of action, despite the prevailing chaos and uncertainty (von Clausewitz, 1968). A more recent account of intuition in military decision making is represented in the OODA-loop by Colonel John Boyd (1927–97). The OODA-loop is a cyclic model of decision making encompassing both analytical assessment and rapid intuitive decision making (NDCSC, 2007).

A military commander faces vast amounts of diverse information during a crisis management operation, typically intelligence (information on the enemy situation), status information on own or subordinate units, and new or adjusted orders or directives from a higher level of command (ibid.). The contemporary military operational doctrine demands of the decision maker that he or she is able to analyse the effects of actions to as full extent as possible, while at the same time cautioning: 'An exaggerated focus on effects can lead to action paralysis' (ibid.: 55). Hodgkinson and Healey (2009) argue that the increasing complexity of the context is countered with increased flexibility in using both analysis and intuition in the decision making. In order to be successful in a dynamic and unpredictable environment, a decision maker must be open to a wide range of possibilities and options, and must also be adaptive to changes (Dane, 2010). There need not be a trade-off between increased expertise and flexibility, as long as the working environment is dynamic, such as in crisis management (ibid.; see also Haerem & Rau, 2007).

In military doctrinal documents we even find descriptions of desired characteristics to general cognitive processing which one assumes would be typical for successful commanders of combat operations (NATO SAS-050, 2007). A higher-level commander (General), for example, should have: experience, creativity, decisiveness, and understanding. A lower-level commander should possess: instinctive grasp of situation (sixth sense, 'fingerspitzengefühl'), flexibility, imagination, experience, creativity, decisiveness, and attention to detail. Soldiers in general should have experience and cognitive flexibility. From this, we see that the demand of officers and soldiers alike is not necessarily a 'clear-cut' analytic or intuitive decision maker, but instead a balanced 'combo' of an experienced and flexible actor that is capable of handling any kind of crisis situation, familiar as well as novel.

Gary Klein, who pioneered the field of naturalistic decision making (NDM), defines intuition as experience translated into action (Klein, 2003). Klein found that the classical (analytical) model of decision making does not describe real-life decision making very well (Klein, 1998, 2003), and proposed an alternative to the analytical model: the recognition-primed decision (RPD) model (Klein, 1998, 2003; Ross et al., 2004). This model combines intuitive with analytical processing, in that the decision maker recognizes patterns from cues in the environment, invoking appropriate action scripts (intuition); then uses mental simulation to critically evaluate courses of action (analysis). Empirical evidence suggests that decision makers naturally behave as predicted by the RPD model in crisis situations (Kaempf et al., 1996), and that when decisions are made in accordance with the RPD model there is a significant increase in speed (Thunholm, 2003) and performance (Johnston et al., 1997), compared to when more elaborate, analytical procedures are used.

Hence, both military practitioners and researchers propose that intuition is important. Yet, the production of methodologically sound empirical studies, testing the effectiveness and importance of intuition in such a setting, is to our knowledge still in an embryonic stage. In the next section we shall discuss the findings of some of the few published empirical studies of intuition and performance in crisis situations.

DO INTUITIVE PEOPLE PERFORM BETTER IN A CRISIS?

As suggested above, there is a small but increasing amount of research pointing to the superiority of intuition and intuitive decision making in crisis situations. The main tenet is that people tend to make better decisions using intuition, when conscious deliberation is hindered due to lack of time or by competing tasks (Evans, 2008). According to the contingency perspective, information processing in decision making is highly dependent on task and context factors (Payne, 1982). Hammond (1996) argued that both intuitive and analytical processing is present in most decisions, and the relative degree of each processing style depends on, for example, time pressure and task complexity (Dunwoody et al., 2000; Witteman et al., 2009). In responding to the question in the header of this section, however, we mainly focus on the individual differences that may play a role in intuitive decision making, and to a lesser extent on the task contingent factors.

There are many individual differences that play a role in the effectiveness of intuitive decision making (e.g., Kahneman & Klein, 2009; Pretz & Totz, 2007). Hodgkinson et al. (2009) point to individual differences in cognitive styles. A person's intuitive cognitive style refers to that person's preference for automatic, rapid and effortless information processing, whereas an analytic cognitive style refers to preferences for conscious, slow and deliberative information processing (Evans, 2008; Pacini & Epstein, 1999). This is in line with Pretz's (2008) definition of cognitive style, as individual differences in preferences to think intuitively or analytically. Both intuitive and analytic cognitive styles are assessed independently of task or situation (Hodgkinson et al., 2008), usually with an instrument such as the Rational–Experiential Inventory (REI; Hodgkinson et al., 2009; Pacini & Epstein, 1999) or the Preference for Intuition or Deliberation (PID; Betsch, 2008; Witteman et al., 2009).

Military commanders, police commissioners, fire marshals, and rescue team leaders also have in common that they acquire their knowledge and skills largely through intensive periods of training and exercise. For intuitive decision making to be effective, it is necessary that the decision maker acquires a certain level of experience. Klein (2003) argues that experience is a prerequisite for recognizing cues and patterns in the first place, and suggests that the ability to become a successful intuitive decision maker may be developed through training. A person who trains in intuitive decision making will learn to size up situations more quickly, recognize problems and anomalies of the situation, and feel confident when selecting the first course of action. He/she will also have a good sense of the next step(s), avoid being overwhelmed by data, and remain calm under uncertainty (ibid.). Klein also points out that intuitive decision making must be accompanied by the ability to think analytically. Ramanathnan (2009) adds that this complementary skill is particularly valuable when the decision maker encounters situations that are novel (see also Baylor, 2001).

Duggan's (2005) concept of 'strategic intuition' in military operations builds on Klein's RPD model, and implies that the decision maker continuously chooses between analysis and intuition, to an extent that both analysis and intuition are in fact used at the same time. Whether decision making at a given step is predominantly analytic or intuitive may depend on time and information available, in addition to the experience and preferences of the decision maker (cf. the 'cognitively versatile' decision maker; Hodgkinson & Clarke, 2007). In short: 'Strategic intuition is how experienced commanders think – and how we want inexperienced commanders to learn to think' (Duggan, 2005: 12).

Seemingly in contrast to what the NDM perspective suggests (e.g., Klein, 1998, 2003), Pretz (2008) found that an analytical style was appropriate for more experienced individuals, whereas the effect was inconclusive for the intuitive style. Haerem et al. (2008), on the other hand, found that the effectiveness of an intuitive cognitive style increased with higher levels of experience. The explanation for these differences in results might be that Pretz's study did not impose time pressure on the task doers, while Haerem et al.'s study did. Since the NDM perspective assumes time pressure we should not interpret Pretz's study as refuting the RPD model, perhaps to the contrary.

In another test of the effectiveness of intuitive style under time pressure, Bakken and Haerem (2010) found that intuitive cognitive style had incremental validity over cognitive ability and degree of experience in predicting task performance in a crisis management simulation. Together these studies provide support for dual process theory and the proposition that decision makers with an intuitive cognitive style (i.e., preferring intuitive decision making) will perform better in crisis situations. In the next section, we shall look more closely at the relationship between intuitive and analytic cognitive styles, as well as between intuitive style and intuitive processing.

INTUITION AND ANALYSIS: RELATIONSHIPS BETWEEN COGNITIVE STYLE AND PROCESSING

Across situations and contexts, some people tend to have a more intuitive cognitive style and others a more analytic cognitive style. It follows from theory that a person's cognitive style should have a direct influence on that person's cognitive processing (e.g., Epstein, 1990), so that a person who prefers intuition should also be more inclined to actually use intuition in decision making.

The Hodgkinson and Clarke (2007) framework of contrasting cognitive strategies and styles is an application of dual process theory to strategic management. The framework proposes that the effectiveness of decision making is contingent on a match between the style of the decision maker and the characteristics of the work setting. For example, 'detail conscious' (i.e., highly analytic) decision makers may perform well in decision problems where detailed, quantitative data are abundant and with ample time to make the decision. Conversely, 'big picture conscious' (i.e., highly intuitive) managers may excel in making decisions of strategic importance based on little data and with a short time to make a decision. However, both types of managers may experience decreased performance if there is a mismatch between style and context. A particularly superior combination in dynamic environments (such as crisis management) is the 'cognitively versatile' decision maker, who much prefers both intuitive and analytic processing. Such a person will have the ability to switch between processing modes as the situation dictates, and thereby attain superior performance in a wide range of different situations and contexts.

This 'versatility' capability may have special importance with respect to Klein's (1998) RPD model, in that the RPD fuses two processes: the first is how a decision maker sizes up the situation to recognize which course of action makes sense, and the second is how the decision maker evaluates a course of action by imagining its consequences.

It is a recognized weakness of existing research on intuition that researchers have consistently failed to distinguish between intuition as cognitive style and intuition as cognitive processing (Sinclair & Ashkanasy, 2005). A recent study by Bakken et al. (2010) investigated the relationship between cognitive style, cognitive processing, and performance in crisis management. They found that intuitive processing partially mediated a positive effect of intuitive cognitive style on task performance, but only for decision makers who were also highly analytic.

In another study, Bakken and Haerem (2010) found that intuitive and analytic cognitive style interacted and predicted task performance, when controlling for ability and experience. More specifically, they identified a positive effect of intuitive cognitive style on task performance, for decision makers who were highly analytic. Furthermore, intuitive cognitive style positively predicted intuitive processing, but only for experienced decision makers.

DISCUSSION AND IMPLICATIONS

In this chapter we have reviewed a growing stream of research on the effects of intuition, in order to provide answers to three questions: (i) How and why is intuition important in crisis management? (ii) Do intuitive people perform better in crises? (iii) What is the relationship between intuitive versus analytic cognitive style, and intuition as cognitive style versus intuition as actual processing? Empirical research on these topics is still relatively scarce. The few studies we have found provide some support for dual process theory (e.g., Epstein, 1990), and the Hodgkinson and Clarke (2007) framework in particular. Although additional research is needed, across a variety of settings, there is some empirical evidence pointing towards the 'cognitively versatile' decision maker as the superior performer in crisis management. Pretz's (2008) study, however, indicates that the contextual factors are critical in reaching that conclusion. Contextual factors, for example time pressure and task complexity, may influence the results so strongly that what is found in one context does not hold in another.

It is interesting to note that the finding of a partial mediation effect of intuitive processing between intuitive cognitive style and task performance (Bakken et al., 2010), indicates not only that intuitive cognitive style has both direct and indirect effects on task performance, but also that the degree of actual usage of intuitive processing is determined by other factors besides cognitive style. An implication of this could be that intuitive processing is beneficial in decision making regardless of cognitive style, possibly due to the nature of decision support, rules and routines prevailing in the situation. There may be situations, particularly in crisis management, where intuitive processing should indeed be encouraged and trained (Johnston et al., 1997).

When it comes to practical relevance for the management of crises, it is also interesting to note that a growing number of documents related to military doctrine make a call for re-examining the conditions under which crisis management operations are planned and conducted, and the implications for selection and training of personnel, as well as implications for organizational development (Alberts et al., 2010; Duggan, 2005; NDCSC, 2007). Based on current research it is difficult to make a clear prescription for decision makers in crisis management. Perhaps the finding with broadest support is that under time pressure, intuitive decision making is well advised. Even this finding, however, is not without reservations: if you are an expert you may do well to trust your intuition, but not if you are a novice.

Overall, it seems that this research area is gaining practical relevance and therefore also a demand for increased progress. In the words of the Norwegian Chief of Defence: 'We have moved from a situation in which the Armed Forces had a clearly defined and all-embracing threat which we were trained and equipped to resist – and which we could actually plan for – to a far more complex and unpredictable spectrum of possible scenarios' (NDCSC, 2007: 3). The Director of the Strategic Studies Institute, US Army War College, comments on what he sees as an increasing gap between formal analytical methods and intuitive decision making in military command organizations, and argues that an effective commander appears to be one who is able to adapt, and also to depart from formal methods of decision making (Duggan, 2005).

This chapter has contributed to clarifying the role and importance of intuition with respect to performance in crisis management decision making, and outlined some of the preconditions for its effective use, especially in a military setting. The progress of this research area will determine to what extent it can be of practical relevance for the management of crises in the future.

REFERENCES

Alberts, D. S., Huber, R. K., & Moffat, J. 2010. *NATO NEC C2 Maturity model (N2C2M2)*. DoD Command and Control Research (NATO SAS-065). Available at: www.dodccrp.org (accessed 16 September 2010).

Bakken, B. T., & Haerem, T. 2010. *Cognitive styles in decision making: Comparing unitary and dual-system approaches to predict performance in simulated crisis management tasks*. Paper presented at the 2010 Annual meeting of the Academy of Management, Montreal, Canada, 6–10 August.

Bakken, B. T., Haerem, T., & Kuvaas, B. 2010. *Intuition and analysis in decision making: Mediated and moderated relationships between preferences, processing and performance* (Research Report). Oslo, Norway: Norwegian School of Management.

Baylor, A. 2001. A U-shaped model for the development of intuition by level of expertise. *New Ideas in Psychology*, 19: 237–244.

Betsch, C. 2008. Chronic preferences for intuition and deliberation in decision making: Lessons learned about intuition from an individual differences approach. In H. Plessner, C. Betsch, & T. Betsch (Eds.), *Intuition in judgment and decision making*: 231–250. New York and London: Lawrence Earlbaum Associates.

Dane, E. 2010. Reconsidering the trade-off between expertise and flexibility: A cognitive entrenchment perspective. *Academy of Management Review*, 35(4): 579–603.

Dane, E., & Pratt, M. G. 2007. Exploring intuition and its role in managerial decision-making. *Academy of Management Review*, 32(1): 33–54.

Department of Homeland Security. 2007. *National preparedness guidelines.* Available at: www.dhs.gov (accessed 12 April 2010).

Duggan, W. 2005. *Coup d'oeil: Strategic intuition in army planning.* Available at: www. StrategicStudiesInstitute.army.mil (accessed 16 September 2010).

Dunwoody, P. T., Haarbauer, E., Mahan, R. P., Marino, C., & Tang, C.-C. 2000. Cognitive adaptation and its consequences: A test of Cognitive Continuum Theory. *Journal of Behavioral Decision Making,* 13: 35–54.

Epstein, S. 1990. Cognitive–Experiential Self-Theory. In L. A. Pervin (Ed.), *Handbook of personality. Theory and research*: 165–192. London: Guilford Press.

Epstein, S., Pacini, R., Denes-Raj, V., & Heier, H. 1996. Individual differences in intuitive–experiential and analytical–rational thinking styles. *Journal of Personality and Social Psychology,* 71(2): 390–405.

Evans, J. St. B. T. 2008. Dual-process accounts of reasoning, judgment and social cognition. *Annual Review of Psychology,* 59: 255–78.

Gigerenzer, G. 2000. *Adaptive thinking: Rationality in a real world.* New York: Oxford University Press.

Haerem, T., Bakken, B. T., & Rau, D. 2008. *Decision making under time pressure: The influence of cognitive styles and expertise on task performance.* Paper presented at the 2008 Annual Meeting of the Academy of Management, Anaheim, CA, 8–13 August.

Haerem, T., & Rau, D. 2007. The influence of degree of expertise and objective task complexity on perceived task complexity and performance. *Journal of Applied Psychology,* 92(5): 1320–1331.

Hammond, K. R. 1996. *Human judgment and society policy: Irreducible uncertainty, inevitable error, unavoidable injustice.* New York: Oxford University Press.

Hidayat, E. R., Putranto, J. P., & Thjahjono, A. E. 2009. Military decision-making for field commanders. The Indonesian National Army's experience. In P. Greener, & J. Stouffer (Eds.), *Decision-making: International perspectives*: 37–60. Kingston, Ontario: Canadian Defence Academy Press.

Hodgkinson, G. P., & Clarke. I. 2007. Conceptual note: Exploring the cognitive significance of organizational strategizing: A dual-process framework and research agenda. *Human Relations,* 60: 243–255.

Hodgkinson, G. P., & Healey, M. P. 2009. Psychological foundations of dynamic capabilities: Reflexion and reflection in strategic management. In G. T. Solomon (Ed.). *Proceedings of the 69th Annual Meeting of the Academy of Management,* Chicago (CD).

Hodgkinson, G. P., Langan-Fox, J., & Sadler-Smith, E. 2008. Intuition: A fundamental bridging construct in the behavioural sciences. *British Journal of Psychology,* 99(1): 1–27.

Hodgkinson, G. P., Sadler-Smith, E., Sinclair, M., & Ashkanasy, N. 2009. More than meets the eye. Intuition and analysis revisited. *Personality and Individual Differences,* 47: 342–346.

Hogarth, R. M. 2001. *Educating intuition.* Chicago and London: University of Chicago Press.

Johnston, J., Driskell, J., & Salas, E. 1997. Research report: Vigilant and hypervigilant decision making. *Journal of Applied Psychology,* 82(4): 614–622.

Kaempf, G. L., Klein, G., Thordsen, M. L., & Wolf, S. 1996. Decision making in complex naval command-and-control environments. *Human Factors,* 38(2): 220–231.

Kahneman, D., & Klein, G. 2009. Conditions for intuitive expertise. A failure to disagree. *American Psychologist,* 64(6): 515–526.

Klein, G. 1998. *Sources of power: How people make decisions.* Cambridge, MA: MIT Press.

Klein, G. 2003. *Intuition at work.* New York: Doubleday.

NATO SAS-050. 2007. *Exploring new command and control concepts and capabilities.* RTO technical report (RTO-TR-SAS-050). Available at: www.rta.nato.int (accessed 16 September 2010).

NDCSC (Norwegian Defence Command and Staff College). 2007. *Norwegian Armed Forces joint operational doctrine.* Defence Staff, Oslo.

NNPD (Norwegian National Police Directorate). 2007. *Politiets beredskapssystem del I (PBS I). Håndbok i krisehåndtering* [The police preparedness system. Handbook of crisis management]. Oslo: Norwegian National Police Directorate.

Nyhus, J. K. 2000. *Intuisjonens rolle ved ledelse og beslutningstaking. En studie av hvordan militære lederes intuisjon påvirker deres effektivitet i operativ stab* [The role of intuition in leadership and decision making. A study of how military leaders' intuition affects their effectiveness in the operative staff]. Oslo: Norwegian Defence Command and Staff College.

Pacini, R., & Epstein, S. 1999. The relation of rational and experiential information processing styles to personality, basic beliefs, and the ratio-bias phenomenon. *Journal of Personality and Social Psychology*, 76: 972–987.

Payne, J. W. 1982. Contingent decision behavior. *Psychological Bulletin*, 92: 382–402.

Pretz, J. 2008. Intuition versus analysis: Strategy and experience in complex everyday problem solving. *Memory and Cognition*, 26(3): 554–566.

Pretz, J., & Totz, K. S. 2007. Measuring individual differences in affective, heuristic, and holistic intuition. *Personality and Individual Differences*, 43: 1247–1257.

Ramanathnan, K. 2009. Building critical thinking and creative thinking in military decision-making. In P. Greener, & J. Stouffer (Eds.), *Decision-making: International perspectives*: 1–17. Kingston, Ontario: Canadian Defence Academy Press.

Ross, K. G., Klein, G. A., Thunholm, P., Schmitt, J. F., & Baxter, H. C. 2004. The Recognition-Primed Decision Model. *Military Review*, July–August: 6–10.

Salas, E., Rosen, M. A., & DiazGranados, D. 2010. Expertise-based intuition and decision making in organizations. *Journal of Management*, 36: 941–973.

Sayegha, L., Anthony, W. P., & Perrewé, P. L. 2004. Managerial decision-making under crisis: The role of emotion in an intuitive decision process. *Human Resource Management Review*, 14: 179–199.

Seeger, M. W., Sellnow, T. L., & Ulmer, R. R. 2003. *Communication and organizational crisis.* Westport, CT: Praeger.

Seiler, S. 2009: The impact of team structure, organization, and communication flow on problem solving activities in working groups: A comparison between military and civilian task forces. In P. Greener, & J. Stouffer (Eds.), *Decision-making: International perspectives*: 85–100. Kingston, Ontario: Canadian Defence Academy Press.

Sinclair, M., & Ashkanasy, N. M. 2005. Intuition. Myth or a decision-making tool? *Management Learning*, 36(3): 353–370.

Thunholm, P. 2003. *Military decision making and planning: Towards a new prescriptive model.* PhD dissertation, Stockholm University, Stockholm.

Von Clausewitz, C. 1968. *On war* (edited by A. Rapaport). Harmondsworth, Middlesex: Penguin Books.

Witteman, C., van den Bercken, J., Claes, L., & Godoy, A. 2009. Assessing rational and intuitive thinking styles. *European Journal of Psychological Assessment*, 25(1): 39–47.

12 The critical decisions vortex – interplay of intuition, reason, and emotion: comparison of three dynamic industries
Jean-Francois Coget

The rational decision-making paradigm has dominated research in decision making for years. Rational decision making is typically described as (i) defining a problem, (ii) identifying relevant criteria dimensions of the problem, (iii) weighing the different criteria in terms of importance, (iv) generating alternative solutions that address the problem, (v) rating each alternative on the relevant criteria, and (vi) choosing the optimal solution (Bazerman, 1998; Kahneman et al., 1987; Simon, 1968). Rational decision-making models have been widely used in economics, management science, sociology, and political science (March, 1991). One of their main benefits is that they allow researchers to model human behavior with a high degree of mathematical formality. They are at the heart of such popular models as game theory (Von Neuman & Morgenstern, 1944) or expectancy theory (Vroom & McCrimmon, 1968).

In spite of their popularity, these models have been criticized for imposing norms such as rationality, conscious and effortful analysis, and choice that individuals often deviate from in practice. Simon's work (1968), for instance, has demonstrated that cognitive limits make it impossible for people to gather complete information and find the optimal solution to a problem. In practice, their rationality is bounded. Kahneman and Tversky (1979) further showed that individuals rely on heuristics that systematically bias their judgment even when they are not overloaded cognitively.

Recently, an alternative model of intuitive decision making has captured the attention of management scholars. It is characterized as a rapid, non-conscious process that produces affectively charged judgments through holistic associations (Dane & Pratt, 2007; Sinclair & Ashkanasy, 2005). This model has been found to be faster and more effective under certain conditions than rational decision making (Dane & Pratt, 2007; Simon, 1987). Furthermore, some managers report that they use it more often than the rational model (Andersen, 2000), and increasingly so as they climb the professional ladder (Sadler-Smith & Shefy, 2004).

Klein (1993) has vividly illustrated the use of intuition in his work with firefighters and soldiers, who, when making decisions in the field, often do not generate multiple alternatives and then choose one among them. Rather, skilled firefighters generate only one feasible course of action and enact it. In intuitive decision making, the cognitive process of rational analysis and choice is replaced by sizing up a situation and matching it with a prototypical situation that evokes a given course of action. Research on expert decision making has clearly established that repeated exposure to specific types of problems through practice and training is related to the ability to excel in a domain of activity (Ericsson & Charness, 1994).

Despite considerable progress in the field, two questions remain unanswered. First, the role that emotions play in intuitive decision making is still unclear, with some researchers regarding emotions as essential to intuition, and others considering them a distraction. Second, little research has investigated how intuitive and rational decision making interact (Dane & Pratt, 2007). Traditionally, emotions were considered to bias rational decisions (e.g., Janis & Mann, 1977). Therefore the advice was to ignore or control them. Recent research on emotional intelligence, however, has started to challenge such wisdom (Goleman, 1995; Salovey & Mayer, 1990). There is now a growing body of research evidencing the positive role that emotion can play in rational decision making (for extensive reviews, see Forgas, 1995; Loewenstein & Lerner, 2003), and intuitive decision making (Burke & Miller, 1999; Hayashi, 2001; Sadler-Smith & Shefy, 2004). Current studies examining intuition and emotion are limited, however, in that they tend to focus on generalized mood rather than on emotion. Moreover, the relationship has been explored primarily in the laboratory rather than in the field, and most studies focus on incidental rather than direct emotional experience.

THE CRITICAL DECISIONS VORTEX MODEL

Coget and Keller (2010) have proposed a model of how rational decision making, intuitive decision making, and emotion supplement, complement, or impede each other: the 'critical decisions vortex' (see Figure 12.1). The critical decisions vortex is a meta-process through which experts continually shift among the three processes of thinking, intuiting, and feeling in order to make the right decisions and take action. The metaphor of a 'vortex' attempts to reflect the relentless shifting that occurs among processes, and the lack of apparent order in which the shifts happen.

While decision-making models typically seek to identify neat causal sequences among their variables of interest, such as thoughts, intuitions, emotions, decisions, or actions, which they describe as discrete phenomena, from a phenomenological point of view, individuals experience reality

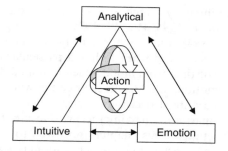

Figure 12.1   The Critical Decisions Vortex Model

in continuous, rather than in discrete terms (Bohm, 1980; Chia, 1994; Derrida, 1981). The subjective, moment-to-moment experience of a decision maker is a flow of thinking, intuiting, feeling, and acting, rather than discrete thoughts, intuitions, emotions, and actions (Chia, 1994; Coget, 2004). While after the fact, decision makers might retrospectively invent an artificial story that connects sequentially a thought to a decision to an action (Weick, 1995), in the moment, the flows of thinking, intuiting, feeling, and acting interact with one another in numerous feedback loops, at times reinforcing, competing, or impeding one another (Coget, 2004; Coget & Keller, 2010).

The critical decisions vortex model was developed in the emergency room context. The vortex has three poles: reasoning, intuiting, and feeling. Coget and Keller (2010) found that when one of the poles is privileged to the exclusion of the others, emergency room doctors risk committing a mistake or decreasing the quality and speed of their diagnosis and treatment. While intuitive and rational decision making can point in different directions, they nonetheless complement each other: intuition can alert physicians to revisit an earlier diagnosis based on rational conclusions, or provide a fast diagnosis in urgent cases where the rational process would be too slow. Rational decision making can take over where intuitive decision making dead-ends, and confirm or refine intuitive conclusions. While overwhelming emotions can interrupt both types of decision making, emotions of lower intensity can initiate intuitive decision making, energize action, facilitate empathy, help doctors recognize their own limits, and help them solve moral dilemmas. In other words, they provide valuable input for rational diagnosis.

Emotion is an affective state accompanied by physiological reactions, such as blushing, acceleration of the heartbeat, trembling, and sweating (James, 1884), triggered by internal or external stimuli, and appraised in terms of its consequences for our well-being (Frijda, 1986; Lazarus, 1999).

Emotions have an intensity – high or low – and a valence – pleasant or unpleasant – (Feldman, 1995; Russell, 1999), and are generally of short duration (Ekman, 1994). Emotional intensity is broadly related to the degree of arousal experienced when feeling a particular emotion (Posner et al., 2005). This is distinct from mood which is more diffuse, less intense, lasts longer than emotion, and has no clear cause, whereas emotion does (Ekman, 1994). The critical decisions vortex model focuses mostly on emotions and examines how they interact with intuition and rationality in different work settings. This chapter endeavors to extend Coget and Keller's (2010) original work in the emergency room to two other dynamic environments: movie sets and wineries.

METHODOLOGY

As stated above, data were collected from three different industry settings: emergency rooms (ERs), in the medical industry, movie sets, in the film industry, and vineyards/wineries, in the wine industry. The ER data were gathered through a series of interviews with an experienced ER doctor, and have been analyzed in detail elsewhere (ibid.). The data concerning movie sets and vineyards/wineries were collected and analyzed through a qualitative method inspired by Coget's (2009) dialogical inquiry paired with a grounded theory approach (Glaser & Strauss, 1967). First, seven movie directors and eight owner/winemakers were interviewed in order to gain insight into their activity and the particular choices they made. They were then shadowed and videotaped in the field (i.e., on set, and at their vineyards/wineries) as they made critical decisions. After analyzing the videos, follow-up interviews were conducted with the subjects about how they made important decisions, captured on video.

THE CRITICAL DECISIONS VORTEX IN MOTION: EXAMPLES FROM ER, MOVIE SETS, AND WINERIES

The Critical Decisions Vortex in the ER

Characteristics of the ER

The ER is a turbulent environment characterized by high stakes, high stress, rapidity, incomplete information, overwhelming data, and overlapping processes (Klein et al., 2006). It is typically the first point of entry in the hospital system for patients suffering potentially serious, or even life-threatening medical conditions (Whittaker et al., 2004). The two main tasks of an ER doctor are to rapidly diagnose patients and treat them. In theory, diagnosis is supposed to happen first and be followed by treatment. In practice, however, the two intersect in multiple feedback loops, treatment often preceding full diagnosis (Coget & Keller, 2010; Groopman, 2007).

How the critical decisions vortex operates in the ER

Diagnosis consists of narrowing down increasing amounts of information about a case to a pattern that can be acted upon, which happens thanks to the three integrated processes of the critical decisions vortex: rational decision making, intuitive decision making, and emotions. Rational decision making is the default pole of the vortex. At the beginning of a diagnosis, when receiving information from the triage nurse, paramedics, or other ER personnel, doctors classify the case based on the key symptom(s), and then follow an algorithm designed to figure out the possible causes of the symptom(s) (Bache et al., 2003). Rational decision making is also the pole of the critical decisions vortex that rookie doctors have to rely on at first, because they do not have enough experience to use intuitive decision making (Groopman, 2007).

As ER doctors garner more and more experience, they increasingly incorporate intuitive decision making (Greenhalgh, 2002). All of the cases they treat get stored in their memory in more vivid detail than abstract knowledge, with their associated symptoms. On noticing subtle patterns, such as the color of skin, activity level, angle of limbs, smells, sounds of different organs, and subjective descriptions of pain, ER doctors are able to immediately diagnose an ailment without conscious need to reason.

Rational and intuitive decision making can interact in different ways (Coget & Keller, 2010). Intuitive decision making can support rational decision making by detecting anomalies that technology and rational analysis fail to detect, thus redirecting a diagnosis away from the wrong algorithm, preventing errors and saving lives. It can also outperform rational decision making in complex, yet urgent situations. In some cases, ER doctors just take a look at a patient and get the correct hunch. Generally the hunch is then confirmed by further analysis. Acting on intuition to treat patients can be essential given the limited time that ER doctors have for treatment and the limited resources of the ER. Intuitive decision making is also useful in synthesizing overwhelming amounts of information, which has become particularly helpful as technology continually increases the level of details available.

Rational decision making can assist intuitive decision making in several ways as well. First, it can confirm an intuitive hunch. This is why doctors order tests to confirm their initial diagnoses. It can also outperform intuitive decision making where the latter fails. Occasionally, an initial diagnosis stops making sense, forcing doctors to find an algorithm that will help them progress in their inquiry.

While strong emotions can impede decision making by blurring judgment, or temporarily paralyzing action, moderate emotions can also enhance it in five ways (ibid.):

1. Emotions can inform judgment by initiating intuitive decision making or providing diagnostic information for rational decision making.
2. Emotions can assist decision making in the ER by energizing action.
3. The particular emotion of empathy is crucial for ER doctors as it helps them relax patients, which facilitates diagnostic communication and the administration of care. Empathy in itself is a form of care that is useful to give patients, although it is often overlooked by the medical community (Maguire, 1999; Morse et al., 2008; Taylor, 1988).
4. Emotions help doctors recognize their limits and manage themselves so that they do not 'spin around', a term used in the ER to refer to moments when a doctor does not know which actions to prioritize any longer and loses precious time hesitating between them, or overtaxes him/her self to the point of making mistakes.
5. Emotions influence doctors' implicit moral judgment when they attribute the limited resources of the hospital and prioritize cases. For more details, see Coget and Keller (2010).

The Critical Decisions Vortex on Movie Sets

Characteristics of movie sets

Like the ER, movie sets are turbulent environments (Coget, 2004). While no human life is at risk, movie sets are nonetheless fraught with time pressures, complexity, ambiguity, and stress. During the production phase of movie making – when a movie is actually shot – expensive equipment, crew, and cast are mobilized to make a film in just a few weeks (Travis, 1999). Because of this, every minute lost on set costs vast amounts of money, which creates a tremendous amount of pressure during the shoot (Coget et al., 2009). Since movie crews are temporary organizations that operate in often unknown terrains, unpredictable circumstances, such as weather events, malfunctioning equipment, or unforeseen legal issues, often disrupt the shooting plan, forcing the director to improvise in urgency (Bechky, 2006). Add to the mix often capricious and emotional cast members and the challenges of a collective creative project, and you have a very turbulent environment (Bart & Guber, 2002). During the production phase, movie directors are in charge of organizing this complex temporary enterprise, leading and managing the crew and cast to produce movies that conform to their vision, the script, requirements of production companies, and that remain on budget (Travis, 1999). At any given moment on set, directors are diagnosing, prioritizing, and addressing a number of issues that they notice or that their crew bring to their attention.

Three key differences can be noted between the ER and movie sets. First, movie directing is not as codified as medicine. While roles are very well determined on movie sets (Baker & Faulkner, 1991; Bechky, 2006), directors are not as extensively and rigorously trained as doctors. There are few prescribed algorithms for solving specific problems. Problem solving is rather communicated through stories and examples (e.g., Bart & Guber, 2002), which makes it more likely that directors will rely on their expertise rather than on formal knowledge, and therefore use intuition when making a decision. Second, unlike the practice of medicine, movie directing is a creative activity. Third, while emotions are accepted as an avoidable part of the ER, emotions hold center stage in the entertainment industry. Indeed, movie directing is often defined as producing emotions (Bart & Guber, 2002; Travis, 1999).

How the critical decisions vortex operates on movie sets

Results show that directors use their intuition in two distinct ways. First, they use their experience to intuitively diagnose and solve small issues, such as adjusting actors, choosing types of shots and coverage, or noticing when a special effect becomes dangerous. Second, directors use their intuition to keep track of the big picture, their vision of the movie, and to update it. Shooting often involves abandoning the plan that was devised in pre-production to accommodate changing conditions, such as the weather or unforeseen issues, or to take advantage of the creative talent of the cast and crew, who might enhance the original vision of the director. For instance, one director who had an argument with an actress on set intuitively decided to 'use' her extreme anger by shooting a scene where she needed to appear angry instead of trying to defuse her anger and delay production.

While most of the rational decision making that directors engage in seems to be happening during the pre-production phase, when they plan their shoot, directors still seem to be using rational decision making on set in two ways. First, they constantly discuss the situation with their crew and cast, who often bring issues to them. These discussions, particularly with the technical crew, such as the director of photography, often allow them to solve issues rationally. Second, directors resort to rational decision making on set when they lack the expertise to make an effective intuitive decision quickly. One director, for instance, decided to empty the set and take the time to rehearse lines with an actress who could not deliver them, based on what she had learned in her film school directing classes because she could not figure out what the problem with the actress was.

Because of the emotional nature of the industry, most directors express their emotions more freely than in other settings. Like in the ER, emotions motivate and sustain directors. They monitor their own emotions to see whether a scene is likely to produce emotion in the public. They then express these emotions to their crew and cast in order to redirect their efforts. Like in the ER, very strong emotions may derail directors. Several directors, for instance, acknowledged their insecurity in dealing with difficult, overly dramatic actors, describing how emotional confrontations kept nagging them during a shoot. Nonetheless, most directors are comfortable with their and others' emotions, and frequently use them. For more details on all these situations, see Coget (2004) and Coget et al. (2009).

In a forthcoming study based on the same dataset, my colleagues and I have paid particular attention to the emotions of anger and fear. We found that moderate fear motivates the use of rational decision making, while moderate anger seems to be associated with the use of expert intuitive decision making (expert IDM). Intense anger or fear, however, are associated with a form of decision making we label emotional intuitive decision making (emotional IDM). Emotional IDM is associated in memory with personal experiences that may be irrelevant to the professional situation and produces impulsive actions that are often less effective than the actions produced by expert IDM.

The Critical Decisions Vortex in Wineries

Characteristics of small vineyards and wineries
The activity of the owner–winemakers of small vineyards and wineries includes viticulture (grape growing) and enology (winemaking). Viticulture focuses on 'vineyard development from initial planning to picking vineyard site selection; choice of rootstock, vine variety, and clone; soil testing and soil preparation; choice of vine density and trellis system; vine planting, training and pruning, control of vine pests, vine diseases, and weeds; fruit sampling and harvest' (Robinson, 1994: 1050). Enology means the study of wine; the practice of which is winemaking. Crushing, fermentation, clarification, stabilization and aging are a series of decisions that determine wine quality (Ough, 1992).

Viticulture is an agricultural process that unfolds over a yearly cycle, and winemaking is a process that lasts several months, sometimes years. Hence, the activity of small winemakers is not as turbulent as that of ER doctors or movie directors. However, during key moments of the winemaking process, such as harvest, their activity becomes somewhat turbulent (Cox, 1998). Once the winemaker has decided to harvest, which is a crucial decision, crews need to move very quickly because grapes are fragile and sensitive to hot temperatures. Equipment malfunction and logistical errors are bound to happen and need to be addressed quickly. Delicate operations, such as storing and sorting need to be coordinated simultaneously, and the process of fermentation, the first step of winemaking, begins. Like the film industry, winemaking is a creative process that involves exploration and innovation. It requires that winemakers make a series of interconnected decisions about how to process their grapes and juice so as to craft the best wine they can (ibid.).

Viticulture and winemaking is an interesting example, lying mid-way between medicine and filmmaking. While both are scientifically studied and have long traditions, they are nonetheless less codified than medicine, and few winemakers have formally studied their craft. Most of them have learned from experience and by exchanging information with their peers (Heimoff, 2007). One of the characteristics that all three settings – the ER, movie sets, and small vineyards/wineries – have in common is that the activity of the focal actors is physical and requires quick logistical decisions. Therefore they are more likely than typical office settings to mobilize intuition and emotions, which are processes that are heavily connected to physiological reactions and the body (Dane & Pratt, 2007; James, 1884).

How the critical decisions vortex operates in the activity of small winemakers

Winemakers use both rational and intuitive decision-making approaches. For example, an important decision in the wine cycle is deciding when to harvest grape berries (Cox, 1998). The berries will provide the best juice, which in turn will contribute to a better wine, when they are ripe. To determine ripeness, winemakers routinely tour their vineyard around harvesting time to taste the berries. They also perform chemical analyses on them to determine their sugar (Brix) and acidity (pH) levels. Many winemakers confide that while numbers matter, they rely more heavily on their intuitive tasting experience of the berries to determine ripeness. Their intuitive experience relies on years of experience in harvesting at different times with different weather patterns. Relying on chemical analysis can be considered a rational approach, while tasting berries is rather an intuitive approach. The same story repeats itself at different stages of the winemaking process, such as during vinification: winemakers rely on both careful chemical analyses of their juice, and impressions garnered through their senses and shaped by years of experimenting with different winemaking decisions. One winemaker, who unlike many others, studied oenology formally, explained that what he learned in school does not help him make good wine. For that, he relies on his intuition, his senses, and experimentation that might go counter to 'established' scientific knowledge. He only resorts to the rational algorithms he learned in school when he has made a big mistake in the winemaking process and has to fix it.

Like movie directors, winemakers are creative, and passionate about their craft. Beyond intuition, emotions and bodily sensations are very important in winemaking and marketing: wine depends on what you taste, and how it feels. Wine tasting has been compared to poetry: what the experience of drinking wine reminds you of determines your subjective tasting experience of the wine, which will determine your evaluation of its quality (Smith, 2007). One winemaker avows that he constantly monitors the emotion he and his workers evince around his wine: he believes that emotions affect the quality of water (Emoto, 2005) and therefore bans negative emotions around his wine. Whether emotions actually reflect in water molecules is beside the point. His care for his wine is communicated to his workers and his clients and positively affects his decision making and results (he produced 95 and 97 Parker-rated wines). All of the winemakers studied tend to freely express emotions that reflect their passion for their wine, which clearly seems to positively influence their marketing image with regard to their customers. Wine is also associated with social moments, which usually bring positive emotions.

CONCLUSION

The critical decisions vortex contributes to the research on decision making by suggesting that the distinction between thought, intuition, emotion, and action is more blurry than often considered in the literature. This chapter has extended the work of Coget and Keller (2010) in ERs and applied the critical decisions vortex to two other environments: movie sets and wineries – comparing and contrasting the dynamics in these three settings. While these two new contexts are quite different from ERs and from each other, they nonetheless reveal that movie directors and winemakers do rely on the meta-process of the critical decisions vortex as well as ER doctors, although in slightly different ways. In particular, emotions are more readily accepted as a central aspect of film- and winemaking and therefore influence thinking and intuiting more strongly in movie directors and winemakers than in ER doctors. Further applications of the critical decisions vortex model to other settings might yield yet more interesting observations and conclusions.

REFERENCES

Andersen, J. A. 2000. Intuition in managers: Are intuitive managers more effective? *Journal of Managerial Psychology*, 15(1): 46–63.

Bache, J. B., Armitt, C. R., & Gadd, C. 2003. *Handbook of emergency department procedures.* London, Mosby Inc.

Baker, W. E., & Faulkner, R. R. 1991. Role as resource in the Hollywood film industry. *American Journal of Sociology*, 97(2): 279–309.

Bart, P., & Guber, P. 2002. *Shoot out: Surviving fame and (mis)fortune in Hollywood.* New York: G. P. Putnam's Sons.

Bazerman, M. H. 1998. *Judgment in managerial decision making*, Vol. 5. New York: John Wiley & Sons.

Bechky, B. 2006. Gaffers, gofers, and grips: Role-based coordination in temporary organizations. *Organization Science*, 17(1): 3–21.

Bohm, D. 1980. *Wholeness and the implicate order.* London: Routledge & Kegan Paul.

Burke, L., & Miller, M. 1999. Taking the mystery out of intuitive decision making. *Academy of Management Executive*, 13(4): 91–99.

Chia, R. 1994. The concept of decision: A deconstructive analysis. *Journal of Management Studies*, 31(6): 781–806.

Coget, J. F. 2004. *Leadership in motion: An investigation into the psychological processes that drive behavior when leaders respond to 'real-time' operational challenges.* Unpublished doctoral dissertation, Anderson School of Management – Human Resources and Organizational Behavior Area – UCLA.

Coget, J. F. 2009. Dialogical inquiry: An extension of Schein's clinical inquiry. *Journal of Applied Behavioral Science*, 45(1): 90–105.

Coget, J. F., Haag, C., & Bonnefous, A. 2009. Le rôle de l'émotion dans la prise de décision intuitive : Zoom sur les réalisateurs en période de tournage. [The role of emotion in intuitive decision making: focus on movie directors on set.] *M@n@gement*, 12(2): 118–141.

Coget, J. F., & Keller, E. 2010. The critical decisions vortex: Lessons from the emergency room. *Journal of Management Inquiry*, 19(1): 56–67.

Cox, J. 1998. *From vines to wines.* North Adams, MA: Storey Publishing.

Dane, E., & Pratt, M. 2007. Exploring intuition and its role in managerial decision-making. *Academy of Management Review*, 32(1): 33–54.

Derrida, J. 1981. *Positions.* Chicago: Chicago University Press.

Ekman, P. 1994. Strong evidence for universal in facial expressions: A reply to Russell's mistaken critique. *Psychological Bulletin*, 115(2): 268–287.

Emoto, M. 2005. *The hidden messages in water.* New York: Atria Books.

Ericsson, K. A., & Charness, N. 1994. Expert performance. *American Psychologist*, 49(8): 725–747.

Feldman, L. A. 1995. Variations in the circumplex structure of emotion. *Personality and Social Psychology Bulletin*, 21(8): 806–817.

Forgas, J. P. 1995. Mood and judgment: The Affect Infusion Model (AIM). *Psychological Bulletin*, 117(1): 39–66.

Frijda, N. H. 1986. *The emotions.* Studies in emotion and social interaction. Cambridge: Cambridge University Press.

Glaser, B., & Strauss, A. 1967. *The discovery of grounded theory.* Chicago: Aldine.

Goleman, D. 1995. *Emotional intelligence.* New York: Bantam Books.

Greenhalgh, T. 2002. Intuition and evidence – uneasy bedfellows? *British Journal of General Practice*, 52(478): 395–400.

Groopman, J. 2007. *How doctors think.* Boston, MA: Houghton Mifflin.

Hayashi, A. 2001. When to trust your gut. *Harvard Business Review*, 78(2): 59–65.

Heimoff, S. 2007. *New classic winemakers of California.* Berkeley and Los Angeles, CA: University of California Press.

James, W. 1884. What is an emotion? *Mind*, 34(April): 188–205.

Janis, I., & Mann, L. 1977. *Decision making: A psychological analysis of conflict, choice, and commitment.* New York: Free Press.

Kahneman, D., Slovic, P., & Tversky, A. 1987. *Judgment under uncertainty: Heuristics and biases.* Cambridge and New York: Cambridge University Press.

Kahneman, D., & Tversky, A. 1979. Prospect theory: An analysis of decision under risk. *Econometrica,* 2(March): 263–292.

Klein, G. 1993. A recognition-primed decisions (RPD) model of rapid decision making. In G. Klein, J. Orasanu, R. Calderwood, & C. Zsambok (Eds.), *Decision making in action: Models and methods*: 138–147. Norwood, CT: Ablex.

Klein, K., Ziegert, J., Knight, A., & Xiao, Y. 2006. Dynamic delegation: Shared, hierarchical, and deindividualized leadership in extreme action teams. *Administrative Science Quarterly,* 51(4): 590–621.

Lazarus, R. 1999. *Stress and emotion: A new synthesis.* New York: Springer.

Loewenstein, G., & Lerner, J. S. 2003. The role of affect in decision making. In R. Davidson, H. Goldsmith, and K. Scherer (Eds.), *Handbook of affective science*: 619–642. Oxford and New York: Oxford University Press.

Maguire, P. 1999. Improving communication with cancer patients. *European Journal of Cancer,* 35(14): 2058–2065.

March, J. G. 1991. How decisions happen in organizations. *Human–Computer Interaction,* 6(2): 95–117.

Morse, D. S., Edwardsen, E. A., & Gordon, H. S. 2008. Missed opportunities for interval empathy in lung cancer communication. *Archives of Internal Medicine,* 168(17): 1843–1852.

Ough, C. S. 1992. *Winemaking basics.* New York: Food Products Press.

Posner, B. Z., Russell, J. A., & Peterson, J. B. 2005. The Circumplex Model of Affect: An integrative approach to affective neuroscience, cognitive development, and psychopathology. *Development and Psychopathology,* 17(03): 715–734.

Robinson, J. 1994. *The Oxford companion to wine.* Oxford: Oxford University Press.

Russell, J. A. 1999. Core affect, prototypical emotional episodes, and other things called emotion: Dissecting the elephant. *Journal of Personality and Social Psychology,* 76(5): 805–819.

Sadler-Smith, E., & Shefy, E. 2004. The intuitive executive: Understanding and applying 'gut feel' in decision-making. *Academy of Management Executive,* 18(4): 76–91.

Salovey, P., & Mayer, J. D. 1990. Emotional Intelligence. *Imagination, Cognition and Personality,* 9(3): 185–211.

Simon, H. A. 1968. *Administrative behavior: A study of decision-making processes in administrative organization.* New York: Macmillan.

Simon, H. A. 1987. Making management decisions: The role of intuition and emotion. *Academy of Management Executive,* 1(1): 57–64.

Sinclair, M., & Ashkanasy, N. M. 2005. Intuition: Myth or a decision-making tool. *Management Learning,* 36(3): 353–370.

Smith, B. C. 2007. The objectivity of tastes and tasting. In Smith (Ed.), *Questions of taste: The philosophy of wine*: 41–78. New York: Oxford University Press.

Taylor, K. M. 1988. 'Telling bad news': Physicians and the disclosure of undesirable information. *Sociology of Health and Illness,* 10(2): 109–132.

Travis, M. 1999. *The director's journey: The creative collaboration between directors, writers and actors.* Studio City, CA: Michael Wiese Productions.

Von Neuman, J., & Morgenstern, O. 1944. *Theory of games and economic behavior.* New York: Wiley.

Vroom, V. H., & MacCrimmon, K. R. 1968. Toward a stochastic model of managerial careers. *Administrative Science Quarterly,* 13(1): 26–46.

Weick, K. E. 1995. *Sensemaking in organizations.* Foundations for organizational science. Thousand Oaks, CA: Sage.

Whittaker, J., Brickwood, A., & Curran, A. 2004. *The emergency department: A survival guide.* Knutsford, UK: PasTest Ltd.

13 Intuitive decision making in emergency medicine: an explorative study

Christian Harteis, Barbara Morgenthaler, Christine Kugler, Karl-Peter Ittner, Gabriel Roth and Bernhard Graf

Emergency physicians undertake demanding and responsible work, often in situations that call for quick and competent actions in order to save life and preserve health. In most cases it is impossible to fully appraise an accident location, to conduct a complete anamnesis or to determine a patient's medical history. Rather, emergency physicians have to initiate appropriate interventions without deliberated analyses by making spontaneous decisions (Leprohon & Patel, 1995). The reliable appropriateness of these decisions determines the quality of the physician's performance. As emergency medicine cases are generally not standard but rather vary with regard to problems and challenges, experience and routines cannot fully explain an emergency physician's capability to cope competently with the demands of an emergency situation. It might be intuition which enables them to perform at a high level under conditions as described above (King & Macleod Clark, 2002).

WHAT EMERGENCY PHYSICIANS NEED: A STABLE AND RELIABLE HIGH PERFORMANCE

Following Posner (1988), expertise is the general basis for enabling individuals to perform consistently at a high level. Hence, this section briefly discusses the state of research on expertise which indicates that intuition is an important component of it. A general idea of information processing provides opportunities for an empirical assessment of the phenomenon of intuition.

Expertise Research

Expertise research usually describes the development of individual knowledge structures during the development from novice to expert. This approach dates from studies on chess which investigated the role of memory

145

for extraordinary performances of perception and recognition (Chase & Simon, 1973a/b). Findings suggest that decision behaviour in reality is not always completely rational (Simon, 1955) and that experts recognize patterns in complex arrangements which enable them to respond spontaneously. Expertise theories such as knowledge encapsulation (Boshuizen & Schmidt, 1992) and learning from experience (Strasser & Gruber, 2004) were developed on the basis of empirical findings from the domains of medicine and counselling, which have received much attention in research literature. These theories explain the growth of expertise by changes in the individual's repertoire and the structure of explicable or declarative knowledge. These theories claim that in progressing from novice to expert, theoretical declarative knowledge is enriched by practical problem solving and through deliberate practice (Patel & Groen, 1991). With an increasing level of expertise, declarative knowledge loses its direct relevance for practical solutions, and instead, case-based patterns of practice emerge that are more likely to be able to respond to non-routine or unfamiliar problems within the domain. At the expert level, declarative knowledge is encapsulated in experience-based memory organization packets – the so-called 'encapsulation' theory (Boshuizen & Schmid, 1992) thus describes how expert knowledge changes in quality if rich experience with domain-specific cases is accessed. Subjects at the expert level, when asked about their ways of problem solving, report less frequently about the use of declarative knowledge than do novices, who still do not have the benefit of a broad scope of practical experience (Patel et al., 1990). The theory of learning from experience describes cognitive processes occurring when practical reality confirms or contradicts an individual's knowledge about procedures and operations, i.e. his/her procedural knowledge. If practice confirms procedural knowledge as being appropriate for achieving action goals, this procedural knowledge is strengthened by reflective confirmation. As a consequence, robust learning from experience occurs – as well as when procedural knowledge fails, which leads to a modification of that knowledge (Kolodner, 1983). These theories describe the permanent growth and change of experts' knowledge during their professional career and explain why emergency physicians act competently and why (probably) the improvement is long-lasting – assuming that they reflect on their performance afterwards (Ericsson, 1996). However, there is still a need to explain how emergency physicians are able to deal with unexpected, challenging and new situations.

Intuition as a Component of Expertise

Based on Simon's (1955) concept of bounded rationality, de Groot (1986) established the idea of intuition as complex pattern recognition which enables experts to analyse situations appropriately without necessarily needing awareness. Dreyfus & Dreyfus (1986) developed a five-step model for the development of expertise. In this model the highest level of expertise is the level of intuitive action which does not demand concentration, reflection or awareness. Experts make use of rich knowledge structures, especially their tacit knowledge developed on the basis of rich experiences reflected in their life history (Neuweg, 2004).

Eraut (1994) reviews research on professional expertise and notes that the developed structures of explicable (declarative and procedural) knowledge describe only one (important) aspect of professional performance, but that intuition is an important supplement. He defines intuition as 'not only pattern recognition but also rapid responses to developing situations . . . based on the tacit application of tacit rules. These rules may not be explicit or capable of reasoned justification, but their distinctive feature is that of being tacit at the moment of use' (Eraut, 2000: 127). Hence, intuition is highly relevant for the domain of medicine in general and particularly in the area of emergency medicine. Intuition can be construed as a condensate of complex knowledge patterns, developed by implicit learning during enculturation processes (Reber, 1993) or by automatization and development of routines (Eraut, 1994). Nonaka and Takeuchi (1995) describe the processes of internalization as a way of transforming explicable into tacit knowledge and enculturation as way of mediating implicit knowledge in the context of professional working life within enterprises.

Klein (2003) suggests the effect of mental models when he tries to explain firemen's capacity to make appropriate decisions under constraints. These mental models are the result of mental simulations of action scripts which professionals experience in their career. If a simulation is successful, a mental model develops which can guide future rapid decisions. Intuition 'is based on extensive experience both in analysis and problem solving and in implementation and to the extent that the lessons of experience are logical and well-founded, then so is the intuition' (ibid.: 19).

Two-systems Theory of Information Processing

Various approaches of decision-making research exist which proclaim two parallel and permanent operating information processing systems (Bruner, 1962; Hogarth, 2005; Sadler-Smith, 2010; Sloman, 2002). An important and convincing reference for two-systems theory consists in optical deceptions. The theory 'that two independent systems are at work depends critically on the fact that the perception and the knowledge are maintained simultaneously' (Sloman, 2002: 385). If they are shown pictures which seem to have lines of differing length only on the basis of three-dimensional illusions, subjects show a tendency to agree with the information that the presented lines are of a similar length but simultaneously try to find reasons for the perception of differing lengths. Similar simultaneous beliefs of contradicting statements could be observed in arguing or concluding with probabilities (Tversky & Kahneman, 1983). In their early common work, Kahneman and Tversky (1972) investigated the phenomenon that people make assessments in a distorted manner in areas where they are usually considered to be competent. They developed the theory of two parallel operating systems of information processing (Sloman, 2002) which is widely applied in research on decision making (Dane & Pratt, 2007; Epstein, 2003; Sadler-Smith & Shefy, 2004). Although using different terminologies, in principle authors agree with the comparison of a mode operating deliberately, rationally, and analytically with a mode working associatively, intuitively, and tacitly. Hammond (1993) claims that these two operation modes can be located at a continuum of consciousness: the intuitive mode is on the unconscious side of the continuum and the rational mode is on the conscious side. The border between these two modes is variable on the continuum between the two poles, which means that intuitive decisions can be conscious (i.e., if a person follows a gut feeling) and that rational decisions can be partly unconscious (e.g., if a person follows a given order). Coget and Keller (2010) additionally discuss the influence of emotions on decision making between these two systems. The two-systems theory implies an empirical design which implements extreme conditions to support intuitive or rational decision making by making either intuitive or rational considerations as unlikely as possible.

AN EXPLORATIVE STUDY

As there are no empirical attempts to investigate the role of intuitive decision making in the domain of emergency medicine, an explorative study was conducted to analyse how subjects of varying levels of expertise (experts, semi-experts, novices) differ in their decision-making behaviour when being prompted to act intuitively and rationally.

Design

Based on patient simulation mannequins, each subject had to deal with two different authentic problem cases: one fostering intuitive decision-making processes and one fostering rational decision-making processes. In the first simulation, time pressure (using CPR: cardiopulmonary resuscitation) was utilized to force subjects to make intuitive decisions by making rational considerations impossible. During the second simulation the subjects had to legitimize their decisions and every step verbally without any time pressure, in order to generate rational decisions and avoid intuitive decisions. Due to these various instructions a comparison between rational and intuitive decision-making processes was possible. The simulations were videotaped and analysed together with the subjects immediately after the exercise. Thus, the motives of their behaviour were reconstructed (stimulated recall), in order to identify the knowledge background of the decision-making processes. For both cases a decision tree (checklist) was developed which provided the foundation for the evaluation of the subjects' performances. The study utilized a 2×3 factorial design (within-subject factor: rational vs. intuitive; between-subject factor: level of expertise).

Sample

Thirty emergency physicians with different professional experiences and duration of professional activity (10 novices, 10 semi-experts, 10 experts) participated in the study. The ratio of assigning subject to these subgroups followed their professional status. Norman et al. (2006) discuss this method of assigning different levels of expertise in the domain of medicine and provide two main arguments for the validity of this procedure. First, physicians usually undergo several years of apprenticeship before entering independent practice. During this apprenticeship they develop and reflect on formal and experiential medical knowledge which is an important part of medical expertise. Second, physicians lacking treatment success would have been removed from the practice system. Thus, the ability to deal with several hundred emergency cases indicates treatment success of sufficient quality for the physician to be validly considered as an expert.

The first group (*novices*) consisted of medical students (during their internship, 11th semester) from the University of Regensburg (female = 6, male = 4; $M_{age} = 25.50$, $SD_{age} = 1.58$). Those students who had already worked as an ambulance officer or a paramedic were excluded from the study.

The second group (*semi-experts*) consisted of licenced physicians from the University Hospital of Regensburg but who had not graduated as medical specialists (female = 6, male = 4; $M_{age} = 29.60$, $SD_{age} = 2.01$). At the time they were being trained as emergency physicians or had just graduated from the training. For this training they had to have treated a certain number of emergency cases. At the time when the study was conducted, the total number of completed cases varied between 0 and 50 (Md = 11.50; Q1 = 0; Q3 = 31.25).

The third group (*experts*) consisted of emergency physicians with a professional experience of two years or more (female = 0, male = 10; M_{age} = 38.50, SD_{age} = 4.88). Their experience ranged between 2 and 21 years (M = 8.10; SD = 6.17), with 150 to 2,000 treated cases (Md = 500; Q1 = 400; Q3 = 1,075).

Measures

1. *Working on the problem cases based on the patient simulator 'SimMan'* Patient simulation mannequins were programmed for two different clinical situations. Because of the human bodily functions of the simulator such as breathing, pulse or blood pressure, the simulations appear authentic, especially as the mannequins react appropriately to intervention procedures (Fritz et al., 2008). The two simulations were developed in close cooperation with emergency medicine experts. The cases should be treated within 10 minutes (factual M = 10.39 minutes; Min = 7.08 minutes; Max = 12.10 minutes) and with the help of one paramedic. Case 1 (applying time pressure) simulated hyperkalemia, case 2 (verbalizing and legitimating actions) simulated hypoglycemia.

2. *Checklists for evaluating performances* Checklists defined the series of necessary decisions for an appropriate handling of the case. For each simulation, subjects scored if they made correct decisions according to the checklists' algorithm. Maximum score was 30 points. A non-participating observer completed the checklist during the exercises.

3. *Expert assessments for evaluating the total quality* In a non-participant observation a medical expert carried out an anonymous evaluation for all 30 subjects. All subjects were assessed on a scale of one to ten in terms of 'effectiveness', 'elegance' and 'holism'. At the end an evaluation of the total quality was made.

4. *'Stimulated-recall'* During stimulated recall interviews, the number of decisions as well as the intuitive and rational decisions could be reflected on with the subjects, by watching the videotaped simulations. The semi-standardized interviews followed directly after the second simulation. The subjects were instructed to stop the video whenever they detected points of decision making.

A typical investigation of a subject lasted about 120 minutes and comprised an introduction to the patient simulation mannequin and the situation, followed by the two simulation exercises. The first applied time pressure to force subjects to evoke intuitive decisions. The second demanded that subjects verbalize and legitimate their actions in order to evoke rational decisions. Checklists were completed and expert assessments made during the simulations by a non-participating observer, and both simulations were videotaped. Finally, stimulated recall interviews were conducted. The audiovisual recordings were analysed together with the subjects in order to identify the number of decisions the subjects could recognize. Furthermore, the motives of the subjects' behaviour were reconstructed, in order to identify the knowledge background of the decision-making processes.

RESULTS

First, a general view of group differences among experts, semi-experts and novices regarding the quality of their intuitive decision making confirms performance differences (measured by the checklist): the results of an ANOVA showed significant differences between the groups ($F(2, 27) = 11.28, p < 0.01$), a *post hoc* test (Bonferroni) revealed that the significant difference occurs between novices and both the other groups (novices: $M = 10.90$, SD $= 2.13$; semi-experts: $M = 15.60$, SD $= 2.72$; experts: $M = 17.40$, SD $= 4.25$).

More detailed analyses addressed the knowledge background of the decision-making processes in both simulations. This background was revealed (a) during the stimulated recall interviews and (b) by the external non-participating observation by an expert. In total, the 30 subjects identified 1,095 decisions while reflecting on the videotapes of the simulations. First, the decisions were distinguished according to their consciousness, and second, these decisions were evaluated by the research team (supported by an expert) regarding their appropriateness. Table 13.1 shows the distribution of the 1,095 decisions across consciousness, level of expertise and decision quality.

Analyses of variance did not reveal any significant differences between experts, semi-experts and novices ($F(2, 27)$ varies between 0.025 and 3.203, all n.s.). The only significant difference could be found in an intra-personal comparison between the decision behaviour in simulations 1 and 2 (two-sided *t*-test for dependent samples, df $= 29$) revealed significant differences regarding the number of unconscious decisions ($T = -2.75, p \leq 0.01$): subjects made unconscious decisions significantly more often during the second simulation.

An external expert observer evaluated the simulations by judging the total quality of the subjects' performance considering criteria such as elegance, efficacy and holism, on a 10-point scale (ranging from 1 to 10). Table13.2 provides the ANOVA statistics for this evaluation.

Post hoc tests (Tukey–HSD) for simulation 1 indicate significant

Table 13.1   Numbers of Decisions by Quality and Level of Expertise

Consciousness	Quality	Experts	Semi-experts	Novices	total
Case 1 fostering intuitive decision making by time pressure					
Conscious	Good	120	102	85	307
Conscious	Bad	8	10	12	30
Conscious	Irrelevant	6	15	11	32
Unconscious	Good	38	39	30	107
Unconscious	Bad	5	9	4	18
Unconscious	Irrelevant	5	4	5	14
	Total	182	179	147	508
Case 2 fostering rational decision making by verbalization and reasoning					
Conscious	Good	123	140	100	363
Conscious	Bad	7	8	8	23
Conscious	Irrelevant	1	1	–	2
Unconscious	Good	59	72	43	174
Unconscious	Bad	4	1	11	16
Unconscious	Irrelevant	3	1	5	9
	Total	197	223	167	587

Table 13.2   ANOVA Statistics for the Observation Evaluation

	Mean (SD) experts	Mean (SD) semi-experts	Mean (SD) novices	F	significance
Case 1	9.0 (0.67)	7.1 (1.67)	5.7 (2.06)	11.055	$p < 0.001$
Case 2	9.8 (0.42)	9.4 (0.97)	7.1 (2.08)	11.724	$p < 0.001$

differences between the experts and the two other groups (novices: 3.30, $p \leq 0.01$; semi-experts: 2.20, $p \leq 0.03$) and for simulation 2 significant differences between the novices and the two other groups (semi-experts: –2.30, $p \leq 0.02$; experts: –2.70, $p \leq 0.01$). Additionally, a t-test for independent samples (two-sided, df = 18) was conducted to compare experts and novices. For both cases, the differences between experts and novices were significant (case 1: $T = -4.83$, $p \leq 0.01$; case 2: $T = -4.03$, $p \leq 0.01$).

DISCUSSION

The results did not confirm the importance of intuition as clearly as expected from a theoretical perspective. However, these findings do not contradict the assumption that intuition is an important component of expertise and high performance for the following reasons:

- The sequence of testing may have an influence on the findings. The laboratory setting demanded a stable sequence of simulations 1 and 2 across all subjects. A quick modification of the simulation was possible only within the parameter of this order. Hence, random changes in the sequences were not an option. Thus, subjects may have become familiar with the simulation as well as with the laboratory setting, and an improved performance may be explained by this.
- Even though the selection and development of both simulations followed the main intention of finding cases of similar severity and complexity, subjects may have perceived different levels of demand. Neither case implemented routine cases for emergency physicians, but some feedback suggested a subjective impression that the second simulation was easier to solve than the first.
- The intended effect of verbalization did not apply. Subjects were not restricted by this setting. There are two possible reasons for this unexpected reaction. First, several subjects did not fully verbalize their actions and decisions but had to be reminded repeatedly during the simulation to keep verbalizing. Second, medicine is a scientific domain which is strictly focused towards rational considerations. Emergency physicians must – at least *ex post* – be able to provide a rationale for their actions. Subjects might be accustomed to legitimating their actions – even during the procedure.

An examination of Table 13.1 reveals the failing effect of verbalization: the subjects decided unconsciously in simulation 2 significantly more often than in simulation 1. However, across all groups most decisions in both simulations are judged as appropriate. It is evident that subjects on all levels of expertise apply medical knowledge so that they act competently.

The expert's evaluations strongly support the theoretical assumptions, because they indicate a distinctive superiority of experts over semi-experts and novices in the intuitive setting. Thus an emergency medical expert's performance appears of extraordinarily high quality – especially with regard to such qualitative evaluation criteria as efficacy, elegance etc. In simulation 2, novices are explicitly inferior in the expert's judgement. Even though there is a possibility that the expert's judgement is biased by a 'halo effect', these findings indicate and confirm earlier experiences (Harteis & Gruber, 2008a/b) that qualitative measures capture an illusive phenomenon such as intuition more explicitly than quantitative measures.

154 *Handbook of intuition research*

The expert's evaluations were treated very carefully in view of the distinction among the three subgroups of subjects. The definition of novices and experts is generally undisputed: novices do not have rich experience in a domain while experts are by and large considered to have at least ten years of experience – an often practised but also vehemently debated research pragmatism (Berliner, 2001). However, it is difficult to delineate the group of semi-experts against novices and experts. Thus, in addition to three group comparisons, *t*-tests between novices and experts were carried out to strengthen the results. These tests confirm conclusions from the three-group comparison. They show a clear distinction between the performance of experts and that of novices, as assessed by an expert.

The quality of the group classification defines a crucial moment in studies on expertise. It raises the question what constitutes expertise (and whether it equates with experience) and how it can be distinguished from semi-expertise. Usually, researchers try to observe subjects who show maximum divergence in performance or domain experience to analyse differences in their knowledge structures. However, constraints in the field may force pragmatic decisions, for example, applying 'half-splits' to distinguish two groups of subjects. Berliner critically discusses the ten-year rule which is often found in research on expertise. In field research it is necessary to consider the constraints of the environmental setting to realize empirical studies. In the study presented here, the distinction between subjects reflected their professional status, which in the context of emergency medicine represents varying degrees of experience. This distinction, however, may not be suitable in other work environments, and calls for a cautious contextualization of expertise in order to make the results meaningful.

CONCLUSIONS

The study demonstrates the high competence of subjects on all levels of expertise in dealing with the simulations. Although the simulations were designed to challenge even experienced emergency physicians, the subjects predominantly acted competently. As the findings reveal that measurement of intuition is not always clear cut, challenges remain for future research on intuition. The strategy of measuring intuitive performance by the implementation of an algorithm did not provide satisfying results. However, the findings do not contradict the assumption that intuition is an important component of expertise and high performance. It is rather the case that the analyses of interpersonal differences revealed advantages of experts within the intuitive laboratory setting, namely by quantitative and qualitative measurement (see external expert evaluation). This can be considered as evidence for the assumption that intuition develops during one's professional career.

The main insight from a methodological perspective, besides the need to clearly delineate semi-expertise, concerns the necessity for variation between simulations and settings. It would have been important to change the sequence as well as the settings in order to avoid the sequence or case effects. Further, the results reveal the general problem of empirically grasping intuitive mental processes through verbalization. Measurements of physical or physiological reactions (e.g., eye movement, brain activity) might be a sounder approach but raise serious problems for the laboratory setting.

REFERENCES

Berliner, D. 2001. Learning about and learning from expert teachers. *International Journal of Educational Research*, 35: 463–482.

Boshuizen, H. P. A., & Schmidt, H. G. 1992. On the role of biomedical knowledge in clinical reasoning by experts, intermediates and novices. *Cognitive Science*, 16: 153–184.

Bruner, J. 1962. *On knowing*. Cambridge, MA: Harvard University Press.

Chase, W. G., & Simon, H. A. 1973a. The mind's eye in chess. In W. G. Chase (Ed.), *Visual information processing*: 215–281. New York: Academic Press.

Chase, W. G., & Simon, H. A. 1973b. Perception in chess. *Cognitive Psychology*, 4: 55–81.

Coget, J.-F., & Keller, E. 2010. The critical decision vortex: Lessons from the emergency room. *Journal of Management Inquiry*, 19: 56–67.

Dane, E., & Pratt, M. G. 2007. Exploring intuition and its role in managerial decision making. *Academy of Management Review*, 32(1): 33–54.

de Groot, A. D. 1986. Intuition in chess. *International Computer Chess Association Journal*, 9: 67–75.

Dreyfus, H. L., & Dreyfus, S. E. 1986. *Mind over machine. The power of human intuition and expertise in the era of the computer*. New York: Free Press.

Epstein, S. 2003. Cognitive–experiental self-theory of personality. In T. Millon, & M. J. Lerner (Eds.), *Comprehensive handbook on psychology, volume 5: Personality and social psychology*: 159–184. Hoboken, NJ: Wiley & Sons.

Eraut, M. 1994. *Developing professional knowledge and competence*. London: Routledge.

Eraut, M. 2000. Non-formal learning and tacit knowledge in professional work. *British Journal of Educational Psychology*, 70: 113–136.

Ericsson, K. A. 1996. The acquisition of expert performance: An introduction to some of the issues. In Ericsson (Ed.), *The road to excellence. The acquisition of expert performance in the arts, sciences, sports and games*: 1–50. Cambridge: Cambridge University Press.

Fritz, P. Z., Gray, T., & Flanagan, B. 2008. Review of mannequin-based high-fidelity simulation in emergency medicine. *Emergency Medicine Australasia*, 20: 1–9.

Hammond, K. R. 1993. Natural decision making from a Brunswikian viewpoint. In G. A. Klein, J. Orasanu, R. Calderwood, & C. E. Zsambok (Eds.), *Decision making in action: Models and methods*: 205–227. Westport, CT: Ablex Publishing.

Harteis, C., & Gruber, H. 2008a. How important is intuition for teaching expertise in the field of adult education? *Studies in the Education of Adults*, 40(1): 96–109.

Harteis, C., & Gruber, H. 2008b. Intuition and professional competence: Intuitive versus rational forecasting of the stock market. *Vocations and Learning: Studies in Vocational and Professional Education*, 1: 71–85.

Hogarth, R. M. 2005. Deciding analytically or trusting your intuition? The advantages and disadvantages of analytic and intuitive thought. In T. Betsch, & S. Haberstroh (Eds.), *The routines of decision making*: 67–82. Mahwah, NJ: Lawrence Erlbaum.

Kahneman, D., & Tversky, A. 1972. Subjective probability. A judgment of representativeness. *Cognitive Psychology*, 3: 430–454.

King, L., & Macleod Clark, J. 2002. Intuition and the development of expertise in surgical ward and intensive care nurses. *Journal of Advanced Nursing*, 37: 322–329.

Klein, G. 2003. *Intuition at work*. New York: Doubleday.

Kolodner, J. L. 1983. Towards an understanding of the role of experience in the evolution from novice to expert. *International Journal of Man-Machine Studies*, 19: 497–518.

Leprohon, J., & Patel, V. L. 1995. Decision making strategies for telephone triage in emergency medical services. *Medical Decision Making*, 15: 240–253.

Neuweg, G. H. 2004. Tacit knowing and implicit learning. In M. Fischer, N. Boreham, & B. Nyham (Eds.), *European perspectives on learning at work. The acquisition of work process knowledge*: 130–147. Luxembourg: Office for offical publications of the European Communities.

Nonaka, I., & Takeuchi, H. 1995. *The knowledge creating company. How Japanese companies create the dynamics of innovation*. Oxford: Oxford University Press.

Norman, G., Eva, K., Brooks, L., & Hamstra, S. 2006. Expertise in medicine and surgery. In K. A. Ericsson, N. Charness, P. J. Feltovich, & R. R. Hoffman (Eds.), *The Cambridge handbook of expertise and expert performance*: 339–353. Cambridge: Cambridge University Press.

Patel, V. L., & Groen, G. J. 1991. The general and the specific nature of medical expertise: a critical look. In K. A. Ericsson, & J. Smith (Eds.), *Towards a general theory of expertise: Prospects and limits*: 92–125. Cambridge: Cambridge University Press.

Patel, V. L., Groen, G. J., & Arocha, J. F. 1990. Medical expertise as a function of task difficulty. *Memory and Cognition*, 18: 394–406.

Posner, M. I. 1988. Introduction: What is it to be an expert? In M. T. H. Chi, R. Glaser, & M. J. Farr (Eds.), *The nature of expertise*: xxix–xxxvi. Hillsdale, NJ: Erlbaum.

Reber, A. S. 1993. *Implicit learning and tacit knowledge. An essay on the cognitive unconscious*. Oxford: Oxford University Press.

Sadler-Smith, E. 2010. *The intuitive mind*. Chichester, UK: Wiley.

Sadler-Smith, E., & Shefy, E. 2004. The intuitive executive: Understanding and applying 'gut feel' in decision-making. *Academy of Management Executive*, 18(4): 76–91.

Simon, H. A. 1955. A behavioural model of rational choice. *Quarterly Journal of Economics*, 69: 99–118.

Sloman, S. A. 2002. Two systems of reasoning. In T. Gilovich, D. Griffin, & D. Kahneman (Eds.), *Heuristics and biases. The psychology of intuitive judgment*: 379–396. Cambridge: Cambridge University Press.

Strasser, J., & Gruber, H. 2004. The role of experience in professional training and development of psychological counselors. In H. P. A. Boshuizen, R. Bromme, & H. Gruber (Eds.), *Professional learning: Gaps and transitions on the way from novice to expert*: 11–27. Dordrecht: Kluwer.

Tversky, A., & Kahneman, D. 1983. Extensional versus intuitive reasoning: The conjunction fallacy in probability judgment. *Psychological Review*, 90: 293–315.

14 Legal intuition and expertise
Andreas Glöckner and Irena D. Ebert

> When I became more familiar with the practices in admiralty and in equity, more especially when, a judge in such cases, I felt the restless, eager ranging of the mind to overcome the confusion and the perplexities of the evidence, or of constricting and outworn concepts, and so to find the hidden truth, I knew that not only was it the practice of good judges to 'feel' their way to a decision of a close and difficult case, but that in such cases any other practice was unsound. (Hutcheson, 1929: 277)

Considering the extensive consequences caused by legal decisions, both practitioners and scholars have dealt with the question of the perfect route to valid legal decisions. That is, how should legal decisions be made? Hutcheson (1929), a chief federal judge of the US 5th Circuit, describes his radical change of mind concerning this question. While starting from the position that all legal reasoning has to be based on logic and deliberate information processes he later came to the conclusion that 'hunches' or 'feelings' play a crucial role and are even necessary for appropriate decision making in difficult legal cases.

Guthrie et al. (2007) have shown that judges heavily rely on intuition. In a set of studies, they used deviations from rational behavior to trace intuition and to identify its downsides (cf. Kahneman et al., 1982). The authors revealed that judges tend to select intuitive (but wrong) answers in the Cognitive Reflection Test (Frederick, 2005), are prone to intuitive influences of anchors when determining the amount of compensatory damages they would award the plaintiff (see also Englich & Mussweiler, 2001), make intuitive judgments in legal cases that indicate the neglect of base rates (see also Bar-Hillel, 1980), and intuitively change their judgments in hindsight (see also Hastie et al., 1999). In further studies, potential jurors working on legal cases were found to change their evaluation of the evidence in the direction of their preferred verdict without recognizing it, which induces more extreme confidence ratings (Holyoak & Simon, 1999; Simon, 2004). Altogether, these results support Hutcheson's *descriptive* claim that intuitive processes play an important role in legal judgments. More generally, recent decision models assume that intuitive processes are activated by default in many kinds of judgments and decisions, whereas deliberate processes are additionally activated only if necessary (see Evans, 2008, for an overview). The above-mentioned effects, however, also show that relying on intuition can result in substantial biases.

Other research supports Hutcheson's *prescriptive* claim that intuitive processes constitute a necessary condition for making valid legal judgments in difficult cases. Indeed, it has been shown that intuitive (automatic) processes allow people to quickly integrate a multitude of information (Glöckner & Betsch, 2008b) in a way that the results obtained approximate a rational solution quite well (cf. Juslin et al., 2009). Due to the fact that legal judgments are usually highly complex, it seems to be quite sensible to use the computational power of a resource-efficient mode as intuition instead of losing substantial parts of the information through the use of a meticulous deliberate mode due to its severe constraints on capacity. Although intuitive processes can lead to biases, in complex cases they seem to be necessary to make sound legal judgments.

This, of course, does not mean that jurors and judges should completely avoid deliberating. It has been argued that to achieve just legal judgments, thorough deliberation should be used on top of intuition to check its foundations, processing and alternative interpretations, and to overwrite biased results if necessary (Guthrie et al., 2007; Simon, 2004). Hutcheson's prescriptive claim was right in that legal intuition seems to be an integral part of legal judgments. However, it must be supplemented by deliberate processes that enable for correcting of biases in addition to multiple further advantages.

Before turning to a more detailed discussion of intuition in legal decision making, we would like to clarify three interrelated conceptual issues concerning the definition and operation of intuition:

- *Definition* Several attempts have been made to define intuition. Dual processing models usually list properties of *System 1* processes (intuition: e.g., automatic, fast, unconscious, associative) and *System 2* processes (deliberation: e.g., controlled, slow, conscious, rule-based) (see Evans, 2008). Some definitions that explain the operation of intuitive processes in a little more detail (i.e., Betsch, 2008; Hogarth, 2001; Klein, 2003; Sadler-Smith, 2008) have been summarized in a common-ground definition (Glöckner & Witteman, 2010: 5–6): '[I]ntuition is based on automatic processes that rely on knowledge structures that are acquired by (different kinds of) learning. They operate at least partially without people's awareness and result in feelings, signals, or interpretations. Assumptions concerning the underlying processes and consequently also concerning further properties of these processes diverge'.
- *Processes of intuition* Intuition is based on various processes of memory and perception that operate differently. There exist

well-specified computational models for each kind of process. It is therefore important to specify which 'kind of intuition' is investigated and to keep in mind what we already know about how to model these processes. We describe a recently developed category system for the different processes of intuition below.

- *Intuition, knowledge structures and expertise* The different processes of intuition automatically combine perceived information and information activated from memory. Knowledge structures resulting from experience and learning constitute the basis on which intuitive processes operate (cf. Holyoak, 1991). Professional legal intuition has to rely on a certain degree of legal expertise (Salas et al., 2010) resulting in explicit and implicit knowledge (Blasi, 1995; Marchant & Robinson, 1999). Although both result from learning, explicit knowledge items can be verbalized, whereas implicit (tacit) items cannot. Professional judges have to know legal codes and legal cases explicitly but also implicitly to do their job. This is not to say that laypeople could not also have a sense of justice. It will, however, rely on a different knowledge base, namely on general knowledge and standards of morality and justice.

In the following we shall describe the role of intuition in legal discourse. Then, we shall discuss the different kinds of intuitive processes that play a role in legal decision making and discuss both the advantages and downsides of using them.

THE ROLE OF INTUITION IN LEGAL DISCOURSE

In legal discourse, intuition is important for various reasons. As illustrated by the example described below, it is used to evaluate legal rules. However, it is also important for decision making in practice as some legal systems oblige judges to rely partially on intuition. We shall exemplify this with a discussion of some aspects of evidence law in the US and in Germany.

Legal Intuition versus Fixed Probability Thresholds for Conviction in US Law

Legal intuition is complex. For instance, it has been shown that it cannot be captured by mere probabilities. Imagine a situation known as the 'blue bus hypothetical' in which an object was damaged by a blue bus. The only fact known is that 85% of blue buses in the city are from company A, the remaining buses are from company B. Obviously the probability that the blue bus was from company A is higher than 50%. Strictly applying the standard of proof of US civil law (i.e., preponderance of the evidence), company A should pay the damage. Now imagine a second situation in which there is an eye-witness who makes 85% correct identifications of buses of company A and B (prior probability). The probability that the accident was caused by a bus from company A is obviously the same in both scenarios. Nevertheless, legal intuition leads to diametrically different judgments. Students without legal knowledge and legal professionals alike mainly acquit in the first but convict in the second scenario (Wells, 1992). This example shows that legal intuition is not just based on estimated probabilities and seems to take into account constellation of the evidence in a more complex manner.

Among legal scholars there has been an intense debate on the rules of evidence that should be applied (see Jackson, 1996, for an overview). Some scholars advocate a Bayesian-probability perspective. That is, convictions should be made by posterior probability (i.e., both bus scenarios should be treated equally). Others argue for an inductive probability approach involving hypothesis testing. In line with the Bayesian-probability perspective, it could be argued that explicit probability thresholds (e.g., in civil cases decide for the side with $p > 0.50$) would improve legal judgments (cf. Kagehiro, 1990). If strictly applied, this would reduce or even eliminate the influence of legal intuition. However, it would also lead to decisions that conflict with it. For many good reasons (e.g., when relying on the probability of buses, only the company A with the majority of buses will be convicted for *all* bus-caused damages, which seems unjust), lawyers are usually reluctant to accept such decisions and legal rules that lead to them (Jackson, 1996).

Intuition in German Legal Procedure

The German legal system tries to solve the issue in a quite different way (Engel, 2009). German legal procedure leaves room for intuitive processes in making judgments. However, it also obliges the judge to re-check it thoroughly and deliberately, and to reveal the underlying argumentation at the end. German law does not set a probability threshold and uses the concept of personal conviction instead (Schoreit, 2003): after thorough consideration of all pieces of evidence, the judge has to be personally convinced of the guilt of the accused to sentence and then must explicate the arguments that led to this decision. Judges have lenience on how to come to their decisions according to the concept of free judgment of the evidence (*freie Beweiswürdigung*). Furthermore, they are obliged by law to take into account their holistic impression of the trial (*Gesamteindruck der Hauptverhandlung*). According to self-report, experienced judges often have a legal intuition (*Rechtsgefühl/Judiz*) after reading the information on a case, which is then checked thoroughly by deliberate processes. Alternative interpretations are considered and, based on some kind of feeling, they are compared with each other in terms of how convincing they are. In the legal evaluation of the facts legal norms are taken into account and checked as to whether they allow for developing a convincing argument in support of the legal intuition. For example, after fact-finding it might be clear that person A took money from person B. The judge might have an (implicit) legal intuition that this was a violation of property law. Nevertheless, he/she can only convict A if he/she is able to build a convincing explicit argument that supports this intuition.

PROCESS MODELS FOR INTUITION AND THEIR APPLICATION TO LEGAL DECISIONS

The Interaction of Intuitive and Deliberate Processes

Dual process models assume that there are two different, and relatively distinct, systems of information processing. Note, however, that this does not mean that the systems work completely separately. Many of the current dual process models are *default–interventionist models* assuming that both systems interact with intuitive processes being activated by default and deliberate processes being activated only if necessary to intervene and correct (see Evans, 2008, for an overview; see also Sinclair & Ashkanasy, 2005). Other models make the slightly different assumption that both systems are activated in parallel (e.g., Sloman, 2002). The default–interventionist perspective has recently been applied to legal decision making in the intuition–override model stating that on the bench also, judges start with an intuitive judgment which can then be overridden (Guthrie et al., 2007).

A Process Differentiation of Intuitive Processes

Intuition is used as an umbrella term. Reviewing process models in cognitive decision research has shown that intuition is likely to refer to quite different processes of perception and memory (Glöckner & Witteman, 2010). The simplest class of intuitive processes, *associative intuition*, refers to relatively direct affective responses to stimuli that result from previous experiences with sufficiently similar stimuli (e.g., Slovic et al., 2002). Associative intuitions might, for instance, result from direct affective reactions towards an accused person who is similar to another person with whom the judge has had experience. The affective response is assumed to be directly activated from memory (ibid.), and some theorists assume that this kind of memory-based effect often plays a dominant role in decision making (Loewenstein et al., 2001). To assure a fair judgment, such direct influences should mainly be avoided in legal reasoning.

Another class of intuitive processes, *matching intuition*, is used to match objects or situations to previous experiences or categories (e.g., Dougherty et al., 1999; Fiedler, 1996; Kahneman & Klein, 2009). Matching intuition might be essential for lawyers, in that it quickly provides them with a feeling of how similar cases have (on average) been decided before. This is particularly important in common-law countries like the US, where legal arguments are heavily based on precedents cases. According to Dougherty et al. (1999), basic processes of memory prompting would thereby produce instant feelings about the number of similar cases and the decisions in these cases. The current case would be used to prompt memory for similar cases, and memory would provide an overall feeling ('echo') that is proportional to the number of related cases weighted by their similarity. Using conditional memory prompts, a rough feeling of the decisions in these cases would be produced. It has also been convincingly argued that connectionist approaches involving matching to categories and analogy construction will be of particular importance for legal judgments (e.g., Marchant & Robinson, 1999; Spellman, 2010; see also the following subsection).

Constructive Intuition

Another class of intuitive processes, *constructive intuition*, constructs consistent interpretations or stories of the evidence (e.g., Holyoak & Simon, 1999; Pennington & Hastie, 1988). Models from this class have been applied most intensively to legal decisions and will therefore be outlined in greater detail here.

Constructive intuition is based on processes similar to perception that relies on construction of best interpretations given the evidence and prior knowledge (interactive activation; McClelland & Rumelhart, 1981). This process often leads to quick holistic impressions that are fundamental for behavioral responses (Kunda & Thagard, 1996). A prominent approach to legal decision making that takes into account such constructive processes is the story model (Pennington & Hastie, 1992: 189–90). This model posits that 'jurors impose a narrative story organization on trial information. . . . Meaning is assigned to trial evidence through the incorporation of that evidence into one or more plausible accounts or stories describing "what happened" during events'. The best story is selected based on coherence, coverage, goodness-of-fit and uniqueness. It is then matched to existing verdict categories and accepted if there is a good fit.

Although the processes of story construction and selection can partially involve deliberation, the feeling of how coherent a story is and how it fits with a certain verdict category will often emerge spontaneously based on constructive and matching intuition.

Parallel constraint satisfaction (PCS) network models have been used to generalize the idea of story construction and to make the underlying holistic process mathematically traceable (Glöckner & Betsch, 2008a; Holyoak & Simon, 1999; Robbennolt et al., 2010; Simon, 2004). According to the Glöckner and Betsch PCS model, for instance, related information in memory is activated as soon as individuals are faced with information about a case. Jointly with the perceived information, these pieces of information form a network (*mental representation*), from which usually only small parts are conscious. As soon as this network is constructed, spreading activation leads to maximizing consistency in the network. Thereby pieces of evidence are put together to fit as well as possible. Initial advantages of the more strongly supported interpretation are automatically accentuated by highlighting the aspects that speak for it and inhibiting information that speaks against it. As a result, people 'see' (have the feeling) that one or the other option, story or categorization is preferable. In some cases this feeling will just be the conscious tip of the iceberg while in others the whole interpretation will become conscious. In cases in which no sufficiently consistent solution is found, deliberate processes are activated to support intuitive processes. The structure of the mental representations constructed will thereby be heavily influenced by experience and the decision makers' level of expertise. In a seminal work, Holyoak (1991) has outlined how PCS models can account for core findings in expertise research that challenge previous models based on heuristic search (Newell & Simon, 1972) and automatic serial production rules (Anderson, 1987).

ADVANTAGES AND DOWNSIDES OF INTUITION

Advantages

One of the core advantages of intuitive processes is that they allow for effectively taking into account a large amount of information that is provided for the case and activated in memory (Glöckner & Betsch, 2008b). Capacity constraints and the complexity of cases do not allow for solving them by mere deliberate calculations. On top of this, constructive intuition can handle incomplete information quite easily. In contrast, incomplete information is a serious challenge for determining guilt by means of deliberate Bayesian calculations (Thagard, 2004).

Downsides

Due to the fact that intuition operates in a less controlled fashion and takes into account related pieces of information, it can be distorted and even manipulated by many different factors. According to the PCS models discussed in the previous subsection, the core challenge is that the mental representation, that is, the structure of the network that is constructed based on perceived and activated information, must appropriately represent the structure of the task. Several factors can influence this, from which a few should be listed, for example:

1.   As introduced above, intuition is based on automatic processes that operate on specific knowledge structures. With increasing experience in 'friendly' environments (i.e., environments with correct feedback and representative task selection), implicit and explicit knowledge bases for intuition will improve and become more reliable (Hogarth, 2001). One problem in the legal domain is that judges and jurors often do not receive feedback on their decisions (or only very delayed feedback), which makes learning harder (Kahneman & Klein, 2009). Learning experiences might be insufficient, sometimes even based on biased feedback or they might not be representative for the task at hand. Hence, mental representations could contain inappropriate links.
2.   The context of the information given for the task leads to the construction of inappropriate mental representations. Specific aspects might be salient, proximate, or for other reasons in the focus of attention, resulting in an overweighting of these aspects. Demonstrations of this are the above-mentioned phenomena of anchoring, hindsight bias, base-rate neglect and other biases such as framing (e.g., Guthrie et al., 2000; Kahneman et al., 1982).
3.   In many situations, numbers and probabilities have to be translated and filled with meaning. For most people it will, for instance, be quite unclear whether 100 mg of a drug are a lot or relatively little. How easy it is to evaluate this information plays a crucial role (cf. Hsee, 1996). In intuitive judgments, many context factors will influence how numbers and probabilities are entered into the mental representation.

A second source of problems is that the processes of information integration themselves cause biases. This is particularly true for well-proven information distortions, induced by PCS, which lead to an accentuation of initial advantages of the preferred option and to more extreme confidence ratings (Holyoak & Simon, 1999).

Several scholars argue that deliberation (e.g., deliberately considering the opposite) usually helps to reduce these errors and make mental representations more appropriate (Guthrie et al., 2007; Mussweiler et al., 2000; Simon, 2004). In some (probably rare) cases, however, deliberation might also lead to the activation of inappropriate mental representations and decrease the quality of decisions, as has been shown for preferential choice (Dijksterhuis & Nordgren, 2006; Wilson & Schooler, 1991; but see also Acker, 2008). For the domain of legal intuition, however, this detrimental effect of deliberation still has to be demonstrated empirically.

SUMMARY

From a psychological perspective, it seems to be clear that intuition can be traced back to basic cognitive processes of perception and memory. These processes can be mathematically modeled. They can be used in different subject domains and act upon different knowledge structures. Nevertheless, the basic processes are similar across different subject domains. Current models, findings and individual reports of legal experts converge in that legal experts often use legal intuition as default, which is then checked, and if necessary, corrected by deliberate processes. Legal intuition allows for handling even complex cases with missing information.

The quality of legal intuition depends on multiple factors. Appropriate implicit and explicit knowledge structures due to expertise in the field are important. Legal decision makers should not be forbidden to use intuition, but they should be informed about the mechanisms, as well as the advantages and downsides of intuition. At the same time, legal institutions should always be combined with the obligation deliberately to re-check and imagine the opposite interpretation. Against the backdrop of the cognitive mechanisms discussed in this chapter, obliging judges and jurors to rely completely on deliberate calculations and specifying probability thresholds seems to be less promising.

REFERENCES

Acker, F. 2008. New findings on unconscious versus conscious thought in decision making: Additional empirical data and meta-analysis. *Judgment and Decision Making*, 3(4): 292–303.
Anderson, J. R. 1987. Skill acquisition: Compilation of weak-method problem solutions. *Psychological Review*, 94(2): 192–210.
Bar-Hillel, M. 1980. The base-rate fallacy in probability judgments. *Acta Psychologica*, 44(3): 211–233.

Betsch, T. 2008. The nature of intuition and its neglect in research on judgment and decision making. In H. Plessner, C. Betsch, & T. Betsch (Eds.), *Intuition in judgment and decision making*: 3–22. Mahwah, NJ: Lawrence Erlbaum Associates.

Blasi, G. L. 1995. What lawyers know – lawyering expertise, cognitive science, and the function of theory. *Journal of Legal Education*, 45(3): 313–397.

Dijksterhuis, A., & Nordgren, L. F. 2006. A theory of unconscious thought. *Perspectives on Psychological Science*, 1(2): 95–109.

Dougherty, M. R. P., Gettys, C. F., & Ogden, E. E. 1999. MINERVA-DM: A memory processes model for judgments of likelihood. *Psychological Review*, 106(1): 180–209.

Engel, C. 2009. Preponderance of the evidence versus intime conviction: A behavior perspective on a conflict between American and continental European law. *Vermont Law Review*, 33(3): 435–467.

Englich, B., & Mussweiler, T. 2001. Sentencing under uncertainty: Anchoring effects in the courtroom. *Journal of Applied Social Psychology*, 31(7): 1535–1551.

Evans, J. St. B. T. 2008. Dual-processing accounts of reasoning, judgment, and social cognition. *Annual Review of Psychology*, 59: 255–278.

Fiedler, K. 1996. Explaining and simulating judgment biases as an aggregation phenomenon in probabilistic, multiple-cue environments. *Psychological Review*, 103(1): 193–214.

Frederick, S. 2005. Cognitive reflection and decision making. *Journal of Economic Perspectives*, 19(4): 25–42.

Glöckner, A., & Betsch, T. 2008a. Modeling option and strategy choices with connectionist networks: Towards an integrative model of automatic and deliberate decision making. *Judgment and Decision Making*, 3(3): 215–228.

Glöckner, A., & Betsch, T. 2008b. Multiple-reason decision making based on automatic processing. *Journal of Experimental Psychology: Learning, Memory, and Cognition*, 34(5): 1055–1075.

Glöckner, A., & Witteman, C. L. M. 2010. Beyond dual-process models: A categorization of processes underlying intuitive judgment and decision making. *Thinking and Reasoning*, 16(1): 1–25.

Guthrie, C., Rachlinski, J. J., & Wistrich, A. J. 2000. Inside the judicial mind. *Cornell Law Review*, 86: 777–830.

Guthrie, C., Rachlinski, J. J., & Wistrich, A. J. 2007. Blinking on the bench: How judges decide cases. *Cornell Law Review*, 93(1): 1–44.

Hastie, R., Schkade, D. A., & Payne, J. W. 1999. Juror judgments in civil cases: Hindsight effects on judgments of liability for punitive damages. *Law and Human Behavior*, 23(5): 597–614.

Hogarth, R. M. 2001. *Educating intuition*. Chicago: University of Chicago Press.

Holyoak, K. J. 1991. Symbolic connectionism: Toward third-generation theories of expertise. In K. A. Ericsson, & J. Smith (Eds.), *Toward a general theory of expertise*: 301–336. Cambridge: Cambridge University Press.

Holyoak, K. J., & Simon, D. 1999. Bidirectional reasoning in decision making by constraint satisfaction. *Journal of Experimental Psychology: General*, 128(1): 3–31.

Hsee, C. 1996. The evaluability hypothesis: An explanation for preference reversals between joint and separate evaluations of alternatives. *Organizational Behavior and Human Decision Processes*, 67(3): 247–257.

Hutcheson, J. C. 1929. The judgment intuitive: The function of the 'hunch' in judicial decision making. *Cornell Law Quarterly*, 14: 274–288.

Jackson, J. D. 1996. Analysing the new evidence scholarship: Towards a new conception of the law of evidence. *Oxford Journal of Legal Studies*, 16(2): 309–328.

Juslin, P., Nilsson, H., & Winman, A. 2009. Probability theory, not the very guide of life. *Psychological Review*, 116(4): 856–874.

Kagehiro, D. K. 1990. Defining the standard of proof in jury instructions. *Psychological Science*, 1(3): 194–200.

Kahneman, D., & Klein, G. 2009. Conditions for intuitive expertise: A failure to disagree. *American Psychologist*, 64(6): 515–526.

Kahneman, D., Slovic, P., & Tversky, A. (Eds.). 1982. *Judgment under uncertainty: Heuristics and biases*. New York: Cambridge University Press.

Klein, G. A. 2003. *Intuition at work*. New York: Doubleday.

Kunda, Z., & Thagard, P. 1996. Forming impressions from stereotypes, traits, and behaviors: A parallel-constraint-satisfaction theory. *Psychological Review*, 103(2): 284–308.

Loewenstein, G. F., Weber, E. U., Hsee, C. K., & Welch, N. 2001. Risk as feelings. *Psychological Bulletin*, 127(2): 267–286.

Marchant, G., & Robinson, J. 1999. Is knowing the tax code all it takes to be a tax expert? On the development of legal expertise. In R. J. Sternberg, & J. S. Horvath (Eds.), *Tacit knowledge in professional practice: Researcher and practitioner perspectives*: 3–20. Mahwah, NJ: Lawrence Erlbaum.

McClelland, J. L., & Rumelhart, D. E. 1981. An interactive activation model of context effects in letter perception: I. An account of basic findings. *Psychological Review*, 88(5): 375–407.

Mussweiler, T., Strack, F., & Pfeiffer, T. 2000. Overcoming the inevitable anchoring effect: Considering the opposite compensates for selective accessibility. *Personality and Social Psychology Bulletin*, 26(9): 1142–1150.

Newell, A., & Simon, H. A. 1972. *Human problem solving*. Oxford: Prentice-Hall.

Pennington, N., & Hastie, R. 1988. Explanation-based decision making: Effects of memory structure on judgment. *Journal of Experimental Psychology: Learning, Memory, and Cognition*, 14(3): 521–533.

Pennington, N., & Hastie, R. 1992. Explaining the evidence: Tests of the Story Model for jury decision making. *Journal of Personality and Social Psychology*, 62: 189–206.

Robbennolt, J., MacCoun, R., & Darley, J. 2010. Multiple constraint satisfaction in judging. In D. Klein, & G. Mitchell (Eds.), *The Psychology of Judicial Decision Making*: 27–40. Oxford: Oxford University Press.

Sadler-Smith, E. 2008. *Inside intuition*. Inside intuition. New York: Routledge/Taylor & Francis Group.

Salas, E., Rosen, M. A., & DiazGranados, D. 2010. Expertise-based intuition and decision making in organizations. *Journal of Management*, 36: 941–973.

Schoreit, A. 2003. StPO § 261 Freie Beweiswürdigung [Free judgment of the evidence]. In G. Pfeiffer (Ed.), *Karlsruher Kommentar zur Strafprozessordnung und zum Gerichtsverfassungsgesetz mit Einführungsgesetz [Karlsruhe commentary on the code of criminal procedure and on judiciary law with the introductory act]*. Munich: C. H. Beck.

Simon, D. 2004. A third view of the black box: cognitive coherence in legal decision making. *University of Chicago Law Review*, 71: 511–586.

Sinclair, M., & Ashkanasy, N. M. 2005. Intuition: myth or a decision-making tool? *Management Learning*, 36(3): 353–370.

Sloman, S. A. 2002. Two systems of reasoning. In T. Gilovich, D. Griffin, & D. Kahneman (Eds.), *Heuristics and biases: The psychology of intuitive judgment*: 379–396. New York: Cambridge University Press.

Slovic, P., Finucane, M., Peters, E., & MacGregor, D. G. 2002. The affect heuristic. In T. Gilovich, D. Griffin, & D. Kahneman (Eds.), *Heuristics and biases: The psychology of intuitive judgment*: 397–420. New York: Cambridge University Press.

Spellman, B. A. 2010. Judges, expertise, and analogy. In D. Klein, & G. Mitchell (Eds.), *The psychology of judicial decision making*: 149–163. Oxford: Oxford University Press.

Thagard, P. 2004. Causal inference in legal decision making: Explanatory coherence vs. Bayesian networks. *Applied Artificial Intelligence*, 18(3–4): 231–249.

Wells, G. L. 1992. Naked statistical evidence of liability: Is subjective probability enough? *Journal of Personality and Social Psychology*, 62(5): 739–752.

Wilson, T. D., & Schooler, J. W. 1991. Thinking too much: Introspection can reduce the quality of preferences and decisions. *Journal of Personality and Social Psychology*, 60(2): 181–192.

15 Intuition in teaching

Paola Iannello, Alessandro Antonietti and Cornelia Betsch

Teaching is conceived traditionally as a process in which teachers proceed step by step so as to make explicit the contents and procedures that students are asked to learn. In turn, students are expected to master such contents and procedures in an explicit way with the help of teachers' actions. That is, students should be able to analyse what they have learned and identify the procedures necessary to process the contents properly. If we define intuition as a mental act that occurs quickly in the student's mind, yields direct evidence and does not require (or requires only limited) awareness of the way s/he reasoned or the need to have the reasons leading to a given conclusion clear in mind (Hogarth, 2001; Khatri & Ng, 2000; Parikh, 1994; Stanovich & West, 2002), one might be inclined to believe that intuition plays a subordinate role in the teaching process. In fact, teachers should not lead learners to grasp concepts or apply procedures in an intuitive manner – that is, in an immediate and automatic way – because this is not the goal of instruction under the assumption that true knowledge can be articulated and supported by arguments.

Moreover, intuition even seems to be a misleading teaching approach. The naive conceptions held by students before becoming involved in the teaching process are usually grounded on intuitions they have about reality. Such conceptions are often wrong and need to be restructured through conceptual changes; and some authors argue that this process is the core process of teaching (Limón & Mason, 2002). Furthermore, some contents to be learned are counter-intuitive. In this case, teaching should be used not only to help students replace intuitions with more-relevant concepts, but also to combat biases produced by the alleged intuitive evidence (Sinatra & Pintrich, 2002).

In any case, even though intuition may lead students to develop correct conceptions, such conceptions do not represent valid knowledge. This is because students cannot articulate and analyse such conceptions explicitly and thus cannot highlight their foundation, probe their truthfulness by means of arguments, or communicate the concepts to others by making clear why they trust their validity.

If we adopt the distinction proposed by Reichenbach (1951), we can say that even if intuition might play a role in the *discovery* context (i.e., the process through which a student comes to understand something), intuition could not play a role in the *justification* context (i.e., the process through which students give an account of what they have learned).

In this chapter we shall attempt to show that, in opposition to the traditional view mentioned above, intuition might represent a fruitful teaching strategy. Intuition can be considered to be either the *goal* of teaching (that is, a skill that can be trained: Hogarth, 2001) or the *means* through which a goal is achieved (such as the use of intuition in decision making or in problem solving and creativity). In this chapter we shall consider intuition to be a means that teachers can apply in order to steer and support students' attempts to comprehend and build knowledge in instructional settings. Such means include, for instance, eliciting learner insights, asking learners to carry out a given task while following the path they perceive to be the most promising, and taking into account students' impressions and spontaneous ideas.

Why might intuition facilitate teaching? According to a constructivist perspective (Von Glasersfeld, 1995), the starting place of teaching should always be the students' pre-comprehension of the concepts to be learned. Indeed, students should not be conceived as empty vases that teachers should fill with new notions. Rather, teachers should be aware that students always have their own view about what teachers are going to say and explain (Gardner, 1999). Thus, pre-conceptions that learners obtain through intuition, irrespective of whether they are true or false, can be the starting point of teaching. Initial student insights do not have to be discarded, since they allow teachers to recognize learners' naive conceptions, providing them with a starting point for interactions with students. This allows teachers to make connections between what learners (naively, perhaps falsely so) believe and what they should (more correctly) know. In other words, intuition can provide teachers with 'advance organisers' (Ausubel, 1968) – that is, reference points whose validity teachers can begin to question by showing inconsistencies or weaknesses, in order to convince students that they need to alter their conceptions.

Second, intuition always involves a selection of reality, since it catches only some features, which may or may not be relevant. In any case, intuition provides individuals with a simplified representation of what is to be learned. This allows learners to apply, without cognitive overload, mental operations that enable them to extend and integrate current knowledge, in the case that intuitions are correct, or amend pre-conceptions, in the case that they are incorrect. Good intuitions usually lead learners to identify the essential aspects of the situation in question. Such a structural representation helps students easily extrapolate the most important elements and schematize them so that salient aspects are kept in mind (Gladwell, 2005).

Due to its holistic nature, intuition facilitates the simultaneous processing of different elements (Antonietti, 1991). As a consequence, intuition leads one to understand relations: the simplification produced by intuition does not isolate an element from its context, but rather places it in relation to other elements, so that a network is highlighted (Gladwell, 2005). The resulting pattern of relations provides a preliminary, general overview of the situation which, in turn, reduces cognitive load and leads to faster cognitive processing.

A further reason supporting the claim that intuition can be beneficial in teaching stems from the fact that intuition refers to a background of knowledge that is familiar to the individual. In this way, intuition provides a sense of certainty (Bechara & Damasio, 2005), which helps reduce the sense of fear and anxiety that might be experienced by learners when facing a new field of knowledge. Finally, intuition is also sometimes accompanied by a sense of trustworthiness (Kuhnle, ch. 19 this volume). This leads students to feel self-confident and, thus, encourages them to become involved in the learning process.

TAKING COGNITIVE STYLES INTO ACCOUNT

On the basis of these remarks, we may rightly believe that intuition plays a role in the teaching process, in the sense that teachers can rely on students' intuitions. It follows that a good teaching strategy frequently evokes intuitions, takes them seriously and encourages learners to work on and through them. However, the role of intuition may be influenced by students' personal characteristics, such as different inclinations to use intuition. In fact, it is well recognized that the actual use of intuition is determined by both contextual and dispositional factors (Burke & Miller, 1999). Even though specific external conditions, such as time pressure (Kuo, 1998) or poorly structured situations (Behling & Eckel, 1991), could induce the use of intuition, it seems that individual preferences are prominent even in situations that explicitly require the employment of a certain strategy (Betsch, 2004). Thus, we must also consider the fundamental role of personal disposition and how such individual differences actually affect the teaching process.

An individual characteristic that represents a critical intervening variable in the study of learning is the way in which individuals process and organize information – also termed 'cognitive style' (Hunt et al., 1989). Individual differences in cognitive functioning may be defined as a cognitive style when the differences are possibly innate, pervasive and stable; that is, they appear consistently in different situations and are fairly fixed characteristics at different times (Ausburn & Ausburn, 1978; Peterson et al., 2009; Riding et al., 1993). Cognitive styles can be described as habitual ways of thinking and transversal dimensions that lead individuals to similar attitudes, behaviours and strategies in a variety of domains. They reflect 'how', rather than 'how well', people process information. Cognitive styles are considered to be ways of *using* instead of *possessing* abilities (Antonietti, 2003) or, alternatively, high-level heuristics that organize lower-level strategies, operations, propensities and abilities in complex processes (Messick, 1976). Whereas the abilities are measured in terms of *level* of performance, styles are measured in terms of *manner* of performance. Moreover, they differ in that abilities are *unipolar* dimensions, whereas styles are *bipolar* or *multipolar* (Antonietti, 2003).

When considering cognitive styles as specific ways in which people habitually process information, it is clear that styles make a difference in behaviour and performance in various domains of life (Zhang & Sternberg, 2009) including learning (Sternberg, 1997; Sternberg et al., 1998). Recent studies have identified cognitive style as a good predictor for academic achievement beyond general abilities (Sternberg & Zhang, 2001).

Styles play an important role in mediating access to both information and performance feedback (Evans et al., 2010; Riding & Rayner, 1998). Moreover, learning outcomes improve when instructional material is customized to one's cognitive style (Riding & Ashmore, 1980; Thomas & McKay, 2010). The so-called 'cognitive style matching hypothesis' (Graff, 2003) suggests that when the features of an instructional setting are consistent with the learner's style (matching condition), better outcomes occur in comparison to mismatching conditions (Ford & Chen, 2001; see also work on decisional fit: Betsch & Kunz, 2008).

Many proposals have been offered for dimensions of cognitive style based on the idea of bipolarity, which is represented by two value-equal opposing poles that correspond to distinctive modes of cognitive functioning, such as field dependent–independent (Witkin, 1962), impulsive–reflective (Kagan et al., 1964), holist–serialist (Pask, 1972), verbalizer–visualizer (Paivio, 1971) and adaptive–innovative (Kirton, 1976, 1989). However, when confronted with a myriad of style dimensions of a common conceptual framework and language, some researchers attempted to integrate different style categorizations into a more unifying intuition–deliberation dimension (Allinson & Hayes, 1996; Cassidy, 2004; Coffield et al., 2004; Entwistle, 1981; Vance et al., 2007; Zhang & Sternberg, 2007). In each of the aforementioned bipolar dimensions, one of the features can be considered typical of the intuitive and analytical constructs. For example, field-dependent individuals tend to show less inclination to separate objects from their environment and thus prefer more global, perhaps intuitive, approaches to cognitive activity. Field-independent individuals, on the other hand, prefer focusing on details and basic relationships, thus adopting a more detailed, perhaps analytical perspective (Witkin, 1962). Impulsive individuals tend to respond quickly to a cognitive task, while reflective individuals pause and reflect before coming to the solution (Kagan et al., 1964). Serialists operate with a step-by-step approach, focusing on small amounts of information at a time before linking these steps. On the contrary, holists consider a large amount of material and attempt to achieve understanding by identifying global and major patterns in the data (Pask, 1972; Pask & Scott, 1972). Finally, visualizers prefer to process information quickly by inspecting (concrete or mental) pictures, whereas verbalizers tend to elaborate information by the mediation of sequential, verbal operations (Paivio, 1971).

Thus, cognitive styles can be considered to be simply different conceptions with specific aspects of the same intuitive–analytical dimension. Specifically, people with an intuitive style tend to approach cognitive tasks in a fast, effortless and automatic way and rely more on sudden feelings and 'gut instincts'. For this reason, the intuitive style has been described as global, impulsive, divergent and inductive. Analytical individuals, on the other hand, prefer to apply logical techniques in a slower, elaborated and planned manner when presented with a cognitive task, leading the analytical style to be classified as sequential, reflective, convergent and deductive (Allinson & Hayes, 1996; Betsch & Iannello, 2010).

Intuition and analysis can be treated as opposite poles along the same bipolar dimension and, therefore, as mutually exclusive (Allinson & Hayes, 1996; Hayes & Allinson, 1994; Myers & McCaulley, 1985; Simon, 1987). However, recent findings (Hodgkinson & Sadler-Smith, 2003) suggest that individual behaviour is better modelled by two separate unipolar scales. In line with dual process theories, this view argues that intuition and analysis are complementary and, as a consequence, can be applied concurrently. Instruments based on this premise measure intuition and analysis separately, since the two constructs are conceived as orthogonal and independent dimensions (Betsch, 2004; Isenberg, 1984; Pacini & Epstein, 1999; Sauter, 1999). This implies that individuals process information with two parallel, interactive systems, which are interconnected despite the fact that they operate in different ways (Epstein, 1994). These two ways of thinking permit individuals to switch back and forth as required between the two modes of processing, albeit moderated to some degree by individual styles and preferences (Dane & Pratt, 2007).

THE CASE OF TEACHING THROUGH HYPERMEDIA

The aforementioned view of the intuitive–analytical style can be exemplified by taking into consideration the role that cognitive styles play when teachers ask students to employ hypermedia tools. Hypermedia tools are instructional devices that present learners with pieces of knowledge expressed in different formats (written texts, spoken discourses, graphs, pictures, movies and so on), which cannot be accessed according to a fixed, linear (that is, sequential) order but rather according to a non-linear order that is chosen by learners themselves (allowing learners to 'jump' from one piece of knowledge to another according to personal preferences). When teachers provide learners with the opportunity to move freely through a hypermedia presentation, learners should develop personal navigation patterns that mirror their own cognitive characteristics. The flexibility offered by hypermedia, according to the matching hypothesis mentioned previously, should enhance learning by customizing the imposed structure of learning materials to learners' own cognitive profiles. In other words, individual differences in cognitive style should lead to distinct navigation patterns, which in turn should result in different learning outcomes.

Consistent with such claims, some authors have found that people with different cognitive styles, if allowed to navigate a hypermedia freely, use different search (Leader & Klein, 1996) or browsing (Palmquist & Kim, 2000) strategies, despite the fact that, in some cases, the match between teacher and student cognitive styles yielded no advantages (Graff, 2003). A lack of relationships between cognitive styles, browsing patterns and learning outcomes were reported in the literature (Liu & Reed, 1994). Riding and Grimley (1999) found that students possessing an analytical cognitive style did not learn as well as students with an intuitive–holistic style when using a multimedia presentation of information that fragmented the text to be learned into several small units. Graff (2003) observed that the best learning results were obtained neither by analysts nor by intuitive–holists but rather by students displaying an intermediate style.

In order to better understand the relations between the tendency to think intuitively and teaching through hypermedia tools, some further studies were conducted by making reference to the right–left thinking distinction proposed by Torrance (1988). Even though some data support the alleged biological basis of such a distinction (Fabbri et al., 2007), and distinct cognitive functions can be attributed to different brain hemispheres (Springer & Deutsch, 1997), the right–left distinction is meant in a metaphoric sense (that is, right thinkers are not considered to be individuals 'using' predominantly the right hemisphere, but rather individuals showing stylistic profiles that roughly correspond to features traditionally attributed to the right hemisphere: Coffield et al., 2004). The right style refers to holistic thinking and implies a preference for visual code and parallel processing: it is distinctive of intuitive individuals. The left style is associated with logical–analytical thinking and implies a preference for sequential processing of information, verbal expression and systematic approach.

Calcaterra et al. (2005) hypothesized that left-thinkers should browse a hypermedia in a linear way, whereas individuals preferring intuitive strategies (right-thinkers) should follow non-linear paths. To test this hypothesis, they assessed the cognitive style using the Italian version (Antonietti et al., 2005) of the Your Style of Thinking and Learning (SOLAT) questionnaire (Torrance, 1988) as well as frequency of computer use and computer skills in more than 300 undergraduates. From the initial sample, 40 students were selected to form four groups with the following characteristics: (a) 10 high computer users –analytical thinkers, (b) 10 high computer users – intuitive thinkers, (c) 10 low computer users – analytical thinkers, (d) 10 low computer users – intuitive thinkers. All participants completed a self-report questionnaire measuring spatial orientation and were then requested to browse freely a hypermedia presentation on the ancient Mayan civilization. Finally, the students completed a post-test to assess recall of the hypermedia presentation and the conceptual organization of the acquired knowledge. Findings indicate that hypermedia navigation behaviour was linked to computer skills rather than to cognitive style; and that learning outcomes were affected by neither cognitive style nor computer skills. However, learning outcomes were positively affected by specific search patterns, that is, by re-visiting hypermedia sections and visiting overview sections in the early stages of hypermedia browsing. Furthermore, the navigation of overview sections and holistic processing fostered knowledge representation in the form of maps. These findings suggest that the way a hypermedia is browsed affects learning outcomes, but the impact of cognitive style on both hypermedia navigation and learning outcomes is less important than predicted.

A further investigation was conducted to study both the effects of the students' style on hypermedia navigation and the effects of some hints aimed at inducing learners to browse the hypermedia according to a given strategy (Fiorina et al., 2007). Two-hundred students were asked to visit a website. Navigation of the website was preceded by some initial tasks (hints) that activated either the intuitive or the analytical thinking style; 50 males and 50 females were randomly assigned to each of the two conditions. Then participants were free to browse the hypermedia while their navigation paths were tracked. Finally, participants completed the SOLAT questionnaire. Navigational patterns were related to the kind of hint received as well as to thinking style. More precisely, the intuitive hints induced learners to navigate the hypermedia more rapidly and follow a higher number of discontinuous sequences. Results showed that hints influenced hypermedia navigation, leading participants to apply strategies consistent with the initial tasks, whereas there was no evidence of any relationships between thinking style and navigation behaviour.

This study suggests that the intuitive style must not be conceived as an internal trait that is independent of task features; rather, it should be conceptualized as a disposition that tends to occur within a given context (Gutiérrez & Rogoff, 2003). As the theorists of thinking styles themselves admit, almost nobody is entirely either an intuitive or an analytical thinker. Everyone normally uses both styles depending on the situation. However, one of the two styles does tend to be privileged if the situation does not suggest explicitly that a particular style is preferable. Moreover, in some contexts or specific situations a person can move from one thinking style to the other or to a more integrated one. This supports the idea that intuition is part of a dual mental system that allows individuals to activate intuitive and analytical processing concurrently, functionally shift from an intuitive way of thinking to an analytical one and vice versa and compensate the weaknesses of one mode of thinking by using parts of the other.

BEYOND THE MATCHING HYPOTHESIS

At the beginning of this chapter, we recognized that the role of intuition in teaching has been neglected by the Western school tradition. This is not true in non-Western cultures, where young people are encouraged to rely on intuition (Antonietti et al., 1995). For instance, in some nomadic tribes shepherds realize that a head of cattle is missing not by counting animals one by one but simply by looking at the flock. In contrast, in Western schools we are taught to apply an arithmetic procedure rather than a quick intuitive act to estimate the size of a group of elements. Such cultural differences regarding the use of intuition may be one reason why children's games in some countries are aimed at training this kind of intuitive skill. For example, in some African villages children collect stones into small piles and then guess how many stones are in each pile: the child who successfully estimated the number of stones at one glance is the winner. Similarly, in Europe during the Renaissance period, the ability to evaluate the quantity and/or size of goods to be purchased was highly appreciated, since merchants were not always able to count and measure them; consequently, apprentices were encouraged to rely on intuitions of this kind.

These ethnographic and historical examples suggest that intuition may play a role in teaching. In this chapter, we attempted to identify possible scientific reasons supporting such a role. We argued that if teachers do not ignore and discard students' naive ideas and perceptions, intuition can provide learners with a preliminary representation of the topic to be taught: such representations are functionally relevant, since they are selective (pragmatic features are stressed and structural aspects highlighted), holistic (include relational patterns), familiar and conducive to confidence and self-efficacy.

On these grounds we maintain that, on the one hand, intuition is useful to bootstrap the teaching process. In this case intuition operates as a kind of thinking that *precedes* the application of analytical reasoning. On the other hand, intuition gives the possibility of *overcoming* the limitations of analytical thinking. This is because the mental steps to be followed have become automatic and, therefore, can be skipped, allowing the student to proceed quickly and directly. The results of an investigation carried out by Antonietti et al. (1998) in the field of mathematics teaching can be used to exemplify this. The authors found that the intuitive thinking style was predominant in both underachievers and overachievers, whereas the analytical style characterized average students. It seems that the intuitive approach is followed by students who are not able to apply the sequential algorithms they were taught (which would have allowed them to reach acceptable learning outcomes), as well as by students who do not need to proceed mechanically step by step, since they can skip some passages. To summarize, intuitive strategies are twofold: they can be implemented both by skilled students and by poor achievers. However, in order to produce good learning outcomes, they must be integrated in analytical ways of thinking, as has taken place in the case of overachievers but not underachievers.

Such a view leads us to go beyond the idea that optimal teaching involves a match between learner style and the way in which learners must be taught. Instead, teachers should allow students to pass from an intuitive to an analytical approach, and vice versa, according to the features of the task, demands, resources available, situational constraints, expected outcomes and so on. Some findings, in this case also those concerning mathematics teaching, support such a claim. Riding and Caine (1993) reported that the best academic performance was obtained by students who integrated intuitive and analytical styles. Similarly, Westman (1993) found that students with the highest grades in mathematics showed a high level of flexibility in thinking. The message is that students should be taught to self-regulate the activation of the two forms of thinking (Boekaerts, 2002) as well as monitor and control the implementation of the intuitive strategies, so that they can learn when intuition can be a productive approach to learning.

REFERENCES

Allinson, C. W., & Hayes, J. 1996. The Cognitive Style Index: A measure of intuition analysis for organizational research. *Journal of Management Studies*, 33: 119–135.

Antonietti, A. 1991. Why does mental visualization facilitate problem-solving? In R. H. Logie, & M. Denis (Eds.), *Mental images in human cognition*: 211–227. Amsterdam: Elsevier.

Antonietti, A. 2003. Cognitive styles assessment. In R. Fernandez-Ballesteros (Ed.), *Encyclopaedia of psychological assessment*: vol. I: 248–253. London: Sage.

Antonietti, A., Angelini C., & Cerana, P. 1995. *L'intuizione visiva* [Visual intuition]. Milano: Franco Angeli Editore.

Antonietti, A., Bartolomeo, A., & Carrubba, L. 1998. Successo-insuccesso in matematica e stile di pensiero [Achievement and underachievement in mathematics and thinking style]. *La Matematica e la sua Didattica*, 4: 423–443.

Antonietti, A., Fabio, R. A., Boari, G., & Bonanomi, A. 2005. Il questionario 'Style of Learning and Thinking' (SOLAT): Dati psicometrici per una validazione e standardizzazione della versione italiana [The questionnaire 'Style of Learning and Thinking' (SOLAT): Psychometric data for the validation and standardization of the Italian version]. *TPM Testing-Psicometria-Metodologia*, 12: 299–316.

Ausburn, L. J., & Ausburn, F. B. 1978. Cognitive styles: Some information and implication for instructional design. *Educational Communication and Technology*, 26: 337–354.

Ausubel, D. 1968. *Educational psychology. A cognitive view.* New York: Holt, Rinehart & Winston.

Bechara, A., & Damasio, A. R. 2005. The somatic marker hypothesis: A neural theory of economic decision. *Games and Economic Behavior*, 52: 336–372.

Behling, O., & Eckel, H. 1991. Making sense out of intuition. *Academy of Management Executive*, 5: 46–54.

Betsch, C. 2004. Präferenz für Intuition und Deliberation. Inventar zur Erfassung von affect und kognitionsbasiertem Entscheiden [Preference for intuition and deliberation (PID): An inventory for assessing affect- and cognition-based decision-making]. *Zeitschrift für Differentielle und Diagnostische Psychologie*, 25: 179–197.

Betsch, C., & Iannello, P. 2010. Measuring individual differences in intuitive and deliberate decision making styles – a comparison of different measures. In A. Glöckner, & C. Witteman (Eds.). *Tracing intuition: Recent methods in measuring intuitive and deliberate processes in decision making*: 251–267. London: Psychology Press.

Betsch, C., & Kunz, J. J. 2008. Individual strategy preference and decisional fit. *Journal of Behavioral Decision Making*, 21: 532–555.

Boekaerts, M. 2002. Bringing about change in the classroom: Strengths and weaknesses of the self-regulated learning approach. *Learning and Instruction*, 12: 589–604.

Burke, L. A., & Miller, M. K. 1999. Taking the mystery out of intuitive decision making. *Academy of Management Executive*, 13: 91–99.

Calcaterra, A., Antonietti, A., & Underwood, J. 2005. Cognitive style, hypermedia navigation and learning. *Computers and Education*, 44: 441–457.

Cassidy, S. 2004. Learning styles: An overview of theories, models and measures. *Educational Psychology*, 24: 419–444.

Coffield, F., Moseley, D., Hall, E., & Ecclestone, K. 2004. *Learning styles and pedagogy in post-16 learning: A systematic and critical review*. London: Learning & Skills Research Centre.

Dane, E., & Pratt, M. G. 2007. Exploring intuition and its role in managerial decision making. *Academy of Management Review*, 32: 33–54.

Entwistle, N.J. 1981. *Styles of teaching and learning: An integrated outline of educational psychology for students, teachers, and lecturers.* Chichester, UK: Wiley.

Epstein, S. 1994. Integration of the cognitive and the psychodynamic unconscious. *American Psychologist*, 49: 709–724.

Evans, C., Cools, E., & Charlesworth, Z. M. 2010. Learning in higher education – how cognitive and learning styles matter. *Teaching in Higher Education*, 15: 467–478.

Fabbri, M., Antonietti, A., Giorgetti, M., Tonetti, L., & Natale, V. 2007. Circadian typology and style of thinking differences. *Learning and Individual Differences*, 17: 175–180.

Fiorina L., Antonietti, A., Colombo, B., & Bartolomeo, A. 2007. Thinking style, browsing primes and hypermedia navigation. *Computer and Education*, 49: 916–941.

Ford, N., & Chen, S. Y. 2001. Matching/mismatching revisited: An empirical study of learning and teaching styles. *British Journal of Educational Technology*, 32: 5–22.

Gardner, H. 1999. *The disciplined mind: What all students should understand.* New York: Simon & Schuster.

Gladwell, M. 2005. *Blink: The power of thinking without thinking.* New York: Back Bay Books.

Graff, M. 2003. Assessing learning from hypertext: An individual difference perspective. *Journal of Interactive Learning Research*, 14: 425–438.

Gutiérrez, K. D., & Rogoff, B. 2003. Cultural ways of learning: Individual traits or repertoires of practice. *Educational Researcher*, 32: 19–25.

Hayes, J., & Allinson, C. W. 1994. Cognitive style and its relevance for management practice. *British Journal of Management*, 5: 53–71.

Hodgkinson, G. P., & Sadler-Smith, E. 2003. Complex or unitary? A critique and empirical reassessment of the Allinson–Hayes Cognitive Style Index. *Journal of Occupational and Organizational Psychology*, 76: 243–268.

Hogarth, R. M. 2001. *Educating intuition.* Chicago, IL: University of Chicago Press.

Hunt, R. G., Krzystofiak, F. J., Meindl, J. R., & Yousry, A. M. 1989. Cognitive style and decision making. *Organizational Behavior and Human Decision Processes*, 44: 436–453.

Isenberg, D. J. 1984. How senior managers think. *Harvard Business Review*, November/December: 81–90.

Kagan, J., Rosman, B. L., Day, D., Albert, J., & Phillips, W. 1964. Information processing in the child: Significance of analytic and reflective attitudes. *Psychological Monographs*, 78: 1–37.

Khatri, N., & Ng, H. A. 2000. The role of intuition in strategic decision making. *Human Relations*, 53: 57–86.

Kirton, M. J. 1976. Adaptors and innovators, a description and measure. *Journal of Applied Psychology*, 61: 622–629.

Kirton, M. J. (Ed.). 1989. *Adaptors and innovators.* London: Routledge.

Kuo, F. Y. 1998. Managerial intuition and the development of executive support systems. *Decision Support Systems*, 24: 89–103.

Leader, L. F., & Klein, G. D. 1996. The effects of search tool type and cognitive style on performance during hypermedia databases searches. *Educational Technology Research and Development*, 44: 5–151.

Limón, M., & Mason, L. (Eds.). 2002. *Reconsidering conceptual change.* Dordrecht: Kluwer.

Liu, M., & Reed, W. M. 1994. The relationship between the learning strategies and learning styles in a hypermedia environment. *Computers in Human Behavior*, 10: 419–434.

Messick, S. 1976. *Individuality in learning* (1st ed.). San Francisco: Jossey-Bass.

Myers, I., & McCaulley, M. H. 1985. *Manual: A guide to the development and use of the Myers-Briggs Type Indicator.* Palo Alto, CA: Consulting Psychologists Press.

Pacini, R., & Epstein, S. 1999. The relation of rational and experiential information processing styles to personality basic beliefs, and ratio-bias phenomenon. *Journal of Personality and Social Psychology*, 76: 972–987.

Paivio, A. 1971. *Imagery and verbal processes.* New York: Holt Rinehart & Winston.

Palmquist, R. A., & Kim, K.-S. 2000. Cognitive style and on-line database search experience as predictors of Web search performance. *Journal of the American Society for Information Science*, 51: 558–566.

Parikh, J. 1994. *Intuition: The new frontier of management.* Oxford: Blackwell Business.

Pask, G. 1972. A fresh look at cognition and the individual. *International Journal of Man–Machine Studies*, 4: 211–216.

Pask, G., & Scott, B. C. E. 1972. Learning strategies and individual competence. *International Journal of Man–Machine Studies*, 4: 217–235.

Peterson, E. R., Rayner, S. G., & Armstrong, S. J. 2009. Researching the psychology of cognitive style and learning style: Is there really a future? *Learning and Individual Differences*, 19: 518–523.

Reichenbach, H. 1951. *The rise of scientific philosophy*. Berkeley, CA: University of California Press.

Riding, R.J., & Ashmore, J. 1980. Verbalizer–visualizer, a cognitive style dimension. *Journal of Mental Imagery*, 1: 109–126.

Riding, R. J., & Caine, T. 1993. Cognitive style and GCSE performance in mathematics, English language and French. *Educational Psychology*, 13: 59–67.

Riding, R. J., Glass, A., & Douglas, G. 1993. Individual differences in thinking: Cognitive and neurophysiological perspectives. *Special Issue: Thinking. Educational Psychology*, 13: 267–279.

Riding, R. J., & Grimley, M. 1999. Cognitive style, gender and learning from multi-media materials in II year old children. *British Journal of Educational Technology*, 30: 42–56.

Riding, R., & Rayner, S. 1998. *Cognitive styles and learning strategies*. London: Fulton.

Sauter, V. L. 1999. Intuitive decision-making. *Communications of the ACM*, 42: 109–115.

Simon, H. A. 1987. Making management decisions: The role of intuition and emotion. *Academy of Management Executive*, February: 57–64.

Sinatra, G. M., & Pintrich, P. R. 2002. *Intentional conceptual change*. Hillsdale, NJ: Lawrence Erlbaum Associates.

Springer, S. P., & Deutsch, G. 1997. *Left brain, right brain: Perspectives from cognitive neuroscience*. New York: Freeman.

Stanovich, K. E., & West, R. F. 2002. Individual differences in reasoning: Implications for the rationality debate? *Behavioral and Brain Sciences*, 23: 645–665.

Sternberg, R. J. 1997. *Successful intelligence*. New York: Plume.

Sternberg, R. J., Torff, B., & Grigorenko, E. L. 1998. Teaching triarchically improves school achievement. *Journal of Educational Psychology*, 90: 1–11.

Sternberg, R. J., & Zhang, L. F. 2001. Thinking styles across cultures: Their relationships with student learning. In Sternberg, & Zhang (Eds.), *Perspectives on thinking, learning and cognitive styles*: 227–247. Mahwah, NJ: Lawrence Erlbaum Associates.

Thomas, P. R. & McKay, J. B. 2010. Cognitive styles and instructional design in university learning. *Learning and Individual Differences*, 20(3): 197–202.

Torrance, E. P. 1988. *Your Style of Learning and Thinking*. Benseville, IL: Scholastic Testing Service.

Vance, C. M., Groves, K. S., Paik, Y., & Kindler, H. 2007. Understanding and measuring linear–nonlinear thinking style for enhanced management education and professional practice. *Academy of Management Learning and Education*, 6: 167–185.

Von Glasersfeld, E. 1995. *Radical constructivism: A way of knowing and learning*. London: Falmer Press.

Westman, A. S. 1993. Learning styles are content specific and probably influenced by content areas studied. *Psychological Reports*, 73: 512–514.

Witkin, H. A. 1962. *Psychological differentiation: Studies of development*. New York: Wiley.

Zhang, L. F., & Sternberg, R. J. 2007. *The nature of intellectual styles*. Mahwah, NJ: Lawrence Erlbaum Associates.

Zhang, L. F., & Sternberg, R. J. (Eds.). 2009. *Perspectives on the nature of intellectual styles*. Heidelberg: Springer.

PART 4

NONLOCAL PERSPECTIVE

16 Intuition and the noetic
Dean Radin

Intuition traditionally refers to a way of knowing through 'immediate apprehension', meaning to know without the usual constraints of space or time, and unmediated by the ordinary senses (Osbeck, 2001). This meaning is similar to the Greek words *noēsis* or *noētikos*, which refer to ways of knowing based on inner wisdom, direct understanding, or impressions that transcend rational analysis. The English version of *noēsis* is the word noetic, described by William James in *The Varieties of Religious Experience* as 'states of insight into depths of truth unplumbed by the discursive intellect. They are illuminations, revelations, full of significance and importance, all inarticulate though they remain; and as a rule they carry with them a curious sense of authority' (James, 1902: 371). Noetic experiences manifest as intuitions that appear in a flash, out of the blue, with correct answers to otherwise intractable scientific or technical problems, or with complete scores to intricate musical compositions, or with optimal solutions to complicated decisions.

Because of the emphasis placed on rational knowing in Western scholarship, and especially because of the scientific tenet of physicalism – the belief that 'mental entities, properties, relations and facts are all physical' (Crane & Mellor, 1990: 185) – the traditional meanings of intuition and noetic ways of knowing came to be regarded as an inferior epistemology at best, and superstitious nonsense at worst. For about half of the twentieth century, the enthusiastic adoption of physicalism led many psychologists to embrace the peculiar Catch-22 whereby minds concluded with great confidence that there were no minds after all.

As the cognitive sciences and neurosciences evolved through the latter half of the twentieth century, the unconscious mind – once the sole province of psychoanalysis – became scientifically palatable in terms of subconscious processing. As a result, the once-taboo topic of intuition also became an acceptable topic of study, not in the traditional noetic sense but rather in the domain of computer-inspired background information processing. This led to studies of intuition involving psychophysiological and cortical markers of implicit learning, the brain circuitry responsible for the 'ah ha' experience, identification of unconscious cognitive biases, sets of heuristics useful for making snap decisions under pressure, and so on (Bechara et al., 1997; Kahneman & Tversky, 1973; Luo & Niki, 2003; Myers, 2002; Plessner et al., 2008).

The new openness to studying intuition is reflected by an explosive increase in journal publications. Based on a search of PubMed.com (on June 23, 2010), before 1970 there were only 37 journal publications with the word 'intuition' mentioned anywhere in the article. In the decade of the 1970s, 48 articles were published. In the 1980s, 150. In the 1990s, 486. From 2001 to mid-2010, 1,174 articles were published.

As the study of intuition continues to expand in energy and scope, and our intuitions about intuition continue to evolve, the time seems right to seriously reexamine the traditional form of noetic intuition. For this idea to gain currency, two capacities would need to be demonstrated: the ability to gain knowledge from a distance without use of the ordinary senses, and that this is not bound by the usual constraints of time.

Investigations exploring such capabilities are seldom reported in the mainstream academic literature, but there is a scientific discipline that has focused on these questions since the late nineteenth century – the discipline of parapsychology – and here one finds a vast literature, including contemporary experiments using the most sophisticated neuroimaging techniques. Thousands of laboratory experiments and over a dozen meta-analyses of these data have been published. The cumulative results provide evidence strongly in favor of the noetic form of intuition (Radin, 1997a, b, 2006). An extensive review of these studies is beyond the scope of this chapter, but discussion of a few types of experiments will serve to illustrate the extant literature.

MIND TO MIND

Anecdotal reports of mind-to-mind interactions have been documented throughout history and in all cultures. Many scientists assume that such stories are solely due to coincidence, misreporting or confabulation. But starting in the mid-1800s, controlled experiments were devised to explicitly test whether it was possible for minds to gain information directly from other minds. Over many decades, methods were repeatedly refined and criticized, and all potential loopholes progressively closed, until a simple but rigorous technique evolved in the 1970s which is still in use today.

The method is known as the *ganzfeld* (German for 'whole field') telepathy experiment. A participant in the ganzfeld condition reclines in an easy chair in a sound-proof room with translucent hemispheres placed over the eyes. The participant's face is illuminated with a soft red light, the eyes remain open, and white noise is played over headphones.

After a few minutes in this state, most participants accommodate to the uniform stimuli and soon begin to experience mild visual and auditory hallucinations.

The experiment involves two people, a nominal 'sender' and 'receiver.' The receiver relaxes in the ganzfeld condition isolated from the sender, who is sequestered in a distant room. The sender views an image or video clip randomly selected out of a large pool of potential target clips. The sender attempts to mentally 'transmit' the contents of the target to the receiver, and the receiver is asked to speak aloud his or her impressions into an audio recorder. A typical sending period lasts about 30 minutes.

Then the receiver is taken out of the ganzfeld condition by an experimenter, who is also blind to the actual target. The receiver's recorded impressions are played back while he or she views four images or video clips in random order, one of which is the actual target along with three decoys. The targets in these target pools are previously arranged to be as different from one another as possible to help the receiver select just the one target which best matches his or her impressions.

Under the null hypothesis of no telepathy, the probability that the receiver will correctly guess the actual target is 1 in 4, for a 25% chance hit rate. Over repeated sessions if the average hit rate is sufficiently above 25%, this provides evidence for a communications anomaly that confirms the essence of anecdotal reports of telepathy.

To provide valid data, diligence must be exercised to prevent any conventional means of communication between sender and receiver. In the best studies, surveillance is employed to detect subject or experimenter fraud, special care is taken to ensure adequate randomization of targets, laboratories are checked by engineers for potential cues carried by sounds, vibrations, odors, lights, or electromagnetic signals, and magicians are asked to assess the setup and protocol for possible means of deception or collusion.

From 1974 to 2008, 32 principal investigators, representing a dozen laboratories located in Europe, North and South America, published 112 articles describing ganzfeld telepathy experiments. Cumulatively they reported 1,498 direct hits in 4,705 trials, resulting in an overall hit rate of 32%, as compared to the chance expected 25%. This hit rate is associated with a p-value of 3×10^{-30}, or odds against chance of a million trillion trillion to one.

This literature has been repeatedly assessed using quantitative meta-analytic techniques to judge whether the reported results are independently repeatable. Six meta-analytical reviews have been published since 1991, including one by a long-term skeptic of telepathy. All six reviews agreed that the cumulative effects were statistically significant and that the reported hit rates were independently repeatable (Bem & Honorton, 1994; Bem et al., 2001; Milton & Wiseman, 1999; Storm & Ertel, 2001; Storm et al., 2010; Utts, 1991). Recently, a team of avowedly skeptical researchers led by Delgado-Romero and Howard (2005) tried to replicate the ganzfeld experiment. They frankly admitted their disbelief in telepathy, but they nevertheless obtained the same, statistically significant, 32% hit rate found by the meta-analyses.

If interpretation of these experiments is correct, then one should expect to find meaningful electrocortical correlates between the brains of isolated people who are asked to keep each other 'in mind.' Such studies have been conducted. Typically one person is exposed to a stimulus, like a light flash, at random times while the brain responses of another, distant and isolated person is monitored. Experiments investigating such correlations using electroencephalographic (EEG) measurements were first reported in student–teacher dyads by Tart (1963) and later in identical twins by Duane and Behrendt (1965), the latter published in *Science*. Those articles stimulated ten replications by eight groups around the world. Of the ten, nine reported positive results, including publications appearing in *Nature* (Targ & Puthoff, 1974), *Behavioral Neuropsychiatry* (Rebert & Turner, 1974), and the *International Journal of Neuroscience* (Orme-Johnson et al., 1982).

In the 1990s, a new series of EEG correlation studies were reported by Grinberg-Zylberbaum et al. (1994) in *Physics Essays*. That report stimulated another round of successful replications (including Radin, 2004a; Standish et al., 2004; Wackerman, 2004; Wackermann et al., 2003). To investigate the source of these EEG correlations in the brain, experiments conducted by Standish et al. (2003) and Achterberg et al. (2005) used functional magnetic resonance imaging (fMRI) and found that the visual cortex of the receiver was significantly activated while the distant sender viewed a flickering checkerboard pattern. This finding was later successfully replicated in another fMRI study (Richards et al., 2005).

Besides the EEG and fMRI experiments, some three dozen other studies conducted by laboratories in the United States, Germany, and the United Kingdom have reported similar effects using autonomic measures, such as skin conductance and heart rate. Meta-analysis of those studies by Schmidt et al. (2004), published in the *British Journal of Psychology*, concluded that they showed significant, repeatable effects, and that alternatives such as selective reporting were insufficient to explain the results.

All of these studies asked whether humans have the capacity to directly apprehend information from a distance, unmediated by the ordinary senses. The data across several classes of experiments consistently indicate that the answer is yes, and the effects are sufficiently robust to allow for successful replication in independent laboratories around the world.

MIND TO MATTER

Another way to study whether the mind has an unmediated way of gaining knowledge from a distance is to take advantage of a curious property of quantum mechanics, namely that quantum objects behave differently when they are observed than when they are not observed. This *quantum measurement problem* violates the common-sense assumption that we live in an objective reality that is completely independent of subjective observers. The measurement problem does not imply solipsism, nor does it support popular enthusiasm about creating one's reality simply by wishing. But it does question the dualistic assumption that subjective and objective are inviolately separate.

Because of the epistemological challenge posed by the quantum measurement problem, virtually all of the founders of quantum mechanics wrote extensively about this issue (Jahn & Dunne, 1986 Wilber, 1984). Some, like Wolfgang Pauli, Pascal Jordan, and Eugene Wigner concluded that consciousness was not merely important, but was fundamentally responsible for how reality manifests (Wigner, 1963, 1964). Jordan wrote, 'Observations not only disturb what has to be measured, they produce it. . . . We compel [the electron] to assume a definite position. . . . We ourselves produce the results of measurement' (Mermin, 1990: 119). This strong view of the role of consciousness in the physical world has been echoed by numerous prominent physicists for over a half-century, from Von Neumann (1955) to d'Espagnat (1976), Squires (1987), Stapp (2001) and many others.

The relevance of the quantum measurement problem to understanding noetic intuition is that if the common-sense distinction between subject and object is wrong (or perhaps a useful but inaccurate approximation of reality), then the concept of unmediated knowledge is no longer unthinkable. This is because 'mediated' in this context refers to connections between subject and object. If instead we live in an intersubjective, holistic medium, which is what quantum theory implies, then mediated connections are not only not required, they are not even possible.

Beyond theoretical conjectures, it is possible to directly test the role of consciousness in the quantum measurement problem (Houtkooper, 2002). Four classes of experiments have been developed: (i) experiments testing the effects of intention on the statistical behavior of random events derived from quantum fluctuations (Bösch et al., 2006; Radin & Nelson, 1989, 2003; Radin et al., 2006), (ii) studies involving macroscopic random systems such as tossed dice and human physiology as 'targets' of intentional influence (Radin & Ferrari, 1991; Schmidt et al., 2004), (iii) experiments involving sequential observation to see whether a second observer could consciously or unconsciously detect if a quantum event had been observed by a first observer (Bierman, 2003; Hall et al., 1977; Schmidt, 1970, 1981; Schmidt et al. 1986; Schmidt & Stapp, 1993), and (iv) experiments investigating conscious influence of photons in optical interferometers (Ibison & Jeffers, 1998; Jahn, 1982; Jeffers & Sloan, 1992).

Together, these studies comprise nearly a thousand experiments, conducted by dozens of investigators over six decades. Collectively they provide independently repeatable evidence that observers do indeed affect the behavior of physical systems. The absolute magnitude of the observed effects tends to be quite small, but from a statistical perspective their existence is unambiguous.

MIND THROUGH TIME

The second major capacity required by noetic intuition is *immediate* apprehension, suggesting a means of perception that transcends time. Numerous experiments have explored whether humans have this ability. One design is based on 'intuition hunch' and 'gut feelings' experiences, which may be described as a sense of foreboding without cognitive content. To detect these unconscious *presentiment* (as opposed to precognitive) effects in the laboratory, one or more measurements of nervous system activity are collected before, during and after a participant is exposed to stimuli of varying emotional affect. The proposed transtemporal effect predicts that the nervous system will respond differently before randomly presented emotional events than before calm events, because of the hypothesis that awareness extends beyond the present moment and into what we normally regard as 'the future', from an ordinary state of awareness.

Presentiment experiments have employed physiological measurements such as skin conductance level (Bierman & Radin, 1997, 1999; McCraty et al., 2004a, b; Parkhomtchouk et al., 2002; Radin, 1997a, 2004a; Vassy, 1978; Wildey, 2001), non-specific skin conductance response (May et al., 2005; Spottiswoode & May, 2003), heart rate (McCraty et al., 2004a, b), brain electrical activity (Hartwell, 1978; Hinterberger et al., 2007; Levin & Kennedy, 1975; Radin & Lobach, 2007), and blood oxygenation levels in the brain as measured with fMRI (Bierman & Scholte, 2002). Stimuli have included emotional vs. calm photographs, stylized happy vs. sad faces, auditory startle tones vs. silence, and electrical shock vs. no-shock. In some studies participants initiated trials of fixed time periods at will, and in others stimuli appeared spontaneously at random times.

As of mid-2010, some two dozen experiments of this type have been reported, and all but one were in the predicted direction. Many of these

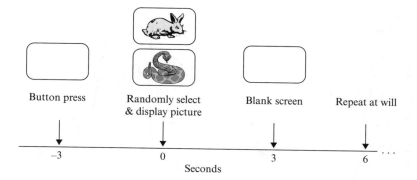

Note: Each trial began with a button press at will (shown at –3 seconds), a photograph was randomly selected and immediately shown at stimulus onset (0 seconds), and then the screen went dark 3 seconds later. Three seconds after that the next trial could begin.

Figure 16.1   Presentiment Study Example

publications included discussions exploring whether the results might be explainable by various artifacts, including subtle cues or anticipatory strategies developed through implicit learning. To date, no artifacts have been identified that can adequately explain these effects via conventional means.

A presentiment study using pupillary dilation as the measurement may be used to illustrate this type of experiment (Radin & Borges, 2009). The study assumed that presentiment effects are largely mediated by the sympathetic nervous system. If this is so, then the pupil would be expected to dilate more before randomly selected emotional vs. calm images. Eye data in this study were collected using a video eyetracking system that provided eye movement direction and pupil diameter measures at 60 samples per second. A computer controlled the random selection and display of picture stimuli, and it coordinated two other computers used to acquire eye-tracking data. The stimuli consisted of color photos from the International Affective Picture System (IAPS; Lang et al., 1999), which provides a wide range of emotional affect and valence.

The experimenter asked a test participant to click a button at will to automatically begin each trial. After the button press a computer screen remained dark for three seconds, then an image was randomly selected from the stimulus set and displayed for three seconds, and then the screen went dark again for three seconds (see Figure 16.1). At this point a message appeared on the screen alerting the participant to continue to the next trial at will.

For purposes of this test 'emotional' was pre-defined as the 5% of contributed trials involving stimulus images with the highest pre-established emotional arousal scores, and 'calm' as the 5% of trials with the lowest

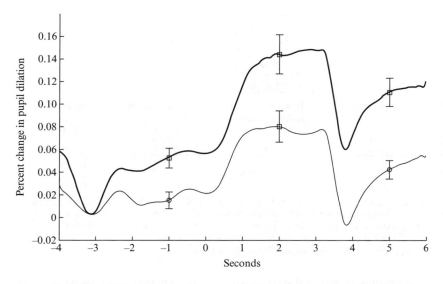

Note: The *bold* (top) line shows average proportional change in pupillary dilation for the 5% most emotional targets; the *thin* (bottom) line shows the same for the 5% calmest targets. Both lines were baseline adjusted to the average pupillary dilation value per trial during the 167 msec prior to the trial-initiating button press (at second –3). Stimulus onset was at second 0 and stimulus offset at second +3. Confidence intervals are plus and minus one standard error, and curves are smoothed 500 msec to clarify the figure.

Figure 16.2   Presentiment Study Results

arousal scores. Results of this test, involving 33 volunteers who together contributed 37 test sessions, showed that the differential change in pupillary dilation during the prestimulus period was significantly positive, as predicted (z = 3.17, p = 0.0008, one-tailed, see Figure 16.2).

DISCUSSION

Most intuition researchers today acknowledge that there is a traditional, 'immediate apprehension' definition of intuition. But the majority have interpreted this idea within the framework of mechanistic, classical physics models of reality. Those models are thought to be incompatible with the possibility of immediate apprehension, and as a result few scientists have been motivated to study whether noetic intuitions are even possible.

As we have seen, experiments have been conducted, and the results do support the traditional notion of intuition. And yet the relevant literature, which was briefly skimmed here, is largely unknown to the larger academic community. On the rare occasion when experimental studies of immediate apprehension or psychic phenomena are discussed at all, they are usually dismissed as mistaken, or of questionable quality, or as non-repeatable. Sometimes this occurs because the authors refer to tertiary sources that misinterpreted or distorted the original work. This seems to be the case of a few conclusions in a scholarly book on the 'powers and perils' of intuition by Myers (2002).

Myers reviewed many approaches to understanding intuition, including the idea that intuition may be a type of psychic phenomenon. Ultimately, this possibility is dismissed with the statement: 'After thousands of experiments, no reproducible ESP phenomenon has ever been discovered' (ibid.: 233). In support of this assertion, Myers cites negative conclusions from reports issued by the US National Research Council (NRC) and the US Central Intelligence Agency (CIA), which were two of several US government agencies in the 1980s tasked with assessing whether psychic phenomena existed (primarily for national security implications).

At first glance, Myers's opinion seems reasonable because at the NRC press conference announcing the report, the chairman of the committee stated that the 'poor quality of psi research was "a surprise to us all – we believed the work would be of much higher quality than it turned out to be."' (News and Comment, 1987: 1502). However, in contrast to that widely publicized statement, the report itself actually reports that 'The best research [in parapsychology] is of higher quality than many critics assume' (Druckman & Swets, 1988: 206). In addition, the press conference failed to mention that the NRC also commissioned an independent assessment of the research quality of these studies. This was performed by two methodology experts from Harvard University, neither of whom had any prior public opinion on this topic. They concluded that in comparison to experiments from four other, non-parapsychological research areas, 'only the ganzfeld ESP [extra-sensory perception] studies regularly meet the basic requirements of sound experimental design', and that the evidence for telepathy was persuasive: 'We feel it would be implausible to entertain the null [hypothesis] given the combined [probability] from these 28 studies' (Harris & Rosenthal, 1988a; see also 1988b, c).

The second report mentioned by Myers was conducted for the CIA at the request of the US Congress. Statistician Jessica Utts of the University of California, Davis, author of numerous university textbooks on statistics and a research design expert, was one of the two principal reviewers. She concluded:

The statistical results of the [remote viewing] studies examined are far beyond what is expected by chance. Arguments that these results could be due to methodological flaws in the experiments are soundly refuted. Effects of similar magnitude to those found in government-sponsored research . . . have been replicated at a number of laboratories across the world. Such consistency cannot be readily explained by claims of flaws or fraud. . . . It is recommended that future experiments focus on understanding how this phenomenon works, and on how to make it as useful as possible. There is little benefit to continuing experiments designed to offer proof . . . (Utts, 1996: 3)

The other reviewer was University of Oregon psychologist Ray Hyman, who, contrary to his previous, uniformly skeptical opinions of ESP research, surprisingly agreed with Utts. He wrote, 'The statistical departures from chance appear to be too large and consistent to attribute to statistical flukes of any sort. . . . I tend to agree with Professor Utts that real effects are occurring in these experiments. *Something* other than chance departures from the null hypothesis has occurred in these experiments' (Hyman, 1996: 57; added italics).

Myers's book also cites a meta-analysis of telepathy studies by Milton and Wiseman (1999). This meta-analysis trumpeted a 'failure to replicate', supporting the orthodox view that psychic effects cannot be repeated in the laboratory, and thus ESP probably does not exist. Few are aware that that article contained a critical flaw, as noted by Delgado-Romero and Howard (2005: 297):

> Milton and Wiseman (1999) employed a rather puzzling form of meta-analysis. They reviewed 30 studies and weighted each study equally . . . rather than the widely accepted procedure of weighting each study by the study's sample size. . . . Thus, one study that ran only 4 pairs of subjects received the same weighting in the overall Effect Size (ES) as did another that tested 100 pairs. Using the more common weighted procedure, the mean ES more than doubled from .013 to .028.

When the proper analysis is employed, Milton and Wiseman's conclusion dramatically flip-flops, shifting from a failure to replicate to a successful replication ($p < 0.05$). This is noteworthy because these telepathy studies followed design protocols that were agreed to in advance by skeptic Ray Hyman in 1986 (Hyman & Honorton, 1986). After that 1986 publication, every one of five published meta-analyses of the ganzfeld telepathy experiments was uniformly positive, unambiguously pointing to the existence of a repeatable effect (Bem & Honorton, 1994; Bem et al., 2001; Storm & Ertel, 2001; Storm et al., 2010; Utts, 1991).

This supports previous conclusions by Child (1985), who reviewed a set of published telepathy experiments for *American Psychologist*, the flagship journal of the American Psychological Association. Child compared what actually took place in those experiments with how they were later described in college psychology textbooks. He concluded that most textbooks contained 'nearly incredible falsification of the facts about the experiments; others simply neglect them' (ibid.: 1228). Roig et al. (1991) later independently conducted a similar analysis, reaching the same conclusion.

From this it seems increasingly likely that as our understanding of the physical world becomes more comprehensive, and as our assumptions of what consciousness is capable of continues to expand, then our understanding of intuition will also be transformed. We shall probably find that some forms of intuition are indeed mediated by mechanistic processes in the nervous system and brain, but there are also other forms of intuition that will require entirely new ways of understanding and apprehending the world.

REFERENCES

Achterberg, J., Cooke, K., Richards, T., Standish, L. J., Kozak, L., & Lake, J. 2005. Evidence for correlations between distant intentionality and brain function in recipients: A functional magnetic resonance imaging analysis. *Journal of Alternative and Complementary Medicine*, 11(6): 965–971.

Bechara, A., Damasio, H., Tranel, D., & Damasio, A. R. 1997. Deciding advantageously before knowing the advantageous strategy. *Science*, 275: 1293–1295.

Bem, D. J., & Honorton, C. 1994. Does psi exist? Replicable evidence for an anomalous process of information transfer. *Psychological Bulletin*, 115: 4–18.

Bem, D. J., Palmer, J., & Broughton, R. S. 2001. Updating the ganzfeld database: A victim of its own success? *Journal of Parapsychology*, 65: 207–218.

Bierman, D. J. 2003. Does consciousness collapse the wave-packet? *Mind and Matter*, 2: 45–58.

Bierman, D. J., & Radin, D. I. 1997. Anomalous anticipatory response on randomized future conditions. *Perceptual and Motor Skills*, 84: 689–690.

Bierman, D. J., & Radin, D. I. 1999. Conscious and anomalous non-conscious emotional processes: A reversal of the arrow of time? In S. R. Hameroff, A. W. Kaszniak, & D. J. Chalmers (Eds), *Toward a science of consciousness III: The Third Tucson Discussions and Debates*: 367–386. Cambridge, MA: MIT Press.

Bierman, D. J., & Scholte, H. S. 2002. *Anomalous anticipatory brain activation preceding exposure of emotional and neutral pictures.* Paper presented at Toward a Science of Consciousness IV conference. Tucson, AZ, April 8–12.

Bösch, H., Steinkamp, F., & Boller, E. 2006. Examining psychokinesis: The interaction of human intention with random number generators – a meta-analysis. *Psychological Bulletin*, 132(4): 497–523.

Child, I. L. 1985. Psychology and anomalous observations: The question of ESP in dreams. *American Psychologist*, 40(11): 1219–1230.

Crane, T., & Mellor, D. H. 1990. There is no question of physicalism. *Mind New Series*, 99(394): 185–206.

D'Espagnat, B. 1976. *Conceptual foundations of quantum mechanics* (2nd ed.). Reading, MA: W. A. Benjamin.

Delgado-Romero, E., & Howard, G. 2005. Finding and correcting flawed research literatures, *The Humanistic Psychologist*, 33(4): 293–303.

Druckman, D., & Swets, J. A. (Eds.). 1988. *Enhancing human performance: Issues, theories, and techniques.* Washington, DC: National Academy Press.

Duane, T. D., & Behrendt, T. 1965. Extrasensory electroencephalographic induction between identical twins. *Science*, 150: 367.

Grinberg-Zylberbaum, J., Delaflor, M., Attie, L., & Goswami, L. 1994. The Einstein–Podolsky–Rosen paradox in the brain: The transferred potential. *Physics Essays*, 7: 422–428.

Hall, J., Kim, C., McElroy, B., & Shimony, A. 1977. Wave-packet reduction as a medium of communication. *Foundations of Physics*, 7: 759–767.

Harris, M. J., & Rosenthal, R. 1988a. *Interpersonal expectancy effects and human performance research*. Washington, DC: National Academy Press.

Harris, M. J., & Rosenthal, R. 1988b. *Postscript to interpersonal expectancy effects and human performance research*. Washington, DC: National Academy Press.

Harris, M. J., & Rosenthal, R. 1988c. *Human performance research: An overview*. Washington, DC: National Academy Press.

Hartwell, J. W. 1978. Contingent negative variation as an index of precognitive information. *European Journal of Parapsychology*, 2: 83–102.

Hinterberger, T., Studer, P., Jäger, M., Haverty-Stacke, C., & Walach, H. 2007. Can a slide-show presentiment effect be discovered in the brain electrical activity. *Journal of the Society for Psychical Research*, 71: 148–166.

Houtkooper, J. M. 2002. Arguing for an observational theory of paranormal phenomena. *Journal of Scientific Exploration*, 16: 171–186.

Hyman, R. 1996. Evaluation of a program on anomalous mental phenomena. *Journal of Scientific Exploration*, 10: 31–58.

Hyman, R., & Honorton, C. 1986. Joint communiqué: The psi ganzfeld controversy. *Journal of Parapsychology*, 50: 351–364.

Ibison, M., & Jeffers, S. 1998. A double-slit diffraction experiment to investigate claims of consciousness-related anomalies. *Journal of Scientific Exploration*, 12: 543–550.

Jahn, R. G. 1982. The persistent paradox of psychic phenomena: An engineering perspective. *Proceedings of the IEEE*, 70(2): 136–170.

Jahn, R. G., & Dunne, B. J. 1986. On the quantum mechanics of consciousness, with application to anomalous phenomena. *Foundations of Physics*, 16: 721–772.

James, W. 1902. *The varieties of religious experience*. Available at: http://www.gutenberg.org/etext/621 (accessed June 25, 2010).

Jeffers, S., & Sloan, J. 1992. A low light level diffraction experiments for anomalies research. *Journal of Scientific Exploration*, 6: 333–352.

Kahneman, D., & Tversky, A. 1973. On the psychology of prediction. *Psychological Review*, 80: 237–251.

Lang, P. J., Bradley, M. M., & Cuthbert, B. N. 1999. *International affective picture system (IAPS): Technical manual and affective ratings*. Gainesville, FL: University of Florida, Center for Research in Psychophysiology.

Levin, J., & Kennedy, J. 1975. The relationship of slow cortical potentials to psi information in man. *Journal of Parapsychology*, 39: 25–26.

Luo, J., & Niki, K. 2003. Function of hippocampus in 'insight' of problem solving. *Hippocampus*, 13: 316–323.

May, E. C., Paulinyi, T., & Vassy, Z. 2005. Anomalous anticipatory skin conductance response to acoustic stimuli: Experimental results and speculation about a mechanism. *Journal of Alternative and Complementary Medicine*, 11: 695–702.

McCraty, R., Atkinson, M., & Bradley, R. T. 2004a. Electrophysiological evidence of intuition: Part 1. The surprising role of the heart. *Journal of Alternative and Complementary Medicine*, 10: 133–143.

McCraty, R., Atkinson, M., & Bradley, R. T. 2004b. Electrophysiological evidence of intuition: Part 2. A system-wide process? *Journal of Alternative and Complementary Medicine*, 10: 325–336.

Mermin, N. D. 1990. *Boojums all the way through: Communicating science in a prosaic age*. Cambridge: Cambridge University Press.

Milton, J., & Wiseman, R. 1999. Does psi exist? Lack of replication of an anomalous process of information transfer. *Psychological Bulletin*, 125: 387–391.

Myers, D. G. 2002. *Intuition: Its powers and perils.* New Haven, CT: Yale University Press.

News and Comment, 1987. Academy helps army be all that it can be. *Science,* 238 (December 11): 1502.

Orme-Johnson, D. W., Dillbeck, M. C., Wallace, R. K., & Landrith, G. S. 1982. Intersubject EEG coherence: Is consciousness a field? *International Journal of Neuroscience,* 16: 203–209.

Osbeck, L. M. 2001. Direct apprehension and social construction: Revisiting the concept of intuition. *Journal of Theoretical and Philosophical Psychology,* 21(2): 118–131.

Parkhomtchouk, D. V., Kotake, J., Zhang, T., Chen, W., Kokubo, H., & Yamamoto, M. 2002. An attempt to reproduce the presentiment EDA response. *Journal of International Society for Life Information Sciences,* 20(1): 190–194.

Plessner, H., Betsch, C., & Betsch, T. 2008. *Intuition in judgment and decision making.* New York: Lawrence Erlbaum Associates.

Radin, D. I. 1997a. *The Conscious Universe.* San Francisco: HarperOne.

Radin, D. I. 1997b.Unconscious perception of future emotions: An experiment in presentiment. *Journal of Scientific Exploration,* 11: 163–180.

Radin, D. I. 2004a. Electrodermal presentiments of future emotions. *Journal of Scientific Exploration,* 18: 253–274.

Radin, D. I. 2004b. Event-related EEG correlations between isolated human subjects. *Journal of Alternative and Complementary Medicine,* 10: 315–324.

Radin, D. I. 2006. *Entangled Minds.* New York: Simon & Schuster.

Radin, D., & Borges, A. 2009. Intuition through time: What does the seer see? *Explore,* 5: 200–211.

Radin, D. I., & Ferrari, D. C. 1991. Effects of consciousness on the fall of dice: A meta-analysis. *Journal of Scientific Exploration,* 5: 61–84.

Radin, D. I., & Lobach, E. 2007. Toward understanding the placebo effect: Investigating a possible retrocausal factor. *Journal of Alternative and Complementary Medicine,* 13: 733–739.

Radin, D. I., & Nelson, R. D. 1989. Evidence for consciousness-related anomalies in random physical systems. *Foundations of Physics,* 19: 1499–1514.

Radin, D. I., & Nelson, R. D. 2003. Research on mind–matter interactions (MMI): Individual intention. In W. B. Jonas, & C. C. Crawford (Eds.), *Healing, intention and energy medicine: Research and clinical implications*: 39–48. Edinburgh, UK: Churchill Livingston.

Radin, D. I., Nelson, R. D., Dobyns, Y., & Houtkooper, J. 2006. Reexamining psychokinesis: Comment on Bösch, Steinkamp, and Boller. *Psychological Bulletin,* 132(4): 529–532.

Rebert, C. S, & Turner, A. 1974. EEG spectrum analysis techniques applied to the problem of psi phenomena. *Behavioral Neuropsychiatry,* 6: 18–24.

Richards, T. L., Kozak, L., Johnson, L. C., & Standish, L. J. 2005. Replicable functional magnetic resonance imaging evidence of correlated brain signals between physically and sensory isolated subjects. *Journal of Alternative and Complementary Medicine,* 11(6): 955–963.

Roig, M., Icochea, H., & Cuzzucoli, A. 1991. Coverage of parapsychology in introductory psychology textbooks. *Teaching of Psychology,* 18(3): 157–160.

Schmidt, H. 1970. Mental influence on random events. *New Scientist and Science Journal,* 50: 757–758.

Schmidt, H. 1981. PK tests with pre-recorded and pre-inspected seed numbers. *Journal of Parapsychology,* 45: 87–98.

Schmidt, H., Morris, R., & Rudolph, L. 1986. Channeling evidence for a PK effect to independent observers, *Journal of Parapsychology,* 50: 1–16.

Schmidt, H., & Stapp, H. 1993. PK with prerecorded random events and the effects of preobservation. *Journal of Parapsychology,* 57: 331–349.

Schmidt, S., Schneider, R., Utts, J., & Walach, H. 2004. Distant intentionality and the feeling of being stared at: two meta-analyses. *British Journal of Psychology,* 95: 235–247.

Spottiswoode, S. J. P., & May, E. C. 2003. Skin conductance prestimulus response: Analyses, artifacts and a pilot study. *Journal of Scientific Exploration,* 17: 617–641.

Squires, E. J. 1987. Many views of one world – an interpretation of quantum theory. *European Journal of Physics*, 8: 173.

Standish, L. J., Johnson, L. C., Richards, T., & Kozak, L. 2003. Evidence of correlated functional MRI signals between distant human brains. *Alternative Therapies in Health and Medicine*, 9: 122–128.

Standish, L. J., Kozak, L., Johnson, L. C., & Richards, T. 2004. Electroencephalographic evidence of correlated event-related signals between the brains of spatially and sensory isolated human subjects. *Journal of Alternative and Complementary Medicine*, 10: 307–314.

Stapp, H.P. 2001. Quantum theory and the role of the mind in nature. *Foundations of Physics*, 31: 1465–1499.

Storm, L., & Ertel, S. 2001. Does psi exist? Milton and Wiseman's (1999) metaanalysis of ganzfeld research. *Psychological Bulletin*, 127: 424–433.

Storm, L., Tressoldi, P. E., & Di Risio, L. 2010. Meta-analysis of free-response studies, 1992–2008: Assessing the noise reduction model in parapsychology. *Psychological Bulletin*, 136: 471–485.

Targ, R., & Puthoff, H. 1974. Information transmission under conditions of sensory shielding. *Nature*, 252: 602–607.

Tart, C. T. 1963. Possible physiological correlates of psi cognition. *International Journal of Parapsychology*, 5: 375–386.

Utts, J. M. 1991. Replication and meta-analysis in parapsychology. *Statistical Science*, 6 (4): 363–403.

Utts, J. M. 1996. An assessment of the evidence for psychic functioning. *Journal of Scientific Exploration*, 10: 3–30.

Vassy, Z. 1978. Method of measuring the probability of 1-bit extransensory information transfer between living organisms. *Journal of Parapsychology*, 43(2): 158–160.

Von Neumann, J. 1955. *Mathematical foundations of quantum mechanics*. Princeton, NJ: Princeton University Press.

Wackermann, J. 2004. Dyadic correlations between brain functional states: Present facts and future perspectives. *Mind and Matter*, 2: 105–122.

Wackermann, J., Seiter, C., Keibel, H., & Walach, H. 2003. Correlations between spatially separated human subjects. *Neuroscience Letters*, 336: 60–64.

Wigner, E. P. 1963. The problem of measurement. *American Journal of Physics*, 31: 6–15.

Wigner, E. P. 1964. Two kinds of reality. *The Monist*, 48: 248–264.

Wilber, K. 1984. *Quantum questions*. Boulder, CO: Shambhala.

Wildey, C. 2001. *Impulse response of biological systems*. Master's thesis, Department of Electrical Engineering, University of Texas at Arlington.

17 Resolving the enigma of nonlocal intuition: a quantum-holographic approach

Raymond Trevor Bradley

The Concise Oxford Dictionary (Fowler & Fowler, 1964: 639) defines *intuition* as 'immediate apprehension by the mind without reasoning, immediate apprehension by a sense, and immediate insight'. Such intuitive experience is quite unlike that of normal conscious awareness, in which the mind's contents are updated incrementally, as the sequences of sensory experience unfold (McCraty et al., 2004a).

The dominant perspective on intuition is a cognitive approach: that intuitive perception is a function of the unconscious mind accessing existing information within the brain from prior experience (e.g., Agor, 1984; Laughlin, 1997; Lieberman, 2000; Mitchell et al., 2005, 2007; Myers, 2002; Simon, 1987). While there is little doubt that information from prior experience – both conscious and unconscious knowledge – is involved, there is, however, a persuasive body of experimental evidence for another informational basis for intuitive perception. This is the *tacit* information about remote or future events which is perceived and processed by the body's psychophysiological systems. Yet despite the voluminous body of rigorous experimental research documenting such nonlocal communication as a scientific fact (Radin, 1997a; Bradley, 2007; Bradley et al., 2010a), the majority of mainstream scientists regard the findings of these studies as anomalous (Walach & Schmidt, 2005).

Although such instances of 'nonlocal intuition' (La Pira & Gillin, 2006) appear to contradict the physical laws of causality, explaining *how* – the mechanisms and processes by which – such space/time-defying interaction occurs has not been possible until relatively recently. Three scientific developments provide the basis for a rational account: the discovery of *holographic organization* (Gabor, 1948); empirical verification of *quantum entanglement* (Aspect et al., 1982; Tittel et al., 1998); and the confirmation of *quantum coherence* (Schempp, 1992). Together, with the psychophysiological evidence on the involvement of passionate attention, these concepts from physics are employed to build a quantum-holographic theory of nonlocal intuition presented in summary form here (see Bradley, 2006, 2007, 2010a; Bradley & Tomasino, 2011; Bradley et al., 2010a, b).

By way of overview, the theory explains how information about a future or distant object/event is quantum-holographically encoded in the radiation of energy as an implicate order, which exists as a domain apart from space/time. The percipient's passionate attentional focus on the object of interest establishes a two-way communication channel, via a process of energetic resonance, between the percipient's psychophysiological systems and the nonlocal object. The body's perception of such implicit information about the object's future is experienced by the individual as an intuition.

THE SCIENTIFIC EVIDENCE – IN BRIEF

Prior Research

Nonlocal communication is a phenomenon that has been consistently documented in rigorous experiments for more than a century (see Radin, 1997a). The key finding is that individuals are able to accurately perceive information from a distant or future source, and that this result *cannot* be explained by researcher/methods artifacts or chance. Moreover, on the basis of results from a series of meta-analyses on the hundreds of studies, involving millions of trials, conducted on three distinct categories of nonlocal communication – person-to-person, place-to-person, and future-to-person information communication – Radin (ibid.) concludes that the likelihood that an intuitive effect is true, *exceeds* the certainty of measurement in experiments verifying quantum mechanics, the most accurate scientific description of reality (see Nadeau & Kafatos, 1999, or Penrose, 1989).

Recent Studies

Using rigorous experimental protocols and electrophysiological instrumentation, researchers have consistently found that the human autonomic nervous system (ANS) unconsciously responds to randomly selected future emotional stimuli (e.g., May et al., 2005; Spottiswoode & May, 2003). In experiments using randomly selected emotionally arousing or calming photographs, Radin (1997a,b) found significantly greater change in electrodermal activity about five seconds before a future emotional picture than before a future calm picture. These results have been replicated (Bem, 2011; Bierman, 2000; Bierman & Radin, 1997; Radin, 2004), and a follow-up study, using functional magnetic resonance imaging (*f*MRI), found brain activation in regions near the amygdala (involved in the processing of strong emotions, such as fear and rage) *before* emotional pictures were shown, but not before the calm pictures (Bierman & Scholte, 2002).

Augmenting Radin's protocol with measures of brain response (EEG) and heart activity (ECG), McCraty et al. (2004a,b; see Figure 17.1a) found that not only did both the brain and heart receive the pre-stimulus information some 4–5 seconds before a future emotional picture was randomly selected, but also that the heart responded about 1.3 seconds *before* the brain. Corroborating evidence of the heart's involvement comes from three new studies: the first involving random presentation of 'pleasant' and 'unpleasant' acoustical stimuli to a sample of Italian participants

(a) Temporal dynamics of heart and brain pre-stimulus responses

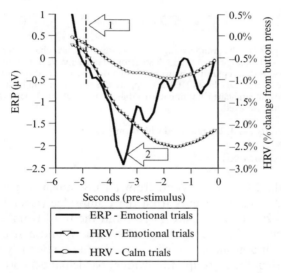

Note: The figure is an overlay plot showing the mean event-related potential (ERP – left vertical ordinate) at FP2 and heart rate deceleration curves (HRV: heart rate variability – right vertical ordinate) for the female subgroup (*n* = 15) in condition 1 during the pre-stimulus period. (The '0' time point denotes stimulus onset.) The heart rate deceleration curve for the emotional trials diverged from that of the calm trials (sharp downward shift) about 4.8 seconds prior to the stimulus (arrow 1), while the emotional trial ERP showed a sharp positive shift about 3.5 seconds prior to the stimulus (arrow 2). This positive shift in the ERP indicates when the brain 'knew' the nature of the future stimulus. The time difference between these two events suggests that the heart received the intuitive information about 1.3 seconds before the brain.

Source: © McCraty et al. (2004b), reprinted with permission.

Figure 17.1   Two Examples of Pre-stimulus Results Involving the Heart

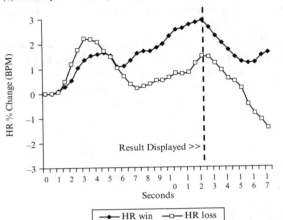

(b) Heart rhythm recordings for repeat entrepreneurs, pre-stimulus period

Note: The figure presents the grand average ($n = 8$) of beat-to-beat change per minute in heart rate (HR % Change) for 'wins' and 'losses' for all participants during the post-bet and post-result periods (the separation between the two time periods is shown by a dashed vertical line labeled 'Result Displayed'). Clearly apparent is the separation between the win and loss curves in the mean heart rhythm patterns that begins at about 6 seconds prior to the outcome result being displayed.

Source: © Bradley et al. (2010a), reprinted with permission.

Figure 17.1   (continued)

(Tressoldi et al., 2009); the second from an investment experiment on repeat (successful) entrepreneurs from the Cambridge (UK) Technopol (Bradley et al., 2010a; see Figure 17.1b); and the third from a study of repeat entrepreneurs in Tehran, Iran, which also found a stronger pre-stimulus effect for a group of 'co-participant' pairs (previously unknown to each other) than for a group of individual participants (Toroghi et al., 2011). Also, in a separate gambling experiment on a US sample of experienced practitioners of emotion self-regulation techniques, Bradley et al. (2010a) found that heart activity patterns in the pre-stimulus period predicted the randomly generated outcome by as much as 12 to 14 seconds.

The consistent finding from the electrophysiological experiments is that the body typically responds to a future emotionally arousing stimulus four to seven seconds prior to experiencing the stimulus. This is well before the half-second anticipatory pre-cortical priming of the brain that occurs before perception of a normal stimulus (Pribram, 1991). The important conclusion is that intuitive foresight is related to the degree of emotional significance of an event to the percipient. Also, instead of evidence of a new so-called 'sixth sense' or a subtle nonlocal information pathway directly into the brain (Bernstein, 2005), the research shows that: stimulus input via normal sensory channels is involved – e.g., visual and acoustical input, at least; known, familiar physiological structures are implicated (brain, heart, and ANS); and the body appears to process intuitive information in the *same* way that it processes ordinary sensory input (McCraty et al., 2004b).

OVERVIEW OF A QUANTUM-HOLOGRAPHIC THEORY OF NONLOCAL INTUITION

Nonlocal communication belongs to a class of consciousness phenomena that has eluded scientific understanding and long remained an enigma. Included in this class are intriguing yet perplexing phenomena such as ESP, clairvoyance, remote viewing, intuition, mind/matter and mind/living systems effects, and other forms of nonlocal interaction, often collectively referred to as *psi* (Radin, 1997a).

Three scientific developments have opened the door to rational explanation (Bradley, 2007). The first is the discovery of the *hologram* – specifically, the principle of distributed organization by which information about the organization and properties of a whole (an object or event) is spectrally encoded throughout a field of potential energy to all points and locations by the radiating oscillations of energy waveforms (Gabor, 1948). The theory that follows utilizes the principles of a special kind of holography – *quantum holography*, discussed momentarily.

The second is the empirical discovery of *quantum entanglement* or nonlocality – that everything in the universe at the subatomic level is interconnected and nonseparable (Aspect et al., 1982; Tittel et al., 1998). The third is the discovery of *quantum coherence* – that subatomic emissions from macro-scale objects (molecular level and above) are not random, but exhibit coherence at the quantum level, reflective of an object's material organization and event history (Schempp, 1992). Coupling these developments in physics with the psychophysiological evidence on the involvement of mental attention and positive emotion in nonlocal interaction provides a key to the door of scientific understanding (Bradley, 2007).

Holographic Theory

The appeal of holographic theory (Gabor, 1948) is the explanatory power of its principle of distributed organization as the information–communication mechanism for nonlocal interaction. Because it is possible to retrieve an image of a whole (object or event) from *any* point or location within a field of potential energy, holographic theory, with its basis in the linear mathematics of the Fourier transform function, has been postulated to provide a reversible physical mechanism by which intuitive information can be encoded, transmitted, received, decoded, and perceived (e.g., Bohm, 1980; Laszlo, 2003; Mitchell, 2004; Tiller, 2004).

Creating a hologram requires two sets of waves: object waves and reference waves. The object wave is directed towards the object. It encodes intensity changes and phase-shifts reflecting the features of the object as the wave interacts with the object, and is then emitted away from the object in all directions. When a reference wave is directed back towards the emitted object wave, it interacts with the object wave and creates an interference pattern that records the phase-shifts of the object wave relative to the reference wave. (Because photographs record the intensity changes and not the phase-shifts of the light waves bouncing off the object, only a two-dimensional image of the object can be recorded.) In short, it is the interference pattern that encodes the phase-shift information from which a three-dimensional image – a *holograph* – of the object can be reconstituted in space–time, via a Fourier transform function (Gabor, 1948; see Bradley, 2010b, Figure 7, for a simple demonstration).

Quantum Holography

Quantum holography is based on Gabor's (1946) energy-based unit of information, the *logon*, which he defines as *the minimum uncertainty with which a signal can be encoded as a pattern of energy oscillations across a waveband of frequencies* (see Figure 17.2a), as in the encoding and transmission of vocal utterances for telephonic communication. He called this unit a *logon* or a *quantum* of information; hence the term 'quantum holography' (Pribram, 1991: Chapter 2). In mathematical terms, the logon is a sinusoidal module variably constrained by space–time coordinates – essentially a *space–time-constrained hologram* (see Pribram, 1991, and Bradley, 2002). It is important to clarify that Gabor's quantum of information is *not* the same as the quantum bit, or *qubit* (see Bradley, 2002).

Gabor's concept of information – the encoding of information in energy oscillations at *any* frequency – is a general concept that applies to energetic information communication at *both* the four-dimensional macro-scale classical world and the micro-scale of quantum reality. Logons are not discrete units of information but overlap, occurring as a modularized series of space–time-constrained sinusoids in which the data in each module are spectrally enfolded, to some degree, into the data of adjoining logons (Figure 17.2b). This overlap has a significant implication for information

(a) Logon–frequency and (space) time limits of measurement

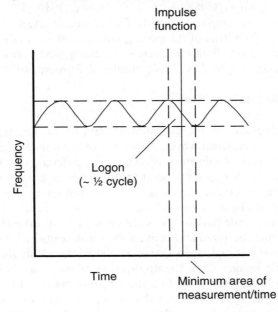

Note: The figure depicts an idealized graphical representation of a Hilbert Space showing a logon – an elementary unit of energetic information – in terms of Gabor's (1946) (energy) frequency and space/time limits of measurement.

Source: © Bradley & Pribram (1998), reproduced with permission.

(b) Overlap among logons

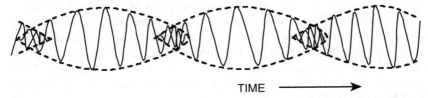

TIME ⟶

Note: The figure depicts a representation of the overlap among a modularized series of logons.

Source: © Bradley & Pribram (1998), reproduced with permission.

Figure 17.2   Gabor's Elementary Unit of Energetically Encoded Information – the Logon

communication from the future, in that each logon, in Gabor's words, contains an *'overlap [with] the future'* (Gabor, 1946: 437; addition in square brackets and emphasis added). This means, in effect, that each unit of information, by virtue of its spectral enfoldment with adjoining units, contains information about the future order energetically encoded into the unit that succeeds it (Bradley, 1998; Bradley & Pribram, 1998).

Explaining Nonlocal Intuition[1]

From the micro-scale of the quantum domain to the macro-scale of the four-dimensional classical world, all objects in the universe are energized in a constant state of vibratory oscillation at different frequencies. The oscillations from all objects generate wave fields of energy that radiate outward and interact. As a wave field of *any* kind interacts with a physical or biological object, a part of the wave is reflected directly from the object's surface, while part of the wave's energy is absorbed, causing the object to become energized and emit another wave outward, back towards the source of the initial wave (Marcer, 2004). Based on the derivation of macro-scale images from the application of quantum holography in *f*MRI studies, it is now known that the returning wave contains nonlocal quantum-level information about the object's internal organization and microscopic features, along with its external and macroscopic features (Schempp, 1992). Moreover, the complete event history of the object's movement in time through its three-dimensional environment is carried by a quantum hologram (Mitchell, 2000). Taken altogether, this produces a holographic process in which micro-scale nonlocal quantum-level information about the object's organization and history is encoded and communicated back to the macro-scale source of the initial wave.

The interaction between these two wave fields generates an interference pattern in which, at the moment of conjunction of object and reference waves – the instant the interference pattern is created – both waves are *spatially and temporally coherent.* As a holograph, the interference pattern spectrally encodes phase-dependent information about the object's internal and external organization, and its event history (Schempp, 1992; Mitchell, 2000). To decode the information a reference wave is required, and Marcer (1995) has established 'that *any* waves reverberating through the universe remain coherent with the waves at the source, and are thus sufficient to serve as the reference to decode the holographic information of *any* quantum hologram emanating from remote locations' (Mitchell, 2000: 302; emphasis added).

At the quantum level, the area of intersection in the interference pattern is a quantum hologram containing quantum-level information reflecting this macro-scale process. Because the area of intersection involves an interaction between wave fronts, in which the radiation of energy in one wave front is modularized by the constraint of the wave front of radiating energy in the other, it is equivalent to Gabor's quantum unit of energetic information, the logon (~ ½ cycle) (Bradley & Pribram, 1998). This means that the quantum hologram is essentially a logon, or a Gaussian-constrained hologram, in Pribram's (1991) terms. And since, by virtue of the overlap among logons, each logon contains spectrally enfolded information about the future (Gabor, 1946), then each quantum hologram also contains quantum-level information about the future organization of the macro-scale object with which it is associated.

Energetic Resonance

Marcer (1995) and Marcer and Schempp (1997) have shown that perception requires both an incoming wave field of sensory information about the object *and* an outgoing wave field of attentional energy, and that a relationship of 'phase-conjugate-adaptive-resonance' (PCAR, Marcer, 1995) must exist between the two wave fields in order to perceive an object in the macro-scale four-dimensional world. Marcer and Schempp (1997) have proposed that 'resonance requires a virtual path mathematically equal but opposite to the incoming sensory information about the object. Further, that it is the incoming space/time information (visual, acoustic, etc.), which decodes the information of the quantum hologram and establishes the condition of *pcar* so that accurate three dimensional perception is possible' (Mitchell, 2000: 297). Thus PCAR is a process in which the incoming and outgoing wave fields are phase-conjoined by the percipient's act of attention, in that s/he tunes into and maintains 'vibratory resonance' with the object's energetic oscillations at the quantum level (Marcer & Schempp, 1997).

When two interpenetrating wave fields are radiating synchronized oscillations at the same energy frequency, the conjunction of individual waves creates a spatially and temporally coherent channel of interaction connecting the object source points of the two wave fields (see Figure 17.3). This channel is essentially a logon pathway for optimal information communication, and it is also generated in systems involving multiple objects with synchronized oscillations at the same energy frequency, such as socially coherent groups (Bradley, 2010b). However, this does not hold for interaction between wave fields radiating energy oscillations at varying frequencies; in such cases effective communication is impeded by spatial and/ or temporal incoherence in the pattern of interpenetration between the wave fields. But when wave fields at different energy frequencies oscillate

Bio-emotional energy fields and communication channels

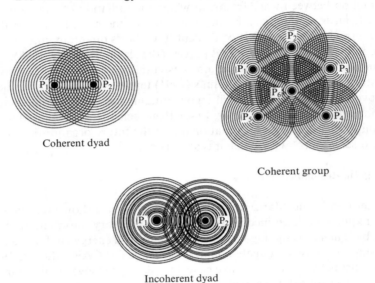

Coherent dyad

Coherent group

Incoherent dyad

Note: The figure shows how a channel of coherent interaction – phase coherence – is generated between two persons (top left; Person #1, P_1, and Person #2, P_2) when their interpenetrating bioemotional wave fields are radiating oscillations at a common resonant energy frequency. This also holds for larger systems composed of wave fields oscillating at the same frequency (top right); where the two wave fields from each pair of individuals interpenetrate coherent channels of interaction are created for each dyadic relation in the system. However, this does not occur for wave fields radiating energy oscillations at different non-harmonic frequencies (bottom); effective communication is impeded by an incoherent pattern of interpenetration between the two wave fields.

Source: © Bradley et al. (2010b); reproduced with permission.

Figure 17.3   Emergence of Coherent Communication Channels Among Interpenetrating Wave Fields of Energy at a Common Resonant Frequency

in *harmonic resonance*, a coherent channel of communication emerges from the radiation of synchronized oscillations across the wave fields (see Bradley, 2007, Figure 8). This provides for a logon pathway of information communication across different scales of organization: from the quantum-level micro-scale domain, to the four-dimensional macro-scale classical world, and vice versa. Since the overlap among logons means that information about future order is spectrally enfolded, this creates an information processing mechanism by which foresight of the future is contained in the logon or nonlocal quantum hologram at hand (Bradley, 2006, 2007).

Passionate Attention and the Heart's Role

As already noted, the act of conscious perception requires both an incoming wave field of sensory information about the object *and* an outgoing wave field of attentional energy. The body's psychophysiological systems generate numerous fields of energy, at various frequencies, that radiate outwards from the body as wave fields in all directions. Of these, the heart generates the most powerful, rhythmic electromagnetic field (Bradley et al., 2010c; McCraty et al., 2009). Not only does a massive deceleration in the heart's pattern of rhythmic activity occur at the moment of mental attention – creating a marked change recorded in the outgoing wave field (McCraty et al., 2004b) – but it is also known that nonlocal perception is related to the percipient's degree of emotional arousal generated by an object (as discussed in the Recent Studies section, above). It is the individual's *passion* or 'rapt attention', as Radin (1997a) calls it – the biological energy activated in the individual's emotional connection to the object of interest – that generates the outgoing attentional wave directed to the object. And since it is well established that the heart's energetic pattern of activity reflects feelings and emotional experience (McCraty et al., 2009; Tiller et al., 1996),[2] it is highly likely that the heart is instrumental in generating the outgoing wave of attentional energy directed to the object.

Directing passionate attentional focus to a nonlocal object establishes a PCAR relationship with the quantum level of the object in question. It is known that attention is significantly enhanced when a self-generated positive emotional state is sustained (Fredrickson, 2002; Isen, 1999; Tomasino, 2007). Maintenance of this state induces a shift to a coherent order in the heart's beat-to-beat pattern – a global state of increased synchronization and harmony in psychophysiological processes, characterized as 'psychophysiological coherence' (McCraty et al., 2009) (see Figure 17.4), which appears associated with intuitive receptivity (Tomasino, ch. 21 this volume); a negative emotional state, like anger or frustration, produces an incoherent order of erratic, irregular beat-to-beat waveforms (Bradley et al., 2010c; McCraty et al., 2009; see Tomasino, Figure 21.1, in this volume). While the interpenetration between the outgoing coherent wave fields generated in the coherence state and the incoming wave fields of quantum coherence from external sources creates an oscillatory channel of energetic resonance for information communication, such communication is impeded during psychophysiological incoherence.

To the degree that a coherent relationship of energetic resonance

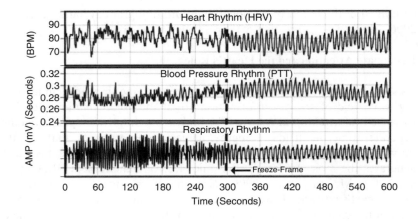

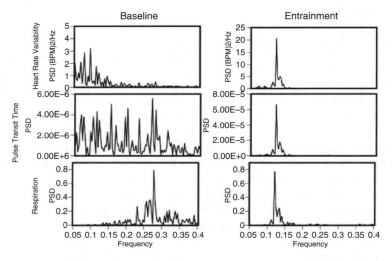

Note: These real-time recordings show an individual's heart rhythm activity (HRV: heart rate variability pattern), pulse transit time (PTT: a measure of beat-to-beat blood pressure), and respiration rhythms over a 10-minute period. At the 300-second mark, the individual used a HeartMath positive emotion self-regulation technique to activate the psychophysiological coherence state, causing these three physiological systems to come into entrainment. The *bottom figures* show the frequency spectra of the same data on each side of the *dotted line* in the center of the *top figures*. Notice that the *figures* on the *right* show that all three systems have entrained to the same frequency (~0.12 Hz).

Source: Adapted from Tiller et al. (1996), © Institute of HeartMath, 1996, reproduced with permission.

*Figure 17.4   Psychophysiological Coherence – A Positive Emotion-
            induced System-wide Shift to Coherent Wave Forms*

between the object and the percipient is maintained – that the object's quantum wave field and the attentional wave field of the percipient are phase-locked in a resonant feedback loop – the individual's psychophysiological system (the brain, the heart, and the body as a whole) can receive and process nonlocal information as quantum holograms. It is the continuous resonant feedback loop between the two that enables the body to receive and process quantum-holographic information from nonlocal sources spectrally encoded in the oscillatory radiation of energy.

One pathway of virtually instantaneous nonlocal information communication is at the quantum level through quantum coherence. Another pathway for information communication at hyper-speeds appears likely when a third emergent wave field is generated by the interaction between incoming and outgoing wave fields at the same frequency, or by harmonic resonance when wave fields of different harmonically-compatible frequencies interact, as described elsewhere (Bradley, 2006, 2007a). Given that the heart receives information about future events *before* the brain (McCraty et al., 2004b), it plays a significant role in the body's sensing and processing of information from nonlocal sources. Indeed, it is likely that the pre-stimulus heart-generated change in afferent neural signals that McCraty et al. (ibid.) observed, is actually a communication to the brain signaling incoming information about the future event. Once received, such quantum-holographically encoded information about a nonlocal object/event is decoded and converted by the brain, through a reverse Fourier transform process, into mental imagery, feelings, and other sensations as detailed by Pribram (1991).

Social Amplification of Nonlocal Effects

The field effects of attentional bio-emotional energy will be significantly stronger when a group's members are bio-emotionally attuned to one another through a fully interconnected network of mutually reciprocated relations of positive affect, modulated by relations of social control, as described elsewhere (Bradley, 1987, 2003; Bradley & Pribram, 1998). By entraining all members to the same resonant socio-emotional frequency, the group creates a powerful collective receptive field of coherent bio-emotional energy through which tacit nonlocal information is accessed and amplified, due to a stronger resonant feedback loop, both to the field of the group and to that of the individual member (Bradley, 2010b). Conversely, in socially incoherent groups, involving relations of discord, disaffection, or conflict, the wave field of collective energy is too disorganized for energetic resonance with the energy wave field from a nonlocal object. This impedes access to information from nonlocal sources.

RECAPITULATION

Focused passionate attention directed to the object of interest attunes the individual's psychophysiological systems to the quantum level of the object, which contains implicit, holographically encoded information about the object's future potential. Such emotional attunement – *coherence* – brings the outgoing wave field of attentional energy from the individual's psychophysiological systems into energetic resonance with the incoming wave field of energy from the object. The energetic resonance between the two wave fields of energy creates an optimal channel for communication of nonlocal information. The body's perception of such implicit information about the object's future is experienced as an intuition. A socially coherent group is optimal, in that the nonlocal interaction effects are amplified by a resonant feedback loop between the collective bio-emotional field of the group and that of the individual member. Finally, while beyond the scope of this work, the same explanatory principles used in this account of non-local intuition may also provide an understanding of 'nonlocal agency', as elaborated elsewhere (Bradley & Tomasino, 2011) – that is, how focused mental intention – *passionate intention* – can exert a measurable effect on changing the future behavior of a physical object/system or a living organism/system, including the human psychophysiological system (Bancel & Nelson, 2008; Jahn & Dunne, 1987; May et al., 2005; Radin, 1997a; Schlitz & Braud, 1997).

NOTES

1. See Bradley (2007a) for a discussion of alternative theories of nonlocal communication to that proposed here.
2. The research shows that information about a person's emotional state is communicated both throughout the body *and* out into the external environment via the heart's pattern of activity. The rhythmic patterns of beat-to-beat heart activity change significantly as we experience different emotions. In turn, these changes in the heart's beating patterns create corresponding changes in the structure spectra of the electromagnetic field radiated by the heart (see the review of research in McCraty et al., 2009).

REFERENCES

Agor, W. 1984. *Intuitive Management: Integrating Left and Right Brain Skills*, Englewood Cliffs, NJ: Prentice-Hall.
Aspect, A., Grangier, P., & Roger, G. 1982. Experimental realization of Einstein–Podolsky–Rosen–Bohm Gedankenexperiment: a new violation of Bell's inequalities, *Physical Review of Letters*, 49: 91–94.

Bancel, P., & Nelson, R. 2008. The GCP experiment: design, analytical methods, Results. *Journal of Scientific Exploration*, 22: 309–333.

Bem, D. J. 2011. Feeling the future: Experimental evidence for anomalous retroactive influences on cognition and affect. *Journal of Personality and Social Psychology*, 100(3): 407–425.

Bernstein, P. 2005. *Intuition: What science says (so far) about how and why intuition works.* In R. Buccheri, A. C. Elitzur, & M. Saniga (Eds.), *Endophysics, time, quantum and the subjective*: 487–506. Singapore: World Scientific.

Bierman, D. J. 2000. Anomalous baseline effects in mainstream emotion research using psychophysiological variables. *Proceedings of Presented Papers*, 43rd Annual Convention of the Parapsychological Association, 17–20 August.

Bierman, D. J., & Radin, D. I. 1997. Anomalous anticipatory response on randomized future conditions. *Perceptual and Motor Skills*, 84: 689–690.

Bierman, D. J., & Scholte, H. S. 2002. Anomalous anticipatory brain activation preceding exposure of emotional and neutral pictures. Paper presented at the Toward a Science of Consciousness IV conference. Tuscon, AZ, 4–8 April.

Bohm, D. 1980. *Wholeness and the implicate order.* Routledge, London.

Bradley, R. T. 1987. *Charisma and social structure: A study of love and power, wholeness and transformation.* New York: Paragon Press.

Bradley, R. T. 1998. Values, agency, and the theory of quantum vacuum interaction. In K. H. Pribram (Ed.), *Brain and values: Is a biological science of values possible?*: 471–504. Mahwah, NJ: Lawrence Erlbaum.

Bradley, R. T. 2002. Dialogue, information, and psychosocial organization. In N. C. Roberts (Ed.), *Transformative power of dialogue*: 243–288. Oxford: Elsevier.

Bradley, R. T. 2003. Love, power, mind, brain, and agency. In D. Loye (Ed.), *The great adventure: Toward a fully human theory of evolution*: 99–150. New York: SUNY Press.

Bradley, R. T. 2006. Psychophysiology of entrepreneurial intuition: A quantum-holographic theory. In M. Gillin (Ed.), *Regional frontiers of entrepreneurship research*: 163–183. Melbourne, Australia: AGSE, Swinburne University of Technology.

Bradley, R. T. 2007. Psychophysiology of intuition: A quantum-holographic theory of nonlocal communication. *World Futures: The Journal of General Evolution*, 63(2): 61–97.

Bradley, R. T. 2010a. Passionate attention and the psychophysiology of entrepreneurial intuition: A quantum-holographic theory. *International Journal of Entrepreneurship and Small Business*, 9(3): 324–348.

Bradley, R. T. 2010b. Detecting the identity signature of secret social groups: Holographic processes and the communication of member affiliation. *World Futures: The Journal of General Evolution*, 66(2): 124–162.

Bradley, R. T., Gillin, M., McCraty, R., & Atkinson, M. 2010a. Nonlocal intuition in entrepreneurs and non-entrepreneurs: Results of two experiments using electrophysiological measures. *International Journal of Entrepreneurship and Small Business*, 10: 324–348.

Bradley, R. T., McCraty, R., Atkinson, M., Tomasino, D., Daugherty, A., & Arguelles, L. 2010c. Emotion self-regulation, psychophysiological coherence, and test anxiety: Results from an experiment using electrophysiological measures. *Applied Psychophysiology and Biofeedback*, published online: DOI, 10.1007/s10484-010-9134-x.

Bradley, R. T., & Pribram, K. H. 1998. Communication and stability in social collectives. *Journal of Social and Evolutionary Systems*, 21(1): 29–81.

Bradley, R. T., & Tomasino, D. 2011. A quantum-holographic approach to the psychophysiology of intuitive action. In L.-P. Dana (Ed.), *World Encyclopedia of entrepreneurship*: 318–347. Cheltenham, UK and Northampton, MA, USA: Edward Elgar.

Bradley, R. T., Tomasino, D., & Gillin, M. 2010b. Transformational dynamics of entrepreneurial systems: Holographic processes and the organizational basis of intuitive action. *International Journal of Entrepreneurship and Small Business*, 11(2): 183–204.

Fowler, H. W., & Fowler, F. G. (Eds.) 1964. *The Concise Oxford Dictionary.* Oxford: Oxford University Press.

Fredrickson, B. L. 2002. Positive emotions. In C. R. Snyder, & S. J. Lopez (Eds.), *Handbook of positive psychology*: 120–134. New York: Oxford University Press.

Gabor, D. 1946. Theory of communication. *Journal of the Institute of Electrical Engineers*, 93: 439–457.

Gabor, D. 1948. A new microscopic principle. *Nature*, 161: 777–778.

Isen, A. M. 1999. Positive affect. In T. Dalgleish, & M. Power (Eds.), *Handbook of cognition and emotion*: 522–539. New York: Wiley.

Jahn, R. G., & Dunne, B. J. 1987. *Margins of reality: The role of consciousness in the physical world*. New York-San Diego, CA: Harcourt Brace Jovanovich.

La Pira, F., & Gillin, M. 2006. Nonlocal intuition and the performance of serial entrepreneurs. *International Journal of Entrepreneurship and Small Business*, 3(1): 17–35.

Laughlin, C. 1997. The nature of intuition: A neuropsychological approach. In R. Davis-Floyd, & P. S. Arvidson (Eds.), *Intuition: The inside story*: 19–37, London: Routledge.

Laszlo, E. 2003. *The connectivity hypothesis: Foundations of an integral science of quantum, cosmos, life, and consciousness*. New York: SUNY Press.

Lieberman, M. D. 2000. Intuition: A social and cognitive neuroscience approach, *Psychological Bulletin*, 126(1): 109–137.

Marcer, P. 1995. A proposal for a mathematical specification for evolution and the Psi field. *World Futures: The Journal of General Evolution*, 44(283), 149–159.

Marcer, P. 2004. *Status of the mission*. Cybernetic Machine Specialist Group, British Computer Society, Available at: www.bcs.org.uk/sggroup/cyber/status.htm (accessed October 16, 2005).

Marcer, P., & Schempp, W. 1997. Model of the neuron working by quantum holography. *Informatica*, 21: 519–534.

May, E., Paulinyi, T., & Vassy, Z. 2005. Anomalous anticipatory skin conductance response to acoustic stimuli: Experimental results and speculations about a mechanism. *Journal of Alternative and Complementary Medicine*, 11(4): 695–702.

McCraty, R., Atkinson, M., & Bradley, R. T. 2004a. Electrophysiological evidence of intuition: Part 1. The surprising role of the heart. *Journal of Alternative and Complementary Medicine*, 10(1): 133–143.

McCraty, R., Atkinson, M., & Bradley, R. T. 2004b. Electrophysiological evidence of intuition: Part 2. A system-wide process? *Journal of Alternative and Complementary Medicine*, 10(2): 325–336.

McCraty, R., Atkinson, M., Tomasino, D., & Bradley, R. T. 2009. The coherent heart: Heart–brain interactions, psychophysiological coherence, and the emergence of system-wide order. *Integral Review*, 5(2): 11–115.

Mitchell, E. 2000. Nature's mind: The quantum hologram. *International Journal of Computing Anticipatory Systems*, 7: 295–312.

Mitchell, E. 2004. Quantum holography: A basis for the interface between mind and matter. In P. G. Rosch & M. S. Markov (Eds.), *Bioelectromagnetic medicine*: 153–158. New York: Dekker.

Mitchell, J. R., Friga, P. N., & Mitchell, R. K. 2005. Untangling the intuition mess: Intuition as a construct in entrepreneurship research. *Entrepreneurship Theory and Practice*, November: 653–679.

Mitchell, R.K., Busenitz, L., Bird, B., Gaglio, C. M., McMullen, J. S., Morse, E., & Smith, J. 2007. The central question in entrepreneurial cognition research. *Entrepreneurship Theory and Practice*, 31(1): 1–27.

Myers, D. G. 2002. *Intuition: Its powers and perils*. New Haven, CT: Yale University Press.

Nadeau, R., & Kafatos, M. 1999. *The nonlocal universe: The new physics and matters of the mind*. New York: Oxford University Press.

Penrose, R. 1989. *The emperor's new mind: Concerning computers, minds, and the laws of physics*. Oxford: Oxford University Press.

Pribram, K. H. 1991. *Brain and perception: Holonomy and structure in figural processing*. Hillsdale, NJ: Lawrence Erlbaum Associates.

Radin, D. I. 1997a. *The conscious universe: The scientific truth of psychic phenomena.* San Francisco, CA: HarperEdge.

Radin, D. I. 1997b. Unconscious perception of future emotions: An experiment in presentiment, *Journal of Scientific Exploration*, 11: 163–180.

Radin, D. I. 2004. Electrodermal presentiments of future emotions. *Journal of Scientific Exploration*, 18: 253–273.

Schlitz, M. J., & Braud, W. 1997. Distant intentionality and healing: Assessing the evidence, *Alternative Therapies*, 3: 87–88.

Schempp, W. 1992. Quantum holography and neurocomputer architectures. *Journal of Mathematical Imaging and Vision*, 2: 109–164.

Simon, H. A. 1987. Making management decisions: The role of intuition and emotion. *Academy of Management Executive*, 1(1): 57–65.

Spottiswoode, S. J. P., & May, E. C. P. 2003. Skin conductance prestimulus response: Analyses, artifacts and a pilot study. *Journal of Scientific Exploration*, 17: 617–642.

Tiller, W. 2004. Subtle energies and their roles in bioelectromagnetic phenomena. In P. G. Rosch, & M. S. Markov (Eds.), *Bioelectromagnetic medicine*: 159–192. New York: Dekker.

Tiller, W. A., McCraty, R., & Atkinson, M. 1996. Cardiac coherence: A new, noninvasive measure of autonomic nervous system order, *Alternative Therapies in Health and Medicine*, 2(1): 52–65.

Tittel, W., Brendel, J., Zbinden, H., & Gisin, N. 1998. Violation of Bell inequalities by photons more than 10 km apart. *Physical Review of Letters*, 81: 3563–3566.

Tomasino, D. 2007. The psychophysiological basis of creativity and intuition: Accessing the 'zone' of entrepreneurship. *International Journal of Entrepreneurship and Small Business*, 4(5): 528–542.

Toroghi, S. R., Mirzaei, M., Zali, M. R., & Bradley, R. T. 2011. Nonlocal intuition in repeat entrepreneurs: A replication and co-subject effects using electrophysiological measures. Paper presented at the 8th AGSE International Entrepreneurship Research Exchange, Melbourne, 1–4 February.

Tressoldi, P. E., Martinelli, M., Zaccaria, E., & Massaccesi, S. 2009. Implicit intuition: How heart rate can contribute to prediction of future events. *Journal of the Society for Psychical Research*, 73(894): 1–16.

Walach, H., & Schmidt, S. 2005. Repairing Plato's life boat with Ockham's razor: The important function of research in anomalies for consciousness studies, *Journal of Consciousness Studies*, 12(2): 52–70.

PART 5

CULTIVATING INTUITION

18 Capturing intuitions 'in flight': observations from research on attention and mindfulness
Erik Dane

Most of us are well acquainted with gut feelings, or intuitions. At various points in our lives, these feelings provide us with guidance as we seek to make critical and oftentimes difficult decisions in work and non-work domains. For most of us, the 'feeling of knowing' that characterizes our intuitions could not be more apparent. As such, we can tell quite easily when such feelings arise. Right?

In this chapter, I challenge the assumption that our intuitions are always obvious to us. To be sure, many of them are likely to be self-evident. However, a growing body of psychological research suggests that we fail to attend to some of our gut feelings (Dijksterhuis & Aarts, 2010; Hofmann & Wilson, 2010; Koch & Tsuchiya, 2006). In other words, our intuitions can recede or dissipate before receiving due consideration. The disconcerting implications of the arguments advanced here raise the question of whether we can become more consciously attentive to our intuitions. On this point, I maintain that individuals are more likely to 'capture' their gut feelings via conscious attention to the extent that they are in a *mindful* state of consciousness in which their attention is directed toward present moment phenomena. Thus, I offer mindfulness as a vehicle by which individuals can achieve greater access to their intuitions and perhaps become more effective decision makers as a result.

INTUITION AND DECISION MAKING

Recent years have witnessed a growth of research on the construct of intuition, or 'affectively charged judgments that arise through rapid, non-conscious, and holistic associations' (Dane & Pratt, 2007: 40). Work in this area has focused on the *nature* of intuitions (e.g., Dane & Pratt, 2009; Hodgkinson et al., 2008; Sinclair et al., 2009), when individuals tend to *use* intuitions to make decisions (e.g., Blume & Covin, 2011; Elsbach & Barr, 1999; Hodgkinson & Sadler-Smith, 2003), and when using intuitions is *effective* compared to employing analytical decision making (e.g., Dane et al., 2009; Hogarth, 2001; Khatri & Ng, 2000). With regard to the topic of intuition effectiveness, researchers have recently questioned a longstanding view advanced by decision-making scholars that intuition is inferior to analysis by arguing that, under certain conditions, intuitive decision making is quite useful. Specifically, researchers maintain that when individuals have a high level of domain expertise and are performing relatively unstructured tasks, intuitions may be remarkably accurate (Dane & Pratt, 2007, 2009; Salas et al., 2010).

At the same time, scholars continue to show that, in a number of cases, intuitions can lead decision makers astray (see Kahneman & Klein, 2009). As such, individuals may benefit from verifying the accuracy of their intuitions before using them as inputs for decision making. Although there has been much discussion concerning whether to probe and, indeed, challenge one's intuitions (e.g., Louis & Sutton, 1991; Miller & Ireland, 2005; Wilson & Schooler, 1991), most research perspectives, regardless of their support for or critique of intuition, hang on a basic assumption – namely, that individuals notice their intuitions when they arise. Intriguingly, emerging research calls this assumption into question.

INTUITION, INFORMATION PROCESSING, AND ATTENTION

Underlying the recent surge of interest in intuition is the claim that humans process information via two relatively distinct cognitive systems – a nonconscious system and a conscious system (see Evans, 2008, for a review of 'dual process' theories of information processing and Keren & Schul, 2009, for a critique of such theories). The nonconscious system, also referred to as 'experiential' (Epstein, 1994), 'associative' (Sloman, 1996), and 'System 1' (Stanovich & West, 2000), tends to operate through relatively simultaneous, effortless, and holistic associations. In contrast, the conscious system, also referred to as 'rational' (Epstein, 1994), 'rule based' (Sloman, 1996), and 'System 2' (Stanovich & West, 2000), tends to operate through relatively sequential, effortful, and discrete connections.

Intuitions are believed to originate in the nonconscious system of processing (Hodgkinson et al., 2008; Hogarth, 2001). When individuals encounter stimuli in their environment that equate with nonconsciously held cognitive structures, holistic associations are drawn that, in some cases, produce intuitions. While this process of 'intuiting' is nonconscious, the outcome of this process, an intuition, or intuitive judgment, arises at a conscious level (Dane & Pratt, 2007). The status of a given intuition in its outcome form as 'conscious' seems to imply that individuals cannot fail

Table 18.1 *Conscious Processing and Attention: Typology for Stimulus Classification*

		Attention	
		High	Little to None
Conscious Processing	Yes	*Quadrant I* Examples Conscious emotions Conscious goals *Consciously attended intuitions*	*Quadrant II* Examples Perceptions of gist *Unattended intuitions*
	No	*Quadrant III* Examples Nonconscious emotions Nonconsciously pursued goals *Suppressed intuitions*	*Quadrant IV* Example Goal-irrelevant stimuli

to notice it. However, as argued here, just because an intuition emerges consciously does not guarantee that it will receive significant attention.

In drawing on research across cognitive, social, and neurological psychology, scholars have recently asserted that attention and conscious processing, though potentially related, are distinct concepts (Dijksterhuis & Aarts, 2010). Attention concerns the degree to which a given stimulus receives information processing; such processing may occur either via the conscious or the nonconscious system. This suggests that psychological stimuli can be mapped onto a 2 × 2 typology such that, at any given point in time, a stimulus may be classified according to whether it is (i) being processed consciously and (ii) receiving high versus low (or no) attention (Dijksterhuis & Aarts, 2010; Koch & Tsuchiya, 2006). Table 18.1 depicts this typology.

Quadrants I and IV concern stimuli that equate with common assumptions about human cognition. First, as represented by Quadrant I, emotions, goals, and intuitions can – and often do – receive a high degree of attention at the conscious level. Not only is this assumption integral to research on each of these concepts, but it is taken for granted in everyday life as evidenced by statements like 'I feel happy today' or 'I have a gut feeling.' Second, because human attention is limited in certain respects (Cowan, 1997; Weber & Johnson, 2009) it is broadly assumed that individuals cannot devote attention to *all* psychological stimuli simultaneously (Pashler, 1998). Hence, as represented by Quadrant IV, it is likely that some stimuli, such as those that bear no relation to one's goals, receive little to no attention at either a conscious or a nonconscious level.

More central to the arguments presented in this section, Quadrants II and III pertain to an intriguing range of research findings worth examining. To begin, although many emotions are consciously attended to, scholars have found that emotions can also exist nonconsciously, such that they consume attentional resources and yet are not consciously perceived (Lambie & Marcel, 2002). Thus, remarkably, an individual can be happy (or sad) and have no awareness of this emotion – a case associated with Quadrant III. Moreover, and also relevant to Quadrant III, a large literature on nonconscious priming indicates that individuals are influenced by stimuli they are not consciously aware of (see Bargh & Chartrand, 1999, for review). The potency of these priming effects rests upon stimuli receiving attention at a nonconscious level – typically because such stimuli either activate or are relevant to a particular goal (Bargh et al., 2001; Fitzsimons & Bargh, 2003; George, 2009). In contrast, when stimuli neither initiate nor relate to goal pursuit, they tend to receive relatively little attention; thus, their impact on behavior is limited (Dijksterhuis & Aarts, 2010; Shah, 2003). As suggested earlier, such stimuli fall in Quadrant IV.

Next, as indicated by Quadrant II, individuals can be conscious of certain stimuli but not attend to them. As shown in this quadrant, visual perceptions of gist often fit this category (Koch & Tsuchiya, 2006). Furthermore, and critical to this investigation, individuals may fail to consciously attend to their intuitions (Hofmann & Wilson, 2010). That is, intuitions may be processed consciously but receive little attention. For example, when an individual directs attention to a demanding work task, an intuition may emerge concerning an unrelated project. Although this intuition arises consciously, the individual may ignore it and continue working on the initial task. This 'unattended intuition' fits Quadrant II in that it is processed consciously but not attended to.

While some intuitions may dissipate entirely after receiving no conscious attention, others may be suppressed to the nonconscious level (Wegner & Smart, 1997), and thus carry the potential to influence behavior. These 'suppressed intuitions' – those that receive nonconscious attention – are categorized in Quadrant III. Because such intuitions have received very little treatment in literature, further research is needed to better understand their nature. Nevertheless, a basic implication of the arguments offered thus far is that, regardless of whether they are ultimately suppressed, extinguished, or both, some intuitions receive little to no attention at the conscious level.

From a decision-making perspective, this notion merits further consideration. Although intuitions are likely to be accurate in certain circumstances and inaccurate in others (Dane & Pratt, 2007), attending to one's intuitions, regardless of their accuracy, may enhance decision-making effectiveness. Taking note of accurate intuitions provides individuals with key inputs to guide their decisions. Equally importantly, attending to inaccurate intuitions offers individuals the opportunity to identify and compensate for them. The latter course of action is critical given evidence that when outcomes of the nonconscious system, such as intuitions, are not consciously attended to, they can still influence decision making via nonconscious pathways (Hofmann & Wilson, 2010). For example, despite failing to consciously attend to a potentially inaccurate intuition about how to price a product, a store manager can be influenced by it in making his or her pricing decision to the extent that it is suppressed to the nonconscious level (cf. Winkielman & Berridge, 2004). In contrast, when individuals are aware of their intuitions, they can endorse, dismiss, or investigate their validity (Kahneman & Frederick, 2005). In doing so, individuals can determine what role, if any, their intuitions should play in their decision-making efforts.

At the same time, consciously attending to one's intuitions may prove costly when two conditions hold. Specifically, when one's intuitions tend to be relatively inaccurate *and* when one tends not to question their accuracy, attending to and taking stock in one's intuitions can be disadvantageous. Research indicates that intuitions tend to be relatively inaccurate among domain novices (Kahneman & Klein, 2009; Salas et al., 2010). Thus, for a domain novice who is relatively unquestioning of the accuracy of his or her intuitive judgments, it may be fortunate that some intuitions receive little to no conscious attention – particularly when these dissipate after attaining Quadrant II status, as opposed to becoming suppressed to the nonconscious level and thus maintaining their potential to influence behavior (Quadrant III).

Summarizing the arguments advanced in this section, individuals may fail to consciously attend to some of their intuitions. Although allocating conscious attention to one's intuitions is not necessarily useful in all cases, evidence suggests that many individuals would benefit from becoming more attuned to their gut feelings as they arise. Therefore, the prospect that some intuitions go unnoticed is problematic from a decision-making standpoint.

CAPTURING INTUITIONS THROUGH MINDFULNESS

The preceding observations raise the following question: how can people become more attuned to their intuitions? Here, I contend that a state of consciousness known as 'mindfulness' plays a key role toward this end. Historically associated with Eastern philosophical traditions, mindfulness is defined as 'a state of consciousness in which attention is focused on present moment phenomena occurring both externally and internally' (Dane, in press; see also Bishop et al., 2004; Brown & Ryan, 2003; Weick & Putnam, 2006). Thus, rather than being preoccupied with thoughts or concerns about the past or the future, one who is in a mindful state of consciousness attends to a number of stimuli and events associated with the present moment (Epstein, 1995; Herndon, 2008). In maintaining this present moment focus, one attends to both *external* (environmental) and *internal* (intra-psychic) phenomena, as each is integral to the moment in which one is engaged (Brown & Ryan, 2003). For this reason, mindfulness has been described as 'the clear and single-minded awareness of what actually happens *to* us and *in* us at the successive moments of perception' (Nyanaponika, 1972: 5; italics added).

In the past decade, there has been an outpouring of research on mindfulness and its potential benefits (Shapiro & Carlson, 2009). For example, researchers have demonstrated that mindfulness increases physical and mental health, interpersonal relationship quality, and behavioral regulation (see Brown et al., 2007). In addition, evidence indicates that, even during short time intervals, mindfulness leads people to notice stimuli in their physical surroundings they might otherwise miss (Slagter et al., 2007).

As noted, mindfulness involves attending not only to a wide range of external events, but also to a broad span of internal phenomena including thoughts, beliefs, and emotions (Kabat-Zinn, 2005). Thus, while in a mindful state of consciousness, individuals tend to notice relatively more internal phenomena than they would otherwise. Supporting this claim, Brown and Ryan (2003) found that mindfulness is associated with high levels of self-concordance with respect to implicit (nonconsciously-based) and explicit (consciously-evaluated) affective states. In particular, they demonstrated that mindfulness leads individuals to evaluate their level of affect (pleasant versus unpleasant) in a manner consistent with their implicit affective state (as assessed by an implicit association measure). In the absence of mindfulness, these two measures (explicit versus implicit) tend to diverge.

Brown and Ryan's results indicate that mindfulness attunes individuals to the outcomes of processes that originate in the nonconscious system of processing. By extension, mindfulness may attune individuals to their intuitions (Dane, in press) – a claim that accords with the observation that mindfulness permits individuals to attend to a wide variety of stimuli including cognitive and emotional phenomena (Kabat-Zinn, 2005; Weick & Sutcliffe, 2006).

In sum, through increasing attunement to the outcomes of nonconsciously-driven processes, mindfulness may enhance the degree to which individuals attend to their intuitions as they arise. Given this proposed role of mindfulness, it bears considering what factors enable individuals to achieve a mindful state of consciousness.

Determinants of Mindfulness

Because mindfulness has long been associated with meditation, it is perhaps not surprising that some practices designed to enhance mindfulness, such as mindfulness-based stress reduction (MBSR: Kabat-Zinn, 1990) and mindfulness-based cognitive therapy (MBCT: Segal et al., 2002), rely heavily on meditative techniques. Drawing on such techniques, Sadler-Smith and Shefy (2007) constructed a training program incorporating the use of meditation to help managers develop their work-related mindfulness. Notably, the broad intent of this program was to attune managers to their intuitions and thus enhance their decision-making effectiveness.

Meditative practice aside, research suggests that even without deliberately seeking to develop mindfulness, individuals may become more mindful at work as they accrue job experience. Specifically, in studying how trial lawyers focus their attention in courtroom settings, Dane (2008) determined that trial lawyers' attentional resources are freed as they gain trial experience. This freeing of attentional resources occurs as one's skills become increasingly automated and as one's stress level diminishes through the acquisition of job experience. As attentional resources are freed, one becomes more capable of focusing attention on a wide range of present moment phenomena, and thus more likely to achieve and maintain a state of mindfulness while performing one's work. Given that Dane's research concerned a highly *dynamic* task environment (i.e., courtroom trials), further investigation is needed to confirm whether the development of mindfulness via job experience occurs in non-dynamic, or *static*, environments.

Research also indicates that, due to dispositional tendencies, some people tend to be in a state of mindfulness more often than others (e.g., Baer et al., 2004; Brown & Ryan, 2003; Giluk, 2009; Lau et al., 2006; Walach et al., 2006). This observation suggests that, far from being a quality that is only accessible following rigorous and lengthy meditation training, mindfulness is a state of consciousness that arises relatively naturally for some people. In addition, in light of the possibility noted above that mindfulness can be developed within a particular context (e.g., one's workplace), it is plausible that the degree to which one tends to be mindful in a given setting is a joint function of one's dispositional tendency for mindfulness and the degree of experience one has accrued in the setting of note.

Without a doubt, more research is needed to better determine what factors cultivate mindfulness. Nevertheless, the factors discussed above provide a foundation upon which to further investigate the circumstances in which both mindfulness and a heighted attunement to intuitions are likely to be found.

CONCLUSION

Although we tend to think of our gut feelings as self-evident, evidence suggests that they can be less apparent than one might assume. As argued in this chapter, individuals fail to attend to a number of their own intuitions, which may compromise their decision-making effectiveness. This observation unveils a new research question: what factors determine whether individuals attend to their intuitions? As suggested here, mindfulness plays a key role in this respect. Through further research, scholars may empirically verify this claim and identify additional conditions favorable for capturing intuitions 'in flight.'

REFERENCES

Baer, R. A., Smith, G. T., & Allen, K. B. 2004. Assessment of mindfulness by self-report: The Kentucky Inventory of Mindfulness Skills. *Assessment*, 11: 191–206.

Bargh, J. A., & Chartrand, T. L. 1999. The unbearable automaticity of being. *American Psychologist*, 54: 462–479.

Bargh, J. A., Gollwitzer, P. M., Lee-Chai, A., Barndollar, K., & Trötschel, R. 2001. The automated will: Nonconscious activation and pursuit of behavioral goals. *Journal of Personality and Social Psychology*, 81: 1014–1027.

Bishop, S. R., Lau, M., Shapiro, S., Carlson, L., Anderson, N. D., Carmody, J., Segal, Z. V., Abbey, S., Speca, M., Velting, D., & Devins, G. 2004. Mindfulness: A proposed operational definition. *Clinical Psychology: Science and Practice*, 11: 230–241.

Blume, B. D., & Covin, J. G. 2011. Attributions to intuition in the venture founding process: Do entrepreneurs actually use intuition or just say that they do? *Journal of Business Venturing*, 26:137–151.

Brown, K. W., & Ryan, R. M. 2003. The benefits of being present: Mindfulness and its role in psychological well-being. *Journal of Personality and Social Psychology*, 84: 822–848.

Brown, K. W., Ryan, R. M., & Creswell, J. D. 2007. Mindfulness: Theoretical foundations and evidence for its salutary effects. *Psychological Inquiry*, 18: 211–237.

Cowan, N. 1997. *Attention and memory: An integrated framework*. New York: Oxford University Press.

Dane, E. 2008. *Examining experience and its role in dynamic versus static decision-making effectiveness*. Paper presented at the Annual Meeting of the Academy of Management, Anaheim, CA.

Dane, E. In press. Paying attention to mindfulness and its effects on task performance in the workplace. *Journal of Management*, DOI: 10.1177/014920631036948.

Dane, E., & Pratt, M. G. 2007. Exploring intuition and its role in managerial decision making. *Academy of Management Review*, 32: 33–54.

Dane, E., & Pratt, M. G. 2009. Conceptualizing and measuring intuition: A review of recent trends. In G. P. Hodgkinson, & J. K. Ford (Eds.), *International review of industrial and organizational psychology*, 24: 1–40. Chichester, UK: Wiley.

Dane, E., Rockmann, K., & Pratt, M. G. 2009. *Should I trust my gut? Evaluating the role of task characteristics and domain expertise in intuitive and analytical decision making.* Working paper. Jesse H. Jones Graduate School of Business, Rice University, Houston, TX.

Dijksterhuis, A., & Aarts, H. 2010. Goals, attention, and (un)consciousness. *Annual Review of Psychology*, 61: 467–490.

Elsbach, K. D., & Barr, P. S. 1999. The effects of mood on individuals' use of structured decision protocols. *Organization Science*, 10: 181–198.

Epstein, M. 1995. *Thoughts without a thinker: Buddhism and psychoanalysis.* New York: Basic Books.

Epstein, S. 1994. Integration of the cognitive and psychodynamic unconscious. *American Psychologist*, 49: 709–724.

Evans, J. St. B. T. 2008. Dual-processing accounts of reasoning, judgment, and social cognition. *Annual Review of Psychology*, 59: 255–278.

Fitzsimons, G. M., & Bargh, J. A. 2003. Thinking of you: Nonconscious pursuit of interpersonal goals associated with relationship partners. *Journal of Personality and Social Psychology*, 84: 148–164.

George, J. M. 2009. The illusion of will in organizational behavior research: Nonconscious processes and job design. *Journal of Management*, 35: 1318–1339.

Giluk, T. L. 2009. Mindfulness, Big Five personality, and affect: A meta-analysis. *Personality and Individual Differences*, 47: 805–811.

Herndon, F. 2008. Testing mindfulness with perceptual and cognitive factors: External vs. internal encoding and the cognitive failures questionnaire. *Personality and Individual Differences*, 44: 32–41.

Hodgkinson, G. P., Langan-Fox, J., & Sadler-Smith, E. 2008. Intuition: A fundamental bridging construct in the behavioural sciences. *British Journal of Psychology*, 99: 1–27.

Hodgkinson, G. P., & Sadler-Smith, E. 2003. Complex or unitary? A critique and empirical re-assessment of the Allinson–Hayes Cognitive Style Index. *Journal of Occupational and Organizational Psychology*, 76: 243–268.

Hofmann, W., & Wilson, T. D. 2010. Consciousness, introspection, and the adaptive unconscious. In B. Gawronski, & B. K. Payne (Eds.), *Handbook of implicit social cognition: Measurement, theory, and applications*: 197–215. New York: Guilford Press.

Hogarth, R. M. 2001. *Educating intuition.* Chicago: University of Chicago Press.

Kabat-Zinn, J. 1990. *Full catastrophe living: Using the wisdom of your body and mind to face stress, pain and illness.* New York: Delacourt.

Kabat-Zinn, J. 2005. *Wherever you go there you are: Mindfulness meditation in everyday life.* New York: Hyperion.

Kahneman, D., & Frederick, S. 2005. A model of heuristic judgment. In K. J. Holyoak, & R. G. Morrison (Eds.), *The Cambridge handbook of thinking and reasoning*: 267–293. Cambridge: Cambridge University Press.

Kahneman, D., & Klein, G. 2009. Conditions for intuitive expertise: A failure to disagree. *American Psychologist*, 64, 515–526.

Keren, G., & Schul, Y. 2009. Two is not always better than one: A critical evaluation of two-system theories. *Perspectives on Psychological Science*, 4: 533–550.

Khatri, N., & Ng, H. A. 2000. The role of intuition in strategic decision making. *Human Relations*, 53: 57–86.

Koch, C., & Tsuchiya, N. 2006. Attention and consciousness: Two distinct brain processes. *Trends in Cognitive Sciences*, 11: 16–22.

Lambie, J. A., & Marcel, A. J. 2002. Consciousness and the varieties of emotion experience: A theoretical framework. *Psychological Review*, 109: 219–259.
Lau, M. A., Bishop, S. R., Segal, Z. V., Buis, T., Anderson, N. D., Carlson, L., Shapiro, S., & Carmody, J. 2006. The Toronto Mindfulness Scale: Development and validation. *Journal of Clinical Psychology*, 62: 1445–1467.
Louis, M. R., & Sutton, R. I. 1991. Switching cognitive gears: From habits of mind to active thinking. *Human Relations*, 44: 55–76.
Miller, C. C., & Ireland, R. D. 2005. Intuition in strategic decision making: Friend or foe in the fast-paced 21st century? *Academy of Management Executive*, 19(1): 19–30.
Nyanaponika, T. 1972. *The power of mindfulness*. San Francisco: Unity Press.
Pashler, H. E. 1998. *The psychology of attention*. Cambridge, MA: MIT Press.
Sadler-Smith, E., & Shefy, E. 2007. Developing intuitive awareness in management education. *Academy of Management Learning and Education*, 6: 186–205.
Salas, E., Rosen, M. A., & DiazGranados, D. 2010. Expertise-based intuition and decision making in organizations. *Journal of Management*, 36: 941–973.
Segal, Z. V., Williams, J. M. G., & Teasdale, J. D. 2002. *Mindfulness-based cognitive therapy for depression*. New York: Guilford Press.
Shah, J. 2003. Automatic for the people: How representations of significant others implicitly affect goal pursuit. *Journal of Personality and Social Psychology*, 84: 661–681.
Shapiro, S. L., & Carlson, L. E. 2009. *The art and science of mindfulness: Integrating mindfulness into psychology and the helping professions*. Washington, DC: American Psychological Association.
Sinclair, M., Sadler-Smith, E., & Hodgkinson, G. P. 2009. The role of intuition in strategic decision making. In L. A. Costanzo, & R. B. McKay (Eds.), *The handbook of research on strategy and foresight*: 393–417. Cheltenham, UK and Northanpton, MA, USA: Edward Elgar.
Slagter, H. A., Lutz, A., Greischar, L. L., Francis, A. D., Nieuwenhuis, S., Davis, J. M., & Davidson, R. J. 2007. Mental training affects distribution of limited brain resources. *PLoS Biology*, 5: 1228–1235.
Sloman, S. A. 1996. The empirical case for two systems of reasoning. *Psychological Bulletin*, 119: 3–22.
Stanovich, K. E., & West, R. F. 2000. Individual differences in reasoning: Implications for the rationality debate? *Behavioral and Brain Sciences*, 23: 645–665.
Walach, H., Buchheld, N., Buttenmüller, V., Kleinknecht, N., & Schmidt, S. 2006. Measuring mindfulness – the Freiburg Mindfulness Inventory (FMI). *Personality and Individual Differences*, 40: 1543–1555.
Weber, E. U., & Johnson, E. J. 2009. Mindful judgment and decision making. *Annual Review of Psychology*, 60: 53–85.
Wegner, D. M., & Smart, L. 1997. Deep cognitive activation: A new approach to the unconscious. *Journal of Consulting and Clinical Psychology*, 65: 984–995.
Weick, K. W., & Putnam, T. 2006. Organizing for mindfulness: Eastern wisdom and Western knowledge. *Journal of Management Inquiry*, 15: 275–287.
Weick, K. W., & Sutcliffe, K. M. 2006. Mindfulness and the quality of organizational attention. *Organization Science*, 17: 514–524.
Wilson, T. D., & Schooler, J. W. 1991. Thinking too much: Introspection can reduce the quality of preferences and decisions. *Journal of Personality and Social Psychology*, 60: 181–192.
Winkielman, P., & Berridge, K. C. 2004. Unconscious emotion. *Current Directions in Psychological Science*, 13: 120–123.

19 The benefit of intuition in learning situations

Claudia Kuhnle

The study of intuition has received considerable attention in the field of management as well as entrepreneurship (e.g., Dane & Pratt, 2007; Hayashi, 2001). Managers report using intuition in problem solving and decision making, which is associated with organizational effectiveness and professional development (e.g., Hayashi, 2001). Especially in situations with high uncertainty, time pressure, or need of creativity, intuition is seen as useful and valuable (e.g., Behling & Eckel, 1991; Dane & Pratt, 2007; Shirley & Langan-Fox, 1996). As a result, its integration in decision-making processes has been encouraged not only in management, entrepreneurship, or marketing (Kirby, 2004; Sadler-Smith & Burke, 2009; Sadler-Smith & Shefy, 2007; Shipp, et al., 1993), but also in other fields like medicine where the use of intuition as a rapid and unconscious decision process is stressed (Greenhalgh, 2002). However, in this respect education and training have been lacking (Sadler-Smith, 2008). It seems that even less is known about the impact of intuition on learning in a school or university context.

Although in their daily life students face complex and often conflicting decisions, which display a number of intuition conducive characteristics, the study of the role of intuition in the learning process is still in its infancy (Kuhnle & Sinclair, 2009). Nevertheless, intuition as a fast and holistic process accompanied by a confirmatory feeling could be beneficial in this respect, for example, when making a decision between a plurality of school or leisure activities. It is postulated in this chapter that an intuitively driven decision, in contrast to a deliberatively driven one, might lower the number of interferences experienced during a performed activity (Hofer et al., 2007), lead to an enhancement of flow (Csikszentmihalyi, 1997; Nakamura & Csikszentmihalyi, 2002), and reduce regret (Gilovich & Medvec, 1995). The experienced quality of performance during the activity can have further implications for regret. A diminished experience during a study task and the later perception of regret are expected to have far-reaching implications for future learning behavior because individuals are likely to make subsequent decisions in accordance with their desire to avoid future regret (Zeelenberg, 1999; Zeelenberg & Pieters, 2007).

At present, individuals face a variety of choice alternatives and decision possibilities whereas they have less time for making decisions (Shirley & Langan-Fox, 1996). These are conditions conducive to the use of intuition. So far, research has focused mainly on management situations (e.g., Dane & Pratt, 2007) but also students deal with a variety of contending actions, for example, leisure activities competing with study demands. This can lead to motivational conflicts, which are becoming more widespread (Fries et al., 2005; Senécal et al., 2003) and tend to result in motivational interference which could have serious consequences for learning behavior (e.g., Hofer et al., 2007).

The information overload in work, study, and daily life situations is hard to evaluate by the conscious information processing system due to its limited capacity (Iyengar & Lepper, 2000; Wilson & Schooler, 1991). Consequently, individuals tend to satisfy rather than maximize in decisions (Sadler-Smith et al., 2008). As a result, dissatisfying decisions occur more often and give impetus to regret (Schwartz, 2004).

This processing restriction is not in line with the premise of homo economicus who is able to evaluate all information without default (Ng & Tseng, 2008); therefore some experts criticized the rationale of this decision-making model as untenable (Simon, 1955). An integration of intuitive and analytical decision making can improve the results (Blattberg & Hoch, 1990; Hodgkinson & Clarke, 2007; Sadler-Smith et al., 2008) since it increases the processing capacity by drawing on conscious and non-conscious resources (e.g., Dijksterhuis, 2004).

This chapter explores whether the employment of intuition, compared to deliberately driven decisions, could enhance one's involvement in a performed task by lowering the occurrence of motivational interferences and thus reinforcing the frequency and length of flow experiences. It appears that such a state would reduce the occurrence of regret, which is likely to have beneficial effects on learning processes and outcomes.

INTUITIVE DECISIONS AND EXPERIENCES DURING AS WELL AS AFTER A LEARNING SITUATION

Intuition

Although there are discrepancies in conceptualizations of intuition, the definition in this chapter is based on its non-conscious nature stressed by most researchers (e.g., Dane & Pratt, 2007; Shirley & Langan-Fox, 1996; Sinclair et al., 2002). Additionally, it takes into consideration the fast manner of intuitive decisions as well as their reliance on holistic associations (Dane & Pratt, 2007). In accordance with Sinclair and Ashkanasy (2005), intuition is viewed as comprising both cognitive and affective elements. The affective elements are of main importance for the postulated relationships between intuition, flow, motivational interference, and regret. It is argued that the confirmatory feeling – experienced in a sense of certitude (Shirley & Langan-Fox, 1996) that accompanies an intuitive decision – should shield against distracting thoughts and negative emotions, including regret.

The use of intuition in decision making is postulated to be beneficial to increase the quality and involvement in a currently performed activity as well as the experience of regret. The quality and depth of the experience of a specific activity following a decision can be characterized by variables such as flow, as a deep involvement in a task at hand (Csikszentmihalyi, 1997), and also by the experience of motivational interference, which describes an impairment of the performed activity due to the valence of a rejected activity (Fries et al., 2008). These phenomena are described in more detail in the following subsections.

Motivational Interference

The experience of motivational interference follows a motivational conflict which arises whenever several goals are pursued, but due to limited resources, only one activity can be performed. In a learning context, school tasks outside of school or university where a high level of self-regulation is necessary are especially prone to this type of motivational conflict (Fries et al., 2008; Hofer et al., 2007). Even after the decision for a specific activity is made, the mere knowledge of attractive alternatives interferes with the performance of the chosen action. This phenomenon is referred to as 'motivational interference' and represents a failure in shielding from the valences of the missed activity. It can be conceptualized as a cognitive, affective, and behavioral destabilization in situations with multiple action opportunities. For students, alternatives can be of an academic and a non-academic nature. Atkinson and Birch (1974) stated in the dynamics of action theory that during one pursued activity other incompatible behavioral tendencies are also activated. These are affected not only by the valence of the currently followed activity but also by the relevance of the alternatives. The opportunity costs that arise from missing out on other opportunities can result in motivational interference (Fries et al., 2008). These costs are expected to increase with more attractive alternatives (Fries & Dietz, 2007). Distracting thoughts about a repressed alternative can interfere with the pursued goal, and thus reduce the working memory capacity (Fishbach et al., 2003; Hofer et al. 2009). For example, the process of learning can be impaired by other contemplated intentions (Cook et al., 2007).

A temptation to interrupt work on a task may occur in the form of a telephone call from a friend, or inviting a student for a meeting (e.g., Hofer et al., 2007). Also working on a computer with access to other alternatives via the Internet can have similar interference effects. The motivation to stay on the learning task can be impeded by the mere presence of temptations (Fries & Dietz, 2007). Following this, it is not unexpected that motivational interference leads to reduced learning time (Hofer et al., 2007) and decreased performance in a learning task (Fries & Dietz, 2007).

Flow

Flow theory has been used to explain intrinsic motivation (see Csikszentmihalyi, 1997; Nakamura & Csikszentmihalyi, 2002). The experience of flow is characterized by the pleasure of engaging in activities for their own sake and is referred to as 'optimal experience'. Csikszentmihalyi (1975a) concluded that flow usually occurs when the ability of the individual and the challenges are balanced. Individuals show a changed time perception, focus only on the task at hand, and are not disturbed by irrelevant thoughts and worries (Csikszentmihalyi et al., 1993). As this is a pleasurable and intrinsically rewarding experience, individuals try to reach this state again (e.g., Csikszentmihalyi, 1997). It is repeatedly demonstrated that flow has beneficial effects on learning and acquisition of skills (e.g., Csikszentmihalyi & Schneider, 2001; Csikszentmihalyi et al., 1993).

Those able to access flow mastered 'directing their awareness so as to limit the stimulus field in a way that allows the merging of action and awareness' (Csikszentmihalyi, 1975b: 55). Attention plays a key role in entering and staying in flow. Hence learning to control attention could increase the possibility of flow (Csikszentmihalyi, 1997). Research found that there is a relationship between self-control ability and the flow experience (Clark, 2002; Kuhnle et al., 2010a). Motivational interference, as a failure in successful self-regulation (e.g., Fries et al., 2008), is therefore expected to prevent the intrinsically rewarding experience of flow. It is proposed here that one possibility for promoting flow experience is to minimize the occurrence of interfering thoughts or feelings.

Regret

The experience of post-decisional regret 'results from the belief or realization that one could have done better by choosing differently' (Sagi &

Friedland, 2007: 516). Regret comprises both cognitive and emotional components, and is therefore often referred to as a cognitively based negative emotion (Gilovich & Medvec, 1995; Landman, 1993; Zeelenberg, 1999). Some researchers suggested that regret and other emotions should be included in theories of rational choice because decisions anticipate not only the possible utility or value of the option but also the emotional reactions (e.g., Zeelenberg, 1999). As the number of possible alternatives increases (Schwartz, 2004), the decision sets rise as well and the experience of regret becomes more likely (Sagi & Friedland, 2007).

Regret should be avoided because negative emotions that pull off resources from the actual goal pursuit can have detrimental effects on students' motivation, resources and also achievement (Pekrun et al., 2002). Furthermore, since regret is unpleasant and often associated with self-blame, individuals try to avoid it (e.g., Zeelenberg et al., 1996). In some instances, individuals avoid making a decision altogether which can have negative effects in the long run (Gilovich & Medvec, 1995; Zeelenberg & Pieters, 2007). The experience of regret has therefore strong implications for the subsequent day-to-day behavior (e.g., Zeelenberg et al., 2001). For example, a lesser absorption in a study activity or the experience of interference can result in regret, which can have detrimental effects on future learning habits. The individual may decide differently next time, for example, for a leisure alternative. Conversely, experiencing flow during an activity can lead to the desire to perform this task again.

Relationships among Intuition, Interference, Flow, and Regret in Learning Situations

The possibility of a supportive effect of intuition on motivational interference and intrinsic motivation (Kuhnle & Sinclair, 2009), and the relationship of regret and intuition and interference have been investigated in previous research (Kuhnle et al., 2010b). The focus of this chapter is to explore the combined effects of these phenomena in a learning context.

Based on the assumption that cognitive resources are restricted and other intentions or active goals can draw resources from an actual pursuit (Cook et al., 2007; Kruglanski et al., 2002), it would be beneficial to reduce interferences during *and* after a performed activity in order to facilitate goal attainment and pleasure from the activity. The ensuing positive affect might promote a further pursuit of goals, which are not necessarily pleasurable but aligned with a long-term goal, such as learning for an exam. Deciding intuitively could be one possibility to reduce interferences, facilitate flow, as well as minimize regret and thus increase positive affect and decrease disturbances during as well as after an activity. One mechanism regarded as relevant for this relationship is the confirmatory feeling which is more affectively driven, whereas the other mechanism – the unconscious and holistic processing mode – is more cognitively driven.

Baron (1998) criticizes intuitive judgment because, due to the subjective experience of certainty, a decision is no longer questioned. Nevertheless, the experience of a positive confirmatory feeling and the knowing with certainty (Shirley & Langan-Fox, 1996; Sinclair, 2003) could lead to a more focused experience of the activity and reduce hesitation about the made decision. This is likely to generate fewer disruptive thoughts or emotions and reduce the sense of loss about missed alternatives which would interfere with the performance of the selected task. Intuitive decisions could shield the learner from interference, and thus enable access to flow and reduce regret. The absence of motivational interference will not automatically result in the experience of flow, but it can facilitate it by successfully shielding the learner from disturbing thoughts or feelings.

In contrast to the widespread opinion that thinking about choice options will lead to a higher contentment, Carmon et al. (2003: 15) found that 'deliberating makes choosing feel like losing'. The decision process can take longer and a tedious analysis of pros and cons may strengthen the attachment to some options in the sense of a prefactual ownership. After the decision, a rejected alternative may appear more attractive than before (Carmon et al., 2003). This increased elaboration of the alternatives could lead to a disturbed experience during the activity itself, because the positive aspects of the rejected alternatives are more accessible and can lead to disturbances. This will trigger interferences, which can impede access to flow. The increased attachment resulting in dissatisfaction with the actual choice and the diminished experience during the activity itself could in turn result in a feeling of regret that this activity was pursued.

Furthermore, a decision might be affected by the holistic approach of intuitive processing. Unconscious thinkers sometimes arrive at better results because they do not focus on a limited number of attributes at the expense of other information (Dijksterhuis, 2004; Wilson & Schooler, 1991). Especially in complex situations, the unconscious can lead to superior decisions (Dijksterhuis, 2004) which can also shield from the experience of post-decisional regret.

In summary, intuitively driven decisions could reduce regret indirectly by supporting the quality of the experience during an activity because of the described buffering effect. Moreover, intuition as fast, holistic, and unconscious information processing should on the one hand be directly related to an increased quality of the decision, due to a more holistic approach. On the other hand it may also have a direct effect on a reduced attachment to other options. Consequently a reduced sense of loss about rejected alternatives is more likely because of the confirmatory feeling and the decreased option attachment. Intuitive decisions should shield against affective and cognitive disturbances during and after an activity. In contrast, deliberatively driven decisions should impair working memory, thus a reduced load on working memory due to the use of intuition can be conducive to the completion of a task.

PRACTICAL IMPLICATIONS

Regret is not only an unpleasant feeling that people try to avoid or alternatively engage in corrective behavior, but it also has a regulative aspect (Zeelenberg & Pieters, 2007). Research showed that not only the experienced but also the anticipated regret can influence behavior (e.g., Zeelenberg, 1999). As the experience of regret is very common (Landman, 1993), it would be beneficial for learners to reduce its occurrence, in particular because a decision to behave differently in order to prevent future regrets seems to have mixed effects. 'It can be counterproductive when this anticipation of regret, for example, leads people to avoid decisions or choose different options' (Zeelenberg & Pieters, 2007: 13). Applied to learning situations, the adaptation of behavior in order to avoid future regret is expected to influence learning habits negatively. More research is needed to gain a better understanding of regret as a basis for interventions and to reveal the expected negative effects on learning.

One possibility for intervention could be to improve the experience during the learning process. Csikszentmihalyi and Schneider (2001) found that adolescents experience flow in their classes as well as when they are doing homework, but the possibility of experiencing flow-like states needs to be further investigated. The promotion of flow during learning activities seems to be possible if educators take into account the appropriate balance between challenge and skills. To promote the acquisition of additional skills, it is optimal to provide a task with a difficulty slightly above the current ability of the student (Shernoff et al., 2003). In contrast, a frequent experience of motivational interference can reinforce the notion that learning is an unpleasant activity (Hofer et al., 2007). Moreover, to support the appropriate use of intuition in different decision situations, the adequacy of deliberative vs. intuitive decisions in a particular situation should be considered.

Intuitive vs. Deliberative Decision Making?

The integration of intuition and deliberation has been recommended in the management decision process (e.g., Blattberg & Hoch, 1990). Also in a learning context, a complementary use of both approaches in a structured manner seems advisable. Intuitive processing can increase the supportive effect of confirmatory feeling. Additionally, the avoidance of excessive deliberation can decrease option attachment and the sense of loss, which is primarily cognitively driven.

One suggestion is to advise a student to make a roughly structured learning schedule in a deliberative way for reaching a long-term goal, for example, a semester final exam. This schedule should also provide a certain degree of freedom to decide intuitively between learning or leisure activities on a daily basis, without losing sight of the long-term goal. This procedure would provide the advantages of both decision systems. Whether to choose analytically or intuitively in day-to-day learning decisions will require future research focusing on school and university context. For example, doing homework for the next day could be a typical situation for deciding analytically, but in the situation of writing an essay with a longer time perspective, more flexible working time, and more creative thinking, the benefit of deciding intuitively could become obvious. The procedure to encourage intuition in management education is more developed. There are concrete suggestions for closing the gap in curricula and incorporating intuition in the education process, for example, how students can become aware of biases. In this area of application, specific business disciplines are recognized where intuition is most supportive (e.g., Sadler-Smith & Burke, 2009).

To gain empirical insight, future research should shed more light upon the relationships among intuition, interference, flow, and regret in a specific learning or working situation. Based on these results, additional intervention methods applicable in the educational or work setting could be proposed.

REFERENCES

Atkinson, J. W., & Birch, D. 1974. The dynamics of achievement-oriented activity. In J. W. Atkinson, & J. O. Raynor (Eds.), *Motivation and achievement*: 271–325. Washington, DC: Winston.

Baron, J. 1998. *Judgement misguided*. New York: Oxford University Press.

Behling, O., & Eckel, N. L. 1991. Making sense out of intuition. *Academy of Management Executive*, 5: 46–54.

Blattberg, R. C., & Hoch, S. J. 1990. Database models and managerial intuition: 50% model + 50% manager. *Management Science*, 36: 887–899.

Carmon, Z., Wertenbroch, K., & Zeelenberg, M. 2003. Option attachment: When deliberation makes choosing feel like losing. *Journal of Consumer Research*, 30: 15–29.

Clark, S. R. 2002. The impact of self-regulated attention control on the amount of time spent in flow. Doctoral dissertation, Northern Arizona University. *Dissertation Abstracts International*, 63: 2615.

Cook, G. I., Marsh, R. L., Clark-Foos, A., & Meeks, J. T. 2007. Learning is impaired by activated intentions. *Psychonomic Bulletin and Review*, 14: 101–106.

Csikszentmihalyi, M. 1975a. *Beyond boredom and anxiety: Experiencing flow in work and play*. San Francisco: Jossey-Bass.

Csikszentmihalyi, M. 1975b. Play and intrinsic rewards. *Journal of Humanistic Psychology*, 15: 41–63.

Csikszentmihalyi, M. 1997. *Finding flow: The psychology of engagement with everyday life*. New York: Basic Books.

Csikszentmihalyi, M., Rathunde, K., & Whalen, S. 1993. *Talented teenagers: The roots of success and failure*. Cambridge: Cambridge University Press.

Csikszentmihalyi, M., & Schneider, B. 2001. *Becoming adult: How teenagers prepare for the world of work*. New York: Basic Books.

Dane, E., & Pratt, M. G. 2007. Exploring intuition and its role in managerial decision making. *Academy of Management Review*, 32: 33–54.

Dijksterhuis, A. 2004. Think different: The merits of unconscious thought in preference development and decision making. *Journal of Personality and Social Psychology*, 87: 586–598.

Fishbach, A., Friedman, R. S., & Kruglanski, A. W. 2003. Leading us not unto temptation: Momentary allurements elicit overriding goal activation. *Journal of Personality and Social Psychology*, 84: 296–309.

Fries, S., & Dietz, F. 2007. Learning in the face of temptation: The case of motivational interference. *Journal of Experimental Education*, 76: 93–112.

Fries, S., Dietz, F., & Schmid, S. 2008. Motivational interference in learning: The impact of leisure alternatives on subsequent self-regulation. *Contemporary Educational Psychology*, 33: 119–133.

Fries, S., Schmid, S., Dietz, F., & Hofer, M. 2005. Conflicting values and their impact on learning. *European Journal of Psychology of Education*, 20: 259–274.

Gilovich, T., & Medvec, V. H. 1995. The experience of regret: What, when, and why. *Psychological Review*, 102: 379–395.

Greenhalgh, T. 2002. Intuition and evidence – uneasy bedfellows? *British Journal of General Practice*, 52: 395–400.

Hayashi A. M. 2001. When to trust your gut. *Harvard Business Review*, 79: 59–65.

Hodgkinson, G., & Clarke, I. 2007. Conceptual note: Exploring the cognitive significance of organizational strategizing: A dual-process framework and research agenda. *Human Relations*, 60: 243–255.

Hofer, M., Schmid, S., Fries, S., Dietz, F., Clausen, M., & Reinders, H. 2007. Individual values, motivational conflicts, and learning for school. *Learning and Instruction*, 17: 17–28.

Hofer, M., Schmid, S., Fries, S., Zivkovic, I., & Dietz, F. 2009. Value orientations and studying in school–leisure conflicts: A study with samples from five countries. *Learning and Individual Differences*, 19: 101–112.

Iyengar, S. S., & Lepper, M. R. 2000. When choice is demotivating: Can one desire too much of a good thing? *Journal of Personality and Social Psychology*, 79: 995–1006.

Kirby, D. A. 2004. Entrepreneurship education: Can business schools meet the challenge? *Education + Training*, 46: 510–519.

Kruglanski, A. W., Shah, J. Y., Fishbach, A., Friedman, R., Chun, W. Y., & Sleeth-Keppler, D. 2002. A theory of goal systems. In M. P. Zanna (Ed.), *Advances in Experimental Social Psychology*: 331–378. San-Diego: Academic Press.

Kuhnle, C., Hofer, M., & Kilian, B. 2010a. *Self-control as predictor of school grades, flow, and life-balance in adolescents*. Manuscript submitted for publication.

Kuhnle, C., & Sinclair, M. 2009. The role of intuition in intrinsic motivation: An organizational and learning perspective. In R. Raj (Ed.), *Intrinsic motivation: An essential key to success*: 174–192. Hyderabad: Icfai University Press.

Kuhnle, C., Sinclair, M., Hofer, M., & Kilian, B. 2010b. *Je ne regrette rien? Variables related to the experience of regret*. Manuscript submitted for publication.

Landman, J. 1993. *Regret: Persistence of the possible*. New York: Oxford University Press.

Nakamura, J., & Csikszentmihalyi, M. 2002. The concept of flow. In C. R. Snyder, & S. J. Lopez (Eds.), *Handbook of positive psychology*: 89–105. Oxford: Oxford University Press.

Ng, I. C. L., & Tseng, L.-M. 2008. Learning to be sociable: The evolution of homo economicus. *American Journal of Economics and Sociology*, 67: 265–286.

Pekrun, R., Goetz, T., Titz, W., & Perry, R. P. 2002. Academic emotions in students' self-regulated learning and achievement: A program of qualitative and quantitative research. *Educational Psychologist*, 37: 91–105.

Sadler-Smith, E. 2008. *Inside intuition*. London: Routledge.

Sadler-Smith, E., & Burke, L. A. 2009. Fostering intuition in management education: Activities and resources. *Journal of Management Education*, 33: 239–262.

Sadler-Smith, E., Hodgkinson, G. P., & Sinclair, M. 2008. A matter of feeling? The role of intuition in entrepreneurial decision-making and behavior. In W. J. Zerbe, C. E. J. Härtel, & N. M. Ashkanasy (Eds.), *Research on emotion in organizations: Emotions, ethics and decision-making*, vol. 4: 35–55. Bingley, UK: Emerald JAI.

Sadler-Smith, E., & Shefy, E. 2007. Developing intuitive awareness in management education. *Academy of Management, Learning and Education*, 6: 186–205.

Sagi, A., & Friedland, N. 2007. The cost of richness: The effect of the size and diversity of decision sets on post-decision regret. *Journal of Personality and Social Psychology*, 93: 515–524.

Schwartz, B. 2004. *The paradox of choice: Why more is less*. New York: HarperCollins.

Senécal, C., Julien, E., & Guay, F. 2003. Role conflict and academic procrastination: A self-determination perspective. *European Journal of Social Psychology*, 33: 135–145.

Shernoff, D. J., Csikszentmihalyi, M., Schneider, B., & Shernoff, E. S. 2003. Student engagement in high school classrooms from the perspective of flow theory. *School Psychology Quarterly*, 18: 158–176.

Shipp, S., Lamb, C. W., Jr., & Mokwa, M. P. 1993. Developing and enhancing marketing students' skills: Written and oral communication, intuition, creativity, and computer usage. *Marketing Education Review*, 3: 2–8.

Shirley, D., & Langan-Fox, J. 1996. Intuition: A review and directions for research. *Psychological Reports*, 79: 563–584.

Simon, H. A. 1955. A behavioural model of rational choice. *Quarterly Journal of Economics*, 69: 99–118.

Sinclair, M. 2003. *The use of intuition in managerial decision-making: Determinants and affective moderators*. Doctoral dissertation, University of Queensland, Brisbane.

Sinclair, M., & Ashkanasy, N. M. 2005. Intuition: Myth or a decision-making tool? *Management Learning*, 36: 353–370.

Sinclair, M., Ashkanasy, N. M., Chattopadhyay, P., & Boyle, M. V. 2002. Determinants of intuitive decision-making in management: The moderating role of affect. In N. M. Ashkanasy, W. J. Zerbe, & C. E. J. Härtel (Eds.), *Managing emotions in the workplace*: 143–163. Armonk, NY: M. E. Sharpe.

Wilson, T. D., & Schooler, J. W. 1991. Thinking too much: Introspection can reduce the quality of preferences and decisions. *Journal of Personality and Social Psychology*, 60: 181–92.

Zeelenberg, M. 1999. The use of crying over spilled milk: A note on the rationality and functionality of regret. *Philosophical Psychology*, 12: 325–340.

Zeelenberg, M., Beattie, J., van der Pligt, J., & de Vries, N. K. 1996. Consequences of regret aversion: Effects of expected feedback on risky decision making. *Organizational Behavior and Human Decision Processes*, 65: 148–158.

Zeelenberg, M., Inman, J. J., & Pieters R. G. M. 2001. What we do when decisions go awry: Behavioral consequences of experienced regret. In E. U. Weber, J. Baron, & G. Loomes (Eds.), *Conflict and tradeoffs in decision making*: 136–155. Cambridge: Cambridge University Press.

Zeelenberg, M., & Pieters, R. 2007. A theory of regret regulation 1.0. *Journal of Consumer Psychology*, 17: 3–18.

20 Integrating intuition into higher education: a perspective from business management
Lisa A. Burke and Eugene Sadler-Smith

The role of intuition pervades various professional domains (e.g., health-care/nursing, finance) and areas of practice (e.g., strategic leadership, management, creativity). Not surprisingly then, intuition has been studied across multiple fields in higher education including physics, math, science, entrepreneurship, business management, journalism, nursing, education, and leadership (see Abbott & Slattery, 1990; Beck, 1998; Burke & Sadler-Smith, 2006; Faiver et al., 2000; Maycock, 1988; Sherin, 2006). Over the last several years, the case for incorporating intuitive approaches in business management education has grown, due largely to the recognition in business that intuition has a role to play in certain decision-making scenarios, especially in undefined, people-related, and/or time-pressured situations.

Given the clarion call for increasing student awareness of intuitive approaches in higher education, we examine how intuition can be inculcated at the student level. Specifically, we discuss increasing students' awareness of intuitive approaches to decision making and summarize various methods for enhancing students' intuitive capacity in business education. For purposes of this chapter, intuition is defined as an affectively charged judgment that arises through rapid, non-conscious and holistic associations (Dane & Pratt, 2007: 40).

STUDENT INTUITION AND HIGHER EDUCATION

Across disciplines in higher education, instructors are concerned with developing students' decision-making skills – is my patient likely to turn worse or better? What factors may be causing the problems with our scientific lab experiment? What type of analogy will my readers really connect to? Decision making is clearly a critical skill to develop in business classes, at both undergraduate and master's levels. As stated by Tichy and Bennis (2008: 3), 'When we ask leaders to list the bad decisions they've made in their lives, many of them will say: I knew in my gut what I should do,

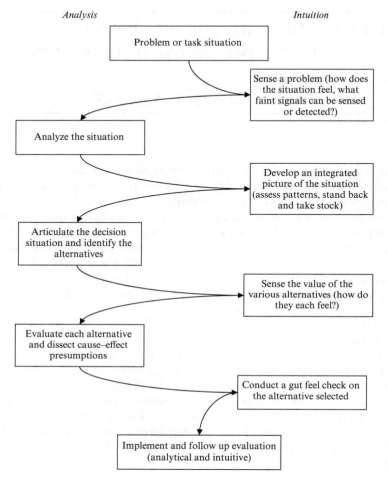

Analysis   *Intuition*

Problem or task situation

Sense a problem (how does
the situation feel, what
faint signals can be sensed
or detected?)

Analyze the situation

Develop an integrated
picture of the situation
(assess patterns, stand back
and take stock)

Articulate the decision
situation and identify the
alternatives

Sense the value of the
various alternatives (how do
they each feel?)

Evaluate each alternative
and dissect cause–effect
presumptions

Conduct a gut feel check on
the alternative selected

Implement and follow up evaluation
(analytical and intuitive)

Source: Adapted from Sadler-Smith & Burke (2009). Reproduced by kind permission of
Sage.

*Figure 20.1   Rational and Intuitive Processes in Decision Making: a
Framework for Use in Higher Education*

but I didn't do it.' While we do not advocate dismissing rational decision
approaches, we do think students should understand the iterative role of
intuitive and rational approaches in effective problem solving and decision
making. As depicted in Figure 20.1, Sadler-Smith and Burke (2009) outlined how rational and intuitive elements comprise the decision-making
process: rational approaches are useful in analyzing the decision situation,

identifying and analyzing decision alternatives, and dissecting cause-and-effect relationships, while intuitive approaches are more useful for sensing the problem at hand, developing an integrated and holistic picture of the problem, sensing the value of various decision alternatives, and conducting a gut check on the decision solution adopted.

Increasingly, more authors are advocating balancing rational and intuitive decision-making approaches in business education and/or have designed the means to measure or build such skills. For example, Shoemaker (2008: 127) suggests in his imperatives for a new business model that managers should 'recognize the importance of intuition and seasoned judgment' while acknowledging its 'heuristic nature'. And helping to advance the measurement of decision styles, Vance et al. (2007) developed and validated the Linear–Nonlinear Thinking Style Profile (LNTSP) inventory, identifying how individuals attend to a particular kind of information source (internal versus external) and the subsequent linear versus non-linear processing of that information. Vance et al. advocate the use of the LNTSP to study management education methods that are most effective in building linear or non-linear skills to achieve greater balance in decision approaches. Next, we summarize methods discussed throughout the business literature for developing students' intuition.

Practical Considerations

In the fields of professional and self-development a number of authors have made suggestions for how intuition can be developed (Duggan, 2007; Robinson, 2006; Tesolin, 2007). Many researchers and practitioners have made innovative and useful recommendations with similar goals (Cappon, 1994; Goldberg, 1985; Klein, 2003; Miller & Ireland, 2005; Rowan, 1986; Weintraub, 1998). In this regard, the work of Taggart is of particular note (Taggart & Robey, 1981; Taggart & Valenzi, 1990; www.the-intuitive-self. org).

Hogarth (2001) concluded that it is possible to educate our 'sixth sense' and offered concrete suggestions and exercises for developing intuitive skills and good habits for learning from experience. Sadler-Smith and Shefy (2004: 76) offered guidelines for developing 'intuitive awareness' so that executives could 'make more effective and intelligent use of intuition in ways that acknowledge its limitations while maximizing its potential.' They argued that intuition and rationality are two parallel systems of knowing, that is they are dual processes (Epstein, 2008) and the challenge for business educators (and managers) is to weave the two systems together in order to develop students who are 'intuitively intelligent' (cf. Hogarth 2001). Analysis and intuition interplay in an iterative fashion in the decision process, based on the assumption that for many real-world business problems neither analysis nor intuition is sufficient (Sadler-Smith & Burke, 2009).

Sadler-Smith and Shefy (2010) furthered the idea of 'intuitive intelligence' when they suggested that: (i) from the perspective of *intuitive expertise* (Dreyfus & Dreyfus, 1986; Klein, 1998) it is possible to develop more finely-tuned, domain-specific intuitive judgment skills (Hogarth, 2001); (ii) managers can build a *knowledge and understanding* of intuition's distinctive features and thus delineate it from related constructs (such as heuristics or insight); and (iii) improved *self-awareness* may help people better understand their own intuiting processes (both cognitive and affective components) and outcomes. Focusing on these three themes, we offer a menu of ideas for educating and developing students' intuition, as summarized in Table 20 1.

Developing Knowledge and Understanding of Intuition

Recent theorizing and research in the field of intuition has tended to adopt a dual process perspective (Hodgkinson et al., 2009). This stance is based on the notion that 'there are two minds [intuitive and analytical] in one brain' (Evans, 2003: 454), generically referred to as System 1 and System 2 (Stanovich & West, 2000). The 'two minds model' comprises two contrasting modes of thinking, namely: analytical (i.e., affect free, serial, slow in operation, fast in formation, detail focused, intentional, cognitively demanding, abstract and/or symbolic based, open to conscious awareness) and intuitive (i.e., affect laden, parallel, fast in operation, slow in formation, holistic, involuntary, cognitively undemanding, imagistic and/or narrative based, unavailable to conscious awareness) (Epstein, 2008; Evans, 2008). This framework of human cognition is a simple, elegant, and powerful theoretical and pedagogical tool for business educators.

Other relevant knowledge and understanding issues for educators include an appreciation of the now widely accepted distinction between insight and intuition (Dane & Pratt, 2007; Hodgkinson et al., 2008; Hogarth, 2001). Sadler-Smith and Burke (2009) offered practical exercises that can be used to illustrate the intuition/insight distinction. Regarding whether intuition is a myth or an effective decision-making tool (Sinclair & Ashkanasy, 2005), Sadler-Smith and Burke (2009) argued that a useful starting point is dispelling the notion of intuition as a mystical, magical, or paranormal phenomenon (Vaughan, 1979), or that it should never be trusted (Bonabeau, 2003). They recommended that instructors use examples and case studies such as Klein's (2003) accounts of experienced

Table 20.1   *Recommendations for Developing Students' Intuition in Higher Education*

Source	Summary of recommendations
Hogarth (2001)	Selecting/creating the right environment for learning (i.e. acquire correct intuitions in appropriate environments)
	Screening automatic actions before following them (i.e. imposing 'circuit breakers')
	Seeking feedback and recognizing if an environment is kind (feedback is critical and functional) or wicked (feedback is faulty)
	Acknowledging emotions as part of intuitive system and treating them as data
	Exploring connections using narrative, imagery, and mental simulation
	Accepting conflict in choice (between analysis and intuition)
	Making the scientific method intuitive (i.e. instruction and practice in scientific reasoning so that it becomes tacit and can be deployed automatically)
Sadler-Smith & Shefy (2004)	Reflecting on experiences of intuition, level of trust placed in gut feel, suppression of hunches, and covertness of reliance on gut feel
	Developing a cognitive appreciation of the differences between instinct, insight, and intuition
	Eliciting reliable feedback on intuitive judgment, building confidence in gut feel, and being in an environment in which good intuitions can be developed
	Benchmarking how reliable one's intuitive judgment is, and identifying how one's intuitive judgment might be improved
	Using imagery rather than exclusively relying on words (i.e. visualizing potential future scenarios and reflecting upon gut responses)
	Testing intuitive judgments by raising objections, generating counter-arguments, and probing the robustness of gut feel to challenges
	Creating conditions for intuition, capturing intuitions before they are censored by the 'analytical mind' and validating intuitions
Sadler-Smith & Burke (2009)	Dispelling myths about intuition: recognizing scientific basis of intuition and contrasting intuitive expertise with magical intuition
	Capturing and analyzing intuitions: developing a systematic approach to recording, interpreting, and articulating intuitions

Table 20.1   (continued)

Source	Summary of recommendations
Sadler-Smith & Burke (2009)	Scrutinizing intuitions and giving feedback: scrutinizing intuition using appropriate questioning techniques; identifying situations where intuition worked and where it failed Being aware of biases: recognizing and countering confirmation bias and other sources of error (e.g. representativeness, availability, and anchoring) Giving the rational mind a reprieve: practicing techniques for mental relaxation and contemplation
Sadler-Smith & Shefy (2010)	Developing intuitive expertise (i.e. knowledge of a domain) Developing intuitive understanding (i.e. knowledge of intuition) Developing intuitive self-awareness (i.e. knowledge of one's intuitive mind)

firefighters deploying intuitive judgment in complex, time-pressured situations, or the story of 'The Getty Kouros' (Gladwell, 2005) as an example of informed intuitions solving complex, high-stake problems. It is important that students appreciate the distinguishing features of different task environments and are able to recognize problems that are likely to yield to intuition (i.e., loosely structured) and those that are not (i.e., tightly structured) (Dane & Pratt, 2009; Klein, 2003).

Developing Intuitive Expertise

From the perspective of 'intuition as expertise', it is importantly acknowledged that intuitive skills are 'based largely on experience and that people's experience differs' (Hogarth, 2001: 23). One challenge therefore in developing intuition is creating the conditions whereby students can have appropriate experiences and learn from them to develop the necessary prototypes and holistic associations upon which the pattern-matching substrates of intuition by recognition (Simon, 1987) may be developed.[1]

Hogarth (2001) suggests that environments in which explicit and implicit learning take place are vital, and distinguishes between kind learning environments (characterized by feedback which is critical and functional) that foster 'good' intuitions and wicked learning environments (characterized by feedback that is faulty and misleading) that foster 'bad' intuitions. Hogarth recommends that students and instructors create the environment for learning good intuitions and that students seek and instructors offer feedback to allow performance-enhancing lessons learned from relevant and timely experiences. Reflecting on students' intuitive 'hits' and 'misses' is a key aspect of building good intuitions, benchmarking the reliability of their intuitions, and identifying the type of situation where gut feel may work.

It is also important for novices, such as undergraduate business students, to accept that: (i) the acquisition of intuitive expertise is a long-term process involving an almost ten-year developmental trajectory in a specific domain (Ericsson et al., 2007); (ii) there are, at times, 'rites of passage' that have to be experienced during skill acquisition (Dreyfus & Dreyfus, 1986); and finally (iii) the process can be accelerated (using some of the aforementioned methods), but there are few if any short cuts. It is through planned, focused, and sustained efforts to accomplish new things in one's domain – but outside of one's 'comfort zone' in a real or simulated setting – that performance capacity is extended (i.e., analogous to developing high-level performance in musical conservatories and sports settings by constantly 'raising the bar').

Developing Skills for Intuitive Self-awareness

The development of intuitive expertise is concerned both with the process of intuiting and its content; by contrast, the development of intuitive self-awareness is concerned more with developing the process. By developing an intuitive self-awareness from an essentially intra-personal perspective, students may arrive at a better understanding of their own attitudes towards intuition, their significant experiences of intuition, and how intuition works for them. The aims of this component for developing students' intuition are: (i) the acquisition of generic intuition skills whereby students may be able to access their 'intuitive mind' and (ii) the capability to deploy skills of both analysis and intuition in ways commensurate with their personal attributes (e.g., style of thinking), circumstances (e.g., level of expertise), and the task at hand (e.g., tightly structured favoring analysis versus loosely structured favoring intuition).

Intuitions are by definition affectively charged (Dane & Pratt, 2007) and in the context of decision making affect is part of the intuitive system and should be treated as data (Hogarth, 2001). However, intuitive feelings are not equivalent to emotional feelings (Sadler-Smith, 2010); hence it is essential not only that students recognize affect as data but also that they are able to distinguish between the stronger affect associated with emotional feelings (for example, fear, love, happiness) and the more subtle affect (e.g., hunch, gut feel, or vibes) associated with the posting of the outputs of intuiting in conscious awareness (Damasio, 1999; Evans, 2003). A related aspect of intra-personal awareness relates to biases; Sadler-Smith and Burke (2009) highlighted the importance of recognizing and countering confirmation bias and other sources of error. Sadler-Smith (2010) also highlights personal fears, prejudices, and wishful thinking as sources of 'feeble' intuitions and enemies of good intuitive judgment. Hogarth (2001: 209) recommended that decision makers become skilled in screening their automatic actions and deliberately impose a 'circuit breaker', 'thereby guiding behavior if not changing underlying attitudes'. In terms of intra- and inter-personal dialogue, the default mode of expression in higher education is often the verbal channel, which tends to be linear; however, other modalities exist such as the visual and kinesthetic. Hogarth (p. 231) recommends making time to 'observe what is around you' (i.e. being mindful) and 'learning to draw or make sketches' as a way of exploring non-linear connections. Specialized applications of visual imagery include: (i) mental simulation techniques (i.e., running a 'DVD in the head') (Klein, 1998, 2003) and (ii) cognitive mapping techniques (Clarke & Mackaness, 2001), which could also be brought into the classroom (Sadler-Smith & Burke, 2009).

Finally, storytelling and metaphorical thinking are important means of expressing intuitions both in intra- and inter-personal dialogue. Students can be trained in the use of narrative, storytelling (Gold & Holman, 2001), and metaphors (Sadler-Smith & Shefy, 2007, 2010). Finally, it may be possible to create the conditions for intuitions by 'quieting the analytical mind', referred to by Sadler-Smith and Burke (2009: 250) as 'giving the rational mind a reprieve'. To this end, Sadler-Smith and Shefy (2007) applied a variety of contemplative and meditative techniques in a management education setting; participants reported positively on the program, and an analysis of diarized accounts of their experiences revealed perceived positive impacts on intra- and inter-personal sensitivities, increased confidence in intuitive judgment, and a heightened awareness of one's own cognitive and affective processes.

SUMMARY

In summary, many techniques and approaches have been offered in the business literature to enhance students' intuitive awareness and skills. As the role of intuition in decision making gains ground in other disciplines, other fields and their instructors may benefit from considering such approaches. The challenge to educators and researchers who are interested in integrating intuition into higher education is to adopt and adapt some of the approaches we have reviewed, design, develop and test new approaches, and rigorously evaluate the effectiveness of such techniques.

NOTE

1. Simon (1987: 63) claimed that 'intuition and judgment – at least good judgment' are 'simply analyses frozen into habit and into the capacity for rapid response through recognition'.

REFERENCES

Abbott, C., & Slattery, K. 1990. Explicit news writing rules and the intuitive 'good ear'. *Journalism Educator*, 45: 51–57.

Beck, C. 1998. Intuition in nursing practice: Sharing graduate students' exemplars with undergraduate students. *Journal of Nursing Education*, 37: 169–172.

Bonabeau, E. 2003. Don't trust your gut. *Harvard Business Review*, 81(5): 116–123.

Burke, L., & Sadler-Smith, E. 2006. Extending intuition in the educational setting. *Academy of Management Learning and Education*, 5(2): 169–181.

Cappon, D. 1994. *Intuition and management: Research and application*. Westport, CT: Quorum.

Clarke I., & Mackaness, W. 2001. Management 'intuition': An interpretative account of structure and content of decision schemas using cognitive maps. *Journal of Management Studies*, 38(2): 147–172.

Damasio, A. R. 1999. *The feeling of what happens: Body, emotion and the making of consciousness*. London: Vintage.

Dane, E., & Pratt, M. G. 2007. Exploring intuition and its role in managerial decision-making. *Academy of Management Review*, 32: 33–54.

Dane, E., & Pratt, M. G. 2009. Conceptualizing and measuring intuition: A review of recent trends. In G. P. Hodgkinson, & J. K. Ford (Eds.), *International review of industrial and organizational psychology*: 1–40. Chichester, UK: Wiley.

Dreyfus, H. L., & Dreyfus, S. E. 1986. *Mind over machine: The power of human intuitive expertise in the era of the computer*. New York: Free Press.

Duggan, W. 2007. *Strategic intuition: The creative spark in human achievement*. New York: Columbia University Press.

Epstein, S. 2008. Intuition from the perspective of cognitive–experiential self-theory. In H. Plessner, C. Betsch, & T. Betsch (Eds.), *Intuition in judgment and decision making*: 23–37. New York: Lawrence Erlbaum.

Ericsson, K. A., Prietula, M. J., & Cokely, E. T. 2007. The making of an expert. *Harvard Business Review*, July–August: 115–121.

Evans, J. St. B. T. 2003. In two minds: Dual-process accounts of reasoning. *Trends in Cognitive Sciences*, 7(10): 454–459.

Evans, J. St. B. T. 2008. Dual-processing accounts of reasoning, judgment, and social cognition. *Annual Review of Psychology*, 59: 6.1–6.24.

Faiver, C., McNally, C., & Nims, P. 2000. Teaching a workshop on creativity and intuition in counseling. *Journal of Humanistic Counseling, Education and Development*, 38: 220–229.

Gladwell, M. 2005. *Blink*. London: Allen Lane.

Gold, J., & Holman, D. 2001. Let me tell you a story: An evaluation of the use of storytelling and argument analysis in management education. *Career Development International*, 6: 384–395.

Goldberg, P. 1985. *The intuitive edge*. Los Angeles: Tarcher.

Hodgkinson, G. P., Langan-Fox, J., & Sadler-Smith, E. 2008. Intuition: A fundamental bridging construct in the behavioral sciences. *British Journal of Psychology*, 99(1): 1–27.

Hodgkinson, G., Sadler-Smith, E., Burke, L., Sparrow, P., & Claxton, G. 2009. Intuition in organizations: Some implications for strategic management. *Long Range Planning*, 42: 277–297.

Hogarth, R. M. 2001. *Educating intuition.* Chicago: University of Chicago Press.
Klein, G. A. 1998. *Sources of power: How people make decisions.* Cambridge, MA: MIT Press.
Klein, G. A. 2003. *Intuition at work: Why developing your gut instincts will make you better at what you do.* New York: Currency Doubleday.
Maycock, F. 1988. *Improving intuitive abilities for a more holistic approach to education.* Paper presented at Meeting of the American Educational Research Association. New Orleans, LA, April.
Miller, C. C., & Ireland, R. D. 2005. Intuition in strategic decision making: Friend or foe in the fast-paced 21st century? *Academy of Management Executive*, 19(1): 19–30.
Robinson, L.A. 2006. *Trust your gut.* Chicago: Kaplan.
Rowan, R. 1986. *The intuitive manager.* Boston, MA: Little Brown.
Sadler-Smith, E. 2010. *The intuitive mind.* Chichester, UK: John Wiley.
Sadler-Smith, E., & Burke, L.A. 2009. Fostering intuition in management education: Activities and resources. *Journal of Management Education*, 33, 239–250.
Sadler-Smith, E., & Shefy, E. 2004. The intuitive executive: Understanding and applying 'gut feel' in decision making. *Academy of Management Executive*, 18: 76–92.
Sadler-Smith, E., & Shefy, E. 2007. Developing intuitive awareness in management education. *Academy of Management Learning and Education*, 6: 186–205.
Sadler-Smith, E., & Shefy, E. 2010. Intuitive intelligence. In J. Gold, A. Mumford, & R. Thorpe (Eds.), *The Gower handbook of management and leadership development*: 387–403. Aldershot: Gower.
Sherin, B. 2006. Common sense clarified: The role of intuitive knowledge in physics problem solving. *Journal of Research in Science Teaching*, 43: 535–555.
Shoemaker, P. 2008. The future challenges of business: Rethinking management education. *California Management Review*, 50: 119–132.
Simon, H. A. 1987. Making management decisions: The role of intuition and emotion. *Academy of Management Executive*, 1: 57–64.
Sinclair, M., & Ashkanasy, N. M. 2005. Intuition: Myth or a decision-making tool. *Management Learning*, 36: 353–370.
Stanovich, K. E., & West, R. F. 2000. Individual differences in reasoning: Implications for the rationality debate? *Behavioral and Brain Sciences*, 23: 645–665.
Taggart, W., & Robey, D. 1981. Minds and managers: On the dual nature of human information processing and management. *Academy of Management Review*, 6: 187–195.
Taggart, W., & Valenzi, E. 1990. Assessing rational and intuitive styles: A human information processing metaphor. *Journal of Management Studies*, 27: 149–172.
Tesolin, A. 2007. Don't stifle intuition in your workplace: How to foster intuition among your employees. *Training and Development*, June: 76–78.
Tichy, N., & Bennis, W. 2008. Making tough calls. *Leadership Excellence*, 25(6): 3–5.
Vance, C., Groves, K., Paik, Y., & Kindler, H. 2007. Understanding and measuring linear–nonlinear thinking style for enhanced management education and professional practice. *Academy of Management Learning and Education*, 6: 167–179.
Vaughan, F. E. 1979. *Awakening intuition.* New York: Doubleday.
Weintraub, S. 1998. *The hidden intelligence: Innovation through intuition.* Woburn, MA: Butterworth Heinemann.

21 The heart in intuition: tools for cultivating intuitive intelligence

Dana Elisa Tomasino[1]

Mainstream science has endeavored to account for intuition purely in terms of cognitive processes within the brain (Baron, 2004; Lieberman, 2000; Mitchell et al., 2005; Simon, 1987). Yet there is a long-held notion, shared by many cultures and civilizations throughout human history, that the heart is involved in intuitive experience: this is the view of the heart as a locus of inner wisdom and insight – a conduit to an *intuitive intelligence* that both transcends and yet also complements the perceptions and understandings of normal awareness (Godwin, 2001; Young, 2003). Ironically, while this ancient understanding of the heart has largely been relegated to metaphor by modern society, new science is now beginning to reaffirm the validity of this age-old concept and to develop an understanding of the heart's central involvement in the psychophysiological and emotional processes that underlie intuition (Bradley et al., 2011; McCraty et al., 2004a; Tressoldi et al., 2009).

Building on this new research, this chapter views intuition as a *whole-body process* in which the heart plays a key role, both in the processes by which intuitive perception occurs and also in the creation of an optimal bodily state – *psychophysiological coherence* – that appears to enhance intuitive receptivity. Activated by positive emotions, this state is marked by a systemic shift toward increased synchronization and harmony in an individual's physiological and psychological processes. Positive emotion-based tools and technologies that activate psychophysiological coherence are discussed as a programmatic means to cultivate intuitive receptivity, and, with sustained practice, to ultimately develop an intuitive intelligence that can inform choice and action across all spheres of life.

INTUITION AND INTUITIVE INTELLIGENCE

Intuition is the capacity for immediate awareness and insight about the totality of an object, event, or situation that transcends the incremental processes involved in normal perception and reasoning (Assagioli, 1971; Myers, 2002). The dominant perspective in intuition research is a cognitive

247

approach, in which intuition is viewed solely as a function of the unconscious mind accessing existing information within the brain from prior experience (Agor, 1984; Mitchell et al., 2005; Myers, 2002; Simon, 1987). While, as Bradley et al. (2011) note, there is little doubt that information stored in memory – both conscious and unconscious knowledge – is involved, there is compelling evidence for another informational basis for intuitive perception. This is the *tacit* information from distant or future (nonlocal) sources which is perceived by the body's psychophysiological systems and registered as a pre-stimulus response, well before the brain's half-second cortical priming; this has been consistently documented in hundreds of rigorous experiments since the middle of the last century (see the reviews by Bernstein, 2005; Bradley, 2007; Radin, 1997a). Therefore, in acknowledging the compelling evidence for such 'nonlocal' intuition (Bradley, 2007), the concept of intuitive perception used in this chapter includes *both* the cognitive processing of existing information stored in the brain and *also* the body's perception of implicit information from nonlocal sources.

There is an inherent intelligence implied in such an expanded concept of intuition, insofar as *intelligence* – the capacity for reasoning, planning, problem solving, and learning from life experience – is viewed not just as a narrow capability but as a 'broader and deeper' capacity for sensing, understanding, and interacting purposefully with objects in our environment (Arvey et al., 1994; Gottfredson, 1997). Rather than intelligence being restricted to the knowledge store from past experience, access to information from nonlocal sources avails the body to another potential source of knowledge based on 'ontologically "*objective*"' information; this information is 'communicated from *real* nonlocal objects' and 'provides a rational basis for intuitive decision and action' (Bradley, 2010: 342, italics added). Thus, access both to stored information about prior experience and to that received by the body from nonlocal sources creates the basis for a more inclusive and fundamental form of intelligence that we call *intuitive* intelligence. When developed, this capacity is manifested as an increasing competence in consistently accessing and using intuition to gain reliable knowledge and insight, and in applying this understanding to greater effect in one's life. Like other forms of intelligence, intuitive intelligence can be developed by intentional practice and honed by application.

THE PSYCHOPHYSIOLOGICAL BASIS OF INTUITION

The findings of recent electrophysiological studies have challenged several commonly held beliefs about intuition – namely: that intuitive perception is purely a function of the unconscious mind accessing stored memories from prior experience; that the intuitive process is localized within the brain; and that the communication of intuitive information does not violate the laws of causality or the physical constraints of space–time (e.g., see Agor, 1984; Laughlin, 1997; Mitchell et al., 2005; Myers, 2002; Simon, 1987). Collectively, these electrophysiological studies have typically shown that the body responds to a future, randomly selected stimulus *4–7 seconds before* the stimulus is experienced (e.g., see Bierman & Radin, 1997; May et al., 2005; Radin 1997a, 2004; Spottiswoode & May, 2003). This electrophysiological pre-stimulus response has been documented not only for the brain and for skin conductance response (a measure of autonomic nervous system activation), but also, most recently, for the heart.

The Surprising Role of the Heart

The first experiments involving the heart (McCraty et al., 2004a, b) adapted an experimental protocol originally developed by Radin (1997b), in which a series of randomly selected photographs of either calm or emotionally arousing stimuli were presented to subjects under controlled conditions while electrophysiological measures were continuously recorded. Measures of both heart (cardiac accelerations/decelerations) and brain (event-related potentials and heartbeat-evoked potentials)[2] activity differed significantly *during the pre-stimulus period* before the presentation of an emotional image, compared to before a calm image. The experiment found that both the heart and brain effectively 'knew' the emotional significance of a future stimulus even before the computer had randomly selected the image to be displayed, and that the heart responded even *before* the brain (McCraty et al., 2004a, b).

Corroborating evidence of the heart's involvement in predicting future events was found by Tressoldi et al. (2009) in Italian research subjects, using random presentation of pleasant and unpleasant acoustical stimuli. Furthermore, a repeated measures study on a US sample, employing a gambling (roulette wheel) protocol, found that heart activity was a more effective predictor of intuitive foresight than skin conductance (Bradley et al., 2011); this study also reported the results from a gambling experiment on repeat entrepreneurs in the UK, in which measures of the heart's activity were found to predict the future randomly generated outcome. Finally, a new study of repeat entrepreneurs in Iran, adapting the McCraty et al. experimental protocol, provided additional evidence of the heart's ability to discriminate between emotional and calm future visual stimuli (Toroghi et al., 2011).

THE HEART AND THE PSYCHOPHYSIOLOGY OF POSITIVE EMOTIONS

To develop an understanding of the heart's role in intuitive experience, it is necessary to examine the extensive interactions among the heart, the emotional system, and cognitive processing. A large body of work in the neurosciences has concluded that the way in which we perceive and process information is mediated by emotional experience (Immordino-Yang & Damasio, 2007; LeDoux, 1994). More specifically, there is evidence that individuals in a positive emotional state display patterns of thought and behavior that are notably creative, flexible, integrative, and open to information (reviewed in Fredrickson, 2002; Isen, 1999); individuals also make more accurate intuitive judgments and display enhanced insight when experiencing positive emotions (Bolte et al., 2003; Subramaniam et al., 2009). While there are clearly multi-system and multi-level processes involved in these relationships, research conducted over the past two decades has identified an intriguing and powerful pathway in which input from the heart plays a key role.

Heart Rhythm Patterns and Emotional States

Work by McCraty and others documents an important relationship between the heart's activity and the generation and experience of emotions (see McCraty et al., 2009). Using a measure of the natural beat-to-beat fluctuations in heart rate, known as 'heart rate variability' (HRV), this research has shown that the *heart rhythm pattern* covaries with emotions in real time, and that distinct heart rhythm patterns characterize different emotional states (McCraty et al., 1995; Tiller et al., 1996).

In general, during stress and negative emotions, the heart rhythm pattern becomes more erratic and disordered, resembling an irregular series of sharp, jagged peaks and valleys (see Figure 21.1). This has been characterized as an *incoherent* pattern of heart rhythm activity and indicates a desynchronization in the activity of the autonomic nervous system. When sustained, such desynchronization impedes the efficient communication and flow of information throughout the psychophysiological systems (McCraty et al., 2009).

By contrast, a very different heart rhythm pattern is observed during positive emotions, such as love and appreciation. In these emotional states, the heart's rhythm resembles a regular series of smooth, cyclic waves, approximating a sine wave (Figure 21.1). Clearly discernible visually as well as by quantitative measurement (McCraty et al., 2009; Tiller et al., 1996), this pattern is referred to as *heart rhythm coherence*; it signifies

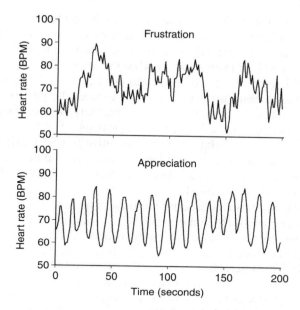

Note: These graphs show examples of real-time heart rate variability patterns (heart rhythms) recorded during self-induced states of frustration and appreciation. The *incoherent* heart rhythm pattern shown in the top graph, characterized by its irregular, jagged waveform, is typical of negative emotions such as anger, frustration, and anxiety. The bottom graph shows an example of the *coherent* heart rhythm pattern that is typically observed when an individual is experiencing a sustained positive emotion, such as appreciation, compassion, or love. The coherent pattern is characterized by its regular, sine wave-like waveform.

Source: Tiller et al. (1996). © Institute of HeartMath.

Figure 21.1   Heart Rhythm Patterns in Different Emotional States

increased synchronization in autonomic nervous system activity and a general shift in autonomic balance toward increased parasympathetic activity.

Heart–Brain Communication

While it is well established that the activity of the heart *responds* to emotions, it is less known that the heart also exerts a unique influence on the very processes that *determine* our emotional and perceptual experience (Damasio, 2003; McCraty & Tomasino, 2006; Pribram & Melges, 1969).

With an intrinsic nervous system that qualifies as a 'little brain' in its own right (Armour & Ardell, 1994), the heart actually sends more information to the brain than the brain sends to the heart (Cameron, 2002). These afferent neurological signals from the heart not only affect the brain's autonomic regulatory centers, but also interact with the higher brain centers involved in emotional and cognitive processing (Frysinger & Harper, 1990; Sandman et al., 1982; van der Molen et al., 1985). As the heart's rhythmic beating patterns change, so does the pattern of neurological information it transmits to the brain centers via the afferent neural pathways. These cardiac afferent neurological signals play an important role in inhibiting or facilitating higher cognitive functions. During emotional stress, the heart's incoherent signal results in the inhibition of higher brain processes involved in cognition and emotion regulation (Bradley et al., 2010; McCraty et al., 2009).

In positive emotional states, by contrast, when the heart generates a harmonious, coherent rhythm of activity, the resulting pattern of cardiac afferent input to the brain contributes to cortical facilitation, whereby higher cognitive faculties are enhanced (Bradley et al., 2010; McCraty et al., 2009). This interaction between the heart and brain may provide a physiological basis for the link between positive emotions and improved creativity, cognitive flexibility, innovative problem solving, and intuition (e.g., see Bolte et al., 2003; Isen, 1999).

PSYCHOPHYSIOLOGICAL COHERENCE: A STATE OF OPTIMAL FUNCTION

As the body's most powerful biological oscillator, the heart effectively 'sets the beat' for the entire body and can frequency-pull or entrain other biological oscillatory systems into synchronization with its rhythm (McCraty et al., 2009). During sustained positive emotional states, when a coherent heart rhythm is maintained, a system-wide phase shift to a distinct, measurable state occurs (Tiller et al., 1996; see Figure 21.2). Distinguished by increased order and synchronization in both physiological and psychological processes, this state has been characterized as *psychophysiological coherence* (McCraty et al., 2009).

The physiological correlates and changes associated with coherence generate an optimal state in which the brain, nervous system, and many bodily processes operate with increased efficiency and harmony. This results in reduced strain on the body's organs and systems, the conservation of metabolic energy, and the enhancement of the body's natural regenerative processes (McCraty et al., 2009; Tiller et al., 1996). Heart rhythm coherence, the key physiological marker of this state, is directly correlated with cognitive function and task performance – improvements

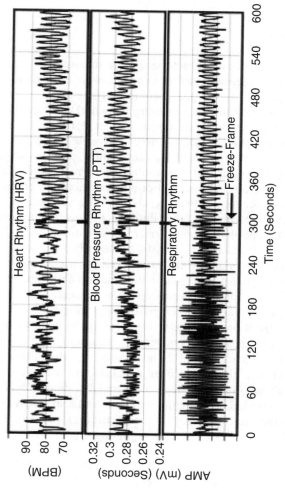

Note: These real-time recordings show an individual's heart rhythm activity (heart rate variability pattern), pulse transit time (a measure of beat-to-beat blood pressure), and respiration rhythms over a 10-minute period. At the 300-second mark, the individual used a positive emotion-based technique to activate the psychophysiological coherence state, causing these three physiological systems to come into entrainment.

Source: Tiller et al. (1996). © Institute of HeartMath.

Figure 21.2   Real-time Shift to Psychophysiological Coherence

in mental focus and attention, speed and accuracy of response, long-term memory, and academic test performance (Bradley et al., 2010; McCraty et al., 2009). At the affective level, the coherence state is associated with greater emotional stability, reduced stress and negative emotions, and an increase in positive emotions (Bradley et al., 2010; McCraty et al., 1998; McCraty & Tomasino, 2006; Tiller et al., 1996).

Coherence and Intuition

Psychophysiological coherence is characterized by certain internal changes conducive to the efficient reception and communication of information by the psychophysiological systems – a quieting of the extraneous inner 'noise' generated by the normal stream of unmanaged mental and emotional activity, in conjunction with a positive emotion-driven global shift toward increased synchronization and harmony in psychophysiological processes. These changes not only enhance cognitive functioning, but also appear to increase sensitivity and receptivity to nonlocal information normally outside the range of conscious awareness. For a description of a potential mechanism for how this occurs, see Bradley, ch. 17 in this volume.

Electrophysiological experiments have illuminated several important connections between psychophysiological coherence and nonlocal intuitive perception. In the McCraty et al. study (2004a, b), described above, analyses of event-related potentials and heartbeat-evoked potentials suggested that the heart's afferent signals likely contain information about the future stimulus, thereby initiating the brain's processing of intuitive perception. Notably, it was further found that in the psychophysiological coherence condition, the processing of pre-stimulus information in the brain's frontal cortex was modified by the heart's afferent signals, suggesting that subjects were more attuned to information from the heart after activating the coherence state (McCraty et al., 2004b). Moreover, results from a roulette experiment with individuals who had practiced coherence-building techniques (described below) for a period of ten years or more found a significant pre-stimulus response in the subjects' heart rhythm recordings, predicting the future randomly generated betting outcome beginning some *12–14 seconds* before the result was known – even before the subjects had made their betting decision (Bradley et al., 2011). This is double the time window of the 4–7 seconds consistently observed in previous studies, suggesting that the body's psychophysiological systems can detect intuitive information *even earlier* in the pre-stimulus period than previously documented.

This connection between coherence and enhanced intuition is also apparent in anecdotal reports from thousands of individuals who have been trained in coherence-building methods (Childre & Martin, 1999;

McCraty & Childre, 2004). A commonly reported experience is a sense of gaining increasing access to a form of internal guidance and discernment that is qualitatively distinct from one's regular cognitive processes and that provides insight and direction with respect to one's self-development, choices, actions, and interactions. Typically, this enhanced capacity to draw on intuition leads to outcomes such as deeper self-awareness, improved emotional balance and mental clarity, more effective decision making and problem solving, greater competence in professional practice, and improved quality of relationships (Childre & Rozman, 2002). These reports and the results above suggest that it may be possible to enhance intuitive intelligence by regular practice of emotion self-regulation techniques that induce psychophysiological coherence. Further research is needed to study this relationship more directly (Bradley et al., 2011; Bradley & Tomasino, 2011; Tomasino, 2007).

COHERENCE-BUILDING TECHNIQUES: TOOLS TO ACCESS 'THE ZONE' OF INTUITION

An important implication raised by these findings is that intuition appears to be a faculty that can be *systematically developed and consciously enhanced* (Tomasino, 2007). One promising means of cultivating intuitive intelligence is the use of emotion self-regulatory techniques that facilitate the activation of positive emotions and induce the psychophysiological coherence state.

Based on an extensive body of research, Childre has developed a system of tools and techniques (Childre & Martin, 1999) that enable individuals to reliably self-generate and sustain psychophysiological coherence and its associated benefits (Tiller et al., 1996; McCraty et al., 1998). These heart-based techniques are designed to help individuals gain greater emotional self-awareness, to manage mental and emotional stress, and to cultivate intuitive intelligence (Childre & Martin, 1999; Childre & Rozman, 2002).

Briefly, these techniques combine a shift in the focus of attention to the area around the heart with the self-induction of a sincere positive emotional state, such as love or appreciation. This shift in focus and feeling significantly changes the pattern of afferent signals sent from the heart to the brain and body and facilitates the natural emergence of the psychophysiological coherence state (see Figure 21.2), which, with practice, can be sustained for extended periods. Studies have shown that the practice of coherence-building techniques significantly reduces stress and negative affect, improves markers of health and well-being, enhances cognitive performance, and leads to significant improvements in psychosocial functioning (see reviews of research in McCraty & Childre, 2004; McCraty & Tomasino, 2006).

The learning and effective use of coherence-building tools can be facilitated by *heart rhythm coherence feedback* technology (McCraty & Tomasino, 2004). Using a noninvasive sensor to measure the pulse wave, this interactive hardware/software technology provides real-time physiological feedback that enables the psychophysiological coherence state to be objectively monitored and quantified. By providing objective validation of coherence, such technology enables individuals to familiarize themselves with the feelings associated with the experiential shift to a psychophysiological state that enhances the likelihood and quality of intuitive experience. In effect, just as athletes train to enter their 'zone' of optimal performance, individuals can learn to access an optimal psychophysiological 'zone' for facilitating creative and intuitive flow (Tomasino, 2007).

Moreover, as people consistently use tools and technologies to facilitate a shift to coherence, the synchronized, harmonious patterns of psychophysiological activity associated with the coherent state become increasingly familiar to the brain and body, and are thereby reinforced in the neural architecture (Bradley et al., 2010; McCraty & Tomasino, 2006). Thus, through a *feed-forward* process, these coherent patterns become established as a new set-point, which the system then automatically strives to maintain. Evidence from research studies suggests that such a system-wide *repatterning process* accounts for the sustained improvements in health, emotional well-being, and performance documented in diverse populations (Bradley et al., 2010; McCraty et al., 1998; McCraty & Tomasino, 2006) and may also explain the development of increased intuitive awareness reported by many practitioners of coherence-building tools.

CONCLUSION: THE HEART AS A CONDUIT TO INTUITIVE INTELLIGENCE

The age-old conception of the heart as a locus of inner wisdom and intuitive insight is validated by a growing body of evidence in new science. Far more than just a pump, the heart is now known to be a complex information processing system with its own intelligence, continuously interacting with the brain and even informing perceptual and cognitive output. Even more intriguing is the recent, growing evidence of the heart's prime role in nonlocal intuition – effectively accessing tacit information about nonlocal objects and events from a domain beyond the constraints of space and time. Finally, research on psychophysiological coherence shows that it is heart-centered positive emotional states that naturally generate an optimal internal milieu: a psychophysiological 'zone' that appears to enhance access to intuitive perception and enables the cultivation of intuitive intelligence.

Rather than being an extraordinary 'gift' innate to a special few, intuition is an inherent natural ability that can likely be developed and improved through use of systematic methods. In this context, the scientific elucidation of a specific bodily state – psychophysiological coherence – is opportune, for it is an internal state that can be intentionally generated and one that appears to be a conduit to intuitive receptivity. Heart-based coherence-building techniques may well hold the key as a practical, effective means of self-activating this state-space to increase access to intuitive experience. Research on these issues is imperative, for not only will it bring us closer to a scientific understanding of the psychophysics of intuition, but it will also inform the ongoing development of applied technologies to facilitate intuitive ability. A long-term goal of such technology is to develop the capacity to utilize this intuitive faculty virtually at will, when intuitive insight and foresight is most needed to inform decisions and shape actions. As we increasingly learn to draw on this *whole-body* intuitive intelligence in all aspects of our lives, we will inevitably evolve into new levels of awareness, connectedness, and potential, both as individuals and as a global society.

NOTES

1. The core idea developed in this chapter of the heart as a source of intuitive intelligence was originally inspired by discussions with D. L. Childre, founder of the Institute of HeartMath, who has spoken and written extensively on the concept of 'heart intelligence.'
   I am grateful to R. T. Bradley for his helpful input on this chapter and his work to elucidate the psychophysics of intuition and nonlocal communication.
2. 'Event-related potentials' are voltage fluctuations in the brain's electrical activity that are associated in time with some physical, mental, or emotional occurrence. These potentials can be recorded from the scalp and extracted from the ongoing electroencephalogram (EEG) by means of filtering and signal averaging. When signal averaging techniques are used to trace the flow and processing of afferent neurological signals from the heart through different regions of the brain, the resulting waveforms are called 'heartbeat-evoked potentials'. In this case the peak of the electrocardiogram (ECG) R-wave is used as the timing source for the signal averaging process (McCraty et al., 2004b).

REFERENCES

Agor, W. 1984. *Intuitive management: Integrating left and right brain skills.* Englewood Cliffs, NJ: Prentice-Hall.
Armour, J. A., & Ardell, J. L. (Eds.). 1994. *Neurocardiology.* New York: Oxford University Press.

Arvey, R. D., Bouchard, T. J., Jr., & Carroll, J. B. 1994. Mainstream science on intelligence. *Wall Street Journal*, June 13: A18.

Assagioli, R. 1971. *Psychosynthesis*. New York: Viking.

Baron, R. A. 2004. The cognitive perspective: A valuable tool for answering entrepreneurship's basic 'why' questions. *Journal of Business Venturing*, 19(2): 221–239.

Bernstein, P. 2005. Intuition: What science says (so far) about how and why intuition works. In R. Buccheri, C. Elitzur, & M. Saniga (Eds.), *Endophysics, time, quantum and the subjective*: 487–506. Singapore: World Scientific.

Bierman, D. J., & Radin, D. I. 1997. Anomalous anticipatory response to randomized future conditions. *Perceptual and Motor Skills*, 84: 689–690.

Bolte, A., Gosche, T., & Kuhl, J. 2003. Emotion and intuition: Effects of positive and negative mood on implicit judgments of semantic coherence. *Psychological Science*, 14(5): 416–421.

Bradley, R. T. 2007. Psychophysiology of intuition: A quantum-holographic theory of nonlocal communication. *World Futures: The Journal of General Evolution*, 63(2): 61–97.

Bradley, R. T. 2010. Passionate attention and the psychophysiology of entrepreneurial intuition: A quantum-holographic theory. *International Journal of Entrepreneurship and Small Business*, 12(3): 343–372.

Bradley, R. T., Gillin, M., McCraty, R., & Atkinson, M. 2011. Non-local intuition in entrepreneurs and non-entrepreneurs: Results of two experiments using electrophysiological measures. *International Journal of Entrepreneurship and Small Business*, 12(3): 343–372.

Bradley, R. T., McCraty, R., Atkinson, M., Tomasino, D., Daugherty, A., & Arguelles, L. 2010. Emotion self-regulation, psychophysiological coherence, and test anxiety: Results from an experiment using electrophysiological measures. *Applied Psychophysiology and Biofeedback*, 35(4): 261–283.

Bradley, R. T., & Tomasino, D. 2011. A quantum-holographic approach to the psychophysiology of intuitive action. In L.-P. Dana (Ed.), *World encyclopedia of entrepreneurship*: 318–347. Cheltenham, UK, and Northampton, MA, USA: Edward Elgar.

Cameron, O. G. 2002. *Visceral sensory neuroscience: Interoception*. New York: Oxford University Press.

Childre, D., & Martin, H. 1999. *The HeartMath solution*. San Francisco: HarperSanFrancisco.

Childre, D., & Rozman, D. 2002. *Overcoming emotional chaos*. San Diego, CA: Jodere Group.

Damasio, A. 2003. *Looking for Spinoza: Joy, sorrow, and the feeling brain*. Orlando, FL: Harcourt.

Fredrickson, B. L. 2002. Positive emotions. In C. R. Snyder, & S. J. Lopez (Eds.), *Handbook of positive psychology*: 120–134. New York: Oxford University Press.

Frysinger, R. C., & Harper, R. M. 1990. Cardiac and respiratory correlations with unit discharge in epileptic human temporal lobe. *Epilepsia*, 31: 162–171.

Godwin, G. 2001. *Heart: A personal journey through its myths and meanings*. New York: William Morrow.

Gottfredson, L. S. 1997. Mainstream science on intelligence: An editorial with 52 signatories, history, and bibliography. *Intelligence*, 24(1): 13–23.

Immordino-Yang, M. H., & Damasio, A. 2007. We feel, therefore we learn: The relevance of affective and social neuroscience to education. *Mind, Brain, and Education*, 1(1): 3–10.

Isen, A. M. 1999. Positive affect. In T. Dalgleish & M. Power (Eds.), *Handbook of cognition and emotion*: 522–539. New York: John Wiley & Sons.

Laughlin, C. 1997. The nature of intuition: A neuropsychological approach. In R. Davis-Floyd, & P. S. Arvidson (Eds.), *Intuition: The inside story*: 19–37. London: Routledge.

LeDoux, J. E. 1994. Cognitive–emotional interactions in the brain. In P. Ekman, & R. J. Davidson (Eds.), *The nature of emotion: Fundamental questions*: 216–223. New York: Oxford University Press.

Lieberman, M. D. 2000. Intuition: a social and cognitive neuroscience approach. *Psychological Bulletin*, 126(1): 109–137.

May, E., Paulinyi, T., & Vassy, Z. 2005. Anomalous anticipatory skin conductance response to acoustic stimuli: Experimental results and speculations about a mechanism. *Journal of Alternative and Complementary Medicine*, 11(4): 695–702.

McCraty, R., Atkinson, M., & Bradley, R. T. 2004a. Electrophysiological evidence of intuition: Part 1. The surprising role of the heart. *Journal of Alternative and Complementary Medicine*, 10(1): 133–143.

McCraty, R., Atkinson, M., & Bradley, R. T. 2004b. Electrophysiological evidence of intuition: Part 2. A system-wide process? *Journal of Alternative and Complementary Medicine*, 10(2): 325–336.

McCraty, R., Atkinson, M., Tiller, W. A., Rein, G., & Watkins, A. D. 1995. The effects of emotions on short-term power spectrum analysis of heart rate variability. *American Journal of Cardiology*, 76(14): 1089–1093.

McCraty, R., Atkinson, M., Tomasino, D., & Bradley, R. T. 2009. The coherent heart: Heart–brain interactions, psychophysiological coherence, and the emergence of system-wide order. *Integral Review*, 5(2): 11–115.

McCraty, R., Barrios-Choplin, B., Rozman, D., Atkinson, M., & Watkins, A. D. 1998. The impact of a new emotional self-management program on stress, emotions, heart rate variability, DHEA and cortisol. *Integrative Physiological and Behavioral Science*, 33(2): 151–170.

McCraty, R., & Childre, D. 2004. The grateful heart: The psychophysiology of appreciation. In R. A. Emmons, & M. E. McCullough (Eds.), *The psychology of gratitude*: 230–255. New York: Oxford University Press.

McCraty, R., & Tomasino, D. 2004. Heart rhythm coherence feedback: A new tool for stress reduction, rehabilitation, and performance enhancement. In *Proceedings of the First Baltic Forum on Neuronal Regulation and Biofeedback*, Riga, Latvia, 2–5 November.

McCraty, R., & Tomasino, D. 2006. Emotional stress, positive emotions, and psychophysiological coherence. In B. B. Arnetz, & R. Ekman (Eds.), *Stress in health and disease*: 360–383. Weinheim, Germany: Wiley-VCH.

Mitchell, J. R., Friga, P. N., & Mitchell, R. K. 2005. Untangling the intuition mess: Intuition as a construct in entrepreneurship research. *Entrepreneurship: Theory and Practice*, November: 653–679.

Myers, D. G. 2002. *Intuition: Its powers and perils*. New Haven, CT: Yale University Press.

Pribram, K. H., & Melges, F. T. 1969. Psychophysiological basis of emotion. In P. J. Vinken, & G. W. Bruyn (Eds.), *Handbook of clinical neurology*, Vol. 3: 316–341. Amsterdam: North-Holland.

Radin, D. I. 1997a. *The conscious universe: The scientific truth of psychic phenomena*. San Francisco: HarperEdge.

Radin, D. I. 1997b. Unconscious perception of future emotions: An experiment in presentiment. *Journal of Scientific Exploration*, 11: 163–180.

Radin, D. I. 2004. Electrodermal presentiments of future emotions. *Journal of Scientific Exploration*, 18: 253–273.

Sandman, C. A., Walker, B. B., & Berka, C. 1982. Influence of afferent cardiovascular feedback on behavior and the cortical evoked potential. In J. T. Cacciopo, & R. E. Petty (Eds.), *Perspectives in cardiovascular psychophysiology*: 189–222. New York: Guilford.

Simon, H. A. 1987. Making management decisions: The role of intuition and emotion. *Academy of Management Executive*, 1(1): 57–65.

Spottiswoode, S. J. P., & May, E. C. P. 2003. Skin conductance prestimulus response: Analyses, artifacts and a pilot study. *Journal of Scientific Exploration*, 17: 617–642.

Subramaniam, K., Kounios, J., Parrish, T. B., & Jung-Beeman, M. 2009. A brain mechanism for facilitation of insight by positive affect. *Journal of Cognitive Neuroscience*, 21(3): 415–432.

Tiller, W. A., McCraty, R., & Atkinson, M. 1996. Cardiac coherence: A new, noninvasive measure of autonomic nervous system order. *Alternative Therapies in Health and Medicine*, 2(1): 52–65.

Tomasino, D. 2007. The psychophysiological basis of creativity and intuition: Accessing 'the zone' of entrepreneurship. *International Journal of Entrepreneurship and Small Business*, 4(5): 528–542.

Toroghi, S. R., Mirzaei, M., Zali, M. R., & Bradley, R. T. 2011. *Nonlocal intuition in repeat entrepreneurs: A replication and co-subject effects using electrophysiological measures.* Paper presented at the 8th AGSE International Entrepreneurship Research Exchange, Melbourne, Australia, 1–4 February.

Tressoldi, P. E., Martinelli, M., Zaccaria, E., & Massaccesi, S. 2009. Implicit intuition: How heart rate can contribute to prediction of future events. *Journal of the Society for Psychical Research*, 73.1(894): 1–16.

van der Molen, M. W., Somsen, R. J. M., & Orlebeke, J. F. 1985. The rhythm of the heart beat in information processing. In P. K Ackles, J. R. Jennings, & M. G. H. Coles (Eds.), *Advances in psychophysiology*, Vol. 1: 1–88. London; JAI Press.

Young, L. 2003. *The book of the heart.* New York: Doubleday.

Index

Aarts, H. 4, 217, 219, 220
Abbott, C. 237
Abramson, L.Y. 48
accuracy 21–6
Achterberg, J. 186
Acker, F. 165
action learning 94
action paralysis 125
activation 102–103
affect 98–9, 189
  influence of valence 41–9
  intensity 9, 37–50
  models 102–105
  negative 42, 44–6, 48–50, 102, 104–105
  positive 42, 44–5, 102, 104–105
  processing styles 4, 8–9, 10
Affect Infusion Model (AIM) 42–3
affective intuition 6, 8, 20
affective matching 8, 9, 11
Agor, W. 197, 248, 249
air traffic control 116
Alberts, D.S. 129
Allinson, C.W. 52, 88–9, 90, 171, 172
Alloy, L.B. 48
alpha waves/activity 61–2, 83–4
analysis 85, 128–9, 172–3
  see also rational/analytic processing (System 2)
analytical cognitive styles 127, 128–9
analytical judgment 21–3
analytical model 125, 126–7
analytical processing 18–19
analytical reasoning 23, 37, 172–3, 175–6
Andersen, J.A. 133
Anderson, J.R. 163
anger 9, 103, 139–40, 207, 251
Ansberg, P. 83
Antonietti, A. 170, 171, 174, 175, 176
anxiety 40–41, 46, 82, 170
approach–avoidance behavior 103
Ardell, J.L. 251

Armour, J.A. 251
army 72, 76, 114, 130
arousal 79, 82–3, 102–103
artificial grammar (AG) algorithm 55
Arvey, R.D. 248
'as-if' loop 9
Ashkanasy, N.M. 5, 8, 122, 123, 128, 133, 161, 229, 240
Ashmore, J. 171
Aspect, A. 197, 201
Assagioli, R. 247
assessment techniques 52, 53–7
associative style 5, 8, 10, 80, 101
associative system 37, 161–2, 218, 222
assumption reversal 91
Atkinson, J.W. 229
attention 230
  capturing intuitions 217–24
  defocused 83–4
  passionate 7, 13, 197–8, 207–209, 210
attentional energy 207–209, 210
Ausburn, F.B. 171
Ausburn, L.J. 171
Ausubel, D. 169
automatic processes 19–20, 37, 38–9
autonomic nervous system (ANS) 198, 201, 249–51
aviation 117–18
awareness 37, 104, 239, 247
  conscious 4, 7, 53–4, 62, 83, 197, 243, 254
  self- 240, 243–4, 255

Baas, M. 102, 103
Bache, J.B. 137
backward-reasoning strategy 23, 91
Baddeley, A. 103
Baker, T. 93
Baker, W.E. 139
Bakken, B.T. 127, 128, 129
Banbury, C. 93
Bancel, P. 210

Horn, J. 80
Houtkooper, J.M. 187
Howard, G. 186, 192
Hsee, C. 164
Huber, R. 81
Hughes, G.D. 91
Hull, C. 82
Human Factors and Ergonomics
 Society 76
Hume, D. 98
hunches 29, 54, 91, 137, 157, 188
Hutcheson, J.C. 157–8
Hyman, R. 192
hypermedia/hypermedia tools 173–5

Iannello, P. 52, 172
Ibison, M. 188
Idson, L.C. 103
IKEA (field study) 32–3
'imagens' 102
'immediate apprehension' 183, 188,
 190–91, 197
'imminence' 54
Immordino-Yang, M.H. 250
implicit knowledge 159, 164, 165
implicit learning 19, 26, 55, 147, 183
implicit processing 22, 54, 222
impression formation 34
incentive level 47, 48–9
incrementalism 6, 10, 93
'incubation' 29, 53
inferential intuition 5, 10, 17–26
information
 acquisition 12, 34
 -based functionality 11–15
 encoding 202–204, 209, 210
 logons 202–207
 modality 101
 processing 4–9, 126, 147–8, 218–21
innovation 82, 89, 93–4
insight 53–4, 56, 62, 71, 197, 240, 247
intellective–judgmental task 100
intellectual behavior 42–3
intelligence, intuitive 240, 247–57
interference 81, 204
 motivational 228, 229–30, 231–3
International Affective Picture System
 (IAPS) 189
'intimation' stage 54
intrinsic motivation 230

intuiting
 deliberative system 4–5
 'in flight' 217–24
 information-based functionality
  11–15
 processing 5–11
intuition
 advantages/downsides 163–5
 benefit (in learning) 227–34
 capturing (in flight) 217–24
 constructive 6, 9–11, 13, 162–3, 169
 in crisis management 122–30
 critical decisions vortex 133–42
 in critical occupations 111–19
 definitions 28, 158, 190, 197, 228,
  237
 'direct' knowing 3–4, 7
 entrepreneurial 6, 88–94
 expert 57–8, 69–76, 79, 140
 in higher education 237–44
 holistic 9, 17–26, 133, 242
 inferential 5, 10, 17–26
 integrated framework 3–15
 investigating 52–63
 learning situations 227–34
 legal 157–65
 noetic 183–93
 nonlocal *see* nonlocal intuition
 psychophysiological basis 183,
  248–9
 role (ethical decisions) 97–105
 strategic 79–85, 127
 types of 17–26
 unconscious thought and 28–35
 zone of 255–6
intuition (in professions/occupations)
 crisis management 122–30
 critical decisions vortex 133–42
 critical occupations 111–19
 emergency medicine 145–55
 legal intuition and expertise 157–65
 teaching 168–76
intuitive competencies 90–91
intuitive creation 6, 12, 13–15
intuitive decision making 145–55,
 233–4
intuitive episodes 59–60
intuitive expertise 4, 12, 13–15, 57–9
 developing 240, 242–3
intuitive foresight 13–15